PORPHYRIUS
THE CHARIOTEER

The new base of Porphyrius, right and front faces

The old base, back and left faces (before restoration)

PORPHYRIUS
THE CHARIOTEER

ALAN CAMERON

OXFORD
AT THE CLARENDON PRESS

OXFORD
UNIVERSITY PRESS

Great Clarendon Street, Oxford OX2 6DP

Oxford University Press is a department of the University of Oxford.
It furthers the University's objective of excellence in research, scholarship,
and education by publishing worldwide in

Oxford New York

Athens Auckland Bangkok Bogotá Buenos Aires Calcutta
Cape Town Chennai Dar es Salaam Delhi Florence Hong Kong Istanbul
Karachi Kuala Lumpur Madrid Melbourne Mexico City Mumbai
Nairobi Paris São Paulo Singapore Taipei Tokyo Toronto Warsaw

with associated companies in Berlin Ibadan

Oxford is a registered trade mark of Oxford University Press
in the UK and in certain other countries

Published in the United States
by Oxford University Press Inc., New York

© Oxford University Press 1973

The moral rights of the author have been asserted
Database right Oxford University Press (maker)

Special edition for Sandpiper Books Ltd., 1999

All rights reserved. No part of this publication may be reproduced,
stored in a retrieval system, or transmitted, in any form or by any means,
without the prior permission in writing of Oxford University Press,
or as expressly permitted by law, or under terms agreed with the appropriate
reprographics rights organisation. Enquiries concerning reproduction
outside the scope of the above should be sent to the Rights Department,
Oxford University Press, at the address above

You must not circulate this book in any other binding or cover
and you must impose this same condition on any acquirer

British Library Cataloguing in Publication Data
Data available

ISBN 0-19-814805-4

1 3 5 7 9 10 8 6 4 2

Printed in Great Britain
on acid-free paper by
Bookcraft (Bath) Ltd,
Midsomer Norton

PREFACE

THIS is a complex book, with a history no less complex. The core of Chapters IV-V began life as one chapter in a volume (still in preparation) with the provisional title *Early Byzantine Epigrams in the Greek Anthology*. While writing it I learned that Louis Robert had identified some of the epigrams in question on a statue base recently excavated in Istanbul. To my surprise and delight he replied to my inquiries by inviting me to publish the monument in his stead.

It soon became clear that the enlarged and more ambitious study which resulted would have to be accommodated in a separate volume, but one consequence of its temporary association with *Early Byzantine Epigrams* remains: this is a literary as well as a social and historical study. It would require greater competence than I can claim in the fields of art history and iconography to do full justice to the reliefs of the base, but I have done my best to explain them and trace their pedigrees.

No one who has studied the hippodrome of sixth-century Constantinople can long escape its notorious so-called 'factions', the turbulent and much misunderstood Blues and Greens. I had originally planned to correct a few relevant misapprehensions in a series of appendices. But as I delved deeper, I came to appreciate more sharply the inadequacies of existing accounts and the impossibility of treating the subject properly except in a far wider perspective. So the process of subdivision had to be carried one stage further; yet another volume therefore (now nearly complete) will trace the evolution and significance of the circus partisans (for so they ought to be styled) from Augustus to Constantine Porphyrogenitus.

Many friends and colleagues have given me the benefit of their advice or assistance in one way or another, notably Robert Aubreton, Robert Browning, Malcolm Colledge, Martin Harrison, John Kent, Denys Page, Werner Peek, Alain Segonds, Jocelyn Toynbee, Michael Vickers, Martin West, and Nigel Wilson. I am particularly grateful to Peter Brown and Cyril Mango, who read the whole book in typescript, and Alan

PREFACE

Griffiths, who did the same in proof. Elisabeth and Andreas Alföldi provided me with all my contorniate illustrations; Ihor Ševčenko with excellent photographs of the inscriptions, a valuable supplement to my own notes and the squeezes of Jeanne Robert in my decipherment. A grant from the Central Research Fund of London University enabled me to visit Istanbul, where I was fortunate enough to profit from the friendly co-operation of Nezih Fıratlı. But my greatest debt is to Louis Robert, who has always been generous with information and advice, and without whom this book would literally not have been written. Not having yet seen it, he cannot be held responsible for any of its shortcomings, but I hope that he will find something on the positive side to justify the confidence he placed in me.

A. C.

Bedford College, London
April 1972

CONTENTS

LIST OF PLATES	ix
LIST OF FIGURES	x
ABBREVIATIONS AND REFERENCES	xi
INTRODUCTION	1
I. THE EXTANT MONUMENTS	3
Disappearance and Discovery	4
The Bases	12
The Frontal Chariot	17
The Tychae	28
The Lower Registers of the Two Bases	30
The Front and Back of the Two Bases	42
The Kathisma Relief on the Back of the New Base	49
The Gate(s) beneath the Imperial Box	55
Rhetoric, whether in Words or Stone	58
II. THE INSCRIPTIONS	65
Left Face	65
Right Face	80
Back Face	82
Front Face	93
III. THE MANUSCRIPT TRADITION	96
The Manuscripts	96
The Relationship between the Manuscripts	99
The Origin of the Collection	105
When were the Epigrams First Transcribed from the Monuments?	109
Conclusion	116

CONTENTS

IV. THE LOST MONUMENTS	117
Porphyrius	121
Other Charioteers	136
V. THE CHRONOLOGY OF PORPHYRIUS	150
The Location of the Monuments on the Spina	180
VI. THE LESSER LIGHTS	188
The Iambic Poems	188
The Paintings	200
The Records	206
Golden Statues	214
CONCLUSION	223
The Scale and Style of the Monuments	223
Other Entertainments	228
Factional Violence	232
Anastasius and the Factions	240
The Victorious Charioteer	244
The Decline of Chariot-Racing	252
APPENDICES	
A. Pl. and L	259
B. Σ^π and Pl.	265
C. The Inscriptions	267
D. Emendations	270
ADDENDA	275
BIBLIOGRAPHY	277
INDEX OF GREEK AND LATIN WORDS	281
GENERAL INDEX	282

LIST OF PLATES

Frontispiece. General view of the two Porphyrius bases (old base before restoration)

(*at end*)

1–10. The new Porphyrius base (unless otherwise stated, photos by courtesy of the Istanbul Archaeological Museum)
    1. Tyche of Nicomedia, with *A. Pl.* 356 (left side)
    2–3. front and back faces, with *A. Pl.* 352 and 353
    4–5. left and right sides, with *A. Pl.* 351 and 356
    6. dancing partisans, with two prose acclamations (left side)
    7. Emperor and party in Kathisma, with *A. Pl.* 353 (back face)
    8. Porphyrius being crowned by a Victory (front)
    9. acclamation from right side (photo by I. Ševčenko)
    10a. *A. Pl.* 351 (right side, top; photo by I. Ševčenko)
    10b: *A. Pl.* 352 (back, top; photo by I. Ševčenko)

11. *A. Pl.* 335–9 in *Laur.* XXXII. 16

12–14. Old base (after restoration)
    12. acclaiming partisans beneath triumphant Porphyrius (left side)
    13. Porphyrius and attendant putti (back)
    14. the *diversium*, beneath Porphyrius and Victories (front)

15–18. The 'Kugelspiel' (photos from Staatliche Museen zu Berlin)
    15. dancing partisans, lot machine, racing quadriga (left side)
    16. dancing partisans, victorious charioteer (*a*) on horseback, (*b*) in quadriga (right side)
    17. ? Kathisma, above arch (front)
    18: racing quadrigae (back)

19–22. Faces A_1, B_1, B_2, and A_2 of the base to the obelisk of Theodosius (photos from Deutsches Archäologisches Institut, Berlin)
    23. Relief below face A_2 of the obelisk base, racing horsemen and coronation scene above racing quadrigae
    24. Mosaic from the Via Flaminia, near Rome
    25. Mosaic from Dougga, Tunisia (photos of both by courtesy of J. M. C. Toynbee)
    26. Aachen–Cluny quadriga textile (photo from Musée de Cluny, Paris)

LIST OF PLATES

27. Münsterbilsen quadriga textile (photo from Musée d'art et d'histoire, Brussels)
28. Fifteenth-century view of Constantinople published by Onufrio Panvinio (after P. Sherrard, *Constantinople* (1965), 21)
29. David, Solomon, and dancers: miniature from MS. Vatic. gr. 699 of Cosmas Indicopleustes
30. David and dancers, miniature from a Carolingian Psalter (Bibl. Nat. Cod. Lat. 1152)
31. Various medallions

LIST OF FIGURES

1. The Porphyrius Monuments: Distribution of Inscriptions   118
2. Distribution of Charioteer Monuments on the Spina   182

CORRIGENDA

p. 4, n. 1: *for* 'appropriate' *read* 'reiterated'.
p. 44, l. 4: delete the second comma.
p. 233, l. 1: *before* 'emperor' *insert* 'Byzantine'.
p. 235, para. 2, l. 14: *for* '610–64' *read* '610–641'.
p. 273, para. 4, l. 5: *for* 'elision' *read* 'hiatus'.
plates 15 and 16: interchange the words 'left' and 'right'.

ABBREVIATIONS AND REFERENCES

Most of the abbreviations I have used for periodicals, collections of inscriptions, and so forth either correspond to the lists in the *Oxford Classical Dictionary* or *L'Année philologique*, or are self-explanatory. The only ones which might cause a moment's pause are the following:

BARB	*Academie royale de Belgique, Bulletin de la classe des lettres et des sciences morales et politiques*
BS	*Byzantino-Slavica*
BZ	*Byzantinische Zeitschrift*
DOP	*Dumbarton Oaks Papers*
Friedlaender, *SG*	L. Friedlaender, *Darstellungen aus der Sittengeschichte Roms*, 9th/10th edition, revised by G. Wissowa, 1919–21.

Malalas and the *Chronicon Paschale* are cited by page and line numbers in the Bonn Corpus editions; the Book of Ceremonies of Constantine Porphyrogenitus, where chapter references are not precise enough, by page and line in the Bonn edition (cited conventionally R for Reiske) and (where available) the Budé text of A. Vogt (V) as well. For references to the charioteer epigrams see p. 1 n. 1. The various *Patria* of Constantinople are quoted by page and line from T. Preger, *Scriptores Originum Constantinopolitanarum* (1901–7).

It might seem unduly perverse of me to have abandoned the convenient Woodward/Wace designation of the four sides of the old Porphyrius base (ABCD) for the cumbersome 'left side', 'right side', 'front', and 'back' that I have employed throughout for both bases and for the so-called Kugelspiel, but I have done so because the concepts of front/back and sides are important for the interpretation both of the reliefs and of the inscriptions of the two bases (see pp. 18, 30–1, 33). Faces of the obelisk base are cited by the notation of G. Bruns, *Der Obelisk und seine Basis* (1935).

INTRODUCTION

THE existence and achievements of Porphyrius and his colleagues have long been known from a fascinating (if little read) series of epigrams in the Greek Anthology.[1] No fewer than thirty-two of these epigrams celebrate Porphyrius himself; the rest, four other charioteers of the period. In addition, we hear something of Porphyrius' firebrand activities outside the hippodrome from an interesting passage in the chronicle of John Malalas.

Shortly before the middle of the last century, however, came more concrete evidence of Porphyrius' fame: the discovery in Constantinople of a massive base (lacking the original statue, alas) to one of the monuments for which these epigrams were written. The inscriptions from the right-hand side were copied by H. Abeken in 1845,[2] and published by W. Henzen in the *Bulletino dell'Instituto di Corrispondenza Archeologica* for 1847. It was not till 1871 that G. Kaibel spotted that the one fragmentary epigram then published could be restored as no. 340 in the Planudean Appendix to the Anthology.[3] Then in 1880 came A. D. Mordtmann's full publication of all the reliefs and inscriptions[4]—revealing that *Anth. Plan.* 342 was also inscribed on the base.

In 1963 a new base was discovered by Dr. Nezih Fıratlı and Mme Andrée Rollas, and announced by them with commendable promptitude in the *Annual of the Archaeological Museums of Istanbul* for 1964.[5] This time the epigrams were recognized (by Professor Louis Robert) as *Anth. Plan.* 351, 352, 353, and 356 in time for the original announcement, though the text of the inscriptions (which include three prose acclamations hitherto unknown) has not yet been published.

[1] *Anth. Pal.* xv. 41–50, *Anth. Plan.* 335–87. Since the numbers in the two series are of a different order of magnitude, and where there is no other possibility of confusion, I normally quote the epigrams for brevity's sake as 41–50, 335–87.
[2] On Abeken see below, p. 275.
[3] *De monumentorum aliquot graecorum carminibus* (Diss. Bonn 1871), 19.
[4] *Athen. Mitteil.* v (1880), 295 f. The base was published again by A. M. Woodward and A. J. B. Wace, in an appendix to W. S. George, *Church of St. Eirene* (1912), 79 f., shamelessly plagiarized by A. A. Vasiliev, *DOP* iv (1948), 29 f.
[5] Signalled briefly too by J. and L. Robert, *Bull. Épigr.* (*REG* lxxviii) 1965, no. 248, p. 129.

INTRODUCTION

The two bases are now reunited in the Archaeological Museum of Istanbul, the old base having been moved there from its original site in the forecourt of the Church of St. Eirene in 1916.[1] For the sake of convenience and brevity I shall distinguish the two henceforth as the 'new base' and the 'old base'—despite the fact (which will emerge in Chapter V) that the new base is actually older than the old base.

Chapters I–II of this book comprise the first full publication of the new base. But their successors investigate a number of wider problems. Since some of these topics may at first sight seem to have little to do with either Porphyrius or his monument, it may be helpful to begin by explaining briefly the purpose of the book as a whole and the interrelationship of its parts.

Chapter I elucidates the reliefs and iconography of the base. Chapter II publishes and explains the inscriptions. In both cases I have found it necessary to consider afresh the reliefs and inscriptions of the old base.

The order of the epigrams as they appear on both monuments is exactly the same as the order in which they appear in the series in the Anthology. That is to say, it looks as though they were copied down into the original version of this series directly from the monuments. Chapter IV suggests that the other epigrams in the series were also copied from monuments of this sort, now lost. That is to say, the existence of lost monuments is inferred from surviving epigrams. This chapter further argues that these epigrams fall into a number of such well-defined and clearly delimited blocks—eleven, to be precise—that it seems reasonable to assume that each block was copied from just one of these now lost monuments. Chapter V attempts to fix the chronology—absolute where possible, relative where not—of both the extant bases and (so far as possible) the five lost bases of Porphyrius. Chapter VI does the same for the one base each of the other four charioteers, reconstructing their careers not so much for their own sake as for the light they cast on Porphyrius. For the nature of the records their epigrams claim, when compared with Porphyrius' records, enables them to be dated relatively to Porphyrius.

The results of the investigation license inferences far transcending the relationship between five charioteers. For it will be

---

[1] J. Ebersolt, *Mission archéologique de Constantinople* (1921), 2.

INTRODUCTION 3

argued that the career of Porphyrius marked a new peak in the fame and material rewards of charioteers—a fame that is less an index of the skill of the charioteers than of the growing importance of the hippodrome in Byzantine life—and of the increasing rivalry of the circus factions. The Byzantines had two heroes, Norman Baynes once remarked: 'the winner in the chariot race and the ascetic saint'.[1] There is a whole literature on the ascetic saint, yet not so much as a single good article devoted to the fame of the charioteer. Much has indeed been written about the factions of the circus—though most of it worthless fiction, presupposing that the racing was a thin façade for social and religious conflict, and altogether ignoring the charioteer.[2] A companion volume will attempt a balanced assessment of the role and significance of the factions. The closing chapter of this book will simply consider some aspects of the phenomenon of the successful charioteer, appropriately enough in the person of Porphyrius, champion of hippodromes all over the Empire for more than forty years.

It will be seen that much of the later part of the book turns on the results claimed in Chapter IV. Hence it is essential to be as sure as we can about the precise order and arrangement of the series of epigrams as they appear in the Planudean Anthology. For this purpose printed editions are almost useless. Chapter III studies the series from every angle, exploiting for the first time three newly discovered (or rediscovered) manuscript sources—all of them either written by Planudes himself or under his supervision. I have thus been able to present a much fuller and more accurate picture of the manuscript tradition. At the same time, of course, the inscriptions on the two bases provide a unique opportunity of checking the manuscript tradition against what—ultimately at any rate—is indisputably its source. So it is that this study of Porphyrius the charioteer embodies the first critical edition of the epigrams known only by a manuscript tradition, as well as the first publication of the new monument.

[1] *The Byzantine Empire* (1925), 33.
[2] Even Romilly Jenkins's lively chapter 'Social Life in the Byzantine Empire', in *Cambridge Medieval History*, IV, *The Byzantine Empire*, ii (1967), 92, could hardly be said to do justice to the importance of the charioteer.

I

THE EXTANT MONUMENTS

DISAPPEARANCE AND DISCOVERY

ALL Henzen says of the circumstances of the discovery of the old base is that it was 'disotterato nel serraglio di Constantinopoli'. Fortunately, however, it is possible to piece together a few facts about the excavations in the Seraglio at this period[1]—facts which may help to explain how it is that two bases put up in honour of Porphyrius in the hippodrome came to be dug up in the Seraglio. The most relevant finds are a number of porphyry sarcophagi of fourth- and fifth-century emperors, discovered in the same area of the Seraglio as the new base and at almost exactly the same time as the old one. An inscription in Turkish dated 15 June 1847 on one of the columns of the portico by the entry to the second court of the Seraglio refers to the excavation near by of these sarcophagi and their removal to St. Eirene (where a sort of private museum was being assembled),[2] pinpointing in addition the location of the lids to two of them which it had not been considered worth extracting from beneath the roots of a magnificent plane tree[3] (as flourishing today as it was then).

Further excavations in the second court in 1959 revealed another imperial sarcophagus of coloured marble,[4] not far from the area where the Porphyrius base was found four years later.[5] In 1969 yet another sarcophagus, plausibly identified as

[1] The facts are collected by Ebersolt, *Mission archéologique*, 2 f., and appropriate by Vasiliev, *DOP* iv (1948), 3 f.
[2] Private, because the Church was still being used as an armoury, and access to it was difficult till 1910. This may be why Abeken only copied the inscriptions from one side, for those on the other side are actually better preserved and more intelligible.
[3] These lids were eventually removed and replaced on their respective sarcophagi in 1916: see the account of the excavation and photographs in Ebersolt, *Mission*, 3 and Pls. ix and x.
[4] All the porphyry sarcophagi ever made—ten—are now accounted for: eight still extant, and the other two last seen in 1750 (C. Mango, *DOP* xvi (1962), 397 f.).
[5] On the circumstances and locations of these two digs see Fıratlı and Rollas, pp. 199–200.

DISAPPEARANCE AND DISCOVERY

Heraclius', was found only yards from the location of the discoveries of 1847.[1] In the absence of any further information relating to the excavations of 1845-7, it seems a reasonable working hypothesis that the old base was found here, and that it was brought to the Seraglio at (approximately) the same time (and for the same reason) as the new base—and the sarcophagi.

The actual statues were broken up, together with countless other bronze statues in the hippodrome, by the Crusaders in 1204, and melted down to be turned into coin.[2] Almost alone among the extensive and magnificent statuary of the hippodrome (much of it genuine ancient workmanship) the four gilded bronze horses (from the period if not the hand of Lysippus) which had stood above the *carceres* were spared the melting-pot and shipped to Venice, where they still stand (after a brief exile in Paris under Napoleon) above the entrance to San Marco. The statues which originally stood on the two extant bases were no doubt such Crusader casualties.

The despoiled and (after the terrible fire of 1203) blackened hippodrome must have looked a sorry sight. Mordtmann argued that most if not all of these despoiled bases and columns would have been cleared out of the hippodrome after the unlamented departure of the Crusaders, to rid the place of these 'sad mementoes of Latin rule' (p. 297). There are several objections to this suggestion.

In the first place, the charioteer bases at least look quite impressive even without their statues, and the amount of masonry to be moved would have been considerable. In the second place, it would probably not have been thought worth while in any event, since the hippodrome seems to have fallen into at least partial disuse. Races might still be held every now and then,[3] but

[1] Cyril Mango, 'A newly discovered Byzantine imperial sarcophagus', *Annual of the Archaeological Museums of Istanbul* xv/xvi (1969), 308-9 with fig. 1.

[2] Nicetas Choniates, *De signis Cpolitanis* 5, cf. 11. 'What has happened to this money minted in Latin Constantinople?' asked Anthony Cutler in the course of a recent analysis of Nicetas' pamphlet (*AJA* lxxii (1968), 116). The answer to this long-standing numismatic puzzle has now been provided by Michael Hendy, *Coinage and Money in the Byzantine Empire 1081-1261* (Dumbarton Oaks Studies xii, 1969), 191 ff., especially p. 206: the coinage of the Latin Empire consisted of *imitations* of the coins of Manuel I and other late twelfth-century Byzantine emperors, not always easy to distinguish from their genuine coinage. I am grateful to Mr. Philip Grierson for explaining this point to me before the appearance of Hendy's book.

[3] Koukoulès, Βυζαντινῶν Βίος iii (1949), 12-13.

they were no longer the occasions they had been in the tenth century, much less the age of Porphyrius. The Latin masters of Constantinople brought their own sport with them—jousting. Even after their departure, this new (and less expensive) western entertainment remained, like other western tastes (the poet Ovid, for example), in favour with Byzantine audiences.[1] Furthermore, an essential feature of the traditional hippodrome ceremonial had been the regular presence and participation of the Emperor, who was able to reach his box without entering the hippodrome in the ordinary way, by a special connecting staircase from his adjacent Palace. After the Byzantine restoration, the emperors, following here the practice of the Comnenian as well as the Latin rulers, preferred to live in the distant Blachernae palace, and the old Grand Palace too fell into partial disuse. Thus the centre of gravity of the city as a whole shifted away from the hippodrome. The result we can see only too clearly in the famous view of an obviously derelict hippodrome copied by Onufrio Panvinio (Pl. 28). The original is generally held to have been made c. 1450, but is probably in fact a few decades later than this—that is to say after, rather than before, the Turkish sack.[2]

There is another way too in which Panvinio's view can help to rebut Mordtmann's suggestion. On the spina of the hippodrome (where the charioteer statues stood) it shows at least a dozen statueless bases of varying sizes—two or three of which could easily be a Porphyrius base. The sketch is not very accurate, since of the three columns that are all that is left on the site of the spina today, it omits no fewer than two (the Serpent column and the so-called obelisk of Constantine VII). Yet this can hardly be allowed to discredit the general accuracy of the sketch. What it does show, surely, is that there were still so many columns on the spina that an artist might feel driven to select.[3] We have three other such selective representations from the sixteenth century:

[1] L. Bréhier, *La Civilisation byzantine* (1950), 102-4, R. Guilland, 'La disparition des courses', *Mél. O. et M. Merlier* i (1955), 31 f., = *Études byzantines* (1959), 89 f. On Ovid, E. J. Kenney, 'A Byzantine Version of Ovid', in *Hermes* xci (1963), 223-4.
[2] Ebersolt, *Constantinople byzantine et les voyageurs du Levant* (1918), 63 n. 1. But see Mango, *REB* vii (1949), 102 n. 5, and *The Brazen House* (1959), 180. There is a good reproduction of Panvinio's view in Philip Sherrard, *Constantinople* (1965), 21.
[3] Similarly, an anonymous Russian pilgrim before the Turkish conquest records 30 columns still standing in the Sphendone arcade (S. Casson, *Preliminary Report upon the Excavations ... in the Hippodrome* (1928), 16), while Panvinio's drawing shows rather fewer.

DISAPPEARANCE AND DISCOVERY

the sketch of Suleiman the Magnificent's procession across the hippodrome made some time between 1526 and 1533 by the Dutchman Pieter Koeck,[1] and two Turkish miniatures of c. 1530 and 1560 respectively.[2] All three show two statueless bases in addition to the three monuments still extant (though in 1544 Pierre Gilles counted seven). Early in the fifteenth century Manuel Chrysoloras referred to the 'extant bases with their epigrams' in the hippodrome as evidence that there must once have been a great many statues there.[3] And in 1422 Buondelmonti explicitly mentions 'columpne marmoree multarum historiarum sculpte, una post alteram'[4] actually on the spina—a perfect description of the rows of charioteer stelae (p. 182) with their tiers of reliefs.

Many columns had been removed by the time Gilles arrived, and he records that many more were carted away during his stay. But the charioteer bases were clearly among those that had already gone: 'Iam vero quid commemorem (he wrote in his *De Topographia Constantinopoleos* (1561), ii. 13) infinitas statuas pugilum, luctatorum, *aurigarum* in hippodromo sitas, quae *etsi dudum perierunt*, tamen recens eorum memoria non perit, retenta *plusquam trecentis versibus etiamnum extantibus*, quibus nonnulli aurigae decantantur.' The charioteer epigrams in the Anthology total 288 lines, to which Planudes added nine four-line poems of more recent origin, making 324 lines in all.[5] There can be little doubt that these are Gilles's 'plusquam trecentis versibus'. That is to say, he knew no more of the charioteer monuments than the epigrams he had read in a printed edition of the Anthology (five editions had appeared by 1544, three more by Gilles's death in 1555).

The evident congestion of the spina in Panvinio's view suggests that few of its monuments can have been removed before the Turkish conquest. And in 1403 the Castilian ambassador Clavijo, *en route* for Samarkand, records on the spina, in addition to the obelisk of Theodosius, sculptures 'recording the great

---
[1] Ibid., fig. 3.
[2] Ibid., p. 15 and figs. 4 and 6.
[3] *Comparison of the Old and New Romes*, PG clvi. 45c.
[4] G. Gerola, 'Le vedute di Constantinopoli di Cristoforo Buondelmonti', *Studi bizantini* iii (1926), 273.
[5] On the distinction between the iambic poems and the inscriptional epigrams see below, Ch. VI.

deeds and acts of the nobles and mighty men of the past'.[1] Of course there were no doubt several columns of which this might have been said, but the two extant Porphyrius bases do answer particularly well to the description—at least to the Greekless beholder. Porphyrius looks a mighty man indeed as he stands in triumphal pose on his chariot with an outsize palm-leaf that looks more like a shield in his right hand.

The balance of probability, I would suggest, is that the bases were removed from the hippodrome not long after the Turkish conquest. This was the tentative suggestion of Woodward and Wace in the standard publication of the old base, though the only reason they gave, that the monuments must still have been *in situ* when Planudes compiled his Anthology (1299), is unfortunately invalid. For Planudes got the epigrams, not from the original monuments, but from an earlier anthology. How much earlier cannot, regrettably, be determined, but hardly later than the end of the ninth century, and possibly much earlier.[2]

But there are arguments in favour of this later date. The objects which kept the bases company under the ground would seem to point to the Turkish rather than the Crusader conquest for the occasion on which they came together in the Seraglio. The great majority of the sarcophagi beyond question came from the Church of the Holy Apostles, where most of the emperors of eight centuries had been laid to rest. The greedy Crusaders rifled them for any treasures they might find inside (Alexius III had already been reduced to removing all external valuables). But they were certainly left *in situ*. A number of fourteenth- and fifteenth-century pilgrims and travellers (Steven of Novgorod, Ignatius of Smolensk, Buondelmonti of Florence, and others) report having seen them in the church (or the mausolea attached to the church),[3] and they were still there for the Turks to open in a further (vain) search for treasure in 1453.[4]

Mehmet the Conqueror at first left the Church of the Holy

---

[1] *Diary*, transl. G. le Strange (1928), 70; cf. Ebersolt, *Constantinople . . . et les voyageurs*, 51: Ebersolt illustrated this page with a photograph of the Porphyrius base, which he evidently took to be one of the columns seen by Clavijo. So too R. Guilland, *BS* xxx (1969), 210–11.
[2] Ch. III.
[3] Ebersolt, *Mission*, 23 for the sources.
[4] *Hist. Pol. Cpoleos*, ed. Bonn, 21, with Ebersolt, *Mission*, 23.

DISAPPEARANCE AND DISCOVERY

Apostles to the Christians, but in 1461 he demolished it and built a mosque on the site.[1] The sarcophagi were dispersed (Gilles saw one just standing outside the new mosque), and a considerable number were placed in the grounds of the Seraglio. It was evidently for their decorative value that they were taken here. Had the intention been merely to dump them, why transport such massive objects intact for two miles to the Sultan's palace instead of finding a nearer dumping ground, or else simply breaking them up on the spot? Several were adapted to serve as fountains—a function which two of them perform to this day.[2]

Furthermore, it was not from the Church of the Holy Apostles alone that imperial sarcophagi were brought to the Seraglio. In 1750 a French traveller, Flachat, saw in the grounds of the Seraglio two porphyry sarcophagi and the lid to a third of green marble, all of which have since disappeared. From Flachat's description Cyril Mango has recently identified the lid as belonging to the sarcophagus of Manuel I (1143–80).[3] Now Manuel was buried in the Pantocrator monastery, and near his tomb stood the stone on which (it was said) the body of Christ was deposed. This latter object later formed part of Sultan Mehmet's collection of Christian antiquities,[4] and it seems a very reasonable assumption that both it and Manuel's tomb were brought to the Seraglio together when the Pantocrator monastery was converted into a mosque, probably not long after the conquest.[5]

This collection of the Sultan's presumably dates from the period towards the end of his reign (1472–8) when he began to build his new palace within the present Seraglio grounds. Its most remarkable feature, an impressive selection of Christian holy relics, in which Mehmet seems to have had an almost

---

[1] R. Janin, *La Géographie ecclésiastique de l'Empire byzantin I: le siège de Constantinople et le patriarchat œcuménique iii: les églises et les monastères* (1953), 50f. On the more general issue of Mehmet's treatment of the population and buildings of Constantinople see now H. Inalcık, *DOP* xxiii/iv (1969/70), 231–49.
[2] Ebersolt, *Mission*, pp. 16 no. E, 19 nos. 2–3, 20 no. 4.
[3] 'Three Imperial Byzantine Sarcophagi discovered in 1750', *DOP* xvi (1962), 397f.
[4] F. Babinger, 'Reliquien am Osmanenhof im XV. Jahrhundert', *Sb. Bay. Akad., Phil.-hist. Klasse* 1956, 2, p. 19 n. 1. That it came from the Pantocrator monastery is stated by Gian-Maria Angiolello († 1525): cf. Babinger, p. 8 n. 2.
[5] Mango, p. 399 n. 14. On both the tomb and the stone see too now the new evidence advanced by Mango in *DOP* xxiii/iv (1969/70), 373–5.

superstitious interest, is attested by a recently published inventory dated to 1489.[1] Among the other items which the collection contained we may surmise to have been a small porphyry altar now in the third court, a white marble baptistery turned into a fountain, perhaps a huge porphyry column of which only a fragment remains, a number of minor items,[2] and—we may surely add— at least two monuments of Porphyrius.

Of course, some of these objects might have been added to the original collection by Mehmet's successors, though none is known to have shared his taste for Christian art—as illustrated by the metre of soil and rubble allowed to accumulate over most of the objects in the second court at least by the first half of the nineteenth century (when the first batch was excavated) and probably very much earlier. Furthermore, some at least of the larger pieces can be proved to go, like the collection of relics, right back to the Conqueror himself. For some of the recent finds had to be left in the second court because they would not pass out through its gate. This gate, euphemistically styled Gate of Peace (where executions took place), was built by Mehmet himself. Evidently he must have begun his collection before he had finished enclosing his palace.

Gilles knew the Anthology intimately. Indeed, the skill and success with which he used the Anthology as a source for the topography of Constantinople has not always been equalled by more recent topographers.[3] In particular, he had evidently read the charioteer epigrams with attention, since he remarks that many great names of the hippodrome were absent from them. He instances a certain Thomas, whose existence he had learned of from a fragment of stone seen in Constantinople with the inscription Θομᾶ ἡνιόχου (to the best of my knowledge no longer extant).[4] Since, then, Gilles was sufficiently familiar with the achievements of Porphyrius to note the absence of his statues

[1] Babinger, pp. 18 f.
[2] Ebersolt, *Mission*, 24–5.
[3] For a few of the shortcomings in use of Anthology evidence which, despite its many other virtues, disfigure even the second edition of R. Janin's *Constantinople byzantine* (1964) see Averil Cameron, *Byzantion* xxxvii (1967), 18 f.
[4] This Thomas the learned zoologist identified with a charioteer called Thomas mentioned in a letter written for Theodoric the Ostrogoth by Cassiodorus (*Var.* iii. 51. 1), between 507 and 511. Since Cassiodorus' Thomas was an easterner ('ex Orientis partibus') the identification is possible, though hardly more, since we have no clue about the date of Gilles's inscription.

DISAPPEARANCE AND DISCOVERY

from the hippodrome, it is likely that he would have been able to identify our two extant bases had they been exposed to view anywhere in the city. Yet in four years of extraordinarily minute and accurate study of the city Gilles did not see them. The simplest explanation is that they had already then been installed in the inaccessible grounds of the Seraglio.

The latest finds from the site offer welcome support to this hypothesis. For in addition to the new sarcophagus, the 1959 excavations brought to light no fewer than nine benches (of varying lengths), evidently, as Fıratlı and Mme Rollas saw, from the hippodrome.[1] We also have two huge capitals,[2] obviously from columns of substantial size, which once supported metal statues. Such columns stood in many places other than the hippodrome, to be sure, but in view of all the other hippodrome material here it is tempting to conjecture that they too might have come from the hippodrome. However, even if only the nine benches and two bases do come from the hippodrome, it is probable that, like the imperial sarcophagi, they were moved together to the Sultan's new palace during or shortly after the dismantling of their original homes.

Perhaps, then, we may picture the visitor to the palace of the Conqueror pausing for a while as he strolled through the splendid gardens of the Seraglio to sit on a hippodrome bench and gaze reflectively at those aptly chosen symbols of an empire that was gone—the glories of emperor and charioteer.

We shall see in Chapter IV that originally there stood five more such bases to statues of Porphyrius in the hippodrome besides the two now known—not to mention several of other charioteers. Were any (or all) of these others brought to the Seraglio too? One might have thought that two would satisfy any man's taste for hippodrome sculpture, but then one might have thought the same about imperial sarcophagi.

These bases were originally deployed together with various other columns along the spina—as illustrated by Panvinio's view. Thus all were exposed equally to the same natural hazards (fires, earthquakes), and all robbed equally of their statues in

---

[1] p. 201, with Pl. xxviii. 2; cf. p. 206 n. 7a for references to other (isolated) finds of hippodrome benches.

[2] One each from the 1959 and 1962 digs: Fıratlı and Rollas, pp. 201–2, with Pls. xxvii. 1 and xxix. 1.

1204. Some may have been more seriously damaged by the fire which scorched two faces of the new base. But others, like the old base, were probably not touched by it (the obelisk base was barely touched). If the two extant bases could survive in such good condition till Mehmet's day, why should not most of the others? All had certainly disappeared by Gilles's arrival a century later, and while a few may have gone to grace the halls of lesser Turkish grandees, there is no record of them, and it is at least as likely that most were transported to the Seraglio together.

The Seraglio grounds have never been systematically excavated. All the sarcophagi, bases, capitals, benches, and other objects discovered in the successive digs of 1845-7, 1959, 1963, and 1969 have come from just one corner of the second court. There may be many other such massive pieces still awaiting discovery. Some will perhaps lurk for ever beneath the numerous buildings dotted over the rambling Seraglio grounds by Mehmet's successors, but others may be within easy reach. The discovery of just one more base of Porphyrius could prove or disprove many of the suggestions put forward in this book.

THE BASES

Since the two bases closely resemble each other, neither can profitably be studied without reference to the other. Indeed, though the primary purpose of this chapter is to publish the new base, it embodies what amounts to a republication of the old base as well, reconsidered in the light of the new one.

The two bases were put up by different factions, the old one by the Blues, the new one by the Greens—though hardly more than a year or so separates them. Both were put up within a range of a year or two either side of A.D. 500.[1] It must also be borne in mind that they stood only a matter of yards from each other on the spina of the hippodrome. We can therefore be certain in a way we seldom can be when comparing two works of art (to use the term generously), that every detail of the new base (the earlier of the two) must have been known to the craftsmen who were making the other. And both sets of craftsmen must also have been familiar with the reliefs on the base of the great obelisk of Theodosius, just over a century old when our two bases were put up,

[1] See below, Ch. V.

one on each side. There is much on the obelisk base which can help to illustrate the reliefs on our two monuments, just as there is much on the monuments to illustrate the base.[1] Other monuments too, western as well as eastern, can help to fill out the picture.

The old base, according to Mordtmann and Woodward–Wace, measures 2·85 m. in height, the new one, according to Fıratlı–Rollas, 3·57 m. It might have seemed that the new base is considerably taller—a quite misleading impression. It is not that the published measurements are inaccurate,[2] but both bases were sunk some distance beneath the surface of the spina, a distance indicated clearly enough by the point below which the stone was left untreated.

From the restored top of the old base to this point is 2·30 m. (7' 8"). From the top of the new base to this level is 2·26 m. (7' 5"). Since we may be missing an inch or so from the top of the new base and since to my eye a shade too much may have been restored on the old base (this damage at the tops must date from the pulling down of the statues by the Crusaders), it is plain that both originally stood as near as makes no difference the same height above ground. This cannot be accidental.

To judge from the fixing holes on top of the bases (those on the old one have now been cemented over), and from the scale of the bases as a whole, the statues must have been of at least life size. Thus when complete with their statues both bases must have stood some 4·50 m. (over 14 feet) high.

Both bases are slightly irregular rectangles in cross-section (the irregularities no doubt accidental). The new base measures at the bottom 0·80 m. (31½") across the front, 0·76 m. (30") at the back, and 0·64 m. (25") on both sides. (On both bases the front is established by the shape and direction of the holes on the top.) The old base is 1·07 m. wide (42") at the front, 1·04 (41") at the back, and 0·81 m. (32") at each side. But since all four corners are cut inwards at a right angle (see Frontispiece), the measure-

---

[1] The only full modern study of the reliefs of the obelisk base is G. Bruns, *Der Obelisk und seine Basis* (Istanbuler Forsch. vii, 1953), a solid and useful work, but unimaginative and blinkered. 'Was man in ihm ganz vermißt', remarked J. Kollwitz (*Gnomon* xiii (1937), 427), 'das ist eine entsprechende Einbeziehung verwandter Denkmäler'—works such as those discussed in this chapter.

[2] Though since both bases are now cemented into the Museum floor it is no longer possible to check the over-all measurements.

ments of the sculptured faces are considerably smaller: front 0·76 m. (30″), back 0·73 m. (29″), sides 0·58 m. (23″).

The new base, according to the preliminary notice of the Roberts in 1965, is 'beaucoup mieux conservée'. Seen side by side as they can be again today in the Room of Christian Antiquities in the Archaeological Museum of Istanbul, there can be no doubt that the new base is much the more impressive of the two. But this is not just or even mainly because the new base is in a better state of repair. It has in fact suffered quite serious damage: the front and right sides were at some time badly scorched by a fire[1] which has spoiled the reliefs, and left little of the inscriptions on the right face and nothing on the front. If there are more inscriptions still legible on the other faces, this is because there were more to start with. There are more reliefs too, bigger and more interesting than those on the old base. Not only are the reliefs on the old base smaller (a consequence of the cutting in of the corners), they also vary in height from side to side, thus creating a less harmonious effect over all.

Each face of both bases is decorated with two or three registers carved in relief, each surmounted by a panel for inscriptions (at least one and usually two per face). On both bases the inscription above the lower relief is sometimes in prose while those above the upper reliefs are always in verse. On no fewer than seven out of the eight faces the upper relief represents Porphyrius standing in his *quadriga* in triumphal pose. Below the lower relief, again on seven out of eight faces, is an almost identical geometrical pattern in low relief: a rosette set in a lozenge set in a rectangle (a very popular motif at the period).[2] The only differences are that on the new base the rosette has four rounded leaves while on the old base it is smaller and has four fleur-de-lis-shaped palmettes; and that on the new base there are palmettes in the angles of the rectangles (except for the bottom left-hand corner on the back, where we find one of the ubiquitous peacocks of the age). The reliefs on the sides of the two bases (both regis-

[1] Perhaps the fire of August 1203, which ravaged the hippodrome: see A. M. Schneider, 'Brände in Konstantinopel', *BZ* xli (1941), 386–7.
[2] Cf. the many panels so decorated in the churches of St. Sophia and St. Eirene, the massive statue base found in the hippodrome in 1951 and now outside one of the main gates of the Istanbul Archaeological Museum, the pedestal in the Museum (Grabar, *Byzantium* (1966), Pl. 310), and another from St. Polyeuctus (*DOP* xx (1966), fig. 31 after p. 238).

THE BASES

ters) are virtually identical, whereas the front and back are in both cases altogether different.

These similarities are no doubt due in part to the makers of the second base directly imitating the first (the new one). But we shall see later (below, p. 163) that the new base was not Porphyrius' first. There was one there already (erected no more than a year or so before the new base) to serve as a pattern to both, and it may well be that both the extant bases look as much like this first one as each other. For example, the care taken to sink the over-all much shorter old base less deep in the spina so as to make it the same height as the new one suggests that this first base may have been the same height too—the common model for both the later bases.

There is little in the reliefs on either base that cannot be paralleled in earlier hippodrome art (by which term I simply mean any representation of a circus subject), but it seems likely that the over-all design and scale of these bases, not least in their sheer accumulation of traditional elements and the remarkable number of epigrams and acclamations inscribed on them, represent something new none the less, something bigger and grander than previous charioteer monuments.

We know of charioteer statues before this, and one or two inscribed bases survive.[1] We also have a few large honorific plaques listing the records of champions like Diocles[2] and Teres[3] at Rome. We have scores of gladiator stelae, some of them with three or four registers of reliefs and one or two inscriptions.[4] We also have a number of inscribed bases to statues of pantomime dancers.[5] But there does not seem to be any precedent for the combination of a rectangular stele more than seven feet tall, with all four faces decorated all over with both inscriptions and reliefs, surmounted by a statue.

In fact the closest parallel is not a monument from the sporting world proper at all: it is a parallel so close—literally so—that

[1] Lucian, *Nigrinus* 29, Galen, xiv. 604 Kühn, cf. *ILS* 5286, and for those in the Gaianum, Hülsen–Jordan, *Topographie Roms* i. 3. 662 n. 104. Cf. too Friedländer, *SG* ii[10]. 27. [2] *ILS* 5287, with Friedländer's full discussion in *SG* iv[10]. 186 f.
[3] Borsari, *Bull. comun.* 1902, 177 f.
[4] L. Robert, *Les Gladiateurs dans l'Orient grec* (1940), *passim*, for full discussion, with supplements in his *Hellenica* iii (1946), v (1948), vii (1949), and viii (1950). *Gladiateurs*, Pl. xxv has four registers, *Hellenica* viii, Pls. xii–xiii three registers.
[5] Robert, 'Pantomimen im griechischen Orient', *Hermes* lxv (1930), 106–22, and in *RÉG* lxxix (1966), 756–9.

one can only be astonished that the extent of its influence has not been perceived. I refer to the obelisk base.[1] There are a number of points of detail in individual reliefs to which we shall come in due course, but for the moment I am only concerned with the disposition of the reliefs as a whole. The top register of each of its four faces is a variation on the same tableau—a tableau in the centre of which stands the subject of the monument, Theodosius. The top registers of all four faces of the new base and three out of four faces of the old base are, again, variations on the same tableau—a tableau in which this time Porphyrius is the central figure. The lower reliefs that Theodosius looks down on are peopled with acclaiming subjects or suppliant barbarians, represented on a diminishing scale further to accentuate Theodosius' own central and dominating position. Porphyrius looks down in all directions at his diminutive acclaiming fans, thus creating exactly the same effect.[2] On the obelisk base as on both Porphyrius bases the lower reliefs on both of the side faces are more or less identical, while those on the back and front are quite different both from the sides and from each other. Given the proximity (and priority) of the obelisk to both bases, these numerous and substantial similarities can hardly be fortuitous.

But for all their similarities the two Porphyrius bases are by no means identical. There is, for example, the cutting in of the corners of the old base; the two extra faces thus created between the main faces are decorated, on the level of the geometrical patterns on the main faces, with two smaller geometrical decorations, a series of lozenges set inside each other within a square. As a result of the cutting away, the reliefs on the sides in particular are much narrower than their counterparts on the new base. Indeed, on the old base reliefs occupy a much smaller area altogether. They do not reach up so high or go down so low, covering barely 1 m. as against almost 2 m. on the front and 1·52 m. on the other three faces of the new base. On the new base the reliefs join their fellows on adjacent faces at the corners, thus (in the case of the lower registers particularly) creating an effect strikingly like that of the reliefs on the obelisk base.

[1] No one but A. Grabar (*L'Iconoclasme byzantin* (1957), 157) seems even to have noticed the parallel.
[2] The same effect is also created by use of the same formula in many contemporary consular diptychs: see J. Beckwith, *Art of Constantinople*[2] (1968), 34–5.

THE BASES

There is one difference between the two bases that particularly catches the eye. On the new base the upper inscription panels are supported at each corner by ungainly caryatids; they stand on the top of the lower inscription panels and look outwards, their legs and arms astride the corners. They are winged Victories, such as the marginally more graceful specimens that hover above Porphyrius on the front face of both bases—and the many more on the columns of Arcadius and Marcian and elsewhere in the art of this period. They are wholly conventional representatives of the genre. Note, for example, the traditional short tunic billowing out just below the bust, and (above all) the way the dress clings to their legs—a stale and inappropriate echo of the classical prototype, where this effect is appropriate enough with one who is flying rapidly through the air. Our four Nikai are not only stationary: they each face in opposite directions.

The two on the front of the old base are no less conventional. For the palm in the left hand of the one on the right of Porphyrius we may compare (out of many examples) the large relief from the Gate of Ayvan Saray (mid fifth century);[1] the other Victory holds a crown in her right—a motif so common on both coins and reliefs as hardly to require specific illustration. By contrast with the caryatids, the legs of the one above Porphyrius on the front of the new base are much too short—and bent backwards at an uncomfortable angle. She too presumably holds a crown, but the relief is too badly damaged at this point to be sure.

Several parallels can be cited for these figures from the relief work of the early to mid fifth century, but there is in every case the same difference. Even the modest degree of freedom and suppleness that informs the earlier reliefs is absent from the stiff ungainly figures of the two Porphyrius bases.

The Frontal Chariot

On all four faces of the new base and on three faces of the old base the central figure in the top register itself is Porphyrius standing full face in his quadriga, always in the same costume and stance; palm in left and crown in upraised right hand, except for the front of the new base where he holds a (now broken away) whip and the right face where he holds both a whip and

[1] Kollwitz, *Oström. Plastik*, 77 f.; Beckwith, *Art of Constantinople*, 23.

a crown. On all four faces of the new base and the front of the old base the bodies of the horses are represented full face (with their heads inclined in varying symmetrical patterns to the side). On the sides of the old base the horses are represented in profile, the pair on the left facing left, those on the right right, with the inside horse in each case looking back over its shoulder. Woodward and Wace contented themselves with quoting the parallel of the Selinus metope for the quadriga *en face*. The history of the motif during the intervening millennium is both interesting in itself and not without relevance to the reliefs on our two bases.

In 1938 G. Hafner collected and analysed more than 150 examples from the archaic period.[1] In all these examples the bodies of the horses are viewed frontally, though the heads are frequently turned to one side. In the classical period this type is joined by what Hafner called the 'gesprengten Schema', the divided pattern: the four horses are split into two pairs facing to the sides and viewed in half or three-quarters profile. After the fourth century B.C. both types seem to die out. They are absent from all hellenistic and early imperial art, but the latter, the divided pattern, reappears early in the third century A.D. on coins and medallions, and is common thereafter.[2] In a paper that appeared almost simultaneously with Hafner's dissertation, H. Seyrig drew attention to an example from a Palmyrene relief of the third century A.D., and compared several later Sassanian examples, postulating a common Parthian model.[3]

It is of course very likely that this postulated Parthian prototype was in origin no more than an 'orientalization' of the classical prototype, but nevertheless it is clearly the oriental rather than the classical tradition that influenced late Roman art. Not only is there the 500-year gap in the classical tradition. There is the fact that all the earliest third-century examples within the Empire come from its eastern provinces. There is no

[1] *Viergespanne in Vorderansicht* (Diss. Berlin 1938); and cf. *AJA* 1972, 4–5
[2] Hafner, pp. 73 f., H. P. L'Orange, *Studies in the Iconography of Sacred Kingship* (1953), 143.
[3] 'Sur quelques sculptures palmyréniennes', *Syria* xviii (1937), 43 f. (cf. now D. Schlumberger, *La Palmyrène du nord-ouest* (1951), 82–3, Pl. xxxviii. 2), cf. too Elisabeth Riefstahl, 'A Coptic Roundel in the Brooklyn Museum', *Coptic Studies in Honor of W. E. Crum* (1950), 531–40, and M. Bussagli, 'The "Frontal" Representation of the Divine Chariot', *East and West* vi (1955), 9–25.

THE BASES

example struck from a Roman mint before the reign of Probus (276–82). More significant still, these examples from within the Empire share with the Palmyrene and Sassanian quadrigae a detail that is wholly foreign to the classical prototype: the representation of the chariot wheels side on. This violation of the ordinary canons of perspective[1] is common to all the late Roman examples, from the third right down to the eighth century. More generally, all are characterized by the rigidity and wholly unrealistic symmetry of the oriental model. There is never any pretence that the quadriga is doing anything but pose—and that very awkwardly—to have its picture taken.

In most of the third-century coins the charioteer is Sol, the sun-god, and his chariot is symbolic. As early as Caracalla (211–17), however, we find that Sol has turned into a Roman emperor, though it is not till the dynasty of Constantine that this way of representing the Emperor becomes standard and common.[2] As the famous medallion of Constantius II well illustrates (Pl. 31.3), perhaps the most striking feature of the type (borrowed from Sol) is the upraised and outstretched right hand, the 'numinous gesture'[3] of power and majesty so common in late imperial art.

A. Grabar has recently underlined the parallelism between the representation of Porphyrius in his quadriga (on the old base) and this imperial type:[4]

Soulignons d'autre part, le lien qui unit l'iconographie triomphale du cocher à celle des empereurs. Il est inutile d'insister sur l'identité iconographique de l'image frontale de l'aurige Porphyre, debout dans

---

[1] I do not wish to suggest that the archaic type was in *true* perspective. No observer can see all four horses of a quadriga frontally at once, and the angle at which the heads are inclined usually lacks 'an anatomical explanation' (see the interesting discussion in J. White, *Perspective in Ancient Drawing and Painting*, Hell. Soc. Suppl. Paper 7, 1956, 11 f.). Yet to the untrained eye the archaic pattern is lifelike in a way that the late antique stereotype is clearly not. See too now (briefly) G. M. A. Richter, *Perspective in Greek and Roman Art* (1970), 16.

[2] L'Orange, *Iconography of Sacred Kingship*, 145 f., R. Brilliant, *Gesture and Rank in Roman Art* (1963), 180. Whether or not Caracalla had any influence on the provincial mint that produced this type, it would certainly have pleased him: for according to Dio (lxxviii. 10. 3) he used to boast that his own style as a charioteer was based on Sol (ἔλεγε κατὰ τὸν Ἥλιον τῇ ἁρματηλασίᾳ χρῆσθαι). It is an interesting coincidence that Caracalla's brother Geta should be the first emperor shown as the Sun-god by an official mint—though not in a chariot: cf. Alföldi, *Röm. Mitt.* l (1935), 107–8.

[3] The phrase is Brilliant's, *Gesture and Rank*, p. 180; much material also in L'Orange, Ch. 16, *passim*.

[4] *L'Iconoclasme byzantin* (1957), 158.

son char et faisant le geste de la victoire, et des images impériales du même sujet : une monnaie de Constance II et une autre de Maurice, des tissus célèbres, donnant au souverain-cocher la même attitude, groupent les chevaux de la même façon et introduisent la même disproportion entre la taille du cocher, trop grand, et ses chevaux trop petits. Comme Dionysos et Mithra dans les arts du Levant, le cocher triomphateur est honoré d'une image qui aurait pu être celle de son souverain.

This is a true and important observation. The quadriga reliefs on the sides of the old base are indeed a classic illustration of the symmetrically divided pattern quadriga that we find on imperial medallions, even down to the transverse wheels. Nevertheless, there are two objections to at least the emphasis of Grabar's analysis.

In the first place, there can be little question of the Porphyrius reliefs being *directly* influenced (as Grabar had assumed) by imperial iconography. The motif had already been adapted to the circus charioteer in the West at least a century before Porphyrius' day. Of this there is abundant documentation in a variety of media.

The circus charioteer in his quadriga (or biga) is of course a frequent sight on the reliefs, mosaics, and paintings of the early Empire—but always in full or three-quarter profile.[1] There is no example of the quadriga *en face* before the first appearance of the motif on coins, that is to say (for the West) in the last quarter of the third century. Not surprisingly, in view of the immense popularity of chariot racing in the West, the motif was almost at once appropriated for real instead of symbolic charioteers. There can, I think, be no doubt that the prototype of the Porphyrius reliefs was firmly established in fourth-century Rome—or that it was from Rome that it reached Constantinople.

One of the best commentaries on the charioteer bases as a whole—a source oddly neglected by earlier commentators—is the contorniates, a series of commemorative medallions struck mostly at Rome but occasionally in other western cities in the late fourth and early fifth centuries.[2] A large proportion of them

---

[1] For an inventory of circus representations see G. Forni, *Enc. dell'arte antica* ii (1959), 649–52. There is a good selection of reliefs and paintings in L. Vogel, *Art Bulletin* li (1969), 155 f.

[2] A. Alföldi, *Die Kontorniaten*, Text und Tafeln, 1942–3. A new and much expanded edition is being prepared by Mrs. E. Alföldi. See too S. Mazzarino's article 'Contorniati' in *Enc. dell'arte antica*.

THE BASES

carry crude and stereotyped representations of the various sorts of popular entertainments of the day—gladiatorial games, wildbeast shows, pantomime dancing, and (of course) chariot-racing. There is on a number of contorniates the exact prototype of the tableaux of the sides of the old Porphyrius base:[1] the charioteer standing full face in his quadriga, his horses in profile symmetrically arranged just as on the base. The wheels of the chariot are likewise shown in profile. The charioteer holds a palm leaf in his left hand and a crown and/or whip in his upraised right. It is always the whip and/or crown that Porphyrius holds in his right hand. He does not (as Grabar alleges) make the imperial gesture of victory.[2] This same quadriga tableau, identical down to almost the last detail, is also portrayed on a number of fourth-century mosaics (mostly from North Africa)[3] and on two engraved glasses of approximately this date.[4]

There is a further detail in which these fourth- and fifth-century western representations provide a particularly good commentary on the side reliefs of the old base. On both sides of the base the names of Porphyrius' horses are inscribed immediately above their heads (see p. 48). On a fourth-century mosaic from Dougga we find exactly parallel inscriptions above the heads of the two inside horses.[5] All four horses are named on one of the glasses, as also on a contorniate,[6] though from considerations of space round the rim, not above their heads. Indeed this naming of race-horses, whether on mosaics, reliefs, lamps, contorniates, knife-handles, and even children's counters,[7] was a well-established western practice.

So even down to such small details as the location of the equine inscriptions and the objects held in the respective hands of the charioteer, the Porphyrius reliefs can be seen to be faithful copies, not of contemporary imperial medallions, but of this western circus prototype. Even the disproportion between driver and team is a regular feature of the contorniate type.

There is another objection to Grabar's view. He quotes

[1] Pl. 31.5, 6, 9.
[2] Contrast the different effect this gesture gives in (say) the medallion of Constantius: Pl. 31.3..
[3] Pl. 25 and cf. *Rev. archéol.* vii (1850), 260, Pl. 143.
[4] Pl. 31.1–2.   [5] Pl. 25.   [6] Pl. 31.9.
[7] See the collection of material in J. M. C. Toynbee, *PBSR* xvi (1948), 32f., with Pls. i–vii.

consular medallions of Constantius II (337–61)[1] and Maurice 583 or 602),[2] and some textiles, not usually now dated before the eighth or ninth century.[3] It might have seemed a reasonable assumption that this motif persisted evenly throughout the period, yet this is not in fact so. After the fourth century it disappears entirely from the repertory of imperial themes till the late sixth. The medallions of Maurice, the only ones extant, were probably modelled on a medallion struck by his predecessor Tiberius II. No specimen has survived, but Gregory of Tours describes the medallions which Tiberius sent the Frankish King Chilperic as having a quadriga on the reverse,[4] and a crude bronze plaque representing a frontal quadriga from a Frankish grave at Monceau may be a local imitation.[5] Then there is a gold plaque in the de Clercq collection in Paris which represents an emperor in frontal six-horse chariot scattering coins, the so-called 'liberalitas' type.[6] It has been argued on stylistic grounds that the emperor is Justin II; if so, the plaque was presumably made by being pressed over a consular medallion issued in 566 or 568.[7] There is a gold bracelet at Dumbarton Oaks with a similar 'liberalitas' scene which was probably made by the same method, to judge from the incomplete lettering taken from a medallion of Maurice.[8] An emperor in quadriga holding a *mappa* on another pressed plaque in the British Museum probably represents Phocas.[9] The very popularity of the motif in the last third of the

[1] Constantius was consul nine times during this period, so the medallion cannot be precisely dated.
[2] That is to say, either his first consulate (Grierson, *DOP* xv (1961), 221 f.) or his second (Grierson again, *Num. Chron.*[6] xv (1955), 61 f.).
[3] For bibliography and arguments on the question see [J. Beckwith], *Masterpieces of Byzantine Art* (1958), no. 56; *Art of Constantinople*, p. 58 and notes.
[4] *Hist. Franc.* vi. 2.
[5] G. Behrens, *Mainzer Zeitschrift* 39/40 (1944/5), 17–19, no. 2a; cf. M. C. Ross, *DOP* xi (1957), 255.
[6] A. de Ridder, *Collection de Clercq* vii. i: *Les Bijoux* (Paris 1911), p. 260, no. 1416, Pl. vii.
[7] Ross, op. cit., 256, with an interesting discussion of late sixth-century medallions and this method of producing gold plaques from them.
[8] Ross, p. 256 and in *Catalogue of the Byzantine Antiquities in Dumbarton Oaks* ii (1965), no. 2, Pl. vi. The pendant intaglio representing an emperor in frontal six-horse chariot acquired by Dumbarton Oaks since the publication of the *Catalogue* (*Handbook of the Byzantine Collection in Dumbarton Oaks*[2] (1967), no. 333, Pl. 333) probably dates from the period of Tiberius and Maurice also—perhaps an imitation of Maurice's 'liberalitas' medallion.
[9] Ross, p. 256, fig. 9.

sixth century underlines its absence from the preceding century and a half, throughout the period in which the long career of Porphyrius falls.

Scholars have debated whether or not the frontal quadriga type refers to a real function of the Emperor: his consular procession, for example. Current opinion seems against this, though the possibility remains open that there is a reference to the procession into the circus on the occasion of the games traditionally given at the consular inauguration.[1] It is strengthened by the coincidence that the quadriga type disappears at the same time as the *pompa circensis* itself, which is never attested in Constantinople. It is obviously tempting to see a link between the two. H. Stern has suggested that the motif was dropped because of the pagan associations of the *pompa circensis*[2] (one thinks of Ovid's account in *Amores* iii. 2. 43 f.). This is a possibility, though hardly a compelling one. Surprisingly enough, no one has referred in this context to the adaptation of the motif to the circus charioteer, particularly on contorniates. Could not this be why it was dropped from the cycle of imperial themes? No emperor would wish to be mistaken for a circus performer. It is significant that while contorniates will often show the Emperor on horseback, whether hunting or trampling on the foe,[3] they never show him in a quadriga, whether frontal or in profile. The quadriga is reserved exclusively for the circus charioteer.

The motif of the Emperor on horseback is indeed common throughout the Byzantine period: its history was admirably traced in an earlier work of Grabar.[4] Naturally enough in view of the importance of chariot racing and the ceremonial of the hippodrome in Byzantine life, there is an official cycle of hippodrome scenes (we can now add to their number the lower relief on the back of the new base). Yet the Emperor is always shown as a *spectator*. The medallions of Maurice and Tiberius seem to be the only examples since the late fourth century of an emperor being shown *in* a quadriga.

There can in fact be little doubt that (for whatever reason) the Emperor in quadriga is one of the many traditional themes

---

[1] Discussion and bibliography in H. Stern, *Le Calendrier de 354* (1953), 158 f., though add J. M. C. Toynbee, *Roman Medallions* (1944), 84 f.
[2] *Le Calendrier*, 161–3.
[3] Alföldi, *Die Kontorniaten*, 117 for a list.
[4] *L'Empereur dans l'art byzantin* (1936), 45 f., 133 f.

of the imperial iconography eliminated between the fourth and sixth centuries. There were more than fifty reverse types to the coinage of Constantius II (337–61), only twenty in the much longer reign of Theodosius II (408–50); in the thirty years of Anastasius the repertory shrank to a mere five.[1] By contrast, under Maurice and Tiberius a number of consular types not seen since the fourth century were briefly resurrected, apparently taken directly from fourth-century models.[2] The quadriga motif is evidently one of these isolated temporary revivals, in the age of Porphyrius barely known outside the circle of coin collectors.

As for the textiles to which Grabar refers, they actually tell against his case. For despite what is often said or assumed, none of them is a straightforward representation of either a Byzantine emperor or a Sassanian sun-god. Indeed, the Aachen–Cluny textile[3] (reputedly from the tomb of Charlemagne) and the Münsterbilsen textile[4] are an excellent commentary on the Porphyrius reliefs.

On both these textiles, as also on a ninth-century fragment from the Victoria and Albert,[5] the reins are taken up and behind the driver's waist, as on the Porphyrius reliefs (and other circus charioteer representations). The reins of the Emperor-charioteer (if shown at all) are not so featured. The circus driver's reins were so fastened to prevent him dropping them in the excitement of the race (he carried a knife to free himself in the event of a crash).

On the Aachen–Cluny textile a youth (? a groom) stands on each side of the quadriga, exactly as on the front of the new Porphyrius base. The left-hand groom on the base holds a palm leaf, the other an object which has been broken off but was no doubt one of the two objects held by his counterpart on the textile, a whip or a crown. Beneath the quadriga are two more youths emptying coins from cornucopiae, a common motif on consular diptychs and of obvious agonistic significance.

On the old base Porphyrius again has attendants, on both front and back, but this time chubby little cupids, putti, as usual holding appropriate objects. We do find on contorniates pantomime dancers attended by putti (usually brandishing crowns).[6]

[1] Grabar, *L'Empereur*, 159.   [2] Ibid. 12–13.   [3] Pl. 26.   [4] Pl. 27.
[5] Grabar, *L'Empereur*, Pl. ix. 2; Pierce and Tyler, *DOP* ii (1941), p. 23 and Pl. 10b.   [6] Pl. 31.7.

And in earlier imperial art putti frequently occur in circus scenes, driving and even pulling chariots on both gems and sarcophagi.[1] But the closest parallel is provided by the Münsterbilsen textile, where winged putti holding crowns flank the charioteer on each side.

The Dumbarton Oaks bracelet in most respects follows the pattern of the Constantius medallions but with the addition of a crown-brandishing attendant on each side of the quadriga as well as a Victory hovering above.[2] Now the detail of the flanking attendants goes right back to the archaic prototype 1,000 years before, and they also appear in several third-century examples.[3] But not on the fourth-century medallions, or indeed (to my knowledge) on any coin or medallion ever struck at Constantinople. Especially in view of their short tunics, which recall the grooms of the Porphyrius reliefs and Aachen–Cluny textile, it seems not impossible that these figures derive, not from the tradition of the Emperor-charioteer, but, if not direct from charioteer-stelae (not necessarily Porphyrius'), medallions, or mosaics, at least from such hybrid quadriga representations as those of our three textiles.

The Münsterbilsen driver, like the Victoria and Albert driver, wears what looks much more like the familiar tunic of the charioteer[4] than anything the Emperor is shown wearing on such occasions. The Aachen–Cluny driver does not wear the charioteer's tunic, but then neither does he wear imperial

[1] Most recent study (omitting gems), L. Vogel, *Art Bulletin* li (1969), 155 f., with earlier bibliography (except for M. Turcan-Déleani, *MEFR* lxxvi (1964), 43 f.); for some of the many gems see H. B. Walters, *Catalogue of the Engraved Gems and Cameos in the British Museum* (1926), nos. 2843 f., with Pl. xxx; P. Fossing, *Catalogue of the Antique engraved Gems and Cameos in the Thorvaldsen Collection* (1929), nos. 726 f.
[2] Above, p. 22 n. 8.
[3] See Hafner's lists, *passim*.
[4] On this see, for example, R. Hanoune, *MEFR* lxxxi (1969), 250; H. Stern, *Recueil général des mosaïques de la Gaule* ii. 1 (1967), 68. See too now the account by M. P. Tambella of the four charioteers from the villa at Baccano (late second/early third century), complete with large colour photographs, in *Mosaici antichi in Italia: Regione settima (Baccano: villa romana)* x, a cura di G. Becatti, etc. (Rome 1970), 71–9, Pls. xxii–xxv. Woodward–Wace, pp. 82–3, give a good description of Porphyrius' outfit (transcribed by Vasiliev, p. 38), to which the reliefs of the new base add nothing. The twisted thongs round the midriff were designed to protect the ribs, as two experienced ancient doctors expressly state: Galen, XVIII. 1. 774–5 Kühn, and a passage of Soranus published by H. Schöne (*JDAI* xviii (1903), 70) with an illustration from the manuscript (Abb. 2).

costume. And like the victorious charioteer but unlike either Emperor or sun-god, he is bare-headed. Porphyrius is bareheaded on every relief where he appears. Like Porphyrius too, neither the Münsterbilsen nor the Aachen–Cluny driver makes the imperial gesture with his right hand: the former indeed brandishes the charioteer's whip.[1]

Previous commentators have drawn attention to certain Sassanian elements in the composition of these textiles,[2] and rightly so. Yet what is not Sassanian owes more to the stereotype of the circus charioteer than to imperial iconography.[3] And if the motif of the Emperor-charioteer was as rare in Constantinople as I have suggested, this is hardly surprising.

The foregoing remarks are not intended to suggest that there are no links at all between the Porphyrius stelae and imperial iconography. Far from it. As emphasized above (p. 16), the structure and arrangement of the reliefs on both bases is clearly influenced by those of the obelisk base, with Porphyrius taking the place of the Emperor. And we shall have occasion to recur to the significance of circus games in the imperial ceremonial, the 'imperial liturgy' of the hippodrome. There was indeed a sense in which it was felt that the Emperor shared in the triumphs of the charioteer.[4] As we can see from the Book of Ceremonies, the victory of a charioteer would give rise to acclamations in honour of the Emperor as well as the charioteer.[5]

All that I dispute is the assumption that Porphyrius was deliberately portrayed in frontal quadriga so as to play on or encourage this identification by recalling the image of the Emperor-charioteer. And I dispute this, not because the notion is implausible in itself, but simply because the charioteer stereotype was in all probability much more familiar to the average circus-mad Byzantine than the imperial quadriga motif. When this average citizen gazed up at the monuments of Porphyrius, he saw (I would suggest), not a charioteer symbolizing in his

[1] See p. 46.
[2] Beckwith, *Art of Constantinople*, 59–60.
[3] W. F. Vollbach's recent study *Early Decorative Textiles* (1969) assumes, without even mentioning the possibility that they might be emperors, that the Aachen–Cluny textile represents a 'circus scene' (p. 114), and that the Münsterbilsen driver, if not a circus charioteer, is Alexander entering heaven (p. 96).
[4] Or rather the other way round: see below, p. 248 ff.
[5] Below, p. 249.

THE BASES

moment of triumph the victories of his Emperor—but just Porphyrius.[1]

The sides of the old base are a classic example (together with the reliefs of the obelisk base) of the 'oriental' inverted perspective that is so striking a feature of Byzantine work. The scene is represented, not as we might expect to see it, but more as Porphyrius himself might have seen it. This is why he towers so disproportionately above his team—and even more so above the (to him) tiny and distant spectators, who are accordingly represented on a lower plane.

It is a measure of what has been called the 'Inkonsequenz'[2] of late Roman art that the front face (like all four faces of the new base) returns to the classical full-face quadriga in orthodox perspective.[3] The bodies of the horses are shown absolutely full face, with only their front legs visible. Their heads (so far as one can discern from the angle of the necks, since the actual heads are now broken away) are only slightly—though of course symmetrically—inclined to the side, most with the team on the back of the new base. I do not recall seeing anything so close to the original prototype of the archaic period in all late Roman and early Byzantine art. The sculptors cannot (of course) be credited with originality in the ordinary sense here. The repetition of the same pattern on five out of eight faces is sufficient commentary. We must assume that they had studied a classical example. And where more likely than that veritable museum of classical statuary, the hippodrome of Constantinople?[4] Naturally one thinks of the great free-standing quadriga above the *carceres*, which would certainly have appeared frontal to anyone working on the spina.

If our sculptors cannot claim originality for their innovation, they do not deserve much praise either (except in so far as the horses—as so often in early Byzantine art—are distinctly freer and more lifelike than the human figures).[5] For they have not,

[1] Accordingly one may perhaps doubt whether Grabar was wholly justified in attributing the significance he did (*L'Iconoclasme byzantin*, 155 f.) to Constantine V's replacement of the images of the ecumenical councils on the ceiling of the Milion with a picture of his favourite charioteer, though there will certainly have been imperial connotations in the victory symbolism (see p. 251).

[2] Hafner, *Viergespanne*, 120.

[3] By 'orthodox' I do not of course mean correct in the accepted sense: see p. 19 n. 1 above.

[4] Mango, *DOP* xvii (1963), 55 f.   [5] Beckwith, *Art of Constantinople*, 13.

of course, produced the classical form pure. In all other respects they retained the lifeless symmetry of the stereotype, transverse chariot wheels and all. For a similar partial use of 'orthodox' perspective compare the quadrigae on the two engraved glasses and the Dougga mosaic, where the bodies of the horses are foreshortened instead of being shown in straight profile, though in other respects corresponding to the 'oriental' stereotype. The result, no doubt the quite unconscious result, is an unhappy combination of very different techniques.[1]

The Tychae

The Tychae, city goddesses, that hover so uneasily above Porphyrius' head on the upper registers of three out of four faces, are absent from the old base, perhaps beneficially so. With Victories at each corner and on the front of the new base, there are quite enough females crowding poor Porphyrius already on the top registers. A large part of each face is covered with wings and draperies of assorted sizes. To make matters worse, the Tychae seem just to spring out of Porphyrius' head. All carry their traditional cornucopiae (indicating that the cities they represent are offering Porphyrius their riches) and wear the traditional mural crown.[2] Fortunately it is possible from (damaged) inscriptions on the ledges above the reliefs to identify two of them: on the right, Nicomedia; on the back, Berytus—both cities well known for their hippodromes. It is a fair guess that the other is Constantinople. Miss Toynbee suggests to me that what appears to be a Nike above Porphyrius' head on the front face might in fact be a winged Tyche of Constantinople. A winged Constantinople would not be entirely unparalleled,[3] and she is certainly wearing a crown, but the fact that the three indisputable Tychae, in other respects corresponding in position and function with the figure on the front face, are all shown without wings perhaps tells against the notion.

Presumably Porphyrius had won great victories at festivals in Nicomedia and Berytus not long before the successes in Con-

[1] What Mango has called a 'troubling disharmony . . . which results from the use of a classical repertoire in a completely unclassical manner' (*Treasures of Turkey* (Skira 1966), 87).
[2] Cf. the relief (of unknown provenance) from *c.* 500 published by A. Grabar, *Sculpture byzantine de Constantinople (IV-X siècle)* 1963, Pl. v. 4, pp. 25 f.
[3] J. M. C. Toynbee, *Studies . . . D. M. Robinson* ii (1953), 276.

stantinople that won him the new base. We know regrettably little about inter-city sport in late antiquity. In hellenistic and early imperial times there had of course been a considerable number of festivals at all the great (and many not so great) cities of Asia Minor and mainland Greece, and we learn from a multitude of honorific inscriptions that it was the normal practice for athletes, dancers, and other performers to travel from one festival to another over the length and breadth of the Empire, accumulating titles and prizes. By Porphyrius' day virtually all these festivals had disappeared, though there is some evidence that charioteers and pantomimes, now the main attractions, performed at more than one city. The great dancers and charioteers of Porphyrius' day came to Constantinople from all corners of the Empire—Alexandria, Cyzicus, Emesa, Nicaea, and Tyre happen to stand on record[1]—no doubt working their way up through the provinces to Antioch and Constantinople. Porphyrius was driving for the Greens at Antioch in 507,[2] several years after he had won the two extant monuments in the capital. Cassiodorus writes of a dancer of the Greens at Rome who had come from the East.[3] A law of 409 (*Cod. Theod.* xv. 5. 3) forbidding provincial governors to court popularity by attracting charioteers and horses from other cities and provinces suggests that such poaching had reached unhealthy proportions. That it did not cease is shown by Justinian's reissue of the ban (*Cod. Just.* xi. 41. 5), adding wild beasts and actors to its scope.

Some games will, as in the earlier period, have been more important than others. A victory at the consular games of Constantinople, for example, must have ranked high. Another occasion often referred to in the chronicles is the festival of the foundation of the city, on 11 May. It could well be that the four cities which honour Porphyrius represented a sort of 'grand slam', like the Olympia, Pythia, Nemea, and Isthmia in the old sacred festivals, or the recognized major championships aimed at by tennis players and racing drivers today.

Such personifications of cities, provinces, etc., were very common in the art and literature of late antiquity, and it is more than likely that the new base is not the first such monument on which they appear. It is the normal practice for inscriptions honouring

[1] Malalas, p. 386; *A.P.* xv. 45. 1; *A. Pl.* 378. 1.
[2] Malalas, p. 395.   [3] *Var.* iii. 51. 1.

athletes and the like to mention prominently the native city to which his victories are such a credit (see below, p. 170), and the extension of this motif from verbal to pictorial form may have been firmly established before Porphyrius' day. An epigram from a monument to another charioteer, a generation or so younger than Porphyrius, Uranius, opens with the following couplet (xvi. 378. 1–2):

Οὐράνιος Νίκαιαν ἔχει πέλας ὁπλοτέρην τε
'Ρώμην, τῆς μὲν ἐών, τῇ δ' ἔνι κῦδος ἑλών.

Commentators have supposed that Uranius stood between *statues* of Nicaea and Constantinople (the 'younger' Rome), but is it not more likely that the two cities were represented doing honour to Uranius on one of the reliefs on the base of his own statue? We might explain similarly the opening words of the following epigram from one of Porphyrius' lost bases (xv. 47. 1–2):

Τοῦτον Πορφύριον Λιβύη τέκε, θρέψε δὲ 'Ρώμη,
Νίκη δ' ἐστεφάνωσεν . . .

Victory crowning Porphyrius, both from the air and on the ground, is represented pictorially on the front of both new and old bases. Perhaps Africa, Constantinople, and Nike were all represented on the relief above xv. 47. Such tableaux are quite common on consular diptychs.[1]

The Lower Registers of the Two Bases

Let us turn now to the lower registers on the side faces of the two bases. On both the scenes are identical (though the treatment varies slightly), and in addition both are devoted, not to Porphyrius (at least not directly), but to the spectators of the hippodrome, acclaiming his victories in different ways.

There is here a link between the reliefs and the inscriptions above them which is not generally so obvious elsewhere on the bases. In each case the inscription is an acclamation from one or other of the factions. A further link between the two bases here is the fact that in both cases one acclamation is put in the mouth of the *opposing* faction. On the left side of the old base (from the Blues) the Greens are represented as begging Porphyrius to ride for them in future (text below, p. 67); on the

[1] Cf., for example, Miss Toynbee, op. cit. 275.

right side of the new base (from the Greens) the Blues admit that the Greens have won the day, and lament their own unsuccessful attempts to enlist Porphyrius as a Blue (text, p. 80). On the left-hand side of the new (Green) base we have the boastful and polemical claim—evidently the sentiments of the Greens themselves this time—that this is Porphyrius' greatest triumph; he has ridden down and enslaved his enemies (text, p. 67). The corresponding inscription on the old base is unfortunately worn away. Woodward and Wace in 1912 contented themselves with the observation that 'Practically all traces of the letters have disappeared'. Mordtmann in 1880 read ΠΟΡ at the beginning of the first line, and ΟΥΠΟΤ at the beginning of what would have been the third line. ΠΟ in line 1 seems reasonably certain to me, followed after a space for one letter by traces consistent with little but a Φ. So Πο[ρ]φ[υρι(ος)] is inevitable—though in the context scarcely helpful. In line 3 ΟΥΠΟ though faint, seems clear enough, and even without Mordtmann's tau, οὔπο[τε] looks almost inescapable. This is much more valuable. For rash, even absurd, though it might seems to infer the gist of a whole inscription from just four letters, granted that it is an acclamation addressed to Porphyrius, and in the light of the corresponding acclamation on the new base, οὔποτε surely suggests something to the general effect: 'never have you won a greater victory'. If this is on the right lines, then we should have an acclamation from the faction who put up the base, just as on the new base. The parallelism between the sides of the two bases would be complete.

It is interesting to compare—or rather contrast—the inscription from the lower panel on the front of the old base. Like the inscriptions on the side panels it is in prose and it is an acclamation. Yet, unlike the acclamations on the side faces, it is not polemical or partisan. It is simply a straightforward claim that Porphyrius has established a record by winning the *diversium* twice (text, p. 208). Unfortunately we are again foiled by an obliterated panel in the corresponding position on the new base, but luckily the series of epigrams in the Anthology makes it virtually certain that the missing inscription was not an acclamation at all, but an uncontentious epigram: see p. 93. It begins to look as if there was a convention, begun perhaps on the first (now lost) of the Porphyrius bases, that the lower half of the sides of the bases was set aside for representations of and acclamations from the factions.

The acclamations from the opposition are still something of a puzzle. Kaibel (who had not seen the base)[1] imagined that the one on the old base was scrawled up unofficially by some rowdies ('a seditiosis clam subscripta')—as if the Blues would have left a whole panel empty for graffiti from the opposition! The parallel of the new base shows that they must have been sanctioned by the faction erecting the monument, but were they fictitious acclamations which they put in the mouth of the opposition, or genuine opposition statements? I would suggest that the tone of the acclamations, the defiance of the old and the disappointment of the new one, strongly favours the second alternative.

If, then, each faction invited the opposition to contribute an acclamation for its monuments, it looks as if such monuments were erected with the consent of *both* factions. We know that the Emperor had to give his consent (p. 227), but it may be that he would not do so unless the defeated faction agreed that the charioteer in question merited a statue. For if they did not agree, then a statue erected under such circumstances would almost certainly cause trouble—and trouble between the factions in the reign of Anastasius usually ended with the imperial guards being sent in to separate the combatants. If this suggestion is correct, it might explain how it was possible for 'envy' to prevent the charioteer Constantine being given a statue (see p. 211). One might not have expected his own faction to envy his success, but the other side might well have done so, to the extent that they refused to allow his just reward.

We may now move on to the reliefs which accompany these acclamations, starting with the new base. On both sides (with minor differences of detail) we have groups of partisans, most of whom are waving what appear to be banners in pairs above their heads (Pl. 15–16).

There does not happen to be an example of this tableau on mosaics or contorniates, but an exact parallel is provided by another object from the hippodrome of Constantinople, a curious

---

[1] *Ep. Gr.* (1878), 935 (p. 389). Not having seen the base, Kaibel could not know that the inscription was neatly set out on a panel of its own.

THE BASES

hollow piece of marble apparently used for some sort of ball game.[1] It measures 0·77 m. high by 0·57/55 m. wide and is decorated with a series of circus scenes in relief on four sides. Since I cannot think of any description in English half as convenient as the name 'Kugelspiel' which German scholars have given it, Kugelspiel it shall be.

The parallel is the more striking in that on the Kugelspiel as on the new base the scene is repeated on both sides. In both cases, moreover, the repetition is not exact: there are the usual slight variations in detail (compare the almost but never quite identical quadriga reliefs on the top registers of the bases, and the four differing views of the Kathisma on the obelisk base).

On the upper register of the right face of the Kugelspiel (Pl. 15) we have two figures in knee-length tunics (as *passim* on the bases) holding each end of a similar banner, the only difference being that this time the banner is sinking downwards instead of billowing upwards. Beneath the arch thus made stand two smaller figures, exactly paralleled by the smaller figure in the middle of the right side of the base, standing, not beneath the arch of a banner, but between two pairs of banner-wavers.

On the upper register of the left face of the Kugelspiel (Pl. 16), we have again two figures holding a banner aloft while two smaller figures stand beneath the arch, only this time there is an additional figure to the left of the tableau, and the left-hand banner-holder and right-hand small figure face to the right. This last-named figure is evidently playing a wind instrument, which for the sake of convenience I shall call a flute. The right-hand figure on the right-hand side of the new base is holding an object (now mostly broken away) in his hands at chest level, his head bent forward so that he is facing the juncture of his hands. Even without the parallel from the Kugelspiel, it is difficult to imagine what he could be doing but playing a flute. The same applies to the figure on the left of this face, and to the diminutive figure in the middle.

Closer inspection of the way the three other miniature figures on the Kugelspiel (all facing the front) stand with both elbows jutting out suggests that they too are flautists—a notion confirmed

[1] O. Wulff, *Beschreibung d. Altchristl. u. Mittelalterl. Byzantin. u. Italien. Bildwerke* i (1909), no. 27, pp. 16–17, and J. Gottwald, *Archäol. Anzeiger* 1931, 152–72. For earlier bibliography, below, p. 63.

by a comparison with the line of hippodrome personnel portrayed along the bottom of face A_1 of the obelisk base (Pl. 19). Three flautists represented in precisely this stance can clearly be discerned. Two together on the left of the organ near the right-hand side, one of whom holds a happily undamaged and plainly visible double flute, while his neighbour's is now only a ridge from his mouth to his chest. Continuing along the line to the left, we meet first four female figures, evidently dancing, then another flautist (the instrument looks like a syrinx), then more dancers.

In fact, with the exception of the tiny figures at each end of the face who are attending to the organs, everyone is either dancing or playing the flute. And surely the same is true of the scenes on both the Kugelspiel and the new base. All the banner-wavers are dancing, and all those not dancing are playing the flute.

The parallelism with the obelisk base can be pushed a little further even. The three figures between the organ and the syrinx-player on the left side of the face are described by G. Bruns,[1] the only commentator to mention them, as dancing girls. The one on the right certainly is, but the other two have no hint of a bust, nor of the delicately pinched waist of their indisputably female neighbour—or the four other dancing girls on the other side of the syrinx-player. But whatever their sex, more significant is the fact that on closer inspection they appear to be waving something above their heads, something each is holding aloft in his outside hand—exactly the pose of the banner-wavers on the other two monuments. In the light of these parallels we may surely conclude that these two also are waving a banner, one less crudely executed than the banana-like objects of the Porphyrius base and the Kugelspiel.

There is another parallel for some elements of this festive tableau: one of the scenes from the series of hippodrome frescoes in the Cathedral of S. Sophia in Kiev. Though distant in time (early twelfth century) and place from Porphyrius, they were executed by workmen from Constantinople—and suggest that little had changed after 500 years. As on the obelisk base (and several contorniates) there is a mobile organ. There are also other instrumentalists and some dancers. In general their dress

[1] *Der Obelisk*, 67.

THE BASES

looks more Russian than Byzantine, but there is one striking common feature. The tiny flautist in the centre on the left side of the base appears to be wearing a pointed hat. The right-hand tiny flautist on the left face of the Kugelspiel seems to have a similar hat. On the Kiev fresco there are two more small flautists wearing pointed hats.[1] In fact the only thing missing is the banner-wavers.

What are these banners, and why are they being waved? Commentators on the Kugelspiel have drawn attention to the *velum* (βῆλον, βηλάριον) mentioned several times in the Book of Ceremonies, which they take to be a sort of awning suspended between columns to protect spectators from the elements. Now it is true that in Gilles's day iron rings, presumably designed for this purpose, were set in the few remaining columns of the sphendone. And on the relief on the right-hand face of the Kugelspiel it certainly looks as if the banner is being lifted in the direction of a column represented in the right corner. J. Gottwald, to whom we owe the only comprehensive interpretation of the monument, assumes that the reliefs represent different stages of a day's racing in sequence.[2] Beginning with the top relief on the right-hand face (Pl. 15) we have what he takes to be the hanging up of the awning, the first event of the day. Then we have below it the lot-casting machine (a popular contorniate type). After lots have been cast for position the race begins, and in the bottom relief we have a quadriga racing at full speed to the right, just behind two more racing across the back face (Pl. 18), while the fourth has just won on the left face, where he is being greeted by a man carrying the palm of victory. Moving upwards again the charioteer does his triumphal lap (as on the front of the new Porphyrius base), and then (according to Gottwald) we have the taking down of the awning, to close the day's proceedings.

The core of this cycle looks valid enough. There seems no trace of a sequence among the reliefs of the two Porphyrius bases and the obelisk base, but this can be sufficiently accounted for by their difference in purpose. Their one overriding purpose was to glorify their honorands. Their literary equivalent is the panegyric, and, like the panegyric, their method is not narrative

---

[1] Grabar, *L'Empereur*, 64, fig. 2; V. Lazarev, *Old Russian Murals and Paintings* (1966), 53 f.
[2] *AA* 1931, 155 f.

but topical. However, granted that the Kugelspiel reliefs are in a cycle, why such emphasis on an awning? Why should an object which would presumably have been put up before the spectators arrived and taken down after they had gone cause such merriment? Nor will this interpretation suit our two new examples of the tableau on the Porphyrius base. For every other scene on both bases was evidently (and naturally) chosen for its relevance to the central theme of Porphyrius' victory. An awning could hardly be held relevant enough to warrant not one but two being depicted on each side.

In any event R. Guilland has shown that the *velum* mentioned in the Book of Ceremonies and the chroniclers is not even an awning.[1] His further argument, that the hippodrome had no awnings at all, surely goes too far. It would be without parallel for an arena in a climate of such extremes not to have offered its patrons any protection against the elements.[2] The fact that the main hippodrome was distinguished from a minor 'covered' hippodrome near by as the 'uncovered' (ἀσκέπαστος) hippodrome only proves (of course) that it was not fully enclosed by a permanent roof or dome, not (as Guilland supposed) that it did not even have movable awnings.

There can be no doubt, however, that the *velum* (sometimes glossed πάνι(ο)ν) was in fact a flag hung above the Kathisma as advance notice of a race day. It will be unnecessary to repeat here the texts analysed by Guilland, though one he missed may profitably be cited. Not simply because it provides explicit confirmation of his interpretation, but because it illustrates one of the recurring incidental themes of this chapter. Once upon a time, according to Cassiodorus (*Variae* iii. 51. 9), Nero, who was devoted to the circus but also fond of his food, was so reluctant to hold up the races till he had finished his lunch that he threw his table napkin (*mappa*) out of the window 'ut libertatem daret certaminis postulati'. 'Hinc', he continues, 'tractum est, ut ostensa mappa certa videatur esse promissio circensium futurorum.' It may be doubted whether there is much truth in this

---

[1] *Speculum* xxiii (1948), 672 f. = *Études topogr.* i (1969), 371 f.

[2] For the abundant evidence relating to the provision of awnings for the theatres and amphitheatres of the West see Balsdon, *Life and Leisure in Ancient Rome* (1969), 257–8. Advertisements for the games at Pompeii regularly specify when awnings are to be provided ('vela erunt') as an extra inducement (for references, Balsdon, p. 297).

THE BASES

aetiology, which purports to explain at one stroke not only the hanging of the flag but also the dropping of the *mappa* to start individual races, but it does at least show that the hanging of the flag was a Roman custom—yet another feature of the hippodrome ceremonial of Constantinople that can be traced back to the Circus of Rome.

So the ceremonial which Gottwald attributed to the hanging of his awning in fact belongs to the hanging of this flag. Nothing remains to suggest that our banners are an awning. The fact that one of the banners on the Kugelspiel seems to touch a near-by column must be written down to coincidence—or blamed on the ineptitude of the craftsman. It would have taken a team of workmen to put up an awning, and it is hardly likely that they would have done anything so energetic dancing to the accompaniment of flutes.

On the other hand our banners cannot be the *velum* either. There was only one flag, and according to the Book of Ceremonies only one man was needed to put it up. There are two banners and four men on each side of the new Porphyrius base.

The answer is that all these tableaux, the Porphyrius reliefs, the obelisk base, the Kugelspiel, the Kiev frescoes, represent a ceremonial dance by circus partisans. We hear of such dances by the Blues and Greens taking place in the Tribunal, a courtyard of the Great Palace, 'up to the reign of Heraclius' (610–41), which suggests that they must have been an important element in imperial ceremonial for some time by then. Later Emperors built special courtyards (Phialai) for the factions.[1] The Book of Ceremonies refers often to such dances as they were performed in the hippodrome in the tenth century,[2] and in all probability they go back, not just to the Roman circus of the principate, but to early republican times. Dionysius of Halicarnassus preserves from Fabius Pictor an account of a *pompa circensis* of the year 499 B.C.[3] Dancers and flautists feature prominently.

---

[1] *Patria Cpoleos*, p. 39, Preger; cf. R. Guilland, 'Les Phiales des Factions', *Étud. topogr.* i (1969), 211–16.

[2] See the passages collected by Guilland, *BS* xxvii (1966), 299—though his references to dancers on p. 294 are not (as Guilland implies) to the dancers who merely performed in the interludes between races in the hippodrome, but to pantomimes, stars of the theatre in their own right.

[3] Dion. Hal., *Ant. Rom.* vii. 71: see A. Piganiol, *Recherches sur les Jeux romains* (1923), 15 f., on the accuracy of Dionysius' account.

THE EXTANT MONUMENTS

To the best of my knowledge there are no examples of dancers in circus contexts on mosaics, contorniates, or other monuments of the early Empire. This is probably due to chance, but perhaps not entirely. The ceremonial role of the factions certainly increased in the later period,[1] and would naturally be reflected more prominently in the art as a consequence.

There are, however, one or two later representations of dancers which deserve brief mention in this connection. First a miniature in the ninth-century Vatican MS. (gr. 699) of the *Christian Topography* of Cosmas Indicopleustes:[2] below David and Solomon, shown (as often in Byzantine art) as a Byzantine Emperor and his Porphyrogenitus, perform two dancers, each swinging the familiar banner above the head. They have been taken for girls.[3] Yet, slender and graceful though they are, they wear short tunics just like the male dancers on our three reliefs, and the one on the right at least might easily be a boy. We may compare a series of miniatures in Carolingian Psalters where in similar tableaux David is always shown with male dancers (still waving the same banner above their heads).[4] Then from a much later period there are the two banner-waving dancing-girls (sex certain) shown together with the Emperor Constantine IX and the Empresses Zoe and Theodora on the so-called crown of Constantine Monomachus, datable between 1042 and 1050.[5] The presence of dancing girls in such company has occasioned surprise.[6] One authority affirms that in Byzantine art dancing-girls are restricted to Biblical representations. There are several examples of 'daughters of Israel' dancing before David, and so the girls on the plaques of the Monomachus crown are 'nothing but the result of transplanting the special way of honouring David into the Byzantine court'.[7] Another writer sees them as evidence of 'Islamic influence'.[8] At this late period there may be something in both explanations, but we should also bear in mind that there

---

[1] See *Circus Factions*, Ch. X. [2] Pl. 29.
[3] M. Bárány-Oberschall, 'The Crown of the Emperor Constantine Monomachos', *Archaeologica Hungarica* xxii (1937), 76; H. Steger, *David: rex et propheta* (1961), 94–5, 153.
[4] Steger, pp. 94 f.: see Pl. 30.
[5] Bárány-Oberschall, Pls. vi and vii.
[6] 'Quite extraordinary', according to K. Weitzmann, *Greek Mythology in Byzantine Art* (1951), 203.
[7] Bárány-Oberschall, p. 76.
[8] Beckwith, *Art of Constantinople*, 108.

THE BASES 39

were female as well as male dancers in the chorus honouring Theodosius I on face A_1 of the obelisk base.

M. Bárány-Oberschall has traced the Monomachus girls back to a prototype in the classical Maenad.[1] The familiarity of Byzantine artists with the figure of the Maenad has been admirably illustrated from MS. illuminations and ivories by K. Weitzmann.[2] Indeed he has postulated a regular 'Dionysiac cycle', of which a good example is provided by an ivory casket in Vienna, which shows on one face a line of flautists and dancing figures waving scarves above their heads.[3] The parallel with the lines of flautists and dancing figures waving scarves on the obelisk base and Porphyrius and Kugelspiel reliefs is obvious. It might be legitimate to see the influence of Weitzmann's 'Dionysiac cycle' here too,[4] so long as we do not doubt that the factions really did dance with scarves to the accompaniment of flutes. In real life the scarves were probably faction banners, green or blue acocrding to the faction.

H. Steger has similarly traced the Carolingian banner-wavers back to the classical Maenad.[5] But he is puzzled by the fact that they are always male, and suggests that this may be a deliberate modification of northern artists, perhaps reflecting a domestic dance in which males alone participated. Surely the males come from Byzantine circus representations of the Emperor and faction dancers. Elsewhere Steger quotes the reliefs of the obelisk base as possible influences on medieval David tableaux, but seems not to have noticed the banner-wavers there, to whom we can now add the Kugelspiel and Porphyrius reliefs. He has also missed a particularly striking literary corroboration of this hypothesis: a Jewish Midrash of the Byzantine period in which Solomon is actually represented in a hippodrome, with both circus performers and spectators divided among the four colours, complete with a characteristically Byzantine explanation of the colours in terms of season symbolism.[6]

[1] Op. cit. 75.   [2] *Greek Mythology in Byzantine Art*, 108 f., 129 f.
[3] Ibid., fig. 231; cf. too fig. 232.
[4] Weitzmann himself traces his cycle back to a second- or third-century Dionysiac epic—earlier, that is, than Nonnus' *Dionysiaca*, which cannot accommodate some of the illustrations in the cycle (ibid. 146, 179 f., 193).
[5] *David: rex et propheta*, 94 f.
[6] E. Patlagean, *Revue des études juives* cxxi (1962), 8–33. Another Byzantine circus motif which appears on Carolingian miniatures is the lot machine (below, p. 63): see O. M. Dalton, *Byzantine Art and Archaeology* (1911), 144.

Let us turn now to the reliefs on the sides of the old base (Pl. 12). On each we have two groups of five figures acclaiming, arranged in one row of two poised rather uneasily above another row of three, the upper row in each case on an appreciably larger scale. The change in scale is not due to the ineptitude of the sculptor, but is a consequence of the principle of 'inverted perspective'. A closer parallel than the reliefs of the obelisk base is provided here by the *oratio* relief on the arch of Constantine in Rome (312–15),[1] where one row of figures is simply placed on top of another, the upper row being again on a larger scale: 'the separate figures', as H. P. L'Orange has recently put it, 'are not gathered in free, natural groups, but are arranged in uniform elements side by side in rows; neither these rows nor the architecture that frames them are free, but everything is strictly subordinated to and symmetrized according to the dominating figure of the Emperor at the center of the relief.'[2] But substitute Porphyrius for Emperor, and you have a perfect description of the Porphyrius reliefs. For the increase in scale in the upper row, which has received less attention than the grouping, a particularly close parallel for Porphyrius' acclaiming fans is the chorus of a pantomime dancer on a contorniate, one row in larger scale on top of another.[3] Compare too the rows of circus spectators in a sixth-century mosaic from Gafsa in North Africa.[4]

Many parallels could be cited for the theme of the group acclamation. One of particular interest is the two registers of acclaiming figures, from their dress senators and commoners respectively, on one of the 'enigmatic panels' of the early fifth-century doors of S. Sabina in Rome.[5] As on the Porphyrius base the figures are divided into groups facing each other. Both groups are acclaiming the figure represented in the top register. E. H. Kantorowicz rightly compared the two scenes,[6] but was surely wrong to infer that Porphyrius was represented *entering* the hippodrome to the cheers of the crowd. He has already won: hence his triumphal stance, and the crowns held by both him and the

---

[1] H. P. L'Orange, *Art Forms and Civic Life in the Late Roman Empire* (1965), fig. 35 (p. 88) and fig. 44 (p. 98).
[2] Ibid. 89–90.   [3] Pl. 31.11.
[4] R. Bianchi Bandinelli, *Rome: the late Empire* (1971), p. 251, Pl. 233.
[5] E. H. Kantorowicz, *Art Bulletin* xxvi (1944), 222, more accessibly and with better illustrations now in his *Selected Studies* (1965), p. 60, with Pl. 19, fig. 40.
[6] *Selected Studies*, 60.

attendant putti and victories. Porphyrius is portrayed simply as the type of the triumphant charioteer, at no particular moment. The abstract character of the scene is illuminatingly underlined by the top relief on the front of the old base, where the quadriga is raised up on a plinth—as though it were already a statue.[1] The acclaiming figures are presumably partisans of the factions. Now we know that the factions sat in special grandstands (confusingly enough called *demoi* like the factions themselves), next to each other on the side of the hippodrome opposite to where the Emperor sat in the Kathisma.[2] The figures in the relief are represented as standing on top of three tiers of benches. Of course, the faction grandstands will in real life have stood considerably higher than this: indeed, they presumably contained several tiers of benches themselves. But is not the placing of the factions on these tiers the artist's schematic way of indicating that they are to be thought of as raised above the level of the mass of the spectators? In short, it is meant to show that they are the factions. The flight of steps is designed to foster this illusion of height.

Compare the middle relief on the front of the new base (Pl. 8). On each side three acclaiming figures face each other, standing on top of two tiers of benches. On the back of the new base we have the imperial box filled with sundry acclaiming figures, all again standing on top of two tiers of benches (Pl. 7). In both cases there are flights of steps to help out the illusion that these groups are elevated above ground level. If we turn now to the representations of the imperial box on the obelisk face, precisely the same phenomenon greets us: on two sides the imperial party and their bodyguards are placed on top of two tiers of spectators, on the third above three tiers. The only difference is that, working as he was in more detail on a wider canvas, the sculptor has filled his benches with spectators. The variation between two and three tiers is probably of no significance.

We know that the factions' grandstands stood opposite the imperial grandstand, and it is likely enough that they were approximately the same height. This, surely, is why the sculptors of the Porphyrius bases and the obelisk base represent both the

---

[1] On this tendency in late Roman art and literature see (briefly) my *Claudian* (1970), 273.
[2] R. Guilland, 'Les dèmes', *Mél. L. Halphen* (1951), 297 f. = *Études topogr.* i (1969), 411 f.

factions and the imperial party raised up on the same number of tiers. We may contrast the dancers and flautists on both the Kugelspiel and the new base, who do not stand on bench tops, and are probably therefore to be thought of as performing at ground level—an inference supported by their position in front of the lower tier of spectators on face A_1 of the obelisk base. Compare too the coronation scene on the middle relief of the front of the new base (Pl. 8): it takes place at ground level between two raised groups.

Mordtmann thought that the two groups on each side of the old base represented, on one side, Greens and Reds; on the other, Blues and Whites. But Reds and Whites are never mentioned in connection with the honours paid to charioteers at this period, and it is more probable that those on the left face are meant to be Greens, those on the right Blues. For the prose acclamations above the reliefs are put into the mouths of the Greens and Blues respectively. The same might well apply to the reliefs on the sides of the new base, for the same reason. Here too left would be Green and right Blue, corresponding to the respective prose acclamations.

Whether the dancers and flautists on the sides of the Kugelspiel are meant to be Greens and Blues respectively is less obvious. The monument has no apparent connection with either faction, and the reliefs may simply be intended to represent the factions in general, performing their dances first before and then after the racing.

The method of acclaiming portrayed on the reliefs of both bases—the raising of one arm—is referred to in a disapproving passage of Procopius (*Anecd.* vii. 12–13), describing how the loose-fitting sleeves of the partisans' tunics billowed out when they waved their arms in the theatres and hippodromes. Corippus describes how they raised and then lowered them again in unison:

<blockquote>emittunt dextras pariter pariterque remittunt.
(*Laud. Just.* ii. 314)</blockquote>

The Front and Back of the Two Bases

It has generally been assumed that the relief on the back of the old base—Porphyrius standing full face—is a copy of the statue that stood on top of the base.[1] It is of course likely that

---

[1] Woodward–Wace, p. 82.

THE BASES

the statue did portray Porphyrius in some such triumphant pose, but if so because both follow a well-established common pattern rather than because the sculptor copied the statue. I do not know of any earlier example in relief, on contorniates, mosaics, etc., but there is a much restored statue in the Vatican of a charioteer of the early Empire holding a palm.[1] At least twenty extant reliefs represent victorious gladiators in exactly this pose, full face and holding a palm aloft.[2] The gladiator is invariably bare-headed, his helmet usually balanced on the shield which rests on the ground beside him. Porphyrius too is bare-headed— his helmet held for him by a little cupid (the motif of the attendant putti has been discussed above).

One of the three constituents of the special outfit presented to the two top charioteers (*factionarii*) according to tenth-century ceremonial was the κασσίδιον, a silver helmet.[3] The helmet held for Porphyrius by the putto is unlike either the crash helmet or the soft turban that most charioteers on reliefs, paintings, or mosaics wear.[4] It might well be this special ceremonial helmet of silver—hence its prominence.

On the lower relief on the front of the old base we have two figures in short tunics each holding the reins of a team of four horses which they are evidently on the point of exchanging. As Mordtmann saw, this must be a schematic representation of the *diversium*, when the victorious charioteer exchanged teams with the man he had beaten and raced him again (see p. 209). As usual the principle of symmetrical grouping has replaced perspective in the arrangement of the horses. The two figures must be representatives of the Blues and Greens respectively—to judge from their dress presumably not the charioteers themselves.

The two lower reliefs on the front face of the new base are relatively straightforward (Pll. 1, 8). The upper one shows Porphyrius on one knee facing left with a palm in upheld right hand while a figure in a long robe standing behind him places what must be a crown on his head. This latter figure is surely not (as Fıratlı and Rollas supposed) the Emperor. It would not be in

---

[1] H. Schöne, *JDAI* xviii (1903), 68.
[2] L. Robert, *Les Gladiateurs* (1940), 47–8 for the list. There are of course further parallels between the gladiator and charioteer stelae: e.g. the Fortuna flanked by Victories of Robert no. 156, p. 170, reappears on the top registers of the new base.
[3] *De Caer.* 330–1 R = ii. 134 V.
[4] See R. Bianchi Bandinelli, *Hellenistic–Byzantine Miniatures of the Iliad* (1955), 110.

keeping with the the Emperor's dignity to descend to the hippodrome, floor to present prizes. By the tenth century an official called the *actuarius* did the job for him.[1] A poem of Sidonius Apollinaris describes how, in mid fifth century, Ravenna the Emperor 'ordered' the victors in a chariot race to be presented with their crowns and palms[2] (which, incidentally, though hardly as ubiquitous in real life as on the Porphyrius reliefs, were real none the less, not symbolic). Not even the consul made the awards at his games. On the diptych of Areobindus (consul at Constantinople in 506) the man who crowns the *venator* in the bottom scene of the right-hand leaf is clearly not the consul himself.[3] On the other side of Porphyrius stands yet another winged Victory, holding an indeterminate object (? yet another crown) in her right hand and a palm in her left.

There is a similar coronation scene on the again badly damaged relief of hippodrome scenes below face A_2 of the obelisk base (Pl. 23). In the middle tableau above the spina we see again the kneeling charioteer (facing right this time), with a standing figure on each side. All three figures are too worn to warrant any firm conclusions about their actions or identity, but G. Bruns was surely wrong to suppose the left-hand figure a man.[4] The waist is narrow and there is an unmistakable bust. In the light of the Porphyrius relief I would suggest that she is a Victory. The outline of her left leg shows clearly through her dress, just as on the Victories of both Porphyrius bases—a cliché of the type mentioned already.

It is possible that in the coronation scene on the front of the base the two acclaiming groups are Greens and Blues respectively, yet if so the representation would be more than ordinarily schematic, since in real life the faction grandstands stood not opposite but next to each other.

In the centre of the relief below the coronation scene is a galloping horseman (evidently Porphyrius again) brandishing another crown in his upraised right hand. On each side stands an acclaiming figure in the usual short tunic. There is a close parallel in the same relief on the obelisk base (Pl. 23). On each side of

---

[1] *De Caer.* 328 R = ii. 132 V.
[2] *Carm.* xxiii. 423 f. See too the Addenda below, pp. 275–6.
[3] R. Delbrück, *Die Consulardiptychen*, Pl. 10, Textband, pp. 72, 112. Though according to Ammianus, xiv. 11. 12, the Caesar Gallus 'capiti Thoracis aurigae coronam imposuit' at Constantinople in 354.   [4] *Der Obelisk*, 60–1.

the coronation scene on this relief is a galloping horseman with a single figure to his left. The figure on the right-hand side is acclaiming (and waving some indistinct object in both hands) like the figure on the right of the Porphyrius tableau. The figure on the left is waving what G. Bruns wrongly took to be a starting-flag. It is of course a whip (races were started at the drop of a *mappa*, not the waving of a flag), that commonest of all motifs in hippodrome art, on mosaics, contorniates, textiles, and reliefs alike. That the figure on the obelisk is indeed waving a whip is confirmed by the whip in the hand of the corresponding figure in the Porphyrius tableau. In both cases, too, the whip itself is not in relief, but cut into the stone.[1]

As a consequence of her interpretation of the whip as a starting-flag, Bruns sees the left-hand horseman on the obelisk relief as just beginning a solo horse-race. In itself this assumption might not seem absurd, yet so far as we know the Byzantines simply did not race horses, any more than the Romans did in the circuses of the West.[2]

The key is provided by a late third-century[3] mosaic found about nine miles north of Rome off the Via Flaminia. At the bottom two *bigae* race from left to right. Over the left-hand pair is written 'Ilarinus Olypio', that is to say 'Hilarinus racing with the horse Oly(m)pius'; over the other pair 'L.... Romano', 'L.... racing with the horse Romanus'. At the top of the mosaic rides a man on a horse waving a crown in his right hand and a palm in his left, while in front of him (on the right) stands a figure waving a whip. Above the horseman is the inscription 'Liber nica', which Miss J. M. C. Toynbee interprets as an exhortation addressed to Liber, 'Liber, win!'[4] Strictly speaking it should mean this, but the *nica* acclamation is often in fact used to address someone who has already won rather than someone who is still racing (pp. 76–9). Compare especially the mosaic from the Via Imperiale to which Miss Toynbee refers, which 'shows eight *quadrigae* racing in the circus, with charioteers and horses named. The victorious charioteer is distinguished by a palm: his

[1] As again on the diptych of Basilius, cos. 480 (Delbrück, *Consulardiptychen*, Pl. 6r).
[2] See (for the Principate) Balsdon, *Life and Leisure*, 323.
[3] Pl. 24; for the inscription, *ILS* 5291a.
[4] *PBSR* xvi (1948), 31. Mommsen's view, to which Miss Toynbee refers, that Nica is a horse's name, is clearly mistaken.

name is in the vocative case, *Aeri* (the other charioteers' names being in the nominative), and is followed by the word *nik*[*a*]'. Aeri(u)s is clearly being acclaimed for his victory.

'L.... Romano' must obviously be restored 'L[iber] Romano'. The mosaic depicts what was no doubt a famous encounter between Liber and Hilarinus, which Liber won. The lower register shows them still racing (with Liber in the lead). The horseman of the upper register is surely not, as Miss Toynbee supposed, a spectator (on a horse!) urging Liber on. He *is* Liber, now represented as the victor (hence the crown and palm) doing a lap of triumph. The figure to his right is a *hortator* cheering him on (the whip being a symbolic representation of his function, rather than what he actually used to perform it).

This is exactly the situation on the obelisk base. On the lower half of the relief we have the race (four quadrigae instead of two bigae), while above are three scenes representing the result. In the middle is the crowning of the winner, on both sides his triumphal lap on horseback, complete with *hortatores*. The front of the new Porphyrius base reproduces both triumphal lap and coronation, while omitting the race. The Kugelspiel omits the coronation, but has both the other two elements. Round the bottom registers runs the race between the four quadrigae (an almost unique example of such a race being shown from right to left), while on the relief above the winning quadriga on the left face we have yet another solo horseman. Once more, surely, the winning charioteer doing his triumphal lap.

Why *two* horsemen on the obelisk base, it might be asked. No doubt quite simply from considerations of symmetry—just as the charioteer of the Münsterbilsen textile holds a whip in both hands, an absurdity only excused by the overriding claims of symmetry. But the double horseman can be traced back to a much earlier period. It has been remarked already that there are a number of second- to third-century sarcophagi representing circus scenes in which the participants are all little cupids.[1] Much scholarly attention has been devoted to unravelling the symbolism of these bizarre tableaux,[2] rather less to their evidence

---

[1] See above, p. 25 n. 1; for an inventory of the sarcophagi, C. Belting-Ihm, *Jahrbuch des römisch-germanischen Zentralmuseums Mainz* viii (1961), 205 f.

[2] For a useful summary of the various views see L. Vogel, *Art Bulletin* li (1969), 159 n. 47 (though add M. Turcan-Déleani, *MEFR* lxxvi (1964), 43 f.).

on circus practice. Such attention as they do receive on this count is directed to the front face, where the four quadrigae or (more usually) bigae race across from left to right, one of them often coming to grief (a realistic detail found in mosaic circus scenes too, but sufficiently disruptive of symmetry to be dropped from the repertoire of Byzantine craftsmen). But on the back of these sarcophagi not infrequently a solo cupid horseman brandishes the victor's crown.[1] On the analogy of our other examples we may surely see him as the winner of the race on the front. And on a recently found third-century specimen at Mainz we find *two* triumphant horsemen-cupids.[2] Since there cannot be two winners (at least not of a symbolic race), both must be the same figure represented twice, as on the obelisk base. In an important study of some of these sarcophagi reliefs published in 1940, G. Rodenwaldt drew attention to a number of features in their composition—frontality, proportioning of figures according to importance, symmetrical arrangement—that anticipated what are held to be the hallmarks of fourth- and fifth-century work.[3] This repetition of the victorious rider provides a striking illustration of his thesis.

Why one horse instead of the whole team for this triumphal lap? A very simple answer suggests itself, nothing to do (for once) with considerations of symbolism or symmetry. There is abundant evidence, literary, archaeological, and epigraphic, for the immense popularity of racehorses in the Roman Empire.[4] Martial wryly remarks that he himself is less famous than Andraemon (a horse of the great Scorpus).[5] And the frequency with which African mosaics in particular show horses on their own—all duly named—proves that they did not derive their fame from their association with this or that charioteer alone. They might be as famous in their own right as any charioteer. Gutta's appropriately named Victor won 429 victories, far more than most charioteers.[6] Assuming that he won one race out of

[1] Belting-Ihm, pp. 206 ff., nos. 9, 10, 14, 17.
[2] Belting-Ihm, Pl. 76. 2–3, with pp. 195 f.
[3] *JDAI* lv (1940), 12–43.
[4] Most of the evidence is collected by J. M. C. Toynbee, *PBSR*, xvi (1948), 24 f. For a very full list of their names see also now J. W. Salomonson, *La Mosaïque aux chevaux de l'antiquarium de Carthage* (1965), 84 f.
[5] *Ep.* x. 9. 5: Andraemon is included in a team of Scorpus' on the inscription to a ruined relief, *ILS* 5289.
[6] Friedlaender, *SG* iv[10]. 185.

every three he ever competed in, this means some 1,300 races, a truly phenomenal performance. Often a mosaic or a relief will name only one horse in a quadriga or biga, the lead horse. The Liber mosaic is a good example: only one of Liber's team is named, Romanus. There is also a sarcophagus relief on which Liber appears with three other drivers of quadrigae. Of his four horses only one again is named: not Romanus, but Jubilator.[1] What more natural and appropriate, when Gutta won with his Victor, Scorpus with Andraemon, Liber with Romanus or Jubilator, than for the driver to do a triumphal lap on the horse that had led his team to victory, so that both celebrities could take their bow together? Not only, then, is the horseman on the Liber mosaic Liber; his horse is surely Romanus.

In tenth-century Constantinople the lap of honour seems to have been done with full quadriga,[2] and it is possible that this postulated Roman custom never existed at Constantinople except in art. Yet Porphyrius' team is fully identified on all three faces where it is represented on the old base. On the left side: Nikopolemos, Radiatos, Purros, Euthunikos; on the right: Halieus, Anthupatos, Kunagos, Pelorios; on the front: Aristides, Palaestiniarches, Purros, and Euthunikos. The fact that Purros and Euthunikos, evidently very strong and superior beasts, featured in two teams is duly recorded. It looks as though horses were still celebrities in their own right as late as Porphyrius' day, and accordingly the scene on the front of the new base might well represent Porphyrius himself on the most popular Blue horse of the season.

The Kugelspiel horseman illustrates a puzzling feature of the mounted Porphyrius. For badly worn though this bottom relief on the front of the base is, it is clear that Porphyrius is holding something else in his hand as well as a crown, what looks like a piece of material billowing out behind him (Pl. 2). The Kugelspiel horseman is holding just such an object in the same hand—perhaps a flag or streamer of some sort. Compare too the triumphal Porphyrius on the back of the new base: he too appears to be holding something of the sort, clearly discernible between his crown and his head. There is also a contorniate where a charioteer

---

[1] *ILS* 5291.
[2] *De Caer.* i. 71, p. 355–7R; ii. 15, p. 590R: cf. R. Guilland, *BS* xviii (1957), 52 (= *Études topogr.* i (1969), 472).

appears to be holding (again in the right hand) something in addition to the usual crown.¹ Finally, the cupid-horseman on the right side of the back of the Mainz sarcophagus is holding something other than a crown in his upraised left hand.² Pantomimes on contorniates sometimes hold a similar indistinct object,³ but this might well be something quite different, a part of their professional equipment (a veil, for example). We can only guess at the identity of the object the charioteers carry, but the most likely guess would seem to be a streamer attached to the crown—no doubt in the colour of the driver's faction.

The Kathisma Relief on the Back of the New Base

We come now to the last and in some ways the most interesting and elaborate of all the reliefs on the new base: the imperial box of the Kathisma represented on the lower register of the back face. Unfortunately, however, the greater detail and elaboration serve only to put the deficiencies of workmanship in a yet sharper light. The contrast with the four representations of the Kathisma on the obelisk base, acknowledged masterpieces of their style, is very revealing in this respect. For example, it is clear from the obelisk reliefs that the Emperor himself and his household sat inside their box, while various ministers, dignitaries, and soldiers stood on either side. There is no such division between the figures on the Porphyrius base: there is a figure half in and half out of the box at each side, so crudely is it defined.

But there are substantial differences between the Kathisma of the Porphyrius and obelisk bases over and above details arising from the sheer ineptitude of execution. There are no pillars at the sides of the box itself, nor does it have a roof. The four

[1] Alföldi, no. LVII. 6. In an interesting article in *Zeitschrift für Numismatik* xxiv (1904), 355 f., R. Zahn drew attention to a fanlike object in the hand of one of the three figures in a charioteer coronation tableau on a late Roman lamp. He quoted a number of parallels, in each case maintaining that the figure in question was a judge or official of some sort. It may be doubted whether he is in every case correct (cf. Alföldi, *Kontorniaten*, 32–3), and our horsemen clearly cannot be judges. They are probably holding something quite different. The difference between the coronation tableau discussed by Zahn and the tableau on the Porphyrius and obelisk bases (above, p. 44) is that in the former the charioteer crowns himself (on this motif see now also L. Robert, *Monnaies grecques* (1967), 107 f., and for the *judex* and his colleague, a herald with a trumpet, see H. Stern, *Recueil général des mosaïques de la Gaule* ii. 1 (1967), 67).
[2] Belting-Ihm, Pl. 76. 3.
[3] Alföldi, nos. LXII. 8 and 9.

decorated panels along the front of the box differ both from one another and from the panels on the obelisk base. On two faces of the obelisk base—A_2 (SW.) and B_2 (NE.)—there is a flight of steps beneath the box leading down to an arch. On the Porphyrius relief there are no steps here, and the top of the arch comes right up to the level of the decorated panels.

The two monuments are separated by some 110 years, and it is conceivable that the Kathisma was destroyed and rebuilt in a slightly different style at some time during this period. But there is no evidence that it was destroyed, nor is any such drastic solution necessary. For while the Kathisma of the Porphyrius relief differs widely from all four representations on the obelisk base, at the same time all four of these representations differ widely from each other. Take the decorated panels in front of the imperial party. In A_1 there are three tall panels (twice as tall, that is, as the panels in front of the dignitaries on either side), of which the middle one is plain. In A_2 there are two rows of three decorated panels. On B_1 just one row of three decorated panels; in B_2 just two such panels. The steps and arch mentioned above are missing from two faces (A_1 and B_1). Which is the 'true' Kathisma? Probably none of them.

Just as the artist varied the number, arrangement, and stances of the imperial party inside the box, so also he quite deliberately varied the details of the box itself. Just as successive panegyrics on a Byzantine emperor differ, not in the essentials of their content, but in details of execution, so must these successive pictorial glorifications of Theodosius be the same yet not quite the same. We have seen already that this holds equally of the upper registers of the Porphyrius bases, almost but not quite identical. In order to make room for his suppliant barbarians on B_1 and his line of dancers and flautists on A_1, the artist was quite prepared to dispense altogether with the steps and arch.

G. Bruns was prepared to accept these variations, but so perturbed was she by the fact that on A_1 alone of the faces the roof of the box was flat, not arched, that she refused to believe that it could be the same box. And since it is on this face alone that the Emperor holds a victor's crown, she ingeniously suggested that he is supposed to be standing in the Stama ($Στάμα$), otherwise known as Pi ($Πί$), where we know that charioteers stopped to be crowned. The name Pi, she remarks, could easily have been suggested by the shape of the box in which the Emperor stands.[1]

This suggestion was well received at the time,[2] but there are two decisive objections. First, Guilland has shown that the Stama/Pi is not at all what Bruns (in company with most earlier scholars) had assumed it to be: viz. a portico directly underneath and attached to the Kathisma. It is in fact a colonnade in front of but quite separate from the Kathisma;[3] in short, nothing like the galleries depicted on A_1. These are clearly represented as being elevated above the ground to the same level as those on the other three faces, with rows of spectators beneath. And there are the same boxes full of dignitaries and guards on either side of the imperial box as on the other three faces. The Emperor himself might have descended to another box, but he would hardly have brought his entire retinue and household with him.

Secondly, Bruns's theory depends on the assumption that the Emperor has changed boxes in order to present the prizes. Yet it is very doubtful whether he is supposed to be doing any such thing. He holds a crown in his right hand not, surely, because he is awarding it, but because he has received it himself.[4] When the central figure of such a tableau holds a crown, this is a symbolic indication that he himself is being acclaimed as a victor. This is why it is at the bottom of this relief and not the other three that we have the line of dancers and flautists, performing in *his* honour, not for some charioteer who is not represented. The scene is exactly parallel to the sides of the new Porphyrius base, where the dancers and flautists perform in Porphyrius' honour, while he towers above them with his victor's crown in upraised right hand. There can be little doubt that these two faces were directly modelled on A_1.

It follows that A_1 too, despite the differences from its fellows, can only be another impression of the Kathisma—differing (like the other faces) because of its different purpose. The relief on the back of the Porphyrius base is yet another impression. But since its artist was more interested in the persons inside the box,

[1] *Der Obelisk*, 61–8.
[2] e.g. E. Wiegand, *BZ* xxxvii (1937), 453.
[3] *Jahrb. d. Österr. Byz. Gesellschaft* vi (1957), 37 f. = *Études topogr.* i (1969), 451 f.
[4] So, without comment, Grabar, *L'Empereur*, 66 (though for 'main gauche' read 'main droite').

and in any case had much less space to work with, he omitted its side pillars and roof. To highlight the imperial party in the centre the dignitaries on either side are simply represented as standing on top of benches, just like the acclaiming figures on the front and those on the sides of the old base. Only the imperial party stands behind decorated panels, of which there appear to be five (one hidden behind the door in the middle), though no obelisk face has more than three. But then no two obelisk faces have the same number and shape of panels. The decoration itself varies, as on three faces of the obelisk base—though on A_2 every panel is the same.

The scale of the Porphyrius relief is of course grotesque, but in this respect it differs from the obelisk reliefs in degree rather than kind. And though the artist has omitted the steps shown below the box in B_2 and A_2, he has two other flights of steps which do not appear anywhere on the four faces of the obelisk base: one flight each side of the box leading down, like the central flight on the obelisk base, to the lower level of the Kathisma. That this detail is more than just a fancy of the Porphyrius artist is strongly suggested by the Kugelspiel, where the opening in the front face is represented as a large door shaped exactly as on the obelisk and Porphyrius reliefs, surmounted by acclaiming figures—and with a flight of steps to each side of the arch, leading, as on the Porphyrius relief, not all the way down to the ground, but only to a lower level than that on which the acclaiming figures stand (Pl. 17). There is no cause to doubt that these steps existed in real life, or to be disturbed at their omission from all the obelisk faces. It could well be that they were justifiably left out as being too far to the right and left respectively of the box in the more realistic proportions of the obelisk reliefs.

Guilland assumed that there were only three floors to the Kathisma:[1] the ground floor, level with the hippodrome floor, which served as a record office;[2] then the imperial box, and above this the παρακυπτικά (see below). Our three monuments surely prove that, however many floors there may have been above the box, the box itself was not (as Guilland assumed) directly above this central door. Both the Kugelspiel and Porphyrius reliefs with their steps at each side and the obelisk reliefs with their central

---

[1] *BS* xviii (1957), 69 f. = *Études topogr.* i (1969), 485 f.
[2] *De Magg.* iii. 19, cf. Guilland, *Études*, 485.

THE BASES

steps are clear evidence that there was another level below the box but well above ground level. It will be seen that on the Porphyrius relief there is in addition a small arch or door beneath the box and to the left of the main door, on the same level as the bottom of the two flights of steps. Guilland further assumed that there were no external steps connecting the different levels of the Kathisma. There may only have been an internal flight connecting the παρακυπτικά with the box, but the variety of steps shown on our three monuments clearly show that there was external communication between at any rate the first and second floors.

The παρακυπτικά is the room or rooms above the box where people could watch the games by looking through (παρακύπτειν) the windows (below, pp. 200–1). It was apparently from behind these grilled windows that court ladies would watch, it not being considered proper for ladies to attend the games in the ordinary way. It is probably such a lady (perhaps a princess) who is shown watching through an open window as the victor rides past on the middle relief of the left face of the Kugelspiel (Pl. 16).

It would be strange for an artist to have shown as much of the Kathisma as he did on the front of the Kugelspiel but to have left off the imperial box itself. It is surely not impossible that the relief originally extended a bit further upwards above the centre of the arch. At present there is between the acclaiming groups on each side of the arch a rectangular area filled with crowns. This obvious symbol of victory is ubiquitous in the agonistic art of the Empire (piles of crowns are especially common, for example, on gladiator stelae), but it is not exclusive to agonistic art. On coins and medallions the crown will symbolize the Emperor's victories, and particularly relevant for our present purpose are the frontal quadriga medallions: below the platform on which the quadriga stands are (together with some palm leaves and other objects) two piles of crowns. Since they are consular medallions, there is of course an agonistic element here, as there is too on the quadriga bracelet cited above (p. 22). Once more a pile of crowns beneath the platform on which the Emperor's quadriga stands. Might it not be that the rectangle of crowns on the Kugelspiel is all that now remains of such a platform for an imperial tableau?

Owing to the attention to detail, the relative excellence of the workmanship, and the good state of preservation of most at least of the obelisk faces, it has proved possible to describe and identify the numerous figures thereon with some accuracy. There is now a fair measure of agreement about the identity of the imperial parties on each face,[1] and J. Kollwitz in particular has managed from their costumes and accessories to specify at least the office or function of a number of the other figures.[2]

Little of the sort, unfortunately, can be done for the crudely executed and worn figures in the Kathisma of the Porphyrius relief. The figure in the centre is evidently the Emperor—that is to say (in *c.* 500) Anastasius. Unlike the Emperor on all four obelisk faces (who wears a *chlamys*), he wears a toga—no doubt the *toga triumphalis* that Emperors often wore in the circus.[3] Though his head is badly worn, there are clear signs of a diadem. The figure to his right again wears a toga and perhaps also a diadem: if so, then it could only be his wife the Augusta Ariadne. The ban on women spectators is not likely to have applied to the wife of two successive Emperors, and we know that she appeared in the Kathisma on 10 April 491 (wearing the imperial *chlamys* herself) to proclaim Anastasius.[4] She is also represented on several diptychs of the period.[5]

The figure to her right, like both the Emperor and Empress, seems to have his arms folded beneath the folds of his costume —though unlike them he wears the *chlamys*. Presumably a high official, since the *chlamys* was the dress of the court dignitary. A list of those who followed Ariadne into the Kathisma in 491 is provided by Peter the Patrician in the Book of Ceremonies (i. 92, p. 418): the two *praepositi*, the *magister officiorum*, the *castrensis*, the quaestor, and 'all the others who are accustomed to watch with the Emperor at chariot races'. From the list of those close to the Emperor at Corippus, *Laudes Justini II* i. 15 f. we may add the praetorian prefect (of the East), and from general considerations of probability the city prefect. The one *chlamydatus* on the relief is presumably one of this band—perhaps the *praepositus*.

---

[1] In addition to Bruns's discussion, see (against Kollwitz's objections in *Gnomon* xiii (1937), 423 f.) S. Mazzarino, *Stilicone* (1942), 101–3 n. 4, and W. Hartke, *Römische Kinderkaiser* (1951), 238–9 (on Eucherius, briefly, my *Claudian* (1970), 47).
[2] *Gnomon* xiii (1937), 423 f.
[3] A. Alföldi, *Röm. Mitteil.* i (1935), 34–6.
[4] *De Caer.* i. 92 (with Bury, *Later Roman Empire* i² (1923), 429 f.—where for December read April).
[5] See Beckwith, *Art of Constantinople*², 37.

THE BASES 55

Praepositi exercised much influence at both the beginning (Urbicius) and end (Amantius) of Anastasius' reign, though it is not known if either was in power *c.* 500. The four figures to the right of the Emperor are all *togati*, as is the one to the left of the *chlamydatus*. One might be the city prefect, who alone of the top court officials traditionally wore the toga,[1] though the rest are probably all senators. A similar preponderance of senators over court officials can be traced on the various faces of the obelisk base: in the front rank of figures on each side of the Emperor we see on A_1 six *togati*; on A_2 two *chlamydati* and one *togatus*; on B_1 four *chlamydati* and one *togatus*; on B_2 again six *togati*. An interesting confirmation of the view recently reaffirmed by H.-G. Beck, that the Senate of Constantinople was not the cipher it is still sometimes imagined to have been.[2]

Unlike the acclaiming figures on all the other faces of both bases, these men are all cheering, not Porphyrius, but the Emperor. This is made quite clear by the way four of them actually face him as they raise their arms in the ritual gesture. The share the Emperor was felt to have in the victories of the charioteer has been alluded to already. It is illustrated on face A_1 of the obelisk base (see p. 19). When *tu vincas* or *nica* are on the lips of all, the Emperor as well as Porphyrius must be in their thoughts. The figure on the extreme right and the two on the left who wear short tunics like the circus partisans seem to fit oddly into such a distinguished and dignified context. Could it be that they are meant to be circus partisans, acclaiming the Emperor here as on other faces they acclaim Porphyrius?

The Gate(s) beneath the Imperial Box

We may conclude this discussion of the Kathisma relief of the Porphyrius base with a thorny and perhaps insoluble issue: the large gate beneath the imperial box. That there was such a gate beneath the Kathisma is known from literary sources. The Book of Ceremonies (i App. p. 507) describes how the Emperor Theophilus rode on horseback beneath the Kathisma (ὑποκάτω τοῦ καθίσματος) into the Daphne courtyard on the far side.

[1] A. Chastagnol, *La Préfecture urbaine* (1960), 196 f.
[2] *Senat und Volk von Konstantinopel* (Sitzb. Bay. Akad., Phil.-hist. Kl. 1966)—with my *Circus Factions*, Ch. XI.

In the course of an elaborate study of the various gates of the hippodrome,[1] R. Guilland has identified this gate with a gate called Karea first mentioned in the late tenth century, and another gate mentioned by Procopius in his account of the Nika revolt in 532. Both identifications seem to me very doubtful.

First Procopius' gate. When Belisarius and his troops, having entered the hippodrome towards its northern end by a circuitous route from the Grand Palace, had reached 'the Blue colonnade, which is on the right of the Emperor's throne, he purposed to go against Hypatius himself first'. Hypatius had by this time ensconced himself in the Kathisma. 'But since there was a small door there', continues Procopius, 'which had been closed and was guarded by the soldiers of Hypatius who were inside, he feared lest while he was struggling in the narrow space the populace should fall on him.'[2] It is plain (a) that this 'little door' ($\pi υλίς$) can hardly be the very substantial looking gate beneath the Emperor's box on all three of our monuments, and (b) that this door was in any case to the right of, not directly beneath, the Emperor's box. Furthermore, Procopius' door evidently led up to this box, where Hypatius was sitting, whereas the gate mentioned in the Book of Ceremonies passed underneath the box and led out to a courtyard on the other side. Clearly we are dealing with two different doors here. The large gate of the Book of Ceremonies and our three monuments is not mentioned by Procopius for the simple reason (I would suggest) that it did not give access to the Kathisma above it. Had Belisarius led his men through it, he would only have found himself on the way back to the Grand Palace which he had (by a more circuitous route) just left.

Now the Karea gate. According to Nicolaus Mesarites,[3] when John Comnenus took the Grand Palace in 1201, he began by forcing the Karea gate and getting control of the Kathisma above (τὰ ὑπερανῳκισμένα τῆς Καρέας βασίλεια, ἐν οἷς οἱ κρατοῦντες προκάθηνται ἱππικοῦ). Evidently then this gate, like Procopius', led up to the Kathisma, not underneath it and out the other side. It could even be Procopius' gate (though things might have

---

[1] *Jahrb. d. Österr. Byz. Gesellschaft* iv (1955), 51 f. = *Études topogr.* i (1969), 509 f. Here, as so often with Guilland's topographical studies, a map or diagram would greatly have aided comprehension.

[2] *Bell. Pers.* i. 24. 48.

[3] p. 24 Heisenberg.

changed in the 670 years that separate these two accounts). But it surely cannot be the gate of our three monuments and the Book of Ceremonies.

Confusingly enough we hear of yet another gate in the Kathisma, again in connection with the Nika riot—and again identified with all the other gates by Guilland. According to the Easter Chronicle[1] and Theophanes[2] (both deriving in the main from the full contemporary account of Malalas[3]) some of the troops who helped Belisarius and Mundus to massacre the rioters entered the hippodrome through the μονόπορτος (μονόπατος Theophanes) τοῦ βασιλικοῦ καθίσματος.

Guilland, for whom this μονόπορτος, like the other two doors, led up to the Kathisma, is obliged to assume that these troops did not enter the hippodrome till after they had ejected Hypatius from the Kathisma. Yet Malalas, the Easter Chronicle, Theophanes, and Procopius, while differing in details of the actual arrest, are all agreed that Hypatius was not arrested till after the fighting was over.[4] These troops cannot then have come through the Kathisma: they must have come round or underneath it.

It is clear from the various accounts of the Nika riot that the Kathisma could be sealed off both from the hippodrome in front and the Grand Palace behind. The front was always vulnerable, however, since there were doors that gave access to the arena and in any case the front of the Kathisma was no more than an open balcony that looked down on the arena from no very great height. Hypatius seems to have experienced no difficulty getting up there, evidently from the hippodrome side. It was thus essential that in an emergency of this sort the Emperor should be able to retire from the Kathisma to the Grand Palace and seal off the Kathisma behind him. This is clearly what happened in January 532. Even after Hypatius had seized the Kathisma, Justinian felt quite safe in debating the crisis, not in the Grand Palace itself, but in a hall which apparently adjoined the Kathisma.[5]

There were of course ways *into* the Kathisma from the Palace

[1] p. 626. 17 Bonn.   [2] p. 185. 21 de Boor.
[3] See Bury's still fundamental analysis in *JHS* xvii (1897), 95 f.
[4] Mal. 476. 10; Theoph. 185. 24; Proc. i. 24. 53; *Chr. Pasch.* 626. 21.
[5] *Chr. Pasch.* 625. 17 f.

side. Belisarius tried one round the side in the hope of catching Hypatius without entering the hippodrome, but the guards stationed here, having decided to wait and see which side won before committing themselves, refused to open it for him. Evidently this gate could only be opened from the outside. Once Justinian had locked it behind himself, there was no way Hypatius could get out of the Kathisma on the Palace side.

It may reasonably be asked, if Theophilus could pass under the Kathisma into Daphne and thence to the Grand Palace, why could not Belisarius have taken his troops into the hippodrome via Daphne and the gate under the Kathisma? The answer is that of course he could have. But once this route was open it could not easily have been closed again if Belisarius had been beaten back, and the rioters would have been able to pour unchecked into the Palace area. So Belisarius took the long route round the north-east fringe of the hippodrome. But once the fighting had begun and it was clear that the loyalist troops were carrying all before them, then the few guards who had remained with Justinian in the Palace could throw open the *monoportos* and attack from beneath the Kathisma.

It might seem that at last we have found the gate below the Imperial box, the gate of our three monuments. Yet caution is necessary. The double gate of the Porphyrius base does not answer very well to the name *monoportos*, and the shape and size of the aperture on both the other monuments also suggest a double, not single gate.

RHETORIC, WHETHER IN WORDS OR STONE

O. Wulff,[1] O. M. Dalton[2], and J. Gottwald[3] all assigned the Kugelspiel to the late fourth century—and all for the same reason. 'The sculptures', said Dalton, 'which are of indifferent quality, recall those of the obelisk base and must be of similar date.' It depends what one means by similar, for Dalton also referred in passing to the old Porphyrius base for comparison—which is of course some 110 years later than the obelisk base. S. Casson, while quoting Dalton as his authority, described the

---

[1] *Altchristl. . . . Bildwerke* (see above, p. 33 n. 1), 17.
[2] *Byzantine Art and Archaeology* (1911), 143.
[3] *AA* 1931, 154. Cf. too *Sport und Spiel bei Griechen und Römern: Bildwerke aus den Staatlichen Museen zu Berlin* (1938), 15, 'um die Wende von 4. zum 5. Jhdt.'.

Kugelspiel as a 'curious monument of the sixth century'.[1] Whether this was just a slip (as seems more likely) or a deliberate correction, the new base of Porphyrius shows that a sixth-century date is certainly possible.

Stylistic dating criteria for works of this sort are highly fallible—and rightly suspect. An outsider, used in his own field to more rigorous standards of proof, may be permitted to smile when he sees art historians solemnly debating on stylistic grounds whether an undated statue from Aphrodisias belongs in 400, 410, 'third decade of the fifth century', or 'second quarter of the fifth century'.[2] Beyond question the study of the art of the late Empire has provided an indispensable key to the understanding of the period as a whole. Yet it would be idle to pretend that it can offer tools sharp enough to date such conventional work to within a decade or two.[3] The blunt truth is that in all this period there is only one absolutely dated and tolerably well-preserved large-scale work for comparison—and that made in Constantinople, not Aphrodisias—the obelisk base. And there have been scholars prepared to ignore the clear prima-facie literary and epigraphic evidence and put even this in the age of Constantine.

So great an authority as A. Grabar remarked not long ago when comparing the old Porphyrius base to the obelisk base that it could hardly be as late as the sixth century.[4] It is not so much the fact that he is wrong to which I call attention; but the confidence with which such an impression is advanced as though it had some basis in facts, if only in relation to other independently dated monuments of the same kind. A colleague of my own has urged me to push the new base back a decade or two earlier than the plain literary and historical facts put it, because of 'stylistic parallels' with the sadly ravaged base of Marcian's column.

It is to be hoped that the firm date for both Porphyrius bases put forward in this book will assist art historians to construct less arbitrary series. The Kugelspiel reliefs, for example, do have stylistic parallels with those of the obelisk base. But surely

[1] *Preliminary Report* . . . (see above, p. 6 n. 3), p. 2.
[2] See the list of authorities quoted by I. Ševčenko, *Synthronon A. Grabar* (1968), 38–9 (an important new contribution to the question of dating the monument and identifying the function of the figure represented).
[3] See the admission of J. Beckwith, *Art of Constantinople*, pp. 27 f.
[4] *L'Iconoclasme byzantin* (1957), 157.

they have more in common over all with the new Porphyrius base. We are now in a position to compare directly the treatment of the same motif in all three—the banner-wavers. Despite Gottwald's warm praise of the 'liveliness and freshness' of the Kugelspiel reliefs,[1] it could hardly be said that they are closer in either style or execution to the obelisk base here than to the two Porphyrius reliefs. Badly weathered though they are they look if anything clumsier than the Porphyrian banner-wavers. And the acclaiming figures on the front of the Kugelspiel are certainly cruder and stiffer versions of the acclaiming figures of both the Porphyrius bases—a far cry from the soft hieratic poses of the obelisk base. Indeed, the close parallel, not just in motif and treatment, but in the repetition of the panel of banner-wavers on opposite sides of both Kugelspiel and Porphyrius base, strongly suggest that one is modelled on the other. And it is not easy to believe that the Porphyrius base was modelled on the humble Kugelspiel. More likely the various reliefs of the Kugelspiel are all copied from one or another of the great series of charioteer stelae that rose in serried ranks from the spina of the hippodrome.

These reliefs are, in fact, like the epigrams which surmount them on both the extant bases, repertories of clichés which span some three centuries virtually unaltered. As L. Robert has remarked in his study of epigrams on imperial officials of the late Empire, it is usually impossible on stylistic grounds alone to date such epigrams to the fourth rather than the sixth century—or vice versa.[2] Their vocabulary, their formulas, their themes, their rhetorical devices change so little over the period. Some are of course better than others, but by no means necessarily the earlier ones. As Mango has well remarked, all the time we are dealing with 'rhetoric, whether in words or in stone'.[3]

The epigrams of the charioteer monuments are composed of just such timeless clichés as the reliefs, though in so far as it is possible to compare the two different art forms, the epigrams are more skilful in their execution than the reliefs. Given their exclusive concentration on the theme of the victorious charioteer, they are of course inevitably repetitious, but they seldom sink below the level of the competent, and from the technical point of

[1] *AA* 1931, 154.   [2] *Hellenica* iv (1948), 108 f.
[3] *Treasures of Turkey* (1966), 84.

RHETORIC IN WORDS OR STONE 61

view many are up to the standards of such polished practitioners of the next generation as Agathias and Paul the Silentiary.[1] The chapters which follow will trace in passing the pedigree of many of the themes in the charioteer epigrams, but let us consider in the present context just one by way of general illustration: *Anth. Plan.* 369, from the base to a statue of Porphyrius' older contemporary Constantine:

ἀντολίης δύσιός τε μεσημβρίης τε καὶ ἄρκτου
σὸς δρόμος ὑψιφαὴς ἀμφιβέβηκεν ὅρους,
ἄφθιτε Κωνσταντῖνε. θανεῖν δέ σε μή τις ἐνίσπῃ·
τῶν γὰρ ἀνικήτων ἅπτεται οὐδ' Ἀΐδης.

Your course, shining afar, has traversed the bounds of east, west, south, and north, immortal Constantine. Let no man say you are dead. Hades himself cannot lay his hands on the unconquerable.

There is nothing new here at either a verbal or a thematic level. Naturally enough our poet is not the first to address a dead man in a sepulchral inscription as ἄφθιτε (e.g. Peek, *GV* 1845. 1). The metrically convenient ἀμφιβέβηκε props up the close of many a line in late epigrams,[2] usually in the general sense 'cover', taking precision from the context (e.g. Kaibel 234. 2, of the second century; Kaibel 473. 3, second century; 1068. 2, fourth to sixth century; *AP* i. 19. 9, *c.* 527; i. 98. 5, *c.* 527). For 'let no man say you are dead' compare Callimachus, *AP* vii. 451. 2, θνῄσκειν μὴ λέγε τοὺς ἀγαθούς, or the adaptation in Peek, *GV* 647. 7–8, from first- or second-century Rome, or in the epitaph for a certain Euprepius on a third-century papyrus (Page, *GLP* i, no. 117. 2. 6, p. 478). With the last line compare especially Parmenio (probably early first century), *AP* vii. 239:

φθίσθαι Ἀλέξανδρον ψευδὴς φάτις, εἴπερ ἀληθὴς
Φοῖβος· ἀνικήτων ἅπτεται οὐδ' Ἀΐδης.

Wholesale though it is, the borrowing is neatly adapted. Constantine is not inappropriately included in the band of the ἀνίκητοι (athletes are actually so styled in inscriptions), the

---

[1] Indeed, Beckby went so far (iv² p. 574) as to suggest that 354 might actually have been written by Agathias (impossibly, of course, since it comes from a monument erected *c.* 500, while Agathias was not born till 531/2: *JHS* 1966, 8 and Averil Cameron, *Agathias* (1970), 140–1).

[2] Never in Nonnus, however, no doubt because of the proparoxytone accent.

sequence of thought is clear, and the borrowed line is not out of keeping with the tone of the poem as a whole.

But the most well-worn line in the poem is the first. Compare first Peek, *GV* 655, from the Trachonitis area of Syria, devoted to a certain Majorinus,

οὗ δύσις ἀντολίη τε μεσημβρίη τε καὶ ἄρκτοι . . .
εὖρύ τε καὶ μάλα καλὸν ἀεὶ κλέος ἀείδουσιν.

Peek, following Kaibel, dated the poem to the second or third century, but Robert has shown on historical grounds that it belongs around the middle of the fourth.[1] Here the line is adequately grafted into its context. In the following sorry effort from fourth-century Lycaonia it stands out as the only metrical line in the poem:[2]

Εὐγένιε, νέος θάνες· ἡελίοιό σε γὰρ ἐγίνωσαν πάντες,
ἀντολίη τε δύσις τε με(σ)ινβρία τε κὲ ἄρκτος . . .

Two lines by Gregory of Nazianzus (late fourth century) open respectively ἀντολίη τε δύσις τε (*carm.* ii. 2. 7. 44) and ἀντολίης δύσιός τε (*AP* viii. 36. 3). The whole line was evidently a stock formula by the fourth century. Nonnus knew it, of course, but (predictably) he expands the bare bones of its basic form into five whole bombastic lines (*Dion.* xli. 283–7). The author of the epigram on Constantine has fitted it into his context and his construction (as a genitive dependent on ὅρους) neatly enough, and no one could possibly have guessed on stylistic grounds that his poem is a century and a half or more later than all the others. He was enough of a craftsman to smooth over the joints and produce, not just the rambling and incoherent string of clichés that so many late inscriptions are, but a real and competent epigram.

The antecedents of the reliefs on the bases go back over a similar distance, geographical as well as chronological. Whatever the exact date of the Kugelspiel, and whatever its exact relationship with the Porphyrius bases, the contorniates cited so often in these pages are mostly a good century or more earlier than the bases—and all of western provenance. One of the reliefs of the Kugelspiel was completely misinterpreted till a contorniate provided the key.

[1] *Hellenica* xi/xii (1960), 302 f.   [2] *SEG* vi. 370. 4–5.

RHETORIC IN WORDS OR STONE

On the middle register of the right-hand face we have two men, one on each side of a rectangular framework, in the centre of which hangs from a sort of axle what looks like a large pot upside down. C. Texier, who first published the monument in 1845,[1] suggested (ingeniously and not absurdly) that it might be a gong to announce the beginning of the races. Then C. Robert drew attention to the contorniate type,[2] of which we have one particularly well-preserved specimen. In the hand of a figure behind the framework a small round object is clearly visible, while on a ledge below there are three more of these objects. Another representation of exactly the same scene has come to light in a recently published fourth-century catacomb painting from Rome.[3] As Robert saw, this is the lot-casting machine, whose operation is fully described in a chapter of the Book of Ceremonies.[4] The lots, balls called σφαίρια, one for each faction, were deposited in an *urna* (ὄρνα) which was then 'rolled'. In the light of these representations it is easy to appreciate the significance of the term κυλίειν ὄρναν. On the right of the Kugelspiel *urna*, as also on all extant contorniate representations, stands a figure holding a whip—no doubt an expectant charioteer. So close is the correspondence between the Kugelspiel and the contorniates, separated by more than a century and half the extent of the Empire.

As for the racing quadriga preceded by acclaiming figure on the bottom register of both left and right faces, there are parallels on mosaics and earlier relief work, but only contorniates, it seems, show the quadriga racing to the *left*. The motif of the solo horseman on the left face has already been traced back to the mosaics and sarcophagi of the third century.

It will not be necessary to recapitulate here the many other motifs of both Kugelspiel and Porphyrius base that can be traced back, often no doubt through many Byzantine intermediaries, to the mosaics, contorniates, sarcophagi, glasses, and so forth of the western provinces in the third and fourth centuries. If

---

[1] *Rev. archéol.* (1845), i. 147–8, with some very inaccurate woodcuts, Pls. xxviii–ix (unfortunately reproduced in Cabrol/Leclercq, *Dict. d'archéol. chrét.* vi. 2 (1925), col. 2390, figs. 5714–6). See rather my Pl. 15.
[2] *Rev. belge de numismatique* xxxviii (1882), 376–80: see Pl. 31.8.
[3] A. Ferrua, *Le pitture della nuova catacomba di via Latina* (1960), Tav. LXXIII.
[4] *De Caer.* pp. 312 f., with Guilland's analysis of the chapter in *BS* xxv (1964), 242–3. See too p. 39 n. 6.

further charioteer bases should ever come to light—and they may—I venture to predict that we shall see among their reliefs the racing quadriga with acclaiming attendant, the lot machine, and that other favourite contorniate type (Pl. 31.10), the movable hippodrome organ, shown twice on the obelisk base (Pl. 19).

The circus factions that meant so much in the life of sixth-century Constantinople go back (if in a different form) to Rome: right up till the tenth century the terminology of the hippodrome remained overwhelmingly Latin; that most Byzantine of phenomena, the 'imperial liturgy' of the hippodrome, has its origins in the ceremonial of the Roman circus; and it is hardly surprising (if interesting and illuminating none the less) that the hippodrome art of sixth-century Constantinople should likewise look back in all essentials to Roman models.

II

THE INSCRIPTIONS

THE left and right faces of the new base each have an epigram above the upper relief and a prose acclamation above the lower relief. This corresponds to a close parallelism between the arrangement of the reliefs on these same faces—a parallelism common to the side faces of both bases.

LEFT FACE

Above the upper relief stands, only slightly damaged, *Anth. Plan.* 356. The letters, here as elsewhere on the base, are on the average 0·015 m. high.[1]

ἄλλοις μὲν γεράων πρόφασις χρόνος· οἱ δ' ἐπ[ὶ νίκαις]
κρινόμενοι πολιῆς οὐ χατέουσι κόμης,
ἀλλ' ἀρετῆς, ὅθεν εὖχος ἀνάπτεται, ἧς ἄπο [τοίων]
Πορφύριος δώρων δὶς λάχεν ἀγλαΐην,
οὐκ ἐτέων δεκάδας, νίκης δ' ἑκατοντάδας [αὐχῶν]
πολλὰς καὶ πάσας συγγενέας Χαρίτων.

1 : γέρας, here as usually in honorific epigrams and invariably in the charioteer epigrams (p. 162), means 'statue'. For the formula ἐπὶ νίκαις see below, p. 265.

3 : Planudes offers εἰς for ἧς, a classic case of iotacism. For ἀγλαΐη at the end of the pentameter (especially in funerary poetry) see L. Robert, *Hellenica* ii (1946), 115–18, and iv (1948), 79.

5 : the metrically convenient ἐτέων δεκάδες is naturally a common way of expressing age in epigrams, especially epitaphs. Gow and Page on Menecrates, *AP* ix. 55. 2 (*HE* 2598), and Philodemus, *AP* v. 13. 8 (*GP* 3175), quote the literary parallels: *AP* vii. 295. 6 (Leonidas); v. 282. 4 (Agathias), from Callimachus fr. 1. 6 Pf.; Gregory Naz., *carm.* ii. 2. 1. 324 (*PG* xxxvii. 1474); add Cyrus (vi s.), *AP* vii. 557. 1. But there are many inscriptional examples too, from the fourth century B.C. on:

[1] See Pl. 1.

Peek 930. 1 (IV s., Peiraeus); 931. 1 (IV s., Eleusis); 986. 1 (II–III s., Sparta); 999. 1 (II s., Myrina); 1000. 1 (II s., Smyrna). It is particularly common and widespread in the Roman period, hardly here under the influence of the greater attention to recording exact ages in Latin epitaphs (a subject excellently studied in I. Kajanto, *A Study of the Greek Epitaphs of Rome*, Act. Inst. Rom. Finl. ii. 3 (1963), 12 f.) since decade-counting inevitably tends to approximation. Cf. Kaibel 366. 7 (late Empire, Cotiaeum); Peek 392. 2 (II s., Athens); 435. 4 (II s., Naples); 506. 2 (I s., Bithynia); 1351. 3 (II s., Paros); a late epigram from Kerak in Palestine published by R. Mouterde, *Mél. Beyrouth* xxxiv (1957), 268, etc. From the charioteer epigrams cf. too 358. 3, ἐξ δ' ἐτέων ἀνύσας δεκάδας, and 372. 3 (on Constantine), πέντε ... δεκάδας τελέσας ἐνιαυτῶν.

5: νίκης δ' ἑκατοντάδας. The numbering of victories in hundreds, neatly though it balances the decades of years, is probably more than a rhetorical flourish. *ILS* 5287. 14 singles out the year when the great Diocles first won 100 victories ('[quo an]no primum centum victorias consecutus est'). Since he won only 1,462 victories in all during a career of 24 years, even Diocles cannot have achieved his century very often. At *ILS* 5287. 11 we hear of horses who are *centenarii*. The next stage (hardly in one session) was to become a *miliarius* (ibid. 18). The inscription of Teres (*Bull. com.* 1901, 178–9) records that '[p]almas sibi complevit c(entesimam) C[alli]d(romo) af(ro), millesimam Hilaro af(ro)' (Callidromus and Hilarus being his lead horses: see above, p. 48). It will be shown in Chapter VI below (pp. 206 f.) that claims to records in these epigrams must be taken seriously, and it is perhaps unlikely that Porphyrius would have been credited—even for the sake of a rhetorical antithesis—with 'centuries' of victories unless he had at least once achieved such a century.

6: Χαρίτων. For the 'grace' of Porphyrius' driving cf. too χάριν in 352. 6 and 342. 3.

The sense of lines 3–4 and the interpretation of the poem as a whole are fully discussed in Chapter IV below for the light they cast on Porphyrius' chronology.

Above the lower relief stands the following in prose (Pl. 6):

† τί πλέον εἶχες τῆς νίκης ταύτης
ἀνθρώποις ἐπιδῖξαι εἰς Πράσινον;

LEFT FACE 67

ἐλαύνων κατεβίβασες τοὺς ἀντὶς σοῦ
καὶ ἔλαβες, Πορφύρι, αἰχμαλώτους
τούς σε μισοῦντας.

1 : τί πλέον εἶχες. ἔχειν is a standard term for the winning of victories in agonistic vocabulary (see the examples collected by L. Robert, *L'Épigramme grecque* (Entretiens sur l'antiquité classique xiv), 1969, 191–2). The inscriptions, both prose and verse, of the old base, Porphyrius' next after this one, show that he was there being honoured for a double success in the *diversium* (see pp. 43 and 209). Unfortunately none of the inscriptions on this base give any clue about the nature of the victory here celebrated, apparently Porphyrius' greatest to date.

2 : εἰς Πράσινον I take to mean 'for the (benefit or glory of the) Greens', translating the whole sentence: 'You have no greater victory than this to show men for the glory of the Greens.' But the phrase is problematic and requires discussion.

It occurs also in the prose inscription on the left face of the old base:

δῆμος Πρασίνων·
ἄγεται οὐκ ἄγεται, οὐ μέλει μοι· δὸς ἡμῖν Πορφύριν,
ἵν' οὓς Πορφύριν
ἔτερψεν εἰς Βένετον τέρψει καὶ εἰς Πράσινον
εἰ δ' αὐτὸς λάβι τὸ δημόσιον.

Every letter is clearly legible, but, short though the text is, it bristles with difficulties. J. B. Bury's 'whether it is in order or not'[1] gives a sense for the first three words which I suspect to be on the right lines, though I cannot provide any clear parallel. 'Whether ... or not, I do not care' (the δῆμος Πρασίνων, the Greens, are speaking). 'Give me Porphyrius, so that those Porphyrius [the second Πορφύριν is presumably a stonecutter's slip for Πορφύρι(ο)ς] has delighted by winning for the Blues he may

[1] *ABSA* xvii (1910/11), 93 n. 3. D. Tabachovitz, 'Zu dem Wagenlenker Porphyrios gewidmeten Inschriften', *Eranos* lvi (1958), 162–3, has confirmed the 'whether ... or not' part of this interpretation (cf. too, for example, the following acclamation addressed to a race-horse (*PBSR* xvi (1948), 32): 'vincas, non vincas, te amamus, Polidoxe'). But I cannot follow him in resurrecting Kaibel's view that ἱππικόν is to be understood with ἄγεται (ἱππικὸν ἄγεσθαι being the standard term for the holding of a race-meeting). Tabachovitz's translation, 'whether races take place or not', is quite inappropriate. The Greens' one desire is that Porphyrius should race for them: obviously he could only do this if races *did* take place.

delight[1] by winning for the Greens. If not,[2] may he [i.e. Porphyrius] take the *demosion* himself.' That is to say, if the Emperor (the addressee of δός, as the corresponding epigram 340. 6 shows) will not give them Porphyrius, they hope that Porphyrius will of his own accord don their colours. For a good commentary on the last line cf. epigram 374. 5–6:

πολλάκι δ' ἀμφοτέρων μερέων ἔρις ἔμπεσε δήμῳ,
τίς μιν ἔχοι· κείνῳ δὲ δόσαν κρίσιν ἐκ δύο πέπλων.

Constantine, the charioteer here in question, is so good that both factions offer him their colours and he has only to choose.[3]

In his recent commentary on this inscription D. Tabachovitz has suggested that εἰς Βένετον and εἰς Πράσινον mean 'as a Blue' (that is to say, driving for the Blues) and 'as a Green' respectively. εἰς+accusative is indeed used in this sense in late Greek[1] (as is *in*+accusative in late Latin).[1] To give but one example, from Malalas (p. 49. 12): ὁ Ζεὺς εἰς Σάτυρον ἔφθειρε τὴν Ἀντιόπην, 'Zeus raped Antiope as [in the form of] a Satyr'. This meaning would fit the new inscription perfectly: 'What greater victory have you won as a Green?'

Yet well-grounded and attractive though this interpretation

[1] τέρψει = τέρψῃ, the aorist subjunctive and future simple being commonly confused at this period: see for example K. Mitsakis, *The Language of Romanos the Melodist* (Byz. Archiv. xi, 1967), § 92. Beckby, iv², p. 574, rashly emends τέρψει to τέρψῃ and οὖς to ὡς to make the inscription correspond more closely with the epigram it complements (see below).

[2] λάβι = λάβῃ, a subjunctive used in the sense of the by now largely defunct classical optative (Mitsakis, *Language of Romanos*, § 102). Vasiliev (*DOP* iv (1948), 36) translated 'if he puts on the costume (of the Greens)', which omits both the δέ and the αὐτός (though admittedly αὐτός is used unemphatically in late Greek), and does not explain the mood of λάβι. Bury's 'then (lit. "if he do so"), let him receive the Demosion himself' (*ABSA* xvii. 93) is possible, but rather flat (if Porphyrius raced for the Greens, then inevitably he would wear their *demosion*). Not without some misgivings I follow Tabachovitz (*Eranos* lvi, 165–7) in taking εἰ δέ as equivalent to εἰ δὲ μή (more parallels would have been desirable). This explains δέ, αὐτός, and the mood, and the alternatives are plausible: the Greens recognize that the Emperor might not *order* Porphyrius to change colours (why should he?), but Porphyrius might *choose* to do so of his own accord (he had after all driven for the Greens in the past—and was in fact to do so often again).

[3] The πέπλος (= δημόσιον) of each faction would be coloured appropriately. This is presumably why the Book of Ceremonies (336. 4 R = ii. 139. 7 V) lays down that when a member of one faction serves as a substitute in another, he must wear the outfit of that faction (i.e. so as not to confuse the spectators).

[4] See the examples and references given by Tabachovitz, pp. 164–5.
[5] Leumann–Hofmann–Szantyr *Latein. Grammatik* ii (1965), 275.

LEFT FACE 69

might seem, I doubt if it is correct. Line 3 must surely be interpreted in the light of the last line of the epigram on the same face (happily intact at this point):

ὡς Βενέτους, τέρψῃ, κοίρανε, καὶ Πρασίνους (34 l. 6)

It is hard to doubt that this is anything but a metrical and more 'classical' version of line 3 of the prose inscription. Βενέτους is governed by ἔτερψεν understood: 'As he [i.e. Porphyrius] delighted the Blues, Lord, so may he delight the Greens.' τέρπειν εἰς Πράσινον evidently means more or less, if not exactly, the same as τέρπειν Πρασίνους.[1]

εἰς Πράσινον (Βένετον) is (on present evidence) confined to the two Porphyrius inscriptions. But with the addition of the definite article the phrase is common in the hippodrome ceremonial of the Book of Ceremonies. Here is a typical brief extract, one that well illustrates the (to modern taste) almost blasphemous mixture of the sacred and the profane that is so characteristic of the unselfconsciously religious Byzantine:[2]

καὶ πάλιν λέγει ὁ θεωρητὴς φωνῇ μεγάλῃ, "ἅγιε τρισάγιε" · καὶ ἀποκρίνονται πάντες καὶ λέγουσι· "Νίκη εἰς τὸ Βένετον" (οἱ Πράσινοι· "εἰς τὸ Πράσινον.") ὁ θεωρητής· "δέσποινα θεοτόκε"· ὁ λαός· "Νίκη εἰς τὸ Βένετον" (οἱ Πράσινοι· "εἰς τὸ Πράσινον"). ὁ θεωρητής· "τοῦ σταυροῦ ἡ δύναμις"· ὁ λαός· "Νίκη εἰς τὸ Βένετον" (οἱ Πράσινοι· "εἰς τὸ Πράσινον") . . .

Here at least there can be no question about the meaning: 'Victory for the Blues (Greens)!' But for the detail of the article, this is the very formula we find on the new base: Porphyrius wins a νίκη εἰς Πράσινον, while in the Book of Ceremonies the factions beg for νίκη εἰς τὸ Πράσινον (Βένετον).

The noun to be understood after Πράσινον/Βένετον in all these examples is μέρος,[3] the normal term for the factions of the

---

[1] The word τέρψις is often applied, not surprisingly, to the entertainments given in the circus and theatre: see (briefly) L. Robert, *Hellenica* xi/xii (1960), 8 n. 4. It would be easy to multiply illustrations: cf. (e.g.) Malalas, p. 285. 20 f., μίμων καὶ ὀρχηστικῶν καὶ τῶν λοιπῶν τέρψεων. One of the officials responsible for public entertainments known from the sixth century known as 'tribunus *voluptatum*' (Jones, *Later Roman Empire* iii (1964), 213 n. 8), where, as John the Lydian remarked to his Latinless readers (*De Mens.* iv. 25), *voluptatum* is used ἀντὶ τοῦ τῶν τέρψεων.
[2] i. 69, 311. 6 f. R = ii. 118. 20 f. V.
[3] Not, or at least not normally, χρῶμα (so A. Maricq, *BARB* xxxvi (1950), 403 n. 3 *ad fin.*).

circus in Byzantine times. This emerges clearly from the formula used by Malalas in his *Chronicle* to describe the factional sympathies of successive Emperors. At p. 263. 3 Domitian is reproached ὡς χαίρων εἰς τὸ Πράσινον. Cf. now p. 295. 15 where Geta ἔχαιρε εἰς τὸ Πράσινον μέρος or p. 379. 19 where Zeno ἔχαιρε... εἰς τὸ Πράσινον μέρος. Other examples show that εἰς + accusative after χαίρω here is simply an alternative for the by now fast disappearing dative. For there is plainly no difference in meaning between the three passages quoted above and the following three: p. 282. 12, ἔχαιρε τῷ Πρασίνῳ μέρει (Marcus); p. 350. 5, ἔχαιρε τῷ Πρασίνῳ μέρει (Theodosius II); p. 368. 13, ἔχαιρε τῷ Βενέτῳ μέρει (Marcian). That is to say Malalas is not intentionally quoting the εἰς τὸ Πράσινον acclamation in the earlier examples, though he may have been unconsciously echoing it.

Although there are no other examples of εἰς Πράσινον (Βένετον) without the article, there is a respectable (if scattered) number of examples of Πράσινον/Βένετον used *tout court* (i.e. without the article) to denote the Greens and Blues. *I. Didyma* no. 611, Πράσινον εἰς τ(?)οὺς αἰῶνας—left unfinished). Galen, *de methodo medendi*, x, p. 478 Kühn, οἱ περὶ Βένετον[1] καὶ Πράσινον ἐσπουδακότες. A curse tablet from Hadrumetum published in *MEFR* xxv (1905), 55 f. curses Ἀρχέλαος ὁ ἡνίοχος Πρασίνου. Then three of the iambic epigrams to be discussed below in Ch. V: *A. Plan*. 384. 1, Λευκοῦ μεθέλκων ἡνίας Κωνσταντῖνος; 386. 3, ἕλκων μεθέλκων Ῥουσίου τὰς ἡνίας (where ἡνίας τοῦ Ῥουσίου or τῶν Ῥουσίων would have scanned equally well) and 381. 1–2, ἡνίας / Πορφύριος Κάλχαντος εἷλκε Βενέτου (where Βενέτων would have scanned equally well). The two turning-points (*metae*, καμπτοί) were called after the Blues and Greens respectively at Constantinople. Usually ὁ καμπτὸς τοῦ Πρασίνου (μέρους) or (τῶν) Πρασίνων, but in Book of Ceremonies 352 R = ii. 154 V we find κάμπτουσιν καμπτὸν Πρασίνου καὶ Βενέτου, and then again κάμπτουσι... καμπτὸν Πρασίνου. Cf. ibid. 313. 2 R = ii. 120. 10 V, δύο κομβινογράφοι, εἷς Βενέτου καὶ εἷς Πρασίνου; 338. 1 f. R. = ii. 140. 20 f. V, ἀπὸ Βενέτου ἵππον ἕνα, ἀπὸ Πρασίνου ἵππον ἕνα, κτλ.

The article is, of course, far more commonly used than not, yet

---

[1] Βαίνετον Kühn, presumably following MS. evidence, but I have ventured to restore what Galen must have written.

there is quite enough evidence to substantiate the usage without, in both prose and verse at all periods. It remains unusual Greek, to be sure, but there is a very simple explanation of this: it is a Latinism.

As *Circus Factions* will illustrate in detail,[1] almost all the terminology of the Byzantine hippodrome is drawn from the circus of Rome, often by straightforward transliteration (e.g. ὄρνα from *urna*, βηγάριος from *bigarius*). The very few terms which are wholly Greek in origin are almost invariably Byzantine innovations of a later age. In the present case it is easy enough to track down the Latin original.

The Emperor Verus, according to *H. A. Ver.* 4. 7, 'amavit et aurigas, *Prasino* favens'. Tertullian describes how 'Russeum alii Marti, alii Album Zephyris consecraverunt, Prasinum vero Terrae matri... Venetum caelo' (*De Spect.* ix. 5). Martial refers to a 'Veneti quadriga' (vi. 46. 1). With ἡνίοχος Πρασίνου of the curse tablet cf. the 'Prasini agitator' of Suetonius, *Nero* 22. 1. Inscriptions record a 'hortator Prasini' (*ILS* 5307), a 'cursor Prasini' (*ILS* 5278), and a 'populus Veneti' (*I. Lat. Afr.* 385). It is the *populus* of this latter formula, or (no less commonly and with no difference in meaning) *populi* in the plural, that gave rise to the use of δῆμος and δῆμοι to denote the circus factions in Byzantine usage. Not realizing this, modern students of the factions call them 'demes', relating them to a postulated 'deme-structure' of their cities, champions of municipal independence against the encroachment of imperial absolutism—all in vain. δῆμος/-οι, like *populus/-i*, simply means 'people'. δῆμος Βενέτου, like *populus Veneti*, of which it is a straightforward calque, means no more than the people, or the fans, of the Blues.[2]

Galen's περὶ Βένετον represents Latin *de Veneto*, as in Martial x. 48. 23,

de Prasino conviva meus Venetoque loquatur.

As A. Maricq has seen (*BARB* xxxvi (1950), 403 n. 2), the noun understood here is *pannus*. Side by side with (e.g.) 'agitator Veneti' we find the full form 'agitator *panni* Veneti' (*ILS* 9348, cf. ibid. 5312, 5313). Cf. Juvenal xi. 197–8, 'fragor aurem / percutit, eventum [= victory] viridis quo colligo panni', and

---

[1] Chapters II–III.
[2] The myth of the demes is fully treated in *Circus Factions*, Ch. III.

with 'Prasino favens' quoted above cf. Pliny, *Ep.* ix. 6. 2, 'favent panno'. Other nouns are found qualified by the colour adjective: namely *factio*, *grex*, and (later) *pars*. But all are feminine, and so could not be supplied with an adjective of masculine termination. This only leaves *pannus*. More sensitive Greek-speakers would tend to add the article, as was their idiom, when adopting these phrases into their language: ἡνίοχος τοῦ Πρασίνου. And it may be in part at least because τοῦ Πρασίνου suggested a nominative τὸ Πράσινον that Greeks came to supply the neuter noun μέρος rather than a Greek transliteration or equivalent of the masculine *pannus*.[1]

I would suggest then that νίκη εἰς (τὸ) Πράσινον (Βένετον) is directly adapted from a Latin circus acclamation 'Victoria [sc. veniat] in Prasinum (Venetum)'. It is not surprising that the Latin original is not attested, since Latin inscriptions normally just list the details of a charioteer's career and records, and none of our literary sources preserves circus cries or acclamations in Latin.

One last argument against Tabachovitz's interpretation may be drawn from a circus formula which does happen to survive. According to Tabachovitz, it will be remembered, εἰς Πράσινον (Βένετον) means 'as (als, en qualité de) a Green (Blue)'. Now the inscriptions in honour of Gutta, Diocles, and Teres[2] record and classify the victories each had won for each of the four factions. Thus they very frequently need to say 'as a Green', 'as a Blue' etc. The phrase they use every time is *in factione Prasina, Veneta, Albata, Russata*. The joint inscription to the monument of Polynices and his son Tatianus (*ILS* 5286) uses instead the shortened version *in Prasino, in Veneto* etc. (as before, supply *panno*). There are contorniates bearing the legend 'Dominus in Veneto' (Alföldi, *Kontorniaten*, Taf. IV. 3; III. 11) and 'Eustorgius in Prasino' (IV. 4). Thus we should expect the Greek version to be ἐν Πρασίνῳ (etc.), not εἰς Πράσινον.[3]

---

[1] μέρος does have its Latin equivalent, *pars*, which seems not to have been used of a circus faction before the late Empire—perhaps replacing *factio*, which fell out of use by the fifth century (*Circus Factions*, Ch. II).
[2] *ILS* 5288 (Gutta), 5287 (Diocles), and L. Borsari, *Bull. Com.* xxix[6] (1901), 177 f. (Teres). The first two are fully discussed in Appendix XIII of Friedlaender's *SG* [9-10].
[3] It would be easy to show that by Porphyrius' day εἰς + accus. was often confused and interchanged with ἐν + dat. (cf. Mitsakis, *Language of Romanos*, §§ 168-9,

The rest of the inscription on the new base need not detain us long. 'By your driving you have brought low your rivals and taken prisoner [i.e. captivated], Porphyrius, those who hate you.'

3: τοὺς ἀντὶς σοῦ. The earliest example of the form ἀντίς. It is regular in some modern Greek dialects and (though absent from Sophocles' Lexicon) well attested in Byzantine Greek by the tenth century and after ('Ιστορικὸν Λεξικὸν τῆς Νέας Ἑλληνικῆς, B (1939), 260), presumably by analogy with μέχρι(s), ἄχρι(s), and ἀμφί(s). There is one other sixth-century example, P. Oxy. 941. 4, a letter to a certain John asking for the use of some land belonging to a monastery: τόπον ὀλίγον ἢ ἀντὶς τοῦ μαρτυρίου ἢ ἐξ ἀρ[ι]στερῶν αὐτοῦ ἤγουν ἐκ δεξιῶν. And we may also add two examples from the so-called glossary of Philoxenus (Corp. Gloss. ii. 60. 55 and 200. 39), a work that has no connection with Philoxenus (cos. 525) but may go back to the sixth or seventh century none the less (we possess the work in a ninth-century manuscript, Par. Lat. 7651). By the eleventh century ἀντίς governs the accusative, but in the Porphyrius inscription, as in P. Oxy. 941. 4, we still find the genitive. Of the later texts it is particularly interesting to compare a series of examples in the Book of Ceremonies[1] where the word is used, as in the Porphyrius inscription, to refer to the rival faction: ὁ ἀντὶς δῆμος at 318. 5 R = ii. 124. 17 V, or just ὁ ἀντίς (317 R = ii. 123. 4 V passim). The Porphyrius inscription suggests that the formula goes back to the late fifth century.

4: τούς σε μισοῦντας. The Blues. Epigram 355. 4 suggests that Porphyrius had left the Blues on bad terms (see p. 163). But τούς σε μισοῦντας may be no more than a stock term for the opposition. Cf. the twin acclamation preserved in the Book of Ceremonies (318. 13 R = ii. 124. 26 V) : τῶν φιλούντων ἡμᾶς πολλὰ τὰ ἔτη. τῶν δὲ μισούντων ἡμᾶς κακὰ τὰ ἔτη.

There are in addition two minor inscriptions. First, on the ridge between the upper inscription panel and the upper relief, the letters NIKOMH. Evidently Νικομή[δεια], identifying the city Tyche below. Porphyrius must have won in the splendid hippodrome of Nicomedia, built by Diocletian and evidently rebuilt after its destruction in the earthquake of 358 (Libanius,Or. lxi. 17).

and for an example in one of the charioteer epigrams, 374. 2). But it would be surprising for a formula of this nature to have been affected by such a tendency.

[1] 318. 5 R = ii. 124. 17 V.

Then, inside the top corner of the lower relief:

† Δάζις λέγω.
νικᾷ¹ ἡ τύχ
η τῶν Πρα
σίνων.

The form of the acclamation is standard all over the eastern provinces of the Empire. There are a number of inscriptional examples,[2] all of them from the late fifth, sixth, or seventh century (none save the one on the new base can be dated more precisely than this). First four from Syria: νικᾷ ἡ τύχη τὸν Βηνήτων (Heliopolis: H. Seyrig, *Syria* xxvii (1950), 248 no. 8 = *IGLS* vi. 2836). νικᾷ ἐ τίχη τὸν Βενέτον and † νικᾷ ἡ τύχε τὸν Βενήτον (Umm idj-Djimâl: E. Littman, D. Magie, D. R. Stuart, *Princeton University Expedition to Syria* III A (1921), 148–9, nos. 256 and 266). νικᾷ εὐτύχη τῶν Βενήτων (Taff, in the Ledjâ: *Syria* III A, no. 804). From Ephesus νικᾷ ἡ τύχι τῶν <νβ> Βενέτων (H. Grégoire, *Recueil I. G. C. As. min.* i, no. 112). From Didyma, νικᾷ ἡ τύχη Πρασίνων and νικᾷ ἡ τύχη Πρασίνον (Grégoire, no. 226. 3 = *I. Didyma* (1958), no. 609, and *I. Didyma*, no. 610). From Stratonikeia (in Caria), νικᾷ ἡ τύχη τῶν Π[ρ]ασίνων (Grégoire, no. 243 *bis*).[3]

Then four more which (like the Porphyrius base) link the factional acclamation with the name of an individual. First the inscription on an ivory comb from Antinoe now in the Louvre. On one side: + νικᾷ ἡ τύχη | + Ἑλλαδίας; and on the other: κέ Βενέτων | + ἀμήν (A. Dain, *Inscriptions grecques du Musée du Louvre: les textes inédits* (1933), 186–7, no. 217). Dain assumed that Helladia was the name of the owner of the comb, but surely she is the dancing-girl depicted on one side of it.[4] Leontius writes of a pantomime called Helladia,[5] and the masculine form Helladius

---

[1] In fact the ν of νικᾷ is written double: ⋈ (see Pl. 6). There is no iota ad- or subscript. (For second thoughts see below, p. 276.)
[2] There is a useful collection of inscriptions relating to the factions by A. Christophilopulu, Χαριστήριον εἰς Α. Κ. Ὀρλάνδον ii (1966), 349 f. (though very confusingly set out and omitting all curse tablets). See too Addenda, p. 276.
[3] I agree with L. Robert, *Hellenica* xi/xii (1960), 492, that the νικᾷ ἡ τύχη formula ought not to be restored (after R. Mouterde, *Mél. Beyrouth* ii (1926), 178 n. 1) in *SEG* viii. 213. So too, independently, A. Christophilopulu, op. cit. 354, suggesting ὀρθοδόξων or φιλοχρίστων before [Β]ενέτ(ω)ν, rather than τῶν (Robert).
[4] An observation I owe to Professor L. Robert.
[5] A. Pl. 284 f., with the commentary by O. Weinreich, *Epigramm und Pantomimus* [cited below, p. 89], 99–111.

is attested for male pantomimes (on the question of these stock professional names see below, p. 171).

From Gortyn in Crete comes the following: + νικᾷ ἡ τύχ[η] Πρασίνων [........] καὶ 'Ιωάννη[ς] (M. Guarducci, *Inscr. Cret.* iv. (1950), 513). Guarducci, followed by S. Spyridakis (*GRBS* viii (1967), 249), assumed that both John and the presumed colleague named in the lacuna were Green charioteers. The same may be true of Lefebvre, *I. G. C. d'Égypte* no. 37, from Alexandria: νικᾷ ἡ τύχη Εὐτοκίου + καὶ Βενέτων + καὶ τοῦ γράψαντος. Eutocius might be a charioteer (or pantomime)—or he might be a local notable. Cf. the following from Didyma: [Γ]εωργίου τοῦ πρ(ωτο)καγκελλαρ(ίου) κ(αὶ) [Β]ενέτων πολλὰ τὰ ἔτη.[1] This George is a high dignitary (*protocancellarius*), probably from the capital.[2] Perhaps he was a patron of the Blues, just as Theodosius II's chamberlain Chrysaphius and Anastasius' city prefect Plato were patrons of the Greens.[3]

Then there are a number of examples of an Emperor's name being linked with one or other of the factions: e.g. νικᾷ ἡ τύχη Κωνσταντίνου (which one?)... καὶ Βενέτων τῶν εὐνοούντων (*CIG* iv. 8788, cf. A. Christophilopulu, op. cit. 356–7; from Constantinople, of uncertain date). Φωκᾶ τῷ θεοστεφῆ κ(αὶ) Βενέτοις Κ(ύρι)ε βοήθη[σον] (Grégoire, no. 113. 3). There are others linking Phocas with the Blues and his successor Heraclius with the Greens: see Y. Janssens, *Byzantion* xi (1936), 526 f., A. Christophilopulu, op. cit. 351 f., and my *Circus Factions*, Ch. V. Here too the Emperor seems to be regarded as the patron of the colour mentioned.

There is little uniformity in this latter batch, nor are any of them exactly parallel to the unusual form of the inscription on the new base, where the acclamation itself is introduced by Δάζις λέγω. Most obviously, Dazis does not include himself in the good fortune he wishes the Greens—as does even the humble anonymous γράψας in the inscription from Alexandria. On a monument wholly devoted to commemorating the triumphs of one charioteer we can surely exclude the possibility that Dazis is another. Nor does he look like a person of real consequence (no grand title).

---

[1] *I. Didyma*, no. 604: correctly restored by Robert, *Hellenica* xi/xii, 490–2.
[2] See Robert, op. cit. 491. So too the Macarius in a parallel inscription from the same pillar (*I. Didyma*, no. 603, with Robert, 491–2).
[3] *Circus Factions*, Ch. II.

Probably not a patron, then. My own guess is that he is just a well-known Green partisan.

There is one other minor problem here—the reason I have transcribed all the other relevant examples of the acclamation. How is the νικα to be accented? Littman, Magie, and Stuart, *Princeton Expedition to Syria* III A (1921), 148, followed by J. Leclercq, *Dict. d'archéol. chrétienne* vi. 2407–9, were for writing νίκα (present imperative) everywhere. E. Stein, *Bas-Empire* ii (1949), 451 n. 1, and L. Robert, *Hellenica* xi/xii (1960), 492 n. 1, νικᾷ (present indicative). The question is obviously little more than academic, not least because in popular speech (Greek and Latin alike) the present indicative was often used instead of and with the same meaning as the imperative.[1] Thus Dazis himself might have written νικᾷ and meant 'win!' Nevertheless there is a genuine distinction to be made between at least two quite different forms of acclamation.

In support of their view Littman, Magie, and Stuart quoted examples such as the triple acclamation on a tablet from Naples (*CIL* x. 2061): 'Venenio nika / Gregori vibas [i.e. vivas] / bibe Secunde.' Or from Antium (*CIL* x. 8303): 'Limeni nica / (Li)meni ζήσῃς.' Undoubtedly *nika* is used here as an imperative, and an educated writer would have accented it paroxytone in Greek. Cf. νίκα Βένετε from the Book of Ceremonies (348. 12 R = ii. 149. 14 V): there is only one manuscript, to be sure, but the accent is obviously correct. Nor do we need the unanimous manuscript authority at Procopius, *BP* i. 24. 10, *Anecd.* 12. 12, 19. 12 and *Aed.* i. 1. 20, not to mention Malalas, p. 474. 12 and other historians of the Nika riot, to reassure us that the watchword of the rioters was νίκα, not νικᾷ. Once more, sense demands it.

The νικᾷ ἡ τύχη formula fits into a different pattern of acclamations, where there is no direct apostrophe. Cf. νικᾷ ἡ τύχη τῶν Ῥωμαίων (*De Caer.* 425. 10 R) or, a few lines after νίκα Βένετε just quoted, νικᾷ ἡ πίστις τῶν βασιλέων, νικᾷ ἡ πίστις τῶν Αὐγουστῶν, νικᾷ ἡ πίστις τῆς πόλεως καὶ τῶν Βενέτων (348. 18 R). There is a whole range of such acclamations,[2] of which the most delightful is a recently published inscription from Didyma:

---

[1] e.g. K. Mitsakis, *Language of Romanos*, § 105; Leumann–Hofmann–Szantyr, *Latein. Grammatik*, 327, § 183a.
[2] See O. Weinreich, *Neue Urkunden zur Sarapis-Religion* (1919), 33–7; E. Peterson, *Εἷς Θεός* (1926), 152–63.

LEFT FACE 77

νικᾷ ἡ τύχη τῶν ἀγάμων (L. Robert, *Hellenica* xi/xii (1960), 494–5), 'long live the bachelors!' Then we have the common type ('Ἰησοῦς) Χριστὸς νικᾷ, with its Latin equivalent 'Christus vincit'.[1] That νικᾷ was understood here as a present is further confirmed by the variation Χριστὸς ἐνίκησεν (e.g. Marcus, V. *Porph. Gaz.* 78, p. 62. 9 Grégoire–Kugener). Christ has conquered (ἐνίκησεν) and therefore is the conqueror (νικᾷ). With this type we may contrast Χριστὲ νίκα in Grégoire, no. 266, parallel to νίκα Βένετε, which in turn is paralleled by (e.g.) ἀγάλλου Βένετε at *Caer.* 357. 11 R = ii. 157. 22 V. The presence of the vocative changes the form of the acclamation, and naturally enough the imperative is used. The point is interestingly illustrated by the following mixture of the two types from Priene: νεικᾷς τύχη Πρασίνων (Grégoire, no. 120 = *I. Didyma*, no. 613). Having used the second person (the equivalent of νίκα), the writer drops the article so that τύχη can stand as a vocative. Cf. the correctly restored νικᾷς Χριστ[έ] of W. K. Prentice, *Syria* III B (1922), no. 26.

According to Malalas, the rioters of 532 chose νίκα as their watchword διὰ τὸ μὴ ἀναμιγῆναι αὐτοῖς στρατιώτας (p. 474. 12). Noting that soldiers always used Latin in their official dealings with the Emperor, Stein inferred that the factions chose νίκα 'par opposition au *tu vincas* latin ... une manifestation contre les troupes'.[2] A strangely fanciful notion for such a sober scholar. Surely the rioters made their choice simply because a word that was so often on their lips in the hippodrome came naturally to their minds at such a moment.

Stein further claims that νίκα was the cry that the factions used for the purposes of their own rivalry, while it was the Latin form that they employed when addressing the Emperor. This generalization is not borne out by the evidence.

In the first place, Leo I, Anastasius, and Justin I are addressed by the formula σὺ νικᾷς no fewer than eleven times in the accounts of their proclamations preserved (from the sixth-century writer Peter the Patrician) in *Caer.* i. 91–3 (410–430 R).[3] On the strength of a solitary *tu vincas* (τούμβηκας) at 424. 12, Stein coolly assumed that the other eleven were originally the

---

[1] See particularly Peterson, *Εἷς Θεός*, 153 f. F. Cabrol, *Dict. d'archéol. chrét.* i. 252, while quoting the Latin version, still expands the ⳨N monogram as Χρ(ιστὸς) ν(ίκα). [2] *Bas-Empire* ii (1949), 450–1, esp. 451 n. 1.
[3] 411. 9; 412. 2; 418. 17; 419. 6; 419. 14; 420. 16; 425. 11; 427. 2; 429. 10; 430. 2, 8 R.

same, but subsequently replaced by the Greek equivalent after the Latin formula had fallen out of use (probably in the eighth century). Now it is true that the greater part of the ceremonial of the Book of Ceremonies did undergo a continuous process of updating and revision—but *not* these chapters. As J. B. Bury so clearly put it in his classic study of the Book of Ceremonies in the *English Historical Review* for 1907 (p. 213): 'Whereas 1–83 are a guide to the actual court ceremonial of the tenth century, 84–95 [the chapters which concern us are 91–3] are of purely antiquarian interest. They not only describe ceremonies which had changed in character, but concern obsolete institutions. . . . 91–5 describe ceremonies as performed on particular historical occasions. In 1–83 the descriptions are always generalized.' Why then should anyone have made such a half-hearted attempt to remove just one trifling anachronism of detail? Why need we hesitate to accept that in the late fifth and early sixth centuries the people addressed their Emperor indifferently with *tu vincas* or σὺ νικᾷς?[1]

Nor is it the case that the factions used only the Greek forms for circus affairs. Cf. σο βίνκας, Πορφύρι written below the prose inscription on the front of the old Porphyrius base. And a glance at the legends of contorniate issues will suggest that in this sphere too people employed Latin and Greek indifferently. Here is a list from charioteer and pantomime contorniates (all of course western):

Aeliani nica (Alföldi, Taf. XXXVI. 8)
Asturi nika (LIX. 3, 8)
Eutime vinicas ([*sic*] LXIII. 7, 8)
Exuperanti vincas (LIV. 6)
Karamalle nicas (LXXII. 7)
Macedoni nika (LXI. 4)
Pannoni nika (XXXVI. 11)
Θεώφιλε nika ([*sic*] LXVII. 10)

Artemi vincas (LXIII. 12, 15)
Bonifati vincas (LXII. 8)
Eutime nica (LXIV. 2, 8)
Iohannes nicas (LXVII. 8)
Laurenti nica (XXXI. 2, 3)
Margarita vincas (LXIX. 2, 3, 7)
Ponpeiane vincas (LIX. 10)
Urse vincas (XXXVI. 10)

---

[1] When Corippus represents the 'vulgus' greeting Justin II 'tu vincas, Justine' (*Laud. Just.* i. 358), this does not exclude the possibility that they also cried σὺ νικᾷς. Writing as he was in Latin, Corippus naturally used the Latin form. Similarly, when '*aurea* plebes / *tempora* principibus . . . optat' at ii. 308–9, this is Corippus' Latin for something like χρυσέους αἰῶνας (from the coronation of Leo I, *Caer.* 412). According to Peter the Patrician (*Caer.* 431. 12 f.) ἔκραζον ὁ μὲν δῆμος ἑλληνιστί . . . οἱ δὲ στρατιῶται ῥωμαϊστί.

Then there is 'Leaeni nica' from one of the late Roman glasses quoted above (*CIL* vi. 2. 10070), 'Gaudenti nica' from *CIL* x. 8059. 177, 'Garamanti nica' and 'Genti nica' from *CIL* vi. 2. 10058—and many others (this list lays no claim to completeness). The regular use of the vocative and evident interchangeability of *nica* (*nika*), *nicas*, and *vincas*[1] confirm that *nica* represents νίκα here, not νικᾷ, though the acclamation is in fact more in the nature of congratulation on past success than hope for the future. Witness 'Liber nica' and 'Aeri nik(a)' inscribed above the *victors* in two chariot-race mosaics discussed earlier (p. 45). The contorniates similarly commemorate victors rather than hopefuls. On the other hand the νικᾷ ἡ τύχη acclamation, despite its present tense, really expresses a wish for the future[2] ('long live the — ' is the natural way of expressing it in English).

The 'Bonifati vincas'-type acclamation does not *prove* that charioteers in Rome were actually acclaimed with '*tu* vincas', but the σο βίνκας of the old Porphyrius base certainly implies that they were. We have seen in Chapter I how much of early Byzantine hippodrome practice, vocabulary, and art goes directly back to Roman precedents, and the chances are surely very high against the paradox of 'tu vincas' being a Byzantine innovation.

And as for Stein's assumption that the νίκα of the Nika rioters represents a protest against the Latin-speaking soldiery, the contorniate legends and other western inscriptions show that 'nica(s)' is not in fact a new acclamation, natural to a Greek-speaking population. Plainly it was already the standard cry of western circus audiences. In fact the use of Greek acclamations in Roman circuses, theatres, and amphitheatres probably goes back to the earliest times. *Nica* was standard in Latin acclamations to gladiators at least by the middle of the first century A.D.[3] The first professionally-trained theatre claques were introduced into Rome by Nero from Alexandria:[4] they will surely have used Greek. When Tertullian denounces the impiety of cheering a gladiator with the same lips that have uttered 'amen'

---

[1] But not (apparently) *vince*.
[2] It should be noted that the present is in fact very frequently used with future reference by this period, the future tense having largely disappeared in popular speech: Mitsakis, *Language of Romanos*, § 92. For the same phenomenon in Latin, Leumann–Hofmann–Szantyr, ii. § 172 (pp. 307–8).
[3] *CIL* iv. 1664; 3950 (from Pompeii, and so of necessity earlier than 79 A.D.).
[4] Suetonius, *Nero* 20, cf. 25: on this subject, see *Circus Factions*, Chs. IX–X.

on receipt of the sacrament, the acclamation he instances is a standard Greek one: εἷς ἀπ' αἰῶνος.[1] Dio records that Commodus, performing in the amphitheatre as a gladiator, was greeted with the cry: νικᾷς, νικήσεις. ἀπ' αἰῶνος, Ἀμαζόνιε, νικᾷς.[2] This is surely the authentic acclamation, not Dio's translation from a Latin original.

RIGHT FACE

Above the upper relief stands the following epigram (= *A. Pl.* 351, Pl. 10*a*):

[ὑμετέρων κήρυκες ἀμεμφέες εἰσὶν ἀγώνων]
 [οἳ καὶ ἀπ' ἀντιβίων] Πορφύριε, στέφανοι·
[πάντας γὰρ σταδίοι]σιν ἀμοιβαδὸν αἰὲν ἐλέγχει[ς]
 [ἀντιτέχ]νους, τῆς σῆς παιγ[νι]ον ἱπποσύνης.
[τοὖν]εκα καὶ ξεῖνον πρ[εσβ]ήϊον εὕρεο μοῦνος,
 εἰκόνα χαλκείην δήμωι ἐν ἀμφοτέρωι.

Diaeresis indicated in l. 4, iotas adscript in l. 6. εὗραο Planudes in l. 6 (see p. 262).

And above the lower relief (Pl. 9):

† παραχοροῦντες Πρασίνοις τὰ τῶν
 ἀγώνων, καὶ παιγνίδιν εἰπόντες τὴν
 πα̣[ρά]δοξον τέρψιν ταύτην, ὡμο-
 λόγ[ησα]ν̣ ν̣ι̣κηθῆναι, οἱ πολλάκις
 Π̣ο̣ρφύρι̣, ζητήσαντές σε.

'Yielding the contests to the Greens, and saying that this outstanding entertainment was (mere) sport (? for Porphyrius), (the Blues) have admitted defeat, they who have often sought you, Porphyrius.'

Concerning the epigram there is little to say. As the last couplet shows, Porphyrius now has the unique honour of a statue from each faction (literally 'in' each faction, i.e. in their 'territory' on the spina: see p. 142). The first couplet alludes to the many

---

[1] *De Spect.* 25; so at least the only MS. (*his apaeonos*), wrongly emended by modern editors: for the numerous parallels, L. Robert, *Études épigraphiques et philologiques* (1938), 108–11.
[2] lxxii. 20. 2; for the numerous Greek acclamations with which Nero was greeted in Rome after his tour of the Greek festivals see Dio liii. 20, with Robert op. cit. 110–11.

RIGHT FACE 81

crowns he has won from the other faction (the Blues), unimpeachable heralds of his triumphs. The middle couplet is the first we hear of the switching from one faction to the other for which Porphyrius was to become notorious.

1: ὑμετέρων. The plural with singular reference is common in Nonnus (Keydell's edition, i (1959), p. 55*) and his successors (e.g. Agathias, *AP* i. 36. 5; xi. 379. 2, 6; Paul, v. 301. 6). ἀμεμφέες, a favourite Nonnian word (twelve times, see Peek's Lexicon, s.v.), used by Agathias again, *A. Pl.* 41. 1 and the late epigram *AP* ix. 495. 1. κήρυκες, obviously metaphorical, but perhaps too alluding to the proclamation of the victor by a herald, certainly the practice in earlier days (lamps and mosaics show the herald with his trumpet: see the references in Robert and Stern quoted above, p. 49 n. 1). Synonyms for ἀντίβιοι are ἀντίτεχνοι (1. 4), ἀντίπαλοι (338. 6; 340. 4; 374. 3; xv. 47. 6), and δυσμενέες (355. 4; 362. 4). One might perhaps have expected the Nonnian ἀμοιβαδίς rather than ἀμοιβαδόν which Nonnus does not use. But cf. xv. 47. 2, from a later monument, again alluding to Porphyrius' switches of colour: ἀμοιβαδὸν ἄλλοτ' ἀπ' ἄλλου (perhaps an echo of Theocritus i. 34, ἀμοιβαδὶς ἄλλοθεν ἄλλος).

2: ἐλέγχεις = defeat, a meaning not well treated by LSJ. The 1968 addenda add Callimachus, frag. 84 Pf. (of an Olympic victor) and Nonnus i. 42. They do not remark that in this, as in the many other examples in Nonnus (viii. 175; x. 210, 317; xi. 389; xii. 160; xxvii. 340; xlii. 424, 459; xlvii. 47), there is always an overtone: either (as, surely, in Pindar *Pyth.* xi. 49, given by LSJ as simply 'get the better of') 'put to shame', or (especially of beauty) 'outshine'. For the latter see too Agathias, *AP* ix. 619. 3.

The prose inscription is an acclamation put into the mouths, not of the Greens who erected the monument, but of their rivals the Blues. In this respect it corresponds to the Green acclamation on the left side of the old base (Ch. I, pp. 45–6). The Blues are represented as admitting defeat: παραχωρεῖν is no doubt the *vox propria* for conceding defeat in a contest. τὰ τῶν ἀγώνων is also probably a stock phrase: cf. the opening words of the factional hymn quoted in the Book of Ceremonies i. 79 (349. 3 R = ii. 149. 28V): οἱ τῶν ἀγώνων σὲ δυσωποῦμεν.

παιγνίδι(ο)ν is explained by l. 4 of the epigram: defeating all comers in turn is a παίγνιον for Porphyrius, mere child's play.

For τέρψις of public entertainments (the standard term) see above, p. 69 n. 1. παράδοξος is the normal sobriquet of the athletic victor, the successful boxer, gladiator, pantomime, etc.: for a selection from the countless inscriptional examples see (e.g.) L. Robert, *BCH* 1928, 419–20; *Hermes* 1930, 112; *Rev. arch.* i (1934), 25 f. As Robert remarks in his *Gladiateurs dans l'orient grec*, 252, the word is used exactly like our modern 'champion'. παράδοξος τέρψις is then 'champion (top-flight) entertainment'.

οἱ πολλάκις, Πορφύρι, ζητήσαντές σε. The restoration of the proper name seems certain. Πορφύρι would be the normal everyday form of the vocative (as in the other prose inscription on this base, and on the front of the old base), though naturally enough the classicizing epigrams always use the full form Πορφύριε (351. 2; 354. 4; 344. 6; cf. Οὐράνιε at xv. 49. 2). The device of apostrophe is particularly common in the charioteer epigrams, Porphyrius being addressed in every one of the five epigrams from his last monument (358–62, cf. pp. 122–3).

The Blues are said to have 'often sought' Porphyrius. One of the epigrams from his next monument (from the Blues) describes how the Greens try to seek him back (δίζοντ' αὖθις ἔχειν, 341. 4). Cf. too xv. 49. 5 (of Uranius), Πρασίνων δέ σε δίζετο δῆμος.

BACK FACE

One epigram above each relief, both almost perfectly preserved. On the ridge between the upper inscription panel and the relief beneath it the letters Υ. ΟϹ are clearly legible, and the other traces consistent with [Βη]ρυτος, i.e. Berytus, identifying the city Tyche below. Porphyrius had no doubt won some notable victories at Berytus, a city with a famous hippodrome (see R. Mouterde, *Mél. de l'Univ. St. Joseph Beyrouth* xv (1930/1), 122–3), and thus a highly probable supplement.

On the upper panel itself stands the following epigram (= *A. Pl.* 352, Pl. 10*b*):

πλάστης χαλκὸν ἔτευξεν ὁμοίϊον ἡνιοχῆι.
εἴθε δὲ καὶ τέχνης ὄγκον ἀπειργάσατο,
ὄγκον ὁμοῦ καὶ κάλλος, ἅπερ Φύσις ὀψὲ τεκοῦσα
ὤμοσεν· "ὠδίνειν δεύτερον οὐ δύναμαι."

ὤμοσεν εὐόρκοις ὑπὸ χείλεσι· Πορφυρίωι γὰρ
πρώτωι καὶ μούνωι πᾶσαν ἔδωκε χάριν.

Now the lower epigram (= *A. Pl.* 353, Pl. 7):

† εἰ Φθόνος ἠρεμέοι, κρίνειν δ᾽ ἐθέλοιεν ἀέθλους,
πάντες Πορφυρίου μάρτυρές εἰσι πόνων.
ναὶ τάχα καὶ φήσαιεν ἀριθμήσαντες ἀγῶνας·
"βαιὸν τοῦτο γέρας τοσσατίων καμάτων."
ὅσσα γὰρ ἡνιοχῆας ἀεὶ μεμερισμένα κοσμεῖ,
εἰς ἓν ἀολλίσσας τηλίκος ἐξεφάνη.

The diaeresis in 352. 1, iota adscript in 352. 5–6, and apostrophe in 353. 1 are all indicated. In 352. 3 Planudes offers ὅπερ for ἄπερ: see p. 269. And on ὑπὸ in 352. 5 see also p. 269.

Number 353 is a competent enough piece, but pretty conventional. Number 352 is distinctly above average: a neat motif embellished with literary allusions, but clearly and simply expressed. Neither is the cento of incoherent clichés that so many late honorific epigrams are—especially when produced in sextuplicate for one monument. In a number of details they anticipate (as do others of the charioteer epigrams) motifs and formulas that we first find otherwise in the highly wrought literary epigrams of Agathias, Paul the Silentiary, and their circle, collected together and published by Agathias under Justin II *c*. 566/7.[1] The commentary will illustrate.

There is another feature too in which the charioteer epigrams anticipate the work of Agathias and their friends: their metre. During the Roman period there were two developments away from the elegiac couplet which in hellenistic times had become established as *the* metre of the epigram. First, towards the hexameter κατὰ στίχον (see A. Wifstrand's chapter 'Ein Geschmackswandel in der Epigrammdichtung', in *Von Kallimachos zu Nonnus* (1933), 155 f.). Secondly, towards the iambic κατὰ στίχον, particularly evident in the late fourth-century epigrams of Palladas, but already noticeable in the poets of Philip's *Garland* (see my remarks in *CQ* 1970, p. 121). Ultimately, of course, the iambic (in the form of the Byzantine twelve-syllable) was to supplant both hexameter and elegiac (see pp. 191 f.).

[1] As shown by my wife and myself in *JHS* lxxxvi (1966), 6–25, cf. ibid. lxxxvii (1967), 131. See also below, p. 90 n. 3.

But the poets of Agathias' circle returned to the elegiac almost (perhaps altogether) without exception. Evidently a conscious purist revival—but not a revival actually initiated by Agathias himself, or by Paul, Julian, Leontius, Macedonius, or any of the other mid-sixth-century epigrammatists. It is already manifest in the charioteer epigrams. Discounting Leontius' poem on Porphyrius and the eight very much later iambic epigrams (380–7: see pp. 191 f.), there are fifty-two inscriptional epigrams in the series, of which fifty are in elegiacs, and only two in hexameters. All fifty-two, moreover, are no less Nonnian in style and metre generally than the work of the *Cycle* poets.

A. Pl. *352*

1 : the πλάστης (used here properly of one who works in bronze) is often directly evoked in late epigrams, copying hellenistic models (with which the authors of the charioteer epigrams seem to have had a close first-hand familiarity, no doubt via the *Garland* of Meleager).[1] Cf. (e.g.) Agathias, *A. Pl.* 332. 1 (imitating Posidippus, *A. Pl.* 119. 1); Julian Aeg., *AP* ix. 796. 1 (imitating Antipater Sid., *AP* ix. 723. 2); and in an epigram from the old base, 342. 2 (direct from Archias, *AP* xv. 51. 2).[2]

2 : αἴθε seems to be the commoner form in late poets (more epic in flavour): always in Nonnus (forty times)[3] and regularly in Agathian poets: *AP* v. 279. 3 (Paul); vii. 565. 1 (Julian); ix. 152. 3 (Agathias); ix. 627. 3 (Marianus); ix. 629. 1 (John Barbucallus). Also at 358. 5 from Porphyrius' last monument. For the same formula introducing the same motif (would that the craftsman could copy more than just his/her physical beauty) cf. Paul, *A. Pl.* 277. 1–2 (with Viansino ad loc.):

σὸν μὲν κάλλος ἔδειξε μόλις γραφίς· αἴθε δὲ τεύχειν
ἔσθενε καὶ λιγυρῶν ἡδὺ μέλος στομάτων.

Note also (written only a year or so before the Porphyrius

---

[1] Which was certainly known to Agathias and his friends a few decades later: Averil Cameron, *Agathias* (1970), 19, 27.

[2] See further below, p. 268. Which of the five or more Archiases represented in the Anthology this is we cannot say: see the discussion in Gow and Page, *Garland of Philip* ii (1968), 432 f. Two at least are Meleagrian, probably none Philippan, so it may have been in Meleager that our poet found his model.

[3] When imitating *AP* v. 84. 1 at *Dion.* xv. 258 f. (cf. W. Peek, *Krit. u. Erklär. Beiträge zu Nonnos* (Abh. Deutsch. Akad. z. Berlin) (1969), 52), Nonnus changed εἴθε to αἴθε.

epigram: see p. 154) Christodorus, *AP* ii. 47–8: ὤφελε χαλκῷ | συγκεράσαι μέλος ἡδύ.
3: ὄγκον ὁμοῦ καὶ κάλλος, the dignity and beauty of his skill. Line 6 adds χάρις; obviously Porphyrius was a stylist.
3–4: cf. anon., *A. Pl.* 302:

εὗρε Φύσις, μόλις εὗρε· τεκοῦσα δ᾽ ἐπαύσατο μόχθων,
εἰς ἕνα μοῦνον Ὅμηρον ὅλην τρέψασα μενοινήν.

The points of contact are several and striking: in both cases Physis gives birth to the subject of the poem after a long labour; in 302 this is stated to be her last (ἐπαύσατο μόχθων), in 352 she vows that it will be her last (ὠδίνειν δεύτερον οὐ δύναμαι); and both poems make use of similar anaphora (302: εὗρε ... εὗρε; 352: ὄγκον ... ὄγκον and ὤμοσεν ... ὤμοσεν). Number 302 is anonymous and undated, but the use of the hexameter κατὰ στίχον suggests a late date,[1] and it might well be an inscription to a statue or painting of Homer in Constantinople known to our poet. There are of course two other possibilities: 302 derives from 352 or both from a common model. Another variation on the theme is presented by a poem of Julian the Egyptian, written at least a decade after the Porphyrius epigram (*AP* vii. 561. 1–2):[2]

ἡ Φύσις ὠδίνασα πολὺν χρόνον, ἀνέρα τίκτεν
ἄξιον εἰς ἀρετὴν τῶν προτέρων ἐτέων.

Paton translated ὀψέ in 352. 3 'late in her life'. μόλις in 302 and πολὺν χρόνον in Julian show that ὀψέ in fact refers to the duration of Physis' labour—the idea being that the more prodigious the child the more arduous the parturition.

Whether or not our poet got the inspiration for his anaphora from 302, he certainly had a more famous model in mind as well, Callimachus' poem *AP* v. 6 (= xxv Pfeiffer = xi Gow and Page):

ὤμοσε Καλλίγνωτος Ἰωνίδι μήποτ᾽ ἐκείνης
ἕξειν μήτε φίλον κρέσσονα, μήτε φίλην.
ὤμοσεν ...

[1] As shown by A. Wifstrand, *Von Kallimachos zu Nonnos* (1933), 155 f., drawing attention on p. 173 to late features on 303 (also on Homer). The similar use of anaphora in 303. 4 suggests the possibility that both are in fact from the same pen.
[2] Julian's earliest datable poems—*AP* vii. 591–2—were written in or after 532 (*JHS* 1966, 13, with McCail, *JHS* 1969, 87); and vii. 590 a year or two at least after 546 (in 1966 I said 548/9, following Haury's chronology for Procopius, *BG* iii. 31. 14: see rather Stein's in his *Bas-Empire* ii (1949), 552–4). It is unlikely that he was writing poems as early as 500, the date of the new base.

86   THE INSCRIPTIONS

The combination of the anaphora and the reference to Physis suggests that the following couplet from the monument to the charioteer Constantine echoes our epigram (373. 1–2):

> ἤθελε Κωνσταντῖνον ἀεὶ πτόλις ἡνιοχεύειν.
> ἤθελεν—ἀλλὰ πόθῳ οὐκ ἐπένευσε φύσις.

The resemblances may not in themselves be decisive, but Constantine's monument was put up not long after and only yards away from Porphyrius', and it is natural to assume that its poet gave our monument a glance.

6: πρώτῳ καὶ μούνῳ—the standard formula for records in agonistic inscriptions (see p. 207), cleverly used here in a non-agonistic context.

A. Pl. 353

The switch from the singular ἠρεμέοι to the plural ἐθέλοιεν[1] is awkward, but presumably influenced by πάντες in the next line. Odd too is the notion of Φθόνος remaining still, implying as it does that she is not usually still. The poet surely has Tyche in mind. Cf. *A. Pl.* 346, from a later monument, where it is Tyche, normally fickle, whose eye now rests on Porphyrius alone:

> πάντα Τύχης ὀφθαλμὸς ἐπέρχεται, ἀλλ' ἐπὶ μούνοις
> Πορφυρίου καμάτοις ἕλκεται ὄμμα Τύχης.

In 353 this motif has been combined, not very harmoniously, with another: the envy generated by the number of Porphyrius' victories. This latter motif appears already in Martial's epitaph for the charioteer Scorpus (x. 53. 3–4):

> Invida quem Lachesis raptum trieteride nona
> [i.e. when he was 27]
> dum numerat palmas credidit esse senem.

The difference here, of course, is that envy of Scorpus is said to have led to his early death (the usual significance of a reference to envy in sepulchral poetry: cf. G. Giangrande, *Hermes* xcvi (1969), 717 f.).

For the additional motif of this couplet of Martial, the number of his victories suggesting that the young charioteer is

---

[1] On the optatives in lines 1 and 3 see below, p. 263.

in fact an old man, cf. two epigrams from Porphyrius' first monument:

εἰ δ' ἐτέων γέρας ἦλθε θοώτερον, ἀλλ' ἐπὶ νίκαις
ὄψιμον, ἀλλὰ μόλις πολλὰ μετὰ στέφεα. (336. 7–8)

In 338. 1–4 Nike counts Porphyrius' victories as Φθόνος does in 353:

Νίκη ... ἀριθμήσασα πολυστεφέας σέο μόχθους
εὗρετο γηραλέων κρέσσονας ἡνιόχων.

O. Weinreich argued on the basis of the latter motif alone that 338 was directly influenced by Martial's poem ('Martials Grabepigramm auf den Pantomimen Paris', *Sitzb. d. Heidelb. Akad. d. Wiss.*, Phil.-hist. Klasse 1940/1, i. 21–2). Even taking into account the envy-counting-victories motif from 352, this conclusion seems a little hazardous. There are other parallels between sixth-century epigrams and Martial, to be sure, and these too Weinreich traces directly to the influence of Martial. In fact we shall see that in all these cases a common Greek model is the more likely answer.

With the following lines from Martial's epitaph on the pantomime Paris (xi. 13. 4 f.),

ars et gratia, lusus et voluptas,
Romani decus et dolor theatri ...
hoc sunt condita, quo Paris, sepulchro,

Weinreich fairly enough compares, from Leontius' poem on the death of the citharode Plato (*AP* vii. 571. 2),

σεῦ δέ, Πλάτων, φθιμένου παύσατο καὶ κιθάρη.

Or (closer to Martial), Julian the Egyptian on the *grammaticus* Theodorus (vii. 595):

κάτθανε μὲν Θεόδωρος· ἀοιδοπόλων δὲ παλαιῶν
πληθὺς οἰχομένη νῦν θάνεν ἀτρεκέως.
πᾶσα[1] γὰρ ἀμπνείοντι συνέπνεε, πᾶσα δ' ἀπέσβη
σβεννυμένου· κρύφθη δ' εἰν ἑνὶ πάντα τάφῳ.

Weinreich had no hesitation in positing Martial as Julian's 'source'. But there are many very similar examples of the motif

[1] πᾶσα refers to the πληθύς of ancient poets, who still lived while Theodorus lived (that is to say through his teaching), but are now irrevocably gone.

in a number of other Agathian poets. First Agathias' own epitaph on the singer Joanna (vii. 612. 3-4):[1]

ὤλετο φορμίγγων τερετίσματα, λῆξαν ἀοιδαί,
ὥσπερ Ἰωάννῃ πάντα συνολλύμενα.

Then there is Paul's epitaph on the *grammaticus* Damocharis (vii. 588: cf. 1. 3, ὤλετο γραμματικῆς ἱερὴ βάσις), and Julian again, on the lawyer Craterus:[2] vii. 562. Once more, too, we find the motif in the charioteer epigrams, this time applied to Porphyrius' contemporary Constantine, cut off in his prime:

ἐξότε Κωνσταντῖνος ἔδυ δόμον Ἄϊδος εἴσω
ᾤχετο σὺν κείνῳ πᾶν κλέος ἡνιόχων. (42)

And from the same monument, *A. Pl.* 366. 5-6:[3]

οὔνεκεν ἱπποσύνης φιλοκέρτομος ὤλετο τέχνη
ἐν σοὶ παυσαμένη πᾶσα καὶ ἀρξαμένη.

Are we really to see the influence of Martial here as well?

Both verbally and thematically closer to the last example than Martial is the following couplet from a monument erected to an engineer *c.* A.D. 200[4] at Hermupolis in Upper Egypt:

ἔγνων, ὦ Μοῖραι· πολυμήχανος ὤλετο τέχνῃ·
τίς τούτῳ ζώντων ἄλλος ὅμοιος ἀνήρ;

---

[1] A. Mattsson (*Untersuchungen zur Epigrammsammlung des Agathias* (Lund 1942), 111) traces the use of the motif in this poem directly to the passage from the *Lament for Bion* 11-12 quoted below—not very plausibly in view of the numerous other examples. Weinreich, at *Epigramm und Pantomimus* (quoted below), 71-2, quotes lines 1-2 of the poem, τὴν λυραοιδὸν | 'Ρώμης καὶ Φαρίης as 'unimpeachable proof' that Agathias knew Martial (cf. his line 3, 'Urbis deliciae salesque Nili'). In fact, of course, the common reference to Egypt merely illustrates what Weinreich himself had admitted in *Martials Grabepigramm*, 12 (quoting H. Bier, *De saltatione pantomimorum* (Diss. Brühl 1920), 91): that good pantomime dancers frequently did come from Egypt, especially Alexandria. I am not myself at all convinced that any of the Agathian poets were familiar with Latin literature: see my wife's brief survey of the literature in *JHS* 1966, p. 211, and for Agathias himself see too *CQ* N.s. XV (1965), 289 n. 3. On the much-discussed case of Paul, *AP* v. 275 and Propertius i. 3 see now R. O. A. M. Lyne, *Proc. Camb. Phil. Soc.* 196 (1970), 60 n. 2, deciding (rightly) for a common hellenistic model.

[2] For some speculations (possible, but not compelling) about the identity of this Craterus see McCail, *JHS* 1969, 88.

[3] Weinreich quotes *A. Pl.* 385 rather than either 366 or *AP* xv. 42, but as we shall see (pp. 191 f.) this is only a ninth- or tenth-century imitation of these two epigrams.

[4] Peek 1846. 3: before 212, according to T. C. Skeat, *JEA* xxviii (1942), 68 accepted by W. Schubart, *Aegyptus* xxxi (1951), 154 (*c.* 200).

Here at least we can surely rule out the possibility of Latin influence.[1] Cf. also two of Gregory Nazianzen's interminable epitaphs on Amphilochius, once a lawyer:

Ἀμφίλοχος τέθνηκεν· ἀπώλετο εἴ τι λέλειπτο
καλὸν ἐν ἀνθρώποις ῥητορικῆς τε μένος.
(*AP* viii. 134. 1–2)

... φθιμένῳ δὲ συνέφθιτο καὶ πυρόεσσα
ῥήτρη καὶ πάτρης εὖχος ἀριστόκου.   (viii. 135. 3–4)

Gregory certainly knew no Latin.

In his paper of 1940/1 Weinreich admirably traced the Latin antecedents of Martial's epitaph on Paris. But, as he admitted in his later study *Epigramm und Pantomimus* (Epigrammstudien I, *Sitzb. Heidelb. Akad. d. Wiss.* 1944–8, i, at p. 70), he had overlooked Alcaeus of Messene's epitaph on the citharode Pylades. Here we find the motif we have been discussing already worked fully out in an epigram of the early second century B.C., subsequently included in the influential *Garland* of Meleager. It will suffice to quote the last couplet (vii. 412. 7–8):

ἔλληξαν δὲ μέλαθρα Διωνύσοιο χορείης,
εὖτε σιδηρείην οἶμον ἔβης Ἀίδεω.

Then there is the probably first-century B.C. Lament for Bion, 11–12:[2]

ὅττι Βίων τέθνακεν ὁ βουκόλος, ὅττι σὺν αὐτῷ
καὶ τὸ μέλος τέθνακε καὶ ὤλετο Δωρὶς ἀοιδά.

It would be natural to suppose that this anonymous poet derived the motif from a hellenistic sepulchral epigram such as that of Alcaeus, a model in which the familiar ὤλετο of the later tradition may already have been present.

Interesting though they are, none of the Latin examples

---

[1] At this date anyway. A century or so later there is some evidence for knowledge of Latin even in Upper Egypt, following official policy after Diocletian: cf. *Historia* xiv (1965), 494 f., *Claudian* (1970), 19 f., and for the influence of Ovid on Nonnus see now the excellent discussion by J. Diggle, *Euripides' Phaethon* (1970), 180–200.

[2] [Moschus] iii. 11–12, cf. 65, πάντα τοι, ὦ βούτα, συγκάτθανε δῶρα τὰ Μοισᾶν. On rather shaky grounds T. B. L. Webster, *Hellenistic Poetry and Art* (1964), 203, has suggested a late second-century date for the *Lament*. But this ignores the tradition (Suidas s.v. Moschos and cf. R. Pfeiffer, *History of Classical Scholarship* (1968), 210–11) that Moschus was a pupil of Aristarchus and the second bucolic poet after Theocritus.

Weinreich quotes is in fact exactly parallel.[1] They all lack two features common to both Martial and the Greek tradition. None contains a precise statement that the art of *x* died with *y*. And the two hellenistic examples, when taken together with Martial's epigram on Paris, the charioteer epigrams, and Agathias on Joanna, all suggest that, though the art in question was early and freely extended to other professions (such as the law and engineering), it was originally and indeed all along predominantly a motif appropriate to the entertainment profession. The hyperbole is, after all, more in keeping with an idol of the theatre or circus than with an engineer or professor of literature.

So far then from Martial's poem being the source of all or even any of the later Greek epigrams quoted above, is it not rather an isolated Latin version[2] of a Greek genre originating in hellenistic times: the epitaph on a popular entertainer so supreme in his art that it could be said to die with him?

It was one of the limited range of hellenistic motifs to catch the fancy of the poets of Agathias' circle at Constantinople,[3] and (as usually happens in such cases) most of them had a go at producing a variation on it. It would hitherto have been supposed that one of their number was the first to give the old motif new currency in sixth-century Constantinople, and that the others took it from him. Yet we are now in a position to see that the motif appears in its classic form (ὤλετο..., applied to a star entertainer) in the charioteer epigrams a full generation before the first of the Agathian poets put pen to paper.

[1] The epitaphs on Naevius and Plautus quoted by Gellius, *NA* i. 24. 2–3 = W. Morel, *Frag. Po. Lat.*[2] (1927), pp. 28 and 32; the epitaphs on Cicero quoted by Seneca, *Suas.* vi. 26–7 = Morel, pp. 118–19.

[2] This is not the place to discuss the more general issue of Martial's debt to Greek epigram: see P. Laurens's recent paper, 'Martial et l'épigramme grecque du Ier siècle après J.-C.', *RÉL* 1966, 315–41. There is also much of relevance in L. Robert's study of Lucillius in *L'Épigramme grecque* (*Entretiens sur l'antiquité classique* xiv, 1969), 181–295.

[3] I use the term 'circle' loosely, since there is little evidence that they formed a regular literary coterie (though some may have). Nevertheless, all or most were professional men or civil servants in Constantinople, and the similarities between their epigrams are many and obvious; partly because they affected common models, partly too because they often imitate each other. The popular notion that they flourished at Justinian's court and through his favour is a mistake. Naturally enough their work reflects some aspects of the age of Justinian (cf. McCail, *JHS* 1969, 94–6), but most of the epigrams were written towards the end of his reign and the *Cycle* itself not published till after his death (above, p. 83, and Averil Cameron, *Agathias* (1970), 12–16).

Another example of the same phenomenon is provided by 353. 3:

πάντες Πορφυρίου μάρτυρές εἰσι πόνων.

Naturally enough, numerous people, places, and things are 'witnesses' to the deeds of the honorand in honorific epigrams. It would be superfluous to cite examples of so common a theme. But the closest parallel I have come across to this formulation of the theme before the Agathian poets is Peek 1937, from second-century Rome:

ἀθάνατ[ος] μερόπων οὐδεὶς ἔφυ· τοῦδε, Σεβήρα,
Θησεύς, Αἰακίδαι, μάρτυρές εἰσι λόγου.

It is thus the more striking that it should be precisely the formulation of 353. 3 that we find adapted a full half-century later by Arabius and Leontius. First Arabius, in a poem written when a certain Longinus was prefect of the city, an office he held in 537–9 and again in 542:[1]

Νεῖλος, Περσίς, Ἴβηρ, Σόλυμοι, Δύσις, Ἀρμενίς, Ἰνδοί...
Λογγίνου ταχινῶν μάρτυρές εἰσι πόνων.

Then Leontius on Peter Barsymes:

Πέτρον ὁρᾷς χρυσέοισιν ἐν εἵμασιν· αἱ δὲ παρ' αὐτὸν
ἀρχαὶ ἀμοιβαίων μάρτυρές εἰσι πόνων.

The ἀρχαί include two praetorian prefectures, the second of which did not begin till 555.[2] In such a situation one would normally guess that all three derive from a common model. But in view of the other examples, and especially if (as suggested with further illustrations below, pp. 113–16) the charioteer epigrams were already circulating in manuscript before the publication of the *Cycle*, there is more than a possibility that both Agathian poets derive from the Porphyrius epigram.

3: ναὶ τάχα. An exclamation of uncertain import much affected by Agathias and his friends: Agathias himself at *AP* iv. 4. 127 (81) and v. 294. 22, ix. 653. 6, xi. 379. 4; Paul, v. 236. 1; Julian, *A. Pl.* 325. 3. Also *A. Pl.* 101. 5, anonymous, but certainly post-Nonnian[3] and quite possibly Agathian. But unlike so many

[1] *A. Pl.* 39. 1–4: *JHS* 1966, 10–11, with McCail, *JHS* 1969, 90–1.
[2] *A. Pl.* 37. 1–2: *JHS* 1966, 15.
[3] Whence γοήμονα... φωνήν in l. 5 (*Dion.* xi. 196, xxiv. 200, i. 127). γοήμων is

phrases in vogue with Agathian poets, ναὶ τάχα is not a Nonnism.[1] The closest Nonnus gets to it is καὶ τάχα at *Dion.* xi. 437 and οὐ τάχα at xlvi. 47. Once more it is the Porphyrius epigram where the phrase first appears.

4: βαιὸν τοῦτο γέρας. A standard formula. Cf. Peek 1936. 4 (from second-century Catania), where a husband mourns his wife, καὶ βαιὴν | στήλῃ τήνδ' ἀπέδωκε χάριν. *TAM* ii. 1173, where a man is honoured with a statue by a city (Olympus in Lycia), βαιὰ χαριζομένη.[2] Sophronius, patriarch of Jerusalem when it fell to the Arabs in 638, dedicated a book to the martyrs Cyrus and John who had cured him of an eye-ailment, βαιὸν ἀμειβόμενος (*AP* i. 90. 4). The epigram to a statue which the council of late fourth-century Sardis erected to Acholius, vicar of Asia, ἀγαθῶν χάριν εἰκόνα βαιήν.[3] Cf. *A. Pl.* 367. 2, from the monument to Constantine: while he lived, the city

εἰκόνα χαλκείην βαιὸν ἔκρινε γέρας.

Strictly speaking, the formula is being misused here. It is properly applied to statues which do exist, but are alleged to be but a paltry reward for the honorand's merits. Not (as here) to explain why he was not given a statue at all. The misuse perhaps suggests that the Constantinian epigram is adapted from 353. 4, and so the later of the two—an inference borne out by other considerations too (p. 215).

4: τοσσατίων. Cf. τοσσατίης at 344. 6. The sort of epic form (first in hellenistic epic, then common in Nonnus: iii. 302; iv. 55, 396; ix. 240 etc.) that was much cultivated in late epigrams: Agathias, *AP* vi. 80. 4; ix. 642. 8, 643. 5: anon., *AP* i. 10. 49 (A.D. 527);[4] and constantly in the work of Dioscorus of Aphro-

not found before Nonnus, who uses it thirteen times (Peek's Lexicon, col. 333). The ναὶ τάχα suggests a *Cycle*-poem which has lost its ascription.

[1] On Nonnian influence on Agathias see Mattsson's full and useful discussion, *Untersuchungen* (above, p. 88 n. 1), 112–71: and G. Viansino's commentaries on Paul (Turin 1963) and Agathias (Milan 1967), with a useful collection of passages, but put together with no method or discrimination.
[2] Cf. L. Robert, *Hellenica* iv (1948), 36 n. 1: *PLRE*, Aquilinus 4.
[3] Early editors gave εἰκόνα χαλκῆν, but W. H. Buckler and D. M. Robinson, *AJA* 1913, 47 f., published the true reading after a re-examination of the stone. Best edition now, with full bibliography, in L. Robert, *Hellenica* iv (1948), 35 f. For the date of Acholius' vicariate see too B. Malcus, *Opusc. Athen.* vii (1967), 137. One might compare the similar use of βαιός in the sepulchral motif from (e.g.) Peek 1924 (Rome, A.D. 94), 53, βαιὸν μὲν τόδε σῆμα, τὸ δὲ κλέος οὐρανὸν ἵκει.
[4] Cf. C. Mango and I. Ševčenko, *DOP* xv (1961), 245.

BACK FACE 93

dito, a pastiche of the clichés of the genre, and so an excellent repertory of its characteristic words and formulas: E. Heitsch, *Die griech. Dichterfragmente der röm. Kaiserzeit* (Abh. Gött. Akad.) 1964², No. XLII. 5. 12; 6. 14; 13. 16; 23. 16.
6: ἀολλίσσας. ἀολλίζω is normally used of assembling people. LSJ do not record it of things before the Agathian epigrammatists. There is one bizarre example in Nonnus,[1] but in normal contexts cf. Macedonius, *AP* ix. 649. 4, and Phocas, ix. 772. 2. Once more, their true predecessor is a Porphyrius epigram.

FRONT FACE

The main inscriptions above both reliefs on this face have been entirely erased by fire (p. 14). But for reasons to be discussed in Ch. IV it seems likely that the missing epigrams are *A. Pl.* 354 and 355, happily copied before the fire:

αἰδομένη χαλκῷ σε πόλις, τριπόθητε, γεραίρει,
ἤθελε γὰρ χρυσῷ, ἀλλ' ἴδεν ἐς Νέμεσιν.
εἰ δὲ τεὴν μέλπων οὐ παύεται ἡθάδα νίκην
εὐγνώμων δῆμος, Πορφύριε, Πρασίνων,
ἔμπνοά σοι ξύμπαντες ἀγάλματα· πᾶς δὲ περισσὸς
καὶ χρυσὸς τούτοις εἰς ἔριν ἐρχόμενος. (354)

οὔπω σοι μογέοντι Τύχη πόρεν ἄξια νίκης·
νῖκαι γὰρ τῆς σῆς μείζονες εὐτυχίης·
ἀλλὰ μέρει πρώτῳ σταθερῷ καὶ ἀρείονι μίμνοις
τὴν φθονερὴν τήκων δυσμενέων κραδίην,
οἵ σέθεν εἰσορόωντες ἀεὶ νικῶσαν ἱμάσθλην
μέμφονται σφετέρην αἰὲν ἀτασθαλίην. (355)

A. Pl. *354*

The city honours Porphyrius in bronze, for gold would have incurred Nemesis. In any case, Porphyrius' fans are living statues; no gold can compete with them. The whole epigram is an apology for not giving Porphyrius a gold statue—a motif which we shall consider fully in a wider context in Ch. VI. Yet another theme that was to be taken up by the Agathian poets (pp. 218 f.).

[1] *Dion.* xl. 378, where the Moon is described as ταυρείην ἐπίκυρτον ἀολλίζουσα κεραίην, i.e. filling out her crescent shape. This extension of meaning in a word Nonnus uses sixteen times elsewhere in its Homeric sense is quite remarkable. Was he perhaps writing with a misremembered echo in his ear of *Iliad* vi. 270 (cf. 287), ἀολλίσσασα γεραιάς (old women)?

Commentators and translators take αἰδομένη in l. 1 in the sense 'reverencing', 'honouring'. This is certainly possible, yet Nonnus uses the word constantly meaning 'ashamed'—particularly often in the feminine, qualifying this goddess or that nymph bashfully hiding her face (see Peek's Lexicon, col. 40). It is used in this sense by Agathias (*A. Pl.* 59. 2) and twice if not all three times by Christodorus (*AP* ii. 200, 219; at 48 commentators again take it as 'reverencing', perhaps wrongly). The influence of Nonnus is strong on educated epigrammatists of the sixth century, and while we must certainly beware of imposing a 'Nonnian strait-jacket' (Giangrande's phrase, *JHS* lxxxix (1969), 142), we must not lightly disregard Nonnian usage in such cases. The Porphyrian poet surely had in mind the shame the city felt at only giving Porphyrius bronze.

A. Pl. *355*

The most polemical of all the epigrams. Porphyrius is urged to stay with this the best faction and consume the envious hearts of the Blues. As they watch his ever-victorious whip they curse their own folly—folly, that is, at letting the Greens get hold of him. The sense of the first couplet is that Fortune has not yet given Porphyrius his just rewards because his victories are greater than the good fortune that has so far come his way, i.e. εὐτυχίη stands for material rewards, not his success numbered in victories.

1: cf. Claudian, *AP* ix. 140. 3, μογέοντι ... πορεῖν.

3: for the meaning of μέρος, conventionally but inaccurately translated 'faction', see *Circus Factions*, Chs. II–III.

4: cf. the distich on φθόνος, *AP* xi. 193 = Kaibel 1115: τήκει γὰρ φθονερῶν ὄμματα καὶ κραδίην. For the φθόνος motif cf. 353. 1.

5: ἱμάσθλην. The whip is almost always featured in artistic representations of the charioteer, whether racing or in triumphal posture.

5–6: it is interesting to see our poet sufficiently interested in such effects to repeat ἀεί/αἰέν with quantities reversed (⌣ – / – ⌣), the artifice of deliberate variation of quantities familiar from Homer's Ἄρες/Ἄρες on, but especially affected by hellenistic poets: see Gow on Theocritus vi. 19, and for a good collection of examples from later poets, Schneider's note on Callimachus *Hymn* i. 55 (pp. 152–3).

FRONT FACE

There are in addition traces of several more inscriptions on this face, the odd letter surviving the fire that scorched the two main panels completely bare: (*a*) on the ridge above the middle relief (Pl. 8); (*b*) on the ridge between the middle and bottom reliefs (Pl. 8); inside the top corners of the bottom relief, (*c*) on the right and (*d*) on the left-hand side.

Of (*a*) all that can now be read is *AI*
NIKH.

Of (*b*) little but a reasonably clear mention of the Greens:
... *AI* .... C .... [T]ΩNΠPACINΩNK[AI ...

Other factional acclamations suggest the possibility of a νικᾷ ἡ τύχη before τῶν Πρασίνων and the name of an individual after the καί. There is barely room for *NΠP* between the first Ω and the *A*.

Of (*c*) virtually nothing can be read save the cross that begins it. The traces of the first letter suggest a *Π* and after space for two letters are traces consistent with a *Φ*. Obviously the chances are high that it is another acclamation naming Porphyrius.

A little more can be made of (*d*) (Pl. 8). Nothing seems to have been lost to the left since the line begins with a clear cross, after which, above and around the head of the *hortator*, the following puzzling traces:

+ CΦΥPI
XICAMMA
.. PIC

All three lines may originally have continued further to the right.

Professors Mango and Harrison draw to my attention the following traces in the top relief, on the right side:

.... Υ
.... C
.... I
.... C

III

THE MANUSCRIPT TRADITION

FOR six of the epigrams on Porphyrius we now have the original inscriptions as well as the manuscript tradition. For twenty-six more (and for twenty-two on other charioteers) we have only the manuscript tradition. This tradition is complex—more complex indeed than has so far been appreciated. Before we can count ourselves in a position to make an analysis of the series as a whole, we must attempt to discover as much as we can about the character, date, and (above all) the arrangement of the collection from which this manuscript tradition descends.

There are three witnesses to this collection, each of which contains a different number of epigrams in a different order. Yet the situation is not so desperate as it might seem. To anticipate my conclusions, it can (I believe) be shown that the fullest witness, the Planudean Anthology, though often inaccurate in points of detail and the latest in date, is nevertheless in essentials a faithful copy of this original collection. Both the other manuscripts contain only rearranged excerpts.

THE MANUSCRIPTS

The fullest and most important collection, containing all fifty-four epigrams of which we have any knowledge, is embodied in the celebrated Marcianus gr. 481 (ff. 43^v–45^v), dated to September 1299:[1] the Planudean Anthology. There are a number of

[1] There is some uncertainty about the interpretation of the date on f. 122^v of the Marcianus. See Beckby, i² (1967), 77 n. 4 and Gow–Page, *Hellenistic Epigrams* i (1965), xxxviii n. 2. The most recent opinion is that of R. Aubreton (*RÉA* lxx (1968), 33): 'il [sc. Planudes] termina son manuscrit en indiquant tout d'abord la date de septembre 1299, qu'il corrigea ensuite en 1301, sans doute après une révision de son œuvre.' What Planudes in fact wrote is 'in the month of September of the thirteenth indiction [i.e. 1299] of the year 6810 [i.e. 1301]'. In such a conflict one would normally accept the former figure, since the indiction system was the one in daily use and errors are not uncommon in *anno mundi* calculations (so P. Maas, *Griech. Paläographie* (Gercke–Norden, *Einleitung* i. 9 (1924)), p. 94). There is no hint of a correction (this is perhaps a misunderstanding of a different—and

THE MANUSCRIPTS

apographs, two of which are especially important, in that they were made within no more than a year or two of their original, one at least and possibly both under Planudes' own supervision: British Museum Additional 16409[1] and the now incomplete Parisinus graecus 2744.[2] These apographs are more than mere copies of their exemplar, and they help to illustrate a hitherto unsuspected stage in the composition of the Planudean Anthology. But for most practical purposes we do not need to go beyond the Marcianus, owing to the happy circumstance that it is both written and revised in Planudes' own hand.[3]

Then there is a selection of twenty-seven included in a much smaller anthology of epigrams in Laurentianus XXXII. 16 (at ff. 383ʳ–384ʳ), the famous collection of classical poets prepared by the school of Planudes between 1280 and 1283 and later purchased from J. Chrysoloras' widow by Filelfo.[4] Like the Marcianus, this collection too was written in Planudes' own hand, early evidence of his interest in a project he was to tackle again on a much larger scale twenty years later. The collection itself has been known for some time, but it is only in the last few years that Planudes' own hand has been recognized,[5] and not till Beckby's second edition (1967) that its readings were published.

Lastly, there are ten added in a later hand on some blank sheets glued to the last quaternion of Palatinus gr. 23 (pp. 707–9), following on Book xv of the *Palatine Anthology* (*AP*). As a result of an early error they are counted in printed editions as *AP* xv.

implausible—suggestion of C. Gallavotti, 'Planudea' (cited below, n. 4), p. 30 n. 10). Nigel Wilson tells me from his wide experience that MSS. are *not* normally redated in this way after revision, and in any case without any indication to the contrary the two dates must surely be taken as (in intention at least) referring to the same occasion. That is to say, the MS. is dated only once, to September (not as Beckby, loc. cit., alleges, to *1* September) 1299.

[1] Discovered by D. C. C. Young, 'On Planudes' edition of Theognis and a neglected apograph of the Anthologia Planudea', *Parola del passato* x (1955), 197 f.
[2] Rediscovered (it was used by Brunck) by R. Aubreton, *Scriptorium* xxiii (1969), 69 f. (cf. *REA* 1968, 40 f.). Folio 81–81ᵛ contains 335–51.
[3] Preisendanz once thought that some leaves were not by Planudes, but later agreed with Young that the entire MS. is indeed his autograph: see Beckby, i², p. 77 n. 5.
[4] Studied by C. Wendel in 'Planudea', *BZ* xl (1940), 418 f., and C. Gallavotti, 'Planudea', *Bollettino del Comitato per la preparazione dell'Edizione Nazionale dei Classici Greci e Latini* vii (1959), 37 f. (cited hereafter simply as 'Planudea'). Pl. 11.
[5] Gallavotti, 'Planudea', 37 n. 18, and (for Preisendanz's opinion) Beckby, i², p. 84. Nigel Wilson has confirmed for me that both the epigrammatic collections in this MS. are indeed in Planudes' hand.

41–50, though in fact they form part of a later collection added at various points on blank spaces and in margins of *AP*, generally known as Σ^π.[1] *AP* itself has in the past been assigned by competent palaeographers to the tenth, Σ^π to the twelfth or thirteenth century. But R. Aubreton has of late advanced grounds for placing *AP* a full century later, and sees Σ^π not as a late addition, but simply as the last stage in the successive revisions which *AP* undoubtedly underwent.[2] He would place Σ^π no later than c. 1080. Whether or not he will persuade palaeographers on at least the first score is as yet uncertain.[3] Gallavotti was prepared to put Σ^π as late as the fourteenth century.[4] My friend Nigel Wilson cannot believe *AP* later than the tenth century, and while he would accept the late eleventh or twelfth for Σ^π, we both agree that it can hardly be regarded as part of *AP* proper. But whether or not Aubreton's date for Σ^π be accepted, it seems likely in any case that it is the earliest of our three collections.

All these sources I have collated for myself: BM Add. 16409 from the original, Σ^π, Laur. XXXII. 16, Marc. gr. 481, and Paris gr. 2744 from photostats. Beckby used collations of the last two made for him by K. Preisendanz (the only published collations, even for the Marcianus), but my own collations show them to be neither full nor accurate. It may be worth adding for the benefit of those unfamiliar with the remarkable publishing history of the *Planudean Anthology* that any variant readings attributed to Planudes in any edition published before 1958 (Beckby's first edition) may safely be dismissed either as modern conjectures or at best as conjectures (or errors) of late manuscript apographs. This book embodies the first reliable text of the charioteer epigrams ever published.

We may now pass to the obvious questions. What is the relationship between and the relative merits of the three manuscript sources, that is to say Σ^π, Laur. XXXII. 16 (L), and the Planudean tradition proper (Pl.), namely Marc. 481 and its two early apographs? Do they have a common source, or do they descend independently from the monuments themselves? If they have a common source, is it the Anthology of Cephalas?

[1] On this collection see now Aubreton, *RÉA* 1968, 69–70.
[2] *RÉA* 1968, 62.
[3] Against Aubreton's date for the Palatinus see *GRBS* xi (1970), 339–50, and H. Hunger, *BZ* lxiii (1970), 370.
[4] 'Planudea', 45.

THE MANUSCRIPTS 99

How many removes are they from the original inscriptions? How far is the manuscript tradition borne out by the inscriptions?

The Relationship between Pl. and L.

Pl. and L share twenty-seven epigrams—and show a considerable number of variants. One might have expected that sometimes L would be right, sometimes Pl.; that Planudes made different slips when writing the two manuscripts at an interval of twenty years. In fact the readings of Pl. are to be preferred throughout (Appendix A). For reasons which will emerge in due course, this can hardly be because Planudes was simply more careless when he wrote L; he was using a different exemplar.

Σ^π and Pl.

There are only ten epigrams for which we have Σ^π as well as Pl., and it reveals certainly two and probably three or four errors in Pl. (Appendix B).

The Inscriptions and the Manuscript Tradition

There are just six epigrams for which we have the (partly preserved) evidence of the inscriptions. Yet they reveal no fewer than seven errors in Pl.; mostly trivial, to be sure, but one affecting the interpretation of a whole epigram—and the dating of the new monument (Appendix C). Obviously we must face the probability of further errors in Pl. where there is no such outside check: Appendix D collects a number of cases where emendation seems called for.

THE RELATIONSHIP BETWEEN THE MANUSCRIPTS

Of our three MS. collections, it looks as if Σ^π, the earliest but unfortunately the smallest, is the most accurate. Both Pl. and (to an even greater extent) L are full of errors. Of these a few are no doubt due to Planudes himself, but the majority were surely present already in his source or sources.

There is little sign that when copying the full collection into the Marcianus Planudes indulged that unhappy flair for conjecture that has made him notorious. If the inscriptions have revealed some errors, they have also confirmed one or two details in Pl. formerly suspected by critics. At 350. 5, presumably faced with an illegible exemplar, Planudes wrote ἐπὶ μένης, scrupulously resisting the inevitable conjecture ἐπιφθιμένης, hitherto ascribed to the *ed. princeps*, though in fact it goes right back to Par. gr. 2744 (the BM apograph left the same gap as its exemplar). No doubt Planudes was hoping to find another exemplar to check it by: it is suggestive that he still left the blank even after the discovery of the new exemplar from which he culled his extensive addenda. Could it be that this second exemplar did not contain the charioteer epigrams, or at most just a selection like L (L omits this poem)? We shall see below that Planudes may have been unjustly blamed for normalization of Doricisms.

Ultimately, the source of all three MSS. was the monuments in the hippodrome. Regrettably, however, it is clear that none of our anthologists did anything so energetic as strolling across to the hippodrome, if only to check their exemplars.[1] Nor does it seem likely even that all three derive from the same written source. Could Planudes have got his error at 46. 1 from the source of $Σ^π$ (pp. 260–1)?

C. Gallavotti, discussing the relationship of L to Pl. in very general terms, left it an open question whether L was based on either of the two sources Planudes later used for the Marcianus.[2] A comparison of their readings for the charioteer epigrams makes it very hard to see a common source behind L and Pl. L contains 150 other epigrams besides the 27 charioteer epigrams, all but a few of which appear in *AP* and Pl. as well. Here again L's readings are often wild and seldom of value. Yet it would be wrong to explain this by supposing that Planudes copied both these and the charioteer epigrams with uniform haste from a source he later used more carefully. As it happens, the pages that carry the bulk of the epigrams (ff. 3–6) are not very tidily written, but the charioteer epigrams are a very neat piece of work, equipped with large decorated initial capitals, a separate lemma for each poem, and a full heading (fuller than the one in the Marcianus) to the series beneath a carefully done ornamental frieze.[3] In any case, it is hardly plausible that Planudes

---

[1] Not that this would have been quite so easy as it sounds: see p. 182.
[2] 'Planudea', 48. [3] See Pl. 11.

THE RELATIONSHIP BETWEEN THE MANUSCRIPTS 101

should have made so many slips and alterations when copying L, *none* of which he repeated in Pl. In particular, we shall see that ζεύγλην at 336. 4 is an ingenious conjecture, certainly worthy of Planudes—but if so forgotten (or repudiated) twenty years later. The simplest explanation, that L and Pl. derive from different sources, can easily be proved.

While most of the epigrams in L duplicated in Pl. come in Pl. *a* (that is to say the Anthology proper, from the first of Planudes' sources), four come only in Pl. *b* (the addenda, which Planudes expressly states to have been taken ἐξ ἑτέρου βιβλίου): *AP* vii. 339, ix. 527, x. 78, xi. 401. Nor can these be isolated additions from a further source; e.g. x. 78 occurs in L as it does in *AP* between x. 76–7 and 79–80. 76–7 and 79–80 are all in Pl. *a*, but 78 he was only able to add from his second source in the addenda. So Pl. *a* drew on an *abbreviated* version of the sequence fully preserved in both L and *AP*.

The remaining possibility, that L drew on the source of Pl. *b*, is ruled out by the fact that we find in L poems absent from both Pl. *a* and Pl. *b*: e.g. *AP* v. 291, vii. 620, xv. 9, xv. 29, Cougny ii. 732, not to mention the run of riddle epigrams from *AP* xiv, and oracles known only from L.[1] So L cannot have drawn on the source of either Pl. *a* or Pl. *b*.

On the other hand, L does have very close affinities with *AP*. For all that it is just a selection, in essentials it follows the arrangement of *AP*; e.g. on ff. 5ᵛ–6ᵛ stand the following epigrams in the following order: *AP* x. 37, 38, 40,[2] 41, 42, 45, 46, 47, 51, 52, 54, 57, 58, 59, 60, 61, 62, 63, 64, 65, 66, 69, 72, 73, 76, 77, 78, 79, 80, 84, 85, 36. On f. 3ᵛ are x. 98 and 104, on f. 4ʳ x. 27, 28, 29, 30, 31, 32, 34, and 35. 3–4. Despite a certain amount of minor rearrangement, there can be little doubt that the source of L contained the series we know as *AP* x in much if not exactly the same form as we have it in *AP*. That (apart from the charioteer epigrams) L has only one of the Planudean poems (*A. Pl.* 27)[3] absent from *AP* is probably of no significance, since virtually all are ecphrastic and L has only three of the Palatine ecphrastica

---
[1] On these see *GRBS* xi (1970), 344 f.
[2] Gallavotti, 'Planudea', 46, mistakenly lists 39 instead of 40.
[3] This epigram (on Sardanapalus) was added later (by Planudes) in a different ink, and since it is known in various forms from a variety of sources (cf. T. Preger, *Inscr. Graec. Metric.* (1891), 232), it could be the fruit of Planudes' casual reading during the composition of L, not from his main source at all.

(ix. 642, 768–9). For poems it shares with both *AP* and Pl. its readings often agree, in both truth, falsehood, and even omissions with *AP* against Pl. (e.g. at *AP* v. 302. 14; ix. 165. 3, 394. 2, 499. 5–6, 642. 4; x. 45. 6–7; xi. 251. 2). The few cases where it preserves the truth with Pl. against *AP* (x. 84. 4; ix. 359. 9–10) are much less striking—and perhaps attributable to Planudean conjecture.

There are several other features linking L with *AP* rather than Pl. The material L shares with *AP* is not restricted to epigrams that both could have obtained from so obvious a common source as the Anthology of Cephalas. L has material from *AP* xiv and xv, books generally agreed to be post-Cephalan. For a long time it was believed that Planudes drew directly on *AP* for the Marcianus anthology, a view now rightly abandoned[1] (other objections apart, both Pl. *a* and Pl. *b* contain material absent from *AP*). We must now inquire whether he drew on *AP* for the Laurentianus anthology. The answer is plain. He did not.

For example, among the seventeen aenigmata on f. 382 of L, all of which appear in the same order in *AP* xiv, stand two additional riddles known only from L,[2] one at the beginning and the other in the middle. There is nothing to suggest that either was inserted from some subsidiary source. The implication is rather that both sequences derive from a common source, which neither L nor *AP* reproduced in its entirety.

Then there are the poems by Gregory Nazianzen which they share. These we may presume with some confidence to have been absent from Cephalas. Of the 260-odd funerary epigrams which constitute *AP* viii only a handful appear in L, but it is otherwise with the *mélange* of Gregory's so-called *dogmatica* and *moralia* at *AP*, pp. 40–8 (conventionally omitted from editions of the Anthology). *AP* contains the following *dogmatica* in the following order: 12, 14, 15, 13, 19, 20, 24, 23, 22, 26, 21, 25, 27. On ff. 362–4 of L we find (in this order): 12, *18*, 20, 24, 22, 26, 21, 25, *23*, 27, and then on f. 385^r: 14, 15, 13, and 19. *AP* has put together what are two separate extracts in L, in both cases with the same variations from the regular order in complete editions of Gregory's

---

[1] As now conclusively demonstrated by F. Lenzinger, *Zur griech. Anthologie* (Diss. Zürich 1965), part ii, and Gow–Page, *Garland of Philip* i (1968), li–liii. I unreservedly withdraw my own earlier adherence to the other view, though the similarities between *AP* and Pl. must not be minimized: see p. 105.

[2] Only, that is, in the epigram tradition: see *GRBS* xi (1970), 348.

poems (the only differences being that *AP* omitted 18 and put 23 after 25 instead of 24). More striking still, both *AP* and L omit the last line of 25. There can be little doubt that here again a common source lies behind L and *AP*, a source that L once again reproduced more fully than *AP*.

But more obvious and more relevant to our present purpose is the case of the charioteer epigrams. L has only 27 of the 54 in Pl. But *AP* has none of them. Or rather they are absent from *AP* proper. There are the 10 added in Σ^{π}, but whether or not Σ^{π} is earlier than L, naturally these 10 cannot be the source of L's 27.

It has indeed been argued that all 54 of the charioteer epigrams together with all the other ecphrastic epigrams in Planudes' Bk. iv which are absent from *AP* once stood together with the ecphrastic epigrams of *AP* ix (584–822)[1] in a lacuna in *AP*. That these two groups were originally united is very probable. It is clear that Planudes took the bulk of the material in his Bk. iv (which includes much of *AP* ix. 584–822 as well as 381 epigrams absent from *AP*) from one source. It is also clear that the second source he used for the addenda was a rather fuller version of the same source. Both these sources were arranged exactly like *AP* ix. 584 f. Since, moreover, the exclusively Planudean material regularly *precedes* the epigrams duplicated in *AP*, it would appear that the Planudean material preceded the Palatine material in Planudes' source(s).[2] Thus its absence from *AP* can be both neatly and plausibly explained by the hypothesis of a substantial loss in the transmission at some stage.

Preisendanz placed the lacuna between *AP* ix. 563 and 564, between two quaternions and where a new scribe begins. In theory several whole quaternions could easily have disappeared at this point without trace, yet, as Wifstrand pointed out,[3] the ecphrastic epigrams do not begin till ix. 584 (epigrams between 564 and 583 Planudes put in his first, not fourth book).[4] It is

---

[1] *AP* ix. 823–7 are wrongly included in *AP* proper, being in fact part of Σ^{π}.

[2] For bibliography and discussion of this complex question see Gow, *The Greek Anthology: Sources and Ascriptions* (1958), 45 f., esp. 52–4, and Aubreton, *RÉA* 1968, 59–60: add Lenzinger, op. cit. 29 and Beckby, iii², pp. 8 f.

[3] *Stud. z. griech. Anthologie* (1926), 81.

[4] The marginal note at the bottom of p. 452 after ix. 563 shows that the scribe expected what we know as ix. 564 to follow. The change of scribes at this point must be explained otherwise than by a lacuna in the exemplar.

between 583 and 584 that the lacuna must be situated. Not, of course, in *AP* itself,[1] where 584 begins on the same page as 583 and ends on the next, but in its source.

So *AP* never contained the charioteer epigrams. The ten of them in Σ^π provide confirmation. Whatever the exact date of the compilation, its compiler's aim was plainly to add material missed by the compilers of *AP*, which he must therefore have read from start to finish. Not all of his material is in fact new. Without the aid of an index of first lines it cannot have been easy to discover whether a given epigram was already included in the 3,700 often very similar epigrams of *AP*. The scribes of *AP* repeated more than 40 epigrams themselves in the course of their long task, and not a few of Planudes' addenda are duplications as well, despite his painstaking rearrangement of the material in his source precisely in order to facilitate the location of individual epigrams.[2] There are one or two such repetitions in Σ^π but it is surely impossible to believe that its compiler could have overlooked the whole series of charioteer epigrams—288 lines!—if it had already been part of *AP*, especially since he included as many as 10 in a collection of only 56 epigrams in all.

It is perhaps from this source of *AP* before its mutilation that L derives, having as it does such striking affinities with *AP* yet not being derivable from *AP* itself. L's source must in any case have been closely related to the source of *AP*.

By a lucky chance Planudes was apparently able to get hold of not one but two similar anthologies. For both his sources are no less closely related to *AP* than L (common errors, common lacunae, common post-Cephalan additions, see p. 106), yet (while lacking much Palatine material) both evidently contained a major part of the material missing from *AP*.

Σ^π too derives from a copy containing 43 poems absent from *AP*, all but four in Pl., most in Pl. *a* but three in Pl. *b*. So Σ^π's source cannot have been identical with either Pl. *a* or Pl. *b*. Nor, more surprisingly, was L's source (p. 101). It is certainly a puzzle that Planudes should not have turned again to the MS. he had copied L from when compiling the Marcianus anthology. Perhaps

---

[1] If I understand him aright this does appear to be Beckby's view (iii², p. 8).

[2] See his methodological statements on f. 2ʳ quoted by Gallavotti, 'Planudea', 31.

THE RELATIONSHIP BETWEEN THE MANUSCRIPTS 105

it contained no more than L¹—or perhaps it was just not available in 1299.

THE ORIGIN OF THE COLLECTION

It is clear that the major part of both *AP* and Pl., as of most of the lesser Byzantine anthologies, goes back to the Anthology of Cephalas. At the same time it is generally allowed that several of the minor books of *AP* are unlikely to be Cephalan: i, iii, xiii, xiv, xv, and even ii (the ecphrasis of Christodorus), present also in Pl. Aubreton has recently suggested that much even of what are usually considered the Cephalan books (v, vi, vii, ix, x, xi) may in fact be later accretion to a Cephalan kernel.[2] He finds internal support in the alternation between order and chaos in the arrangement of these books, and external support in the greater interval that his later date for *AP* would allow for such a process of accretion.

More proof is required to establish the latter point, and as for the former, it could just be that Cephalas did not make a very good job of his anthology. But whatever our final decision about the structure of the 'Cephalan' books, it is clear that there is much in *AP* that is non-Cephalan over and above the minor epigrammatic books. For example, in addition to Christodorus' ecphrasis there are others by Paul the Silentiary (before *AP* i) and John of Gaza (between *AP* xiv and xv). Then there is Nonnus' metrical paraphrase of St. John's Gospel, missing from *AP* as we have it but listed in the table of contents and evidently lost in a (genuine) lacuna before Paul's ecphrasis. It is present in Pl., written after the addenda and so perhaps known to Planudes only from Pl. *b*.

It looks, then, as if *AP* and Pl. derive, not independently from Cephalas with idiosyncratic additions and omissions of their own, but in their essential features from a common tradition of amplified editions of Cephalas, accompanied by a stiff lacing of early Byzantine ecphrastic poetry.

Christodorus' poem entered the tradition early. This is shown by the fact that in *AP* it lacks eight lines present in the Planudean version. Both must derive from a common source that is earlier

---

[1] Though the charioteer epigrams in L have the appearance of being a selection from a larger collection: see p. 145.

[2] *RÉA* 1968, 56 f.

than *AP*. It was surely too long ever to have been a part of Cephalas' actual anthology, but evidently it was early copied into codices containing Cephalas (thus probably paving the way for the even longer ecphrases of Paul the Silentiary and John of Gaza). The reason for its entry into the tradition in the first place is obvious to anyone who has read it in the Palatinus or Marcianus rather than in printed editions. It is treated there (as in the Loeb alone of modern texts) *not* as a continuous ecphrasis, but as a series of 65 ecphrastic epigrams (each equipped with a regular lemma) on the individual statues in the Bath of Zeuxippus. Since the hexameter κατὰ στίχον was commonly used for epigrams at this period, each unit really is indistinguishable from a regular epigram. This is clearly why Planudes incorporated it into the seven books of his anthology proper.

Other post-Cephalan material in *AP* that is also probably pre-Palatine has been mentioned already: the *aenigmata* in *AP* xiv and the *mélange* of Gregory's *dogmatica*, both recurring with material absent from *AP* in L. So Christodorus, Gregory's *dogmatica*, and the *aenigmata* at least were probably all in what we may call 'Cephalas auctus' before *AP*.

It has sometimes been suspected that Planudes himself inserted the charioteer epigrams into the Marcianus from some quite separate source.[1] This seems quite unfounded. The presence of a good selection in both L and Σ^π shows that they too were firm early members of the Cephalan tradition. Whether they actually go right back to Cephalas or not can hardly be proved one way or the other—nor does it very much matter. But on the assumption that the Cephalan books of *AP* do fairly reflect the contents and character of Cephalas' anthology, I can see no insuperable objection to supposing that the charioteer epigrams did form a part of it.

In printed editions of the Planudean Anthology they appear in Bk. v together with Christodorus, the sole occupants of that book. Had this been the original order, then it might have been argued that Planudes found them, not integrated with the Cephalan material in his anthology source proper, but in a separate book, as he probably did Christodorus (a separate book in *AP*).

As late as Jacobs and Dübner it was assumed that the arrange-

[1] Cf. Beckby, iv², p. 304, Gow, *Greek Anthology* (1958), 58 n. 2.

ment of the printed editions was the true Planudean order. Study of the Marcianus revealed that Planudes himself put them in his Bk. iv together with all his other ecphrastica. Or to be more precise, the inscriptional epigrams proper 335-78 are to be found in section 3 of Bk. iv, the nine later poems (see p. 190) in section 6. But the uniting of these two groups and the transferring of them both to Bk. v (till then considerably the shortest of Planudes' books) does not originate (as was assumed so recently as Gow's study of 1958) with the printed editions. According to Gallavotti it is to be found in some late MS. apographs.[1] Aubreton has recently announced that the uniting of the two groups (still left in Bk. iv) goes back to Parisinus graecus 2744.[2] I can add that it goes right back to BM Add. 16409.

BM Add. 16409 is an early, probably the earliest, apograph of the Marcianus, taken before Planudes made his own final revisions (it contains matter he later erased),[3] presumably in c. 1300. The addenda at ff. 82^r–100^v were left as addenda in this MS.; its scribe cannot have seen in time Planudes' instructions on f. 81^v to unite the addenda with the appropriate sections of the anthology.[4] In Parisinus graecus 2744 not only are the addenda duly dispersed where they belong in the body of the anthology: in what survives we can trace all the other modifications of arrangement (except for the transposition of the charioteer epigrams to Bk. v) that we know from the printed editions.

Young opined that the Parisinus was from the same hand as the BM MS.[5] Nigel Wilson doubts this, but agrees that it is of the same period.[6] It would appear that BM Add. 16409 did not

[1] 'Planudea', 35, citing Vat. Barb. gr. 123 and 'others' unspecified. Without referring to Gallavotti, Aubreton maintains in *Scriptorium* 1969, 79, that this was an innovation of the *editio princeps*. Many of these later apographs have never been properly examined: for a useful list see J. Hutton, *The Greek Anthology in Italy to the Year 1800* (1935), 30–1.

[2] *Scriptorium* 1969, 78.

[3] Young, *Parola del passato* 1955, 205; as Young points out, excisions of this sort must be Planudes' own.

[4] Though it has not hitherto been noticed that he did make the other modifications of order suggested by Planudes on f. 46^v.

[5] Op. cit. 198; cf. Aubreton, *Scriptorium* 1969, 70 n. 9. At p. 84 Aubreton left it an open question whether the Parisinus was copied from the BM apograph or the Marcianus itself: the latter is the case, as I shall show elsewhere.

[6] According to G. Rochefort (quoted by Aubreton, *Scriptorium* 1969, 71–2) it is the hand of a scribe 'qui a dû commencer sa carrière dans le troisième tiers du XIIIe s., entre 1260 et 1280'. But Rochefort also thinks that *AP* is a book of the late eleventh century.

satisfy Planudes; he got another pupil to do the job again—properly this time. Since the identification of Planudes' hand in the Marcianus, scholars have understandably ignored its apographs. Why go beyond a carefully revised and legible autograph? Yet after discovering his second source Planudes himself seems to have treated the Marcianus as a *Vorarbeit* to an anthology rather than a finished product. Even after compiling the addenda and having the BM apograph made, he further revised the Marcianus, making a number of minor corrections and also excising some lines that he apparently now regretted having included. When making the addenda he left half a page blank at the end of each book, presumably in case he should come across yet another anthology from which to augment his still further. In this hope at least he was frustrated, and the definitive edition of his anthology appeared (probably before his death in 1305) in the now sadly mutilated Parisinus 2744. It is this MS., not the Marcianus or its much closer BM apograph, that was evidently considered *the* Planudean Anthology, to be copied and recopied over the next two centuries and finally—in 1494—printed by Janus Lascaris.

All that directly concerns us here is the fact that before these final editorial rearrangements, the charioteer epigrams were firmly embedded in the middle of Planudes' ecphrastica, the vast majority of which seem to be of unimpeachably Cephalan origin. To judge from the Cephalan books of *AP*, Cephalas regularly included long and relatively undisturbed sequences of 50 or more epigrams from the *Garlands* of Meleager and Philip and the *Cycle* of Agathias—and nearly 50 consecutive epigrams on philosophers from Diogenes Laertius.[1] When added to the Palatine and other Planudean ecphrastica, the charioteer epigrams would raise the total to only 619, suggesting (with an allowance for further losses) a Cephalan book of less than 700, a perfectly acceptable figure compared with the Cephalan books of *AP*. So the charioteer epigrams would not be either too long or too homogeneous a block for Cephalas to have incorporated undisturbed. And undisturbed it remained (as the next chapter will illustrate at length) till as late in the tradition as the source of Planudes.

[1] See below, p. 148.

WHEN WERE THE EPIGRAMS FIRST TRANSCRIBED FROM THE MONUMENTS?

Certainly by the eleventh century (if that is the date of Σ^p), and by *c.* 900 if they were included by Cephalas. Cephalas' teacher Gregorius Magister made a collection of inscriptional epigrams from various localities in Greece, Thessaly, Macedonia, and Asia Minor,[1] the result of epigraphic forays on the grand scale, an achievement of Byzantine scholarship at this period that has scarcely yet received due attention. Whether the not inconsiderable epigraphic material from Constantinople itself in *AP* and Pl. Bk. iv stems from Gregorius or Cephalas himself is anybody's guess, but much of it was probably collected at this date.

The age of Gregorius Magister and Photius, of Cephalas and the various enterprises of Constantine Porphyrogenitus, would certainly seem the natural context for the transcription of the charioteer epigrams. There are pointers, however, to a considerably earlier date.

First, a passage in that bizarre sketch of the origins, history, and sights of Constantinople, the anonymous Παραστάσεις σύντομοι χρονικαί (§ 38, p. 41. 19 f. Preger), describes one of the sights, a statue of a four-horse chariot of the Sun at the Milion (a sort of double arch of triumph decorated with many splendid statues) where it is alleged that the Emperor Constantine the Great was acclaimed by the Greens after a victory. Here is the relevant passage:

Κωνσταντῖνος ὁ μέγας εὐφημίσθη μετὰ τὸ νικῆσαι Ἀζώτιον καὶ
Βύζαν καὶ Ἄντην, κράζοντος τοῦ Βενέτου μέρους,

"εἷλες παλίνορσον ἱμάσθλην,
ὡς δὲ δὶς ἡβήσας μαίνεαι ἐν σταδίῳ,"

τοῦ δὲ Πρασίνου μέρους λέγοντος "οὐ χρήζομέν σε, λῶβε· οἱ θεοὶ ἀνώτεροι αὐτοῦ εἷλον". (p. 42. 2–8)

The verse quotation is from the last couplet of one of the epigrams on Porphyrius (xv. 44. 5–6). Strange words with which to greet

---

[1] See R. Weisshäupl, *Die Grabgedichte der griech. Anthologie* (Abh. d. archäol.-epigr. Semin. d. Universität Wien vii) 1889, 29 f.; Stadtmueller's edition ii. 1 (1899), ix–x; Beckby i², p. 75, ii², p. 9.

Constantine the Great even if they had not been written 200 years after his death. The *Parastaseis* are so stuffed with such staggering absurdities and confusions (especially where Constantine is concerned) that it is seldom worth even attempting to explain them, much less sift out the few grains of historical fact behind them.[1] But it is possible to make a plausible guess at the source of part at least of this particularly dazzling fatuity.

The complete collection of charioteer epigrams contains, in addition to thirty-two epigrams on Porphyrius, fourteen on another sixth-century charioteer, one Constantine. Now the statue in the *Parastaseis* is of a four-horse chariot, and it is associated with a Constantine and a victory. A different Constantine, of course, and not a victory in the hippodrome. Nor is the epigram in question even about Constantine the charioteer in the first place. But for someone who was familiar with the epigrams, the preliminary confusion between the charioteers Porphyrius and Constantine is at least comprehensible. A direct confusion between the charioteer Porphyrius and the Emperor Constantine is not.

So our author quoted this couplet because he misremembered it as referring to a Constantine whom (of a piece with the fantastic ignorance that brightens his every page) he cheerfully took to be Constantine the Great!

The seventeenth-century commentator Lambecius, having identified the quotation and recognized its true subject, supposed that our author was in fact describing, not a military victory by the Emperor Constantine, but a hippodrome victory by Porphyrius. And since 'Constantine' (i.e. really Porphyrius) was acclaimed by the Blues, he took Azotius to be the Green driver. Byzas and Antes would then be the Red and White drivers. An ingenious suggestion. But alas, Byzas and Antes at least are wholly mythical, the founders of Byz-Antium! They are mentioned elsewhere in the work (pp. 41. 17, 48. 4), and at p. 54. 20 f. we are treated to a solemn account of the battle between Byzas and Constantine which allegedly preceded Constantine's refounding of the city—a devastating commentary on the historical perspective of an eighth-century Byzantine.

When his two colleagues in defeat melt away so swiftly and

[1] For a good brief characterization of the *Parastaseis* see Mango, *DOP* xvii (1963), 60–1.

decisively, Azotius' position as charioteer of the Greens in the early sixth century begins to look less secure. I know of no other text that mentions him, but one thirteenth-century MS. (Paris. gr. suppl. 657) of the version of the same incident in the tenth-century *Patria* of Pseudo-Codinus glosses Azotius ἀρχηγὸς Βύζαντος, thus relegating him also firmly to the land of myth.

Even the colours are wrong. It can be shown (see p. 169) that the epigram in question comes from a monument put up to Porphyrius by the Greens, not the Blues at all. The supposed counter-acclamation of the Greens, with its reference to 'the gods', is intriguing. No more appropriate to a victorious Emperor than the Porphyrius epigram, though conceivably a genuine circus acclamation.[1] But it would be a bold man who attempted to draw the line between fact and fancy here.[2]

We can go no further in the interpretation of this tantalizing passage. But one question does remain worth asking: where did the author get his quotation?

Naturally we cannot rule out personal study of the monuments themselves *in situ*—but hardly casual observation. For the *spina* (or Euripus as the Byzantines called it)[3] on which the bases stood rose fifteen feet above the ground.[4] Thus the epigrams would have been some twenty feet above ground level, quite invisible to any but those who took the trouble to climb up on to the *spina*. Towards the end of the tenth century Pseudo-Codinus refers to the ἡνιοχευτικαὶ στῆλαι in the hippodrome σὺν ταῖς βάσεσιν αὐτῶν ταῖς ἐνιστόροις (p. 191. 9 Preger), though ἐνιστόροις probably refers to the reliefs rather than the epigrams.[5] And no one looking at the Porphyrius bases where charioteers and racing scenes are represented on every face (not to mention the statues on top)

---

[1] Like many others quoted in the *Parastaseis*: see *Circus Factions*.

[2] None but the curious will choose to bother with J. Jarry's attempt (*BIFAO* lxii (1964), 138–41) to salvage the whole story as authentic historical fact: the Porphyrius epigram plagiarizes an epigram originally written for the Emperor Constantine, Byzas, Antes, and Azotius were all generals of Constantine's rival Licinius . . .

[3] Mango, *RÉB* vii (1949), 180 f.

[4] See below, p. 181. But the hippodrome was always accessible, even outside racing hours, since the gates were left permanently open: see R. Guilland, *Jahrb. Österr. Byz. Gesell.* iv (1955), 76 f. = *Étud. topogr.* i (1969), 532 f.

[5] Cf. the introductory lemma to *AP* iii, according to which the epigrams it contains were inscribed on tablets containing ἀναγλύφους ἱστορίας, i.e. the reliefs the epigrams describe, not the epigrams themselves.

could have thought that the addressee of the epigrams was an Emperor.

The simplest way to explain our author's confusion (even allowing an uncommon measure of sheer stupidity) is to suppose that he had read the epigram in question along with many others on a variety of subjects in a MS. anthology. Byzantines seldom bothered to append much in the way of lemmata and ascriptions to individual epigrams in anthologies: there are hardly any in the earliest we know of, the *Sylloge Euphemiana* of *c.* 900, and virtually none in any of the later anthologies apart from *AP* and Pl.[1] The anthology I am postulating no doubt contained (like *AP* and Pl.) epigrams on Emperors as well, and a lemma of the form εἰς Κωνσταντῖνον (all the information provided by Pl. and L) could easily have misled a man who worked like the author of the *Parastaseis*.

If the epigrams were not first copied from the monuments during the ninth-century renaissance,[2] then the chances are that the work was done, not in the dark seventh and eighth centuries, but already in the sixth, a period when the ecphrastic epigram was cultivated as never before in the literary circles of Constantinople. Agathias collected into his *Cycle* the work of almost thirty practitioners from the reigns of Justinian and Justin II, and we have in addition (largely from the Anthology, since so few original inscriptions from Constantinople survive) a number of anonymous but often elegant and ambitious epigrams from monuments of the same period.

We have no grounds for supposing that Agathias' was the only or even the first anthology of sixth-century epigrams. Technically speaking the workmanship of the charioteer epigrams is of a uniformly high order. Their highly wrought literary character has been remarked on already and will be further illustrated in later chapters. Add to this the sheer length and number of epigrams to each monument. We may probably assume that some at least were the work of known poets, not the stonemason's hack responsible for the crudely functional epigrams on such far more important monuments of earlier days, the obelisk of

---

[1] Gow, *Greek Anthology* (1958), 26 n. 5.
[2] The *Parastaseis* were probably written during the reign of Constantine V (741–75): so Mango, *The Brazen House* (1959), 10. G. Millet fancied that he could narrow the termini to between 743 and 746 (*BCH* lxx (1946), 393–402).

FIRST TRANSCRIPTION OF EPIGRAMS 113

Theodosius[1] and the column of Marcian.[2] The Porphyrius and Constantine epigrams, with their erudite allusions to Homer and the Alexandrians and Nonnus (and even Gregory Nazianzen)[3] were obviously intended to do more than merely identify Porphyrius and Constantine. And they were not intended to languish unread twenty feet up in the air.

We may take another example. Excavations in and since 1960 have confirmed the statement of the lemmata that all 76 lines of *AP* i. 10 were inscribed in and around the great church of St. Polyeuctus. To judge from the size of the letters on the fragments so far found, the whole poem would have covered some 250 metres![4] It cannot have been easy to read *in situ*: from any one point much would inevitably have been hidden, and few would have had the time or patience to track it all down. It is an elegant, ambitious piece of work, and (more important) a powerful and detailed eulogy of the noble stock and good works of the great lady who rebuilt the church: Anicia Juliana. It must surely have been circulated in MS. also, as a poem in its own right.

The authors of the epigrams from the charioteer monuments will have circulated copies of their handiwork too, just as Agathias and his friends did half a century later. And once the spate of charioteer monuments had ceased, around the middle of the century (pp. 223 f.), why should not someone have done for their epigrams what Agathias did for the work of his friends? Fifty-four epigrams (totalling 288 lines), quite long enough for a separate publication.

Two lines of reasoning support this hypothesis. First, the numerous indications that the Agathian poets knew the charioteer epigrams. Several themes, several turns of phrase that are characteristic of *Cycle* poems first appear in the charioteer epigrams.[5] In at least one case the debt of the Agathian poet is beyond question.

A. Pl. 337 opens with the following mythological comparison before moving on to the more prosaic matter of Porphyrius' victories in the *diversium*:

---

[1] *ILS* 821, Kaibel 1061: see my commentary in *Athenaeum* xliv (1966), 33–6.
[2] *ILS* 824: see E. Gren, *Eranos* xliv (1946), 226.
[3] 336. 1–2 echoes Gregory, *Carm.* ii. 1. 16. 21/2 and 60/1: cf. *Circus Factions*, Ch. IV.
[4] See the calculations of Mango and Ševčenko in *DOP* xv (1961), 246.
[5] See Ch. II above, at pp. 83 f.

Ἀγχίσην Κυθέρεια καὶ Ἐνδυμίωνα Σελήνη
φίλατο. καὶ Νίκη νῦν τάχα Πορφύριον...

Compare now *A. Pl.* 357, by Leontius Scholasticus:

Ἀγχίσην Κυθέρεια καὶ Ἐνδυμίωνα Σελήνη
φίλατο· μυθεῦνται τοῖα παλαιγενέες.
νῦν δὲ νέος τις μῦθος ἀείσεται, ὡς τάχα Νίκη
ὄμματα καὶ δίφρους φίλατο Πορφυρίου.

Now there are many formulas common to epigrams on charioteers, just as there are to epigrams on provincial governors[1] or pantomime dancers[2]—or to erotic[3] or funerary epigrams.[4] But clearly the similarity between Leontius' poem and 337. 1–2 goes far beyond use of a common motif. Both apply the same motif in the same words to the same charioteer. One must be directly imitating the other.

In 1964 my wife and I decided for the priority of Leontius, mainly because his poem seems so neat and self-contained while the first couplet of 337 sits awkwardly in such a workmanlike piece mainly devoted to the *diversium*.[5] But an imitation does not have to be inferior to the poem imitated. *Cycle* poets often adapted the work of their predecessors, refining it to the sophisticated (i.e. verbose) taste of their own day. And 337 can now be shown (see p. 135) to belong to Porphyrius' very first monument, erected not more than a year or so after A.D. 500 at latest. All Leontius' datable poems fall in the second half of the reign of Justinian, his earliest after 543, his latest after 555—and these are only *termini post quem*. The chances are high that he was not even born by 500—let alone the author of poems that other men imitated.

There is a further parallel between Leontius and a charioteer epigram. Because of his countless victories, says *AP* xv. 48. 3–4 from the monument to Uranius, the people

ἠγαθέου Πέλοπος θῆκεν ἐπωνυμίην.

---

[1] L. Robert, 'Épigrammes du Bas-Empire', *Hellenica* iv (1948), *passim*.
[2] O. Weinreich, *Epigramm und Pantomimus* (Sitz.-Ber. Heidelberg 1944–8), *passim*.
[3] See particularly G. Giangrande, 'Sympotic Literature and Epigram', *L'Épigramme grecque* (1969), 93–172.
[4] R. Lattimore, *Themes in Greek and Latin Epitaphs* (1942). I cite these works merely *exempli gratia*: there are of course many other studies on the formulas and *topoi* of the various genres. [5] *JHS* 1966, 16.

FIRST TRANSCRIPTION OF EPIGRAMS 115

Leontius' poem on the royal baths of Prusa[1] (*AP* ix. 630) opens as follows:

θερμὰ τάδ' ἀτρεκέως βασιλήϊα· τήνδε γὰρ αὐτοῖς
οἱ πρὶν ἀγασσάμενοι θῆκαν ἐπωνυμίην.

After this poem Agathias put one of his own on the Agamemnonian baths of Smyrna, ending ἀντὶ δὲ τιμῆς | τὴν Ἀγαμεμνονέην εὗρον ἐπωνυμίην (*AP* ix. 631. 5–6). Agathias plainly took the formula from Leontius, just as Leontius had taken it in turn from the Uranius epigram.[2] We should bear in mind here that Leontius is one of the two Agathian poets to use the formula μάρτυρές εἰσι πόνων from one of the epigrams on the new monument (p. 91). Other parallels between the *Cycle* and charioteer epigrams are collected in Ch. II above (pp. 83–94). For a likely echo of another epigram from Uranius' monument (376. 4) in Agathias himself (*A. Pl.* 41. 4) see below, p. 274. Uranius' is the last monument in the series.

But there is another factor too. Leontius' poem on Porphyrius does not appear in a context of *Cycle* poems, but together with the other poems on Porphyrius—and not at random. It is neatly placed between blocks of epigrams deriving from two different monuments. We can recognize this today only because the discovery of the new base has revealed that the six epigrams which precede Leontius' poem in *A. Pl.* all come from the same monument. How could a Byzantine anthologist be expected to see (what no modern scholar has) that all the charioteer epigrams are authentic inscriptions and that they are grouped in undisturbed blocks of varying length from their respective monuments (I am anticipating here the demonstration of the following chapter)? If he did not see this, then the chances are against him putting 357 where he did rather than one or two places earlier or later, thereby spoiling either the sequence 351–6 or 358–62. If we may rule out pure coincidence, then it looks as if the man who put 357 where he did was the man who transcribed the epigrams from the monuments.

If so, then two further possibilities offer. Either this man got Leontius' epigram from the *Cycle*, in which case his collection

---
[1] On which cf. L. Robert, *Hellenica* ii (1946), 96–102.
[2] For another possible echo of a charioteer epigram in Leontius see p. 153.

would be later than the *Cycle* (566/7).[1] Or he had access to Leontius' poems before they were collected together in the *Cycle*: perhaps an acquaintance—conceivably Leontius himself (his other poems bear abundant witness to his enthusiasm for the theatre and circus). In view of the signs that other *Cycle* poets knew the charioteer epigrams besides Leontius, the second alternative seems preferable. The collection may already have been in existence by (say) the 550s.

CONCLUSION

This chapter has sought to establish that our three extant MSS. derive, not independently from the monuments, but from a common source in the Anthology of Cephalas or an early amplification thereof, which in turn probably derived from a still earlier MS. source. Where we do not have the original inscriptions, we must expect all the hazards of a regular MS. tradition. Yet the corruptions, numerous though they are, are nevertheless of a relatively minor nature, and the next chapter will argue that the *arrangement* of the epigrams has survived the vicissitudes of time and scribes undisturbed.

[1] To judge from what we can glean about the arrangement of the *Cycle* (admirably analysed by A. Mattsson, *Untersuchungen zur Epigrammsammlung des Agathias* (Diss. Lund 1942), 1–15), the charioteer epigrams would definitely have constituted too long and (in the strict sense) monotonous a block for Agathias to have included it himself.

IV

THE LOST MONUMENTS

THE fact that the epigrams still preserved on the old monument occur so close together in the Planudean series (340 and 342) suggested already to Woodward 'the strong presumption that they were entered in that collection in the exact order in which they were copied in the Hippodrome'.[1] The natural inference is that the two missing epigrams were 341 and either 339 or 343 (in fact, as we shall see, 343). This presumption is turned into virtual certainty by the discovery of the new monument. Numbers 351, 352, 353, and 356 can still be read there, and, on the only face where two are still preserved, in the order 352–3. This time the inference seems inescapable: 354 and 355 stood originally on the now worn front face of the monument (see Fig. 1). Evidently the man who collected the epigrams from the monuments did indeed copy them down in the order he found them inscribed thereon. This is, after all, what one might have expected him to do. It was the obvious way to go about the job if he was not going to risk missing the odd epigram. So (naturally enough) he systematically copied each epigram on one face before progressing to the next, and then moving on to the next monument.

This discovery immediately prompts a further query. If our collector pursued this obvious and natural method for epigrams 339–42 and 351–6 from the two monuments which have survived, did he not pursue it also for the other monuments whose epigrams he has preserved? It is surely overwhelmingly probable that he did.

G. Kaibel, indeed, in his dissertation of 1871, argued that only a very few of the series were genuine inscriptional epigrams: the rest, he claimed, were epideictic imitations, 'a Porphyrii aetate longius remoti', betraying their character by a series of crass blunders.[2] For example, one of them (he alleges) made the

---
[1] *ABSA* xvii (1910/11), 90.
[2] G. Kaibel, *De monumentorum aliquot graecorum carminibus* (Bonn 1871), 29—an opinion perhaps reflected in Norman Baynes's remark (*The Byzantine Empire*
[*cont. on p. 119*]

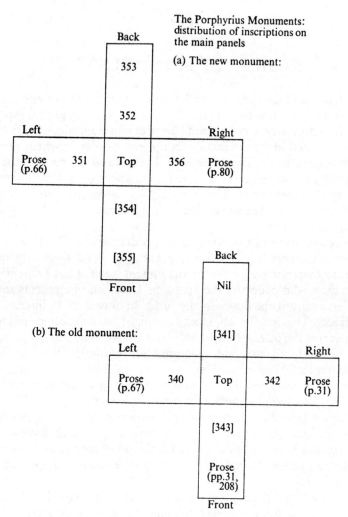

FIG. 1. The Porphyrius Monuments: Distribution of Inscriptions

THE LOST MONUMENTS

outrageous error of supposing that Porphyrius could have been granted a statue by both Greens and Blues, 'quo in tantis factionum simultatibus falsius cogitari nihil potest'. It so happens that the epigram in question (351) is now clearly visible on the top left-hand face of the new monument. We need not spend time on the 'slips' and 'absurdities' he detected in the other epigrams condemned as Byzantine imitations. The complex question of the relationships between the factions was still imperfectly understood in Kaibel's day—still is today in many crucial respects. It will be shown in the following chapters that everything the various epigrams say about Porphyrius' relationship to the Blues and Greens is not merely perfectly comprehensible but highly illuminating—and proves them all beyond doubt authentic.[1]

Of the fifty-four consecutive epigrams included in the series, two short blocks, not consecutive, neither at the beginning nor end, can be assumed to come direct from the original monuments. That the rest were likewise copied direct from their respective monuments is not just a reasonable working hypothesis. It can, I think, be proved by a careful analysis of the series as a whole. I propose, then, to work through the entire series, pointing out where each block begins and ends, so far as possible dating (both relatively and, where possible, absolutely) the monument from which each block was copied.

Vasiliev remarked that 'generally speaking, the epigrams dealing with Porphyrius follow his life almost chronologically'.[2] *Very* generally speaking, they do. The first group in Planudes' series is probably the first chronologically, the last is probably the last chronologically. But there are a number of exceptions in between.

Vasiliev approached the problem as a historian, with no knowledge of the MS. basis of modern printed editions of the Anthology. And it is doubly unfortunate that he was content to use the Loeb edition, which for all its merits is useless for critical

(1925), 33), 'to the charioteer ... the *littérateurs* addressed their choicest epigrams', since I cannot think of any other Byzantine epigrams in honour of charioteers (Christopher of Mitylene no. 6 Kurtz is satirical, not honorific).

[1] I have explained many other seemingly puzzling allusions and details in the charioteer epigrams in my *Circus Factions*: for 336. 4, 337. 4–6, and 47. 5–6 see Ch. IV.
[2] *DOP* iv (1948), 41.

purposes.[1] He simply considered the series 335–62 in the Planudean appendix, and then added the three (there are in fact four, see p. 127) from the brief series of ten at *AP* xv. 41–50. But these ten belong together with their fellows in the Planudean series, where they are all repeated. Indeed (as we have seen) they do not belong to *AP* proper at all, but to Σ^π.[2] Now Σ^π is a selection from the full series preserved by Planudes. It comprises: three epigrams on Constantine (41, 42, 43), one on Porphyrius (44), one on Julian (45), two more on Porphyrius (46, 47), two on Uranius (48, 49) and one given as anonymous in Σ^π, but in fact (as we shall see) on Porphyrius again (50).

In Planudes' series the four epigrams on Porphyrius occur at logical points in Planudes' series of Porphyrius poems, not broken up between other poems in the apparently aimless order of Σ^π.[3] The same applies to the three on Constantine and the two on Uranius, all together with the other poems on Constantine and Uranius in Planudes. And in Planudes the one poem on Julian occurs right at the end, not in the middle.

Since Jacobs's second edition it has been conventional to print the Palatine Anthology in full, and then add in an appendix (now generally, if erroneously, known as '*AP* xvi') the extra poems in Planudes' Anthology. Since the two Anthologies have some two thousand epigrams in common and the Palatine is bigger, this is perhaps inevitable and certainly a convenience. Obviously it would be wasteful to print Planudes entire any more, but the present arrangement does have its disadvantages. Since xv. 41–50 have been held in the past (wrongly, but it is too late to do anything about that now) to form part of *AP*, they have in all editions since Jacobs's second been extracted from their rightful places in the series as it stands in Planudes, and printed as *AP* xv. 41–50. As a result the full series has not been printed in its proper order since the edition of H. de Bosch, the relevant volume of which (iii) appeared in 1798. Brunck (1772–6 and 1785) and Jacobs in his first edition (1794) did print xv. 41–50 in position among the Planudea, but broke up Planudes' arrangement in another way, by placing the iambic epigrams on Por-

---

[1] By this I mean that it gives no indication which poems in *AP* are also transmitted in *A. Pl.*, nor does it reproduce accurate information about the ascriptions supplied in the two anthologies.
[2] On Σ^π see above, p. 98.   [3] On which see p. 144.

THE LOST MONUMENTS

phyrius, Faustinus, Constantine, and Julian (380-7) among the inscriptional epigrams on each of the four respectively.

The following table intercalates *AP* xv. 41-50 where they belong among the Planudea. In addition I have divided the entire series thus constituted into the blocks into which (I believe) it naturally falls, and numbered each with a letter of the alphabet to facilitate reference. The arabic numbers in brackets refer to the chronological order of the blocks (as it will be established in Ch. V): that is to say, A (1) is the first block in the series and also the earliest; B (3) is the second in the series but third in chronological order, and so on. The discussion that follows will touch only on certain links in form and subject-matter between the epigrams of each block. Chapters V–VI, though primarily concerned with wider issues, will supply abundant incidental confirmation of the block-divisions laid down in this chapter.

PORPHYRIUS

A (1) 335, 336, 337, 338, 339: from the Blues, when Porphyrius was very young.

B (3) 340, 341, 342, 343: from the Blues. No direct reference to Porphyrius' age. The old monument.

C (4) ⟨46⟩, 344, ⟨47⟩: from the Blues. Porphyrius is still very young, but has already changed colours several times.

D (6) 345, 346, ⟨44⟩: no colour mentioned, but Porphyrius is an old man, emerging from retirement at popular request.

E (5) 347, 348, 349, ⟨50⟩, 350: from the Greens, after the suppression of the revolt of Vitalian in 515. No reference to age.

F (2) 351, 352, 353, 354, 355, 356: from the Greens. Porphyrius is young, but the first person ever to have won a statue from both Blues and Greens (351. 5-6). Has recently changed colours (355. 3-4). The new monument.

G   357: by Leontius Scholasticus (from a literary source, the *Cycle* of Agathias).

H (7) 358, 359, 360, 361, 362: from the Blues again. Porphyrius is now over 60.

OTHER CHARIOTEERS

I 363-4: to Faustinus, now an old man.

J ⟨41, 42⟩, 365, ⟨43⟩, 366, 367, 368, 369, 370, 371, 372, 373, 374, 375: all on Constantine. Erected on the occasion of his death, at age 50, while still competing.

K ⟨49⟩, 376, 377, ⟨48⟩, 378: to Uranius, on his (second) retirement, having won two statues each from both Blues and Greens.

L ⟨45⟩: to Julian, on his retirement.

PORPHYRIUS (A-H)

For reasons which will emerge as the discussion proceeds, it will be best to begin with the last Porphyrius block (H) and work backwards to A. It will then be possible to dispose of I-L more briefly.

(H)

> Πρεσβυτέρους κοῦρος μὲν ἐών, πρέσβυς δέ τε κούρους
> νικᾷς, τεθρίππων κέντορας ἀθλοφόρων.
> ἐξ δ' ἐτέων ἀνύσας δεκάδας, στήλην ἐπὶ νίκαις
> εἷλες, Καλλιόπα, νεύματι κοιρανίης,
> ὄφρα μένοι καὶ ἔπειτα τεὸν κλέος. αἴθε τοι εἴη,
> ὡς κλέος ἀθάνατον, καὶ δέμας ἀθάνατον. (358)

1: cf. Peek 658. 6 (Kaibel 655) (Rome, ? III-IV s.), ὡς πρέσβυς κοῦρος ἐὼν κρατέες.
2: κέντωρ: in Homer and Callimachus, but cf. rather Agathias, *AP* vii. 578. 2.
4: cf. Kaibel 915. 6 (Athens, IV s.). νεύματι Θευδοσίου: Heitsch xlii. 3. 33 (Dioscorus, VI s.), νεύματα [πα]μβ[α]σιλῆος: and for νεῦμα of imperial approval in ceremonial contexts in general cf. O. Treitinger, *Oström. Kaiser- und Reichsidee* (1938), 54, and below, p. 227.

> Σῆς τόδε διφρελάτειρα τὸ χάλκεον ἄνθετο Νίκα
> δείκηλον μορφᾶς, Καλλιόπα, ζαθέας,
> πρέσβυς ὅτι σφριγόωντας ἐν ἱπποδάμῳ πλέον ἀλκᾷ
> νίκησας, γεραροὺς δ' ὧν νέος ἐν σοφίῃ.
> ἔνθεν ἐλευθερόπαις Βενέτων σέο πήξατο δῆμος
> δοιά, τὰ μὲν τέχνας ἆθλα, τὰ δὲ σθένεος. (359)

2: δείκηλον (or δείκελον) is one of the regular words for statue or painting in late Greek poetry: *AP* ix. 153. 3 and xvi. 332. 2 (Agathias), ix. 505a. 2 (anon., IV-VI s.), Nonn., *Dion.* 48. 697, Paul, *Ecphr.* 693 (276).

Σὸν γῆρας νεότητα τεὴν ὑπερέδραμε νίκαις,
καὶ πάντων κρατέεις πάντοτε, Καλλιόπα.
ἔνθεν Ἄναξ καὶ δῆμος ἐλεύθερος αὖθις ἐγείρει
τοῦτο γέρας, σοφίης μνῆμα καὶ ἠνορέης.   (360)

Οὗτος, ἐγερσιθέητρε, τεὸς τύπος ὅν τοι ἐγείρει
ἑσμὸς ἀριζήλων, Καλλιόπα, στεφάνων.
οὔτε γὰρ ἡνίοχός σε παρήπαφεν, οὔτε χαλινοῖς
δύστομος ἱππείη σοῖς ἀπίθησε γένυς.
μοῦνος δὴ νίκης γέρας ἄρνυσαι. ἦ παρὰ πᾶσι
δόξαν ἔχεις ἀέθλων ἆθλα λιπεῖν ἑτέροις.   (361)

1: for the text, p. 260.
2: for ἑσμός cf. 370. 4, with p. 215 below.
6: for the text, below, p. 263.

Καλλιόπα κλυτόμοχθε, τί σοι πλέον, ὅττι γεραίρει
εἰκόνι χαλκοτύπῳ σοὺς Βασιλεὺς καμάτους,
δῆμος ὁ μυριόφωνος, ὅλη πτόλις; εὖτε καὶ αὐτὴ
δυσμενέων παλάμη σοῖς ἐπένευσε πόνοις.   (362)

1: cf. 348. 3, τί γὰρ πλέον, ὅττι γεραίρει, and *A. Pl.* 267. 5 (Synesius Schol., VI s.), ὅττι γεραίρων.
3: the spelling πτόλις here and at 373. 1 (though not required by the metre) is confirmed by L: elsewhere always πόλις in both MSS.

The most obvious common feature shared by all five of these epigrams is that in only these five of all the Porphyrius epigrams is he called by the name Calliopas alone. From 349. 4 we learn that he was known by both names:

ᾔνεσε [sc. δῆμος] Καλλιόπαν καὶ πάλι Πορφύριον,
διπλόον οὔνομα τοῦτο . . .

Malalas calls him just Calliopas. But apart from the one epigram 349 (where, as we shall see, the author had a special reason for alluding to Porphyrius' double name), all the remaining epigrams call him just Porphyrius. Whether the use of Calliopas in these epigrams was just a whim of the poet employed, or whether Porphyrius himself renounced the name under which he had won his greatest triumphs at the end of his career (for reasons it would be idle even to guess at), nevertheless it does constitute an obvious and striking link between all five.

In addition, the first three all emphasize that Porphyrius is now old. Number 358 indeed states that he is sixty—a fine age for any man still to be braving the hazards of the hippodrome.

Only one of the five states which colour—the Blues—erected the monument they adorned (359. 5). But there is an obvious and close parallelism between the way the Blues are there described as ἐλευθερόπαις Βενέτων ... δῆμος and the description δῆμος ἐλεύθερος (without specification of colour) at 360. 3. And at 363. 3 they are δῆμος ὁ μυριόφωνος—again without specification of colour, which could evidently be taken for granted. In only one other in the whole series of charioteer epigrams (338. 7) is either colour designated by so fanciful a periphrasis.

There is one more interesting link between 359 and 360. 359. 6 says that the Blues have given Porphyrius two prizes, one for his skill and one for his strength: δοιά, τὰ μὲν τέχνας ἆθλα, τὰ δὲ σθένεος. What exactly this means is uncertain, but for the same motif of the statue representing these two aspects of Porphyrius compare 360. 4 σοφίης μνῆμα καὶ ἠνορέης.

With five epigrams on what was probably (like the two extant ones) a rectangular monument, obviously one face must have carried two epigrams—perhaps the front (as on the new monument). The three sides with only one epigram may, of course (like both extant monuments again), have carried prose inscriptions as well, naturally omitted by our collector.

(G)

Number 357 is not from a monument at all, but is a literary piece by Leontius Scholasticus. As remarked already, it is striking that this one literary poem by a known writer is placed between one obvious block and another. For the block immediately preceding 357 comprises the epigrams we know for certain to have formed a homogeneous block from one monument—those from the new monument. So the only literary poem in the series has been neatly intercalated between two inscriptional blocks. It is hard to believe this a coincidence. The person who put it there knew that he was dealing, not just with a number of loose epigrams about the same charioteer, but with blocks of epigrams. And he knew exactly where each block began and ended. Ruling out pure coincidence, there are two possible explanations: either the original collection transcribed from the monuments was equipped with lemmata indicating when the blocks began and ended (such detailed lemmata would be unparalleled in a Byzantine anthology—and conspicuous by their absence in our three extant MSS.); or the man who put Leontius' poem where he did was the man who made the original collection (pp. 115–16).

(F)

Numbers 351–6, the new monument. For the full text of all six see pp. 65, 80–3, 93. It is in some ways fortunate that this, rather than one of the other blocks, was the one to be rediscovered on its original monument. For although all six bear a certain general similarity in tone and phraseology to each other, there are no common features idiosyncratic to this group (i.e. not shared by all the Porphyrius epigrams) quite so striking as in the cases of Blocks E, H, or even C. All six epigrams have the same number of lines (six each) but since as it happens this is true of only one of the other blocks (C), nothing firm could have been based on it.

Number 351 claims that Porphyrius now has a statue from both Blues and Greens, and 356 (with the true text and punctuation restored) that it celebrated Porphyrius' second monument. Now that we know both come from the same monument, we have the key to the chronology of Porphyrius' early monuments (which it will be more convenient to discuss more fully together with the chronology of Porphyrius' career as a whole in the next chapter). Yet before that knowledge was given to us by the monument, constructions built on the linking of the two poems (separated as they are by four other poems) would not have been securely founded. The εἰκόνα χαλκείην δήμῳ ἐν ἀμφοτέρῳ of 351. 6 *need* not have referred to just one statue in each faction. Porphyrius might (say) have had two statues from the Blues before winning his first from the Greens and still made the same boast.

Grateful though we shall be for any further monuments that may come to light in the future, we must be especially grateful for this one, providing as it does the key to the structure of the whole series.

(E)

Nos. 347, 348, 349, 50, 350. Let us consider 350 first:

Οὐ μόνον ἐν σταδίοις σε κατέστεφε πότνια Νίκη,
ἀλλὰ καὶ ἐν πολέμοις δεῖξεν ἀεθλοφόρον,
εὖτ' ἄρ' ἄναξ πολέμιζεν ἔχων Πρασίνους ὑποεργοὺς
ἄγρια μαινομένῳ ἐχθρῷ ἀνακτορέῳ,

καὶ πέσεν αἰνοτύραννος ἐπιφθιμένης τότε 'Ρώμης,
ἦμαρ δ' Αὐσονίοις ἦλθεν ἐλευθερίης.
τοὔνεκα τοῖς μὲν ἔδωκεν ἄναξ γέρας, ὡς πάρος εἶχον,
σόν δὲ τύπον τέχνη ἔξεσε, Πορφύριε.

1: cf. Kaibel 933. 1 (Athens, III s. A.D.), ἄλλοτε μ[ὲν σταδίοις με κατέ]στεφεν Ἑλλὰς ἅ[πασα], and 934. 1 (Olympia, II–III s.), ἔστεφε Πῖσα (both of charioteers). Πότνια Νίκη is obviously likely to be a formula of the genre (epigrams in honour of victorious charioteers, athletes, etc.) rather than a reminiscence of the oracle quoted in Herodotus viii. 77 (as suggested by D. Tabachovitz, *Eranos* lvi (1958), 160–1).
7: recalling Solon, *Eleg.* fr. 5. 1 Diehl[3], δήμῳ μὲν γὰρ ἔδωκα τόσον γέρας, ὅσσον ἀπαρκεῖ, possibly known to the author, since Solon is often quoted in late commentators (see Diehl's testimonia).

Clearly Porphyrius has played a part in the suppression of some usurper (line 5—the invariable meaning of τύραννος at this period). Beckby, following Jacobs, suggests Hypatius, during the Nika revolt of 532. To this several substantial objections can be raised. First, it would be very late in the day for Porphyrius to be doing anything so active (see p. 160). Secondly, the Nika revolt arose in the first instance out of the discontent of the circus factions. The usurpation of Hypatius was a later development during the crisis.[1] Would then Justinian have claimed, in a monument commemorating his victory, that the Greens had been his *helpers*—especially since he was notoriously a partisan of the *Blues*? And the allusion to a 'day of liberty' does not really square with the circumstances of Hypatius' ill-fated (and unwilling) attempt.

Vasiliev suggested Vitalian, author of a massive rebellion against Anastasius in 513–15. He also drew into this connection Vitalian's claim to be defending orthodoxy against the monophysitism of Anastasius. The Greens (he alleged) favoured monophysitism, and so 'naturally supported Anastasius in his war against the Orthodox ... Vitalian' (p. 44). As it happens, the epigram does indeed refer to Vitalian's rebellion, but on the evidence available to him—and especially on his own chronology of Porphyrius (see pp. 150 f.)—Vasiliev's confidence was hardly justified. There is no evidence whatever that the Greens favoured monophysitism,[2] and no evidence that Anastasius favoured the Greens.[3]

[1] See *Circus Factions*, Ch. XI.   [2] *Circus Factions*, Ch. VII.
[3] See p. 241.

Fortunately, the necessary supplementary evidence is provided by another epigram, overlooked by Vasiliev and not explained by Beckby. It has been ignored because in modern editions it is printed as xv. 50, and the charioteer it celebrates is left anonymous:

"Ὤφελες ὅπλα φέρειν, οὐ φάρεα ταῦτα κομίζειν
ὡς ἐλατὴρ τελέθων καὶ πολέμων πρόμαχος.
εὖτε γὰρ ἦλθεν ἄνακτος ὀλεσσιτύραννος ἀκωκή,
καὶ σὺ συναιχμάζων ἥψαο ναυμαχίης·
καὶ διπλῆς, πολύμητι, σοφῶς ἐδράξαο νίκης,
τῆς μὲν πωλομάχου, τῆς δὲ τυραννοφόνου.

As printed in xv, neither poem nor lemma names Porphyrius, and it in fact follows after two epigrams on another charioteer, Uranius. There is however no suggestion in the MS. that Uranius is the subject of 50 too, though Beckby assumes that he is. The subject was a soldier as well as a charioteer (l. 2, cf. 4), and fought against a usurper (ll. 3, 5). Now improbable though it might seem that two different charioteers should have fought in a battle against a usurper, clearly the possibility cannot formally be ruled out. Thus the identification of the subject of 50 with Porphyrius might be held an attractive conjecture, but no more. In fact, we do not need to resort to conjecture. We have seen already that these poems from xv can be replaced where they belong in Planudes' series. And this one belongs, precisely, between 349 and 350. Both 349 and 350 explicitly name Porphyrius, and 350 is equipped with a lemma εἰς τὸν αὐτόν indicating that the subject of 50 was the same as the subject of 350; and 50 where it appears in Planudes' series has a similar lemma linking it to the subject of 349. Obviously, then, for Planudes (and for his source, ultimately the common source of Planudes and Σ^{π}) there was no question but that the subject of 50 was Porphyrius. And since 50 directly precedes 350, it seems inevitable to conclude that they refer to the same event—and so to the same usurper.

From 50 we gain one additional and vital scrap of information: the battle against the usurper was a *sea-battle* (cf. *ναυμαχίης*, l. 4). Now sea-battles were few and far between in the sixth-century Mediterranean world. Despite the assumptions of some scholars, the Byzantines did not yet possess anything that really deserved the name of navy at this period, and we hear little of naval engagements of any sort. Yet it so happens that Vitalian did launch a massive naval attack on Constantinople: unsuccessfully, for his fleet was largely destroyed at the mouth of the Golden Horn.[1] There is no other record of a usurper being defeated by sea at this period, nor is it at all likely that there was another. There can be no doubt, then, that it is to the revolt of Vitalian, suppressed in 515, that both our epigrams refer.

The location of the battle helps to explain an otherwise puzzling detail in 360. In normal circumstances what place would there be for the civilians who constituted the circus factions (here the Greens) in the imperial navy? But in the case of an attack on the city itself, naturally things would be very different. It can be added that these two epigrams provide the earliest (and hitherto overlooked) evidence for the military activity of the factions, not otherwise attested before 559.[2]

Clearly, then, both stood on the same statue base, commemorating Porphyrius' victory at the victory games. What of the other epigrams in the block I am postulating? Do they allude to Porphyrius' double victory? Let us turn first to 347:

Σὴν τροχαλὴν μάστιγα καὶ ἀσπίδα δῆμος ἀγασθεὶς
ἤθελέ σε στῆσαι διπλόον, ὥσπερ ἔδει,
ἡνίοχον κρατερὸν καὶ ἀριστέα· διχθὰ δὲ χαλκὸς
οὐχ ἐχύθη ψυχὴν σεῖο τυπωσάμενος.

1: cf. v. 202. 1, πορφυρέην μάστιγα καὶ ἡνία σιγαλόεντα (Asclepiades or Posidippus).
3: διχθὰ δέ, cf. Il. xvi. 435; Nonnus, xxxviii. 368.
4: for τυπωσάμενος in this sedes see p. 268.

Once more the theme of the double victory: Porphyrius is both charioteer and warrior. This is why the people admire his shield (not part of the charioteer's usual equipment) as well as his whip. They would have liked to catch both aspects in the one statue, but, alas, the bronze would not flow in the two directions at once. Now 348:

Πορφύριον σταδίοισι τίνος χάριν ἡνιοχῆα
δῆμος ὁ πρῶτα φέρων ἄνθετο τῶν Πρασίνων;
αὐτὸς ἄναξ κήρυξε. τί γὰρ πλέον, ὅττι γεραίρει
εἵνεκεν εὐνοίης, εἵνεκεν ἱπποσύνης;

[1] Stein, Bas-Empire ii (1949), 184.
[2] Fully discussed in Circus Factions, Ch. VI.

4: cf. (from II s. Rome) Peek 1522a. 2, εἴνεκ' ἐνηνείας, εἰναικά τ' ἀγ(λ)αΐης, and (from I–II s. Saqqarah in Egypt) SEG viii. 530. 10, εἴνεκ' εὐφροσύνης, εἴνεκεν ἀγλαΐης.

The epigram is cast (like 344) in the form of someone asking why Porphyrius has been honoured. But whereas in 344 the answer to the question τίς ... τίμησεν; had been just ἄναξ χάριν ἱπποσυνάων, in 348 the answer is εἴνεκεν εὐνοίης as well as εἴνεκεν ἱπποσύνης. Now εὔνοια is not a virtue one would expect to be singled out for comment in a charioteer epigram. One might look for it rather in a simple epitaph such as the following, dedicated to a faithful servant by his master in second- or third-century Naples:

Σῆμα Φιλείνῳ τοῦτο φίλῳ δεῖμεν θεράποντι
Ἱπποκράτης πάσης εἵνεκεν εὐνοΐης (Peek 213).

εὔνοια in Porphyrius' case is surely an allusion to his loyalty in supporting Anastasius against the usurper. A less obvious allusion than in the other epigrams to be sure, but no less plain to contemporaries, who (naturally) did not have to have the point spelt out in full *every* time. They had only to walk round the base and read 347, 350, and 50 for further details.

It is, then, a fair conjecture that 347, 348, 350, and 50 all featured on this Vitalian monument. 349 will have to be added to their number, if only because of its position between 348 and 350. But there is in fact another reason too.

Πορφυρίῳ μετ' ἄεθλα γέρας πόρεν ἄξιον ἔργων
κοίρανος ὁ Πρασίνοις τοῦτο χαριζόμενος·
πολλάκι γὰρ δῆμος προφερέστερα ἔργα κομίζων
ἤνεσε Καλλιόπαν καὶ πάλι Πορφύριον·
διπλόον οὔνομα τοῦτο, τόπερ λάχε χάλκεος ἥρως
οὗτος ὁ τεθρίπποις κῦδος ἑλὼν ἀρετῆς.

3: for the text see below, p. 273.

After the reference at xv. 50. 5 to Porphyrius' double victory, and at 347. 1–3 to his double role as warrior and charioteer, it would have been natural enough for a poet hard pressed after four epigrams on the same theme for fresh variations to turn to Porphyrius' other double feature: his two *names*. Certainly, no other Porphyrius epigram makes a play on his double name in this way. In addition, like both 348 and 350, it mentions the Greens as the dedicating faction. And lastly, a small point, it would be a six-line poem to match 50. To judge from the two extant monuments a certain symmetry seems to have been aimed at in the arrangement of the epigrams round the base. For example, the epigrams from the old monument have, respectively, 4, 6, 4, and 6 lines: those from the new monument, all 6. Numbers 347 and 348 would make a pair of four-line epigrams, 50 and 349 a pair of 6 lines each, leaving 350 with its 8 lines and more full and explicit account of Porphyrius' role in the rebellion in a position of special prominence on the front.

There is another interesting thematic link between 347 and 50. 347 laments that the bronze could not be made to represent Porphyrius as charioteer and warrior simultaneously. 50 also regrets that Porphyrius is not shown as a warrior (ὤφελες ὅπλα φέρειν, οὐ φάρεα ταῦτα κομίζειν). Evidently the statue on this base did in fact represent Porphyrius in the traditional garb of the charioteer.

E, then, is a block taken from a monument erected to Porphyrius by the Greens shortly after the suppression of Vitalian's revolt in 515.

(D)

These three epigrams (345, 346, 44) do not have any very obvious common features, but equally have no links with either of the very clearly defined blocks which precede and follow. Here are 345 and 346 (for 44 see pp. 167 f.)

Ἐγγύθι τῆς Νίκης καὶ Ἀλεξάνδρου βασιλῆος
ἔστης ἀμφοτέρων κύδεα δρεψάμενος. (345)

Πάντα Τύχης ὀφθαλμὸς ἐπέρχεται, ἀλλ' ἐπὶ μούνοις
Πορφυρίου καμάτοις ἕλκεται ὄμμα Τύχης. (346)

The link of 345–6 with 44 may be tenuous, but their link with each other is stronger: they are the only two-line Porphyrius epigrams, juxtaposed. There is no allusion to his age in 345–6, but from 44 we learn that Porphyrius had been living in retirement till he was recalled to the arena of Constantinople by popular demand (δήμου βοόωντος). It could be that 345–6 come from one monument and 44 from another, but since no other Porphyrius monument has fewer than three epigrams, I have preferred to assume that all three do come from the same monument.

(C)

Πορφύριος Λίβυς οὗτος· ἀεθλοφόρων δ' ἐπὶ δίφρων
μοῦνος παντοδάπους ἀμφέθετο στεφάνους.
νίκη γὰρ βασίλεια μεριζομένη κατὰ δῆμον
χρώμασι καὶ πέπλοις συμμετέβαλλε τύχας·
ἥρμοσε δ' αὐτὸν ἔχειν Βενέτοις πλέον, ἔνθεν ἀνέστη
χρύσεος ἀντ' ἀρετῆς, χάλκεος ἀντὶ πόνων. (46)

Τίς τελέθεις, φίλε κοῦρε, γενειάδος ἄκρα χαράσσων;—
"*Ὦ ξένε, Πορφύριος."—Τίς πατρίς;—" Ἡ Λιβύη."—
Τίς δέ σε νῦν τίμησεν;—"Ἄναξ χάριν ἱπποσυνάων."—
Τίς μάρτυς τελέθει;—"Δῆμος ὁ τῶν Βενέτων. —
ἔπρεπέ σοι Λύσιππον ἔχειν ἐπιμάρτυρα νίκης
τοσσατίης πλάστην ἴδμονα, Πορφύριε. (344)

Τοῦτον Πορφύριον Λιβύη τέκε, θρέψε δὲ Ῥώμη,
Νίκη δ' ἐστεφάνωσεν ἀμοιβαδὸν ἄλλοτ' ἀπ' ἄλλου
χρώματος ἄκρα φέροντα καρήατι σύμβολα νίκης.
πολλάκι γὰρ δήμους ἠλλάξατο, πολλάκι πώλους·
νῦν μὲν ἐὼν πρῶτος, τοτὲ δ' ἔσχατος, ἄλλοτε μέσσος
πάντας ὁμοῦ νίκησε καὶ ἀντιπάλους καὶ ἑταίρους. (47)

The statue is this time of gold and bronze[1] (46. 6—see below, p. 169). All three epigrams have six lines each, and are stylistically very similar, among the smoothest and most fluent of all the Porphyrius epigrams. Furthermore we have in each one (and in no other Porphyrius epigram) the clear statement that Porphyrius was born in Libya. For some reason this interest in his native land (on which see also below, p. 170) must have been particularly relevant or topical at the time this monument (not his first) was put up. It was put up by the Blues (46. 5, 344· 4), and a further link between 46 and 47 is that both describe in similar and emphatic terms how frequently Porphyrius has been

[1] Does this mean gilded bronze, or bronze with details (face, forearms, whip) picked out in gold? Surely the latter. What catches the eye in a gilded bronze statue is the gold, not the bronze, and it is not surprising that all the inscriptions to gilded statues quoted below (pp. 217 f.) describe those statues as simply χρύσεος, *auratus*, etc., with no mention of the bronze which must usually have underlain the gold.

changing his colours of late. Indeed, it will be shown later (pp. 165 f.) that all three present a new yet consistent attitude to Porphyrius' relations with the Blues and Greens. Their tone is quite different from that of any of the epigrams in groups A, B, and F. For a conjecture about one of the reliefs on this monument (based on 47. 1–2) see above, p. 30.

(B)

The old monument. Only 340 and 342 are still (partly) visible:[1]

[Ἄλ]λοις παυσαμένοισιν, ἀ[εθλεύοντι δὲ μούνῳ]
[Π]ορφυρίῳ βασιλεὺς τοῦτο δ[έδωκε γέρας.]
πολλάκι νικήσας γὰρ ἑοὺς πό[ρεν ὠκέας ἵππους]
λάζετο δ' ἀντιπάλων καὶ πάλ[ιν ἐστέφετο.]
ἔνθεν ἔην Πρασίνοις ἔρις ἄσπε[τος, ἔνθεν ἀϋτή.]
ὡς Βενέτους, τέρψῃ, κοίρανε, κα[ὶ Πρασίνους.]   (340)

1: for the motif see p. 206.
6: for the text see pp. 267–8 below.

[Αὐτὸν] Πορφύριον μὲν ἀπηκρείβωσατο χ[αλκῷ]
[ὁ π]λάστας ἐνπνοῦν οἷα τυπωσάμενος.
[τί]ς δὲ χάριν, τίς ἄεθλα, τίς ἔνθεα δήνεα τέχνης
τεύξει, καὶ νίκην οὔποτ' ἀμειβομένην;   (342)

1–2: for the orthography see p. 268.
2: borrowed from AP xv. 51. 2 (p. 268).
3: cf. πολύτροπα δήνεα τέχνης, Oppian, Hal. i. 7, and AP i. 10. 69 (of A.D. 527).

One of the two epigrams which originally stood on the now broken-away panels at the top of the front and back faces will have been (as Woodward realized) 341:

Αἱ πάντων ψῆφοί με καὶ εἰσέτι διφρεύοντα
ἔστησαν Νίκης ἐγγύθι Πορφύριον·
δῆμος μὲν γὰρ ἐμὸς γέρας ᾔτεεν, οἱ δ' ἕτεροί με
δίζοντ' αὖθις ἔχειν νεῖκος ἀπειπάμενοι·

[1] It will be appreciated, of course, that the 'restorations' in both epigrams are derived from the manuscript tradition. As remarked below (p. 268), editors of the Anthology seem not to have noticed that 342 is preserved on the monument as well as 340.

μήτι δ' ἡνιόχων περιγίγνομαι, οἷσι καὶ ἵππους
κρείσσονας ἀντιπορῶν δεῖξα χερειοτέρους.

5: cf. Il. xxiii. 318.
6: cf. 43. 4.

Line 1 plainly links the poem to 340. 1, with its exactly similar reference to Porphyrius not having retired yet, and the reference in lines 3–4 to 'the others seeking me' is perfectly explained by the envious Green cry recorded at 340. 5–6. The allusion to the *diversium* (in which a successful charioteer would race his opponents again after exchanging teams) in lines 5–6 is paralleled by the similar allusions in both 340. 3–4 and 342. 4.

Woodward and Wace left it an open question whether the other missing epigram was 339 or 343, but our choice is in fact clear. For 343 refers to a bronze statue (line 1), and cannot therefore belong with the following block C, which celebrates a statue of bronze and gold (46. 6). On the other hand, 342. 2 does plainly indicate a bronze statue for B:

Εἰκόνι χαλκείῃ τὸν χάλκεον ἡνιοχῆα
ἄνθετο νικήτην κοίρανος Αὐσονίων
ὡς σοφόν, ὡς Βενέτοις πεφιλημένον· ἀλλ' ἐπὶ νίκαις
Πορφυρίου πολλὰς εἰκόνας ὀψόμεθα. (343)

2: for the text see p. 270.

Woodward and Wace argued that the large relief of Porphyrius on the back face is a copy of the statue, and that 343, with its allusion to the statue, would thus be very suitable for the panel above this relief. They further argue that 341, alluding as it does to the *diversium*, would be appropriate for the panel above the lower relief on the front face, which appears to represent the *diversium* (p. 43). They could be right on both counts (their arguments are accepted—or rather transcribed—by Vasiliev without qualification). Yet it should be noted that 340 too devotes a whole and rather more explicit couplet to the *diversium* (3–4), though the relief it stands above does not represent the *diversium*. And 342 contains a much more elaborate account of the statue than 343 (in any case it is an over-simplification to suggest that the back relief is a 'copy' of the statue; see p. 42). In fact, as can be seen from comparing the epigrams on the new monument with the reliefs they stand above, there is seldom any close correspondence between relief and epigram.

Before taking our leave of B, there is a point of interpretation in 342. 4. Paton translates the phrase νίκην οὖποτ' ἀμειβομένην 'victory that never varied', Beckby 'den Sieg, der ihn niemals verließ'. Woodward and Wace presumably interpreted it similarly, since they remark that it is not the sort of phrase 'used of a man at the beginning of his career'. In fact there is more to it than this. The author is alluding to a phrase from an earlier monument (in fact Porphyrius' first), 339. 3-4:

> ἀμφοτέραις γὰρ ἀμειβομένοις ἐπὶ πώλοις
> κυδιάει νίκαις, οἷς πόρεν, οἷς ἔλαβεν.

ἀμειβομένοις ἐπὶ πώλοις is here an allusion to the changing of horses involved in the *diversium* (evidently a speciality of Porphyrius). Now there are two unmistakable allusions to the *diversium* in the epigrams of the old monument as well as a representation of it on one of the reliefs. So anyone walking round the monument reading its epigrams would be well prepared for this more oblique allusion in 342. Porphyrius might win ἀμειβομένοις πώλοις, but the νίκη he won was οὖποτ' ἀμειβομένη.

(A)

By a process of elimination, we are now left with 335, 336, 337, 338, and 339. But this is by no means the only reason for taking them together as a block:

> Πορφύριον Κάλχαντος ἄναξ καὶ δῆμος ἐγείρει
> πολλοῖς εὐκαμάτοις βριθόμενον στεφάνοις,
> πᾶσι μεθ' ἡνιόχοισι νεώτατον, ὅσσον ἄριστον.
> ἀλλὰ τόσον νίκης κάρτος ἐνεγκάμενον
> ἔπρεπέ μιν χρυσέῳ ἐν ἀγάλματι, μὴ δ' ἐνὶ χαλκῷ
> τοῦτον τοῖς ἄλλοις εἴκελον ἑσταμέναι.   (335)

3-5: for the text and punctuation see p. 272.

> Τέτραχα μὲν, τὸ πάροιθε διακριδόν, ἴαχε δῆμος
> τὸν Καλχαντιάδην Πορφύριον ποθέων·
> αὐτὰρ ὁ δεξιτεροῖσιν ἀνακτορέοιο θοώκου
> ἡνία καὶ ζώνην ἱππότιν ἀνθέμενος,

κεῖθεν ἐπισπέρχων ἐλάᾳ· μεσσηγὺ δ' ἀέθλων
χάλκεος ἱδρύνθη πρῶτον ἴουλον ἔχων.
εἰ δ' ἐτέων γέρας ἦλθε θοώτερον, ἀλλ' ἐπὶ νίκαις
ὄψιμον, ἀλλὰ μόλις πολλὰ μετὰ στέφεα. (336)

1: for the punctuation and interpretation see *Circus Factions*, Chapter IV.
7: cf. in this ἦλθε Θοώτερον in this sedes at Nonnus, *Deon*. xlviii. 851.

Ἀγχίσην Κυθέρεια καὶ Ἐνδυμίωνα Σελήνη
φίλατο, καὶ Νίκη νῦν τάχα Πορφύριον,
ὃς καὶ ἑοὺς ἵππους καὶ ὁμόφρονος ἡνιοχῆος
ἐξ ἑτέρων ἑτέρους αἰὲν ἀμειβόμενος
πολλάκι κρᾶτα πύκασσε πανημερίοισιν ἀέθλοις
οὐ μογέων, ἑτάρου μοῦνον ἐφεσπομένου. (337)

5: the usual formula is στεφάνοις κρᾶτα πυκάζειν (-εσθαι), illustrated by A. Wilhelm, '*Αἰγυπτιακά*', *Sitzb. Wien* 1946, p. 68.
6: the ἕταρος is Porphyrius' colleague in the 'minor' colour, in this case White: see *Circus Factions*, Chapter IV.

Τοῦτό σοι ἠιθέῳ Νίκη γέρας, ὃ χρόνος ἄλλοις
ὀψὲ μόλις πολιοῖς ὤπασε, Πορφύριε·
καὶ γὰρ ἀριθμήσασα πολυστεφέας σέο μόχθους
εὕρετο γηραλέων κρέσσονας ἡνιόχων.
τί πλέον, ὅττι καὶ αὐτὸς ἐπευφήμησεν ἀύσας
σὸν κλέος ἀντιπάλων δῆμος ἀγασσάμενος;
ὀλβίη ἡ Βενέτων πανελεύθερός ἐστι γενέθλη,
ᾗ σε μέγας Βασιλεὺς δῶρον ἔνευσεν ἔχειν. (338)

3: cf. 353. 3 and p. 87.
4: cf. 371. 2.
5: ἀγασσάμενος, a common clausula to late honorific epigrams: *A. Pl.* 35. 2 (Caria, ? VI s.); Kaibel 909. 4 (Megara, IV s.), and 377. 6 below.

Ἄλκιμοι ἀλκήεντα, σοφοὶ σοφόν, υἱέα Νίκης
οἱ Νίκης παῖδες Πορφύριον Βένετοι
ἄνθεσαν· ἀμφοτέραις γὰρ ἀμειβομένοις ἐπὶ πώλοις
κυδιάει νίκαις, οἷς πόρεν, οἷς ἔλαβεν. (339)

335. 3, 336. 6–8, and 338. 1–4 all refer very specifically to Porphyrius' youth, and 337. 1–2 likewise implies that Porphyrius is a handsome youth, such as even a goddess might fall in love with. There is no such cluster of allusions to his youth in any other sequence of as many epigrams. Indeed, it seems very probable that they were the inscriptions to Porphyrius' very first

monument. ὀψὲ μόλις at 338. 2 and ὄψιμον ἀλλὰ μόλις at 336. 8 (even though the meaning is slightly different in each case) constitute a verbal link between two poems of the block. Then from 335. 5 and 336. 6 we learn that the statue was bronze, from 338. 7 and 339. 2 that it was put up by the Blues. Again, Porphyrius' father Calchas is named in two epigrams from this block (335. 1 and 336. 2) and in no other Porphyrius epigram. There is too a symmetry between the first four, comprising as they do 6, 8, 6, and 8 lines respectively, one on each face, perhaps, with the quatrain 339 making up a pair on the front.

OTHER CHARIOTEERS (I–L)

The same method can be employed—with the same results—on the rest of the Planudean series, the epigrams on Faustinus, Constantine, Uranius, and Julian.

(I)

There are only two epigrams on Faustinus (363–4, quoted together at p. 208 below), but both celebrate him as an old man whose racing days are nearly, if not altogether, done. Note also the parallelism between the third line of the two poems, underlining what were evidently felt to be Faustinus' two great qualities: δεύτερα δ' εὕρετο πάντα τέος πόνος (364. 3) and ἰλήκοι, Φαυστῖνε, τέος νόος (363. 3). It was the normal practice of the age to inscribe two epigrams on a statue base (see p. 224), and it seems almost inevitable to assume that both these epigrams once adorned the same base.

(J)

On Constantine, Faustinus' son, there are no fewer than fourteen epigrams, and incredible though it may seem, the inference seems inescapable that all fourteen originally stood on one and the same base.

For, as the first epigram in the series makes clear, no statue of Constantine was erected in his lifetime:

> Χάλκεος οὐκ ἔστης βιόων ἔτι, Κωνσταντῖνε·
> ἀντὶ γὰρ εὐκλείης ἤρκεσε βασκανίη.
> ὡς δὲ θάνες, τότε δή σε πόλις ξύμπασα γεραίρει,
> οἷς δύναται. τί δὲ σῆς ἄξιον ἱπποσύνης; (41)

OTHER CHARIOTEERS

Line 2 means (as Paton translates), 'for envy prevailed against fame'. The same point emerges no less clearly from the first couplet of 367 (quoted below). And since more than half the other epigrams either state or imply that Constantine has only very recently died (42, 365, 43, 368, 369, 373, 375), it seems inevitable to conclude that all came from the monument erected to commemorate his death: his one and only, posthumous, statue.

Furthermore, if they are read in order, it will be seen that there are, as in the case of the successive Porphyrius blocks, some obvious links between adjacent epigrams, suggesting that they may have been intended to be so juxtaposed on the monument. Rather than suppose up to four epigrams on each of four faces, it would seem more plausible to picture a hexagonal base, with two or three on each face. Anyone copying the inscriptions from such a base would naturally have done best to proceed in a methodical fashion, and it is hardly surprising that these links should still be visible.

First, compare numbers 2 and 3 in the series:

Ἐξότε Κωνσταντῖνος ἔδυ δόμον Ἄϊδος εἴσω,
ᾤχετο σὺν κείνῳ πᾶν κλέος ἡνιόχων. (42)

Ἐξότε Κωνσταντῖνος ἔδυ δόμον Ἄϊδος εἴσω,
πλῆτο κατηφείης ἱπποσύνης στάδιον·
τερπωλὴ δ' ἀπέλειπε θεήμονας, οὐδ' ἐν ἀγυιαῖς
κείνας τὰς φιλίας ἐστὶν ἰδεῖν ἔριδας. (365)

The reference to the strife of the hippodrome in 365. 4 is picked up in 366. 5, and 366 is linked in turn to 43 by a common use of the formula καὶ μετὰ πότμον:[1]

Χρύσεον ἀντ' ἀρετῆς γέρας ἔπρεπε Κωνσταντίνῳ,
οὐδένα τῆς τέχνης τοῖον ἐνεγκαμένης.
κουρίζων νίκησεν ἀειδομένους ἐλατῆρας,
γηραλέος δὲ νέους δεῖξεν ἀφαυροτέρους.
ὄντινα καὶ μετὰ πότμον ἀειμνήστῳ τινὶ θεσμῷ
δῆμος καὶ βασιλεὺς ἵδρυσαν ἀζόμενοι. (43)

1–2: see p. 215.
4: cf. 341. 6, δεῖξα χερειοτέρους.

[1] Illustrated below, p. 259.

Εικόνα, Κωνσταντίνε, τεήν ανέθεντο πολίται
μυρόμενοι, ψυχής τέρψιν αποιχομένης·
σοι κλέος όππότε δήμος επεσφρήγιζε θανόντι,
μνήσατο σών καμάτων και μετά πότμον άναξ,
ούνεκεν ιπποσύνης φιλοκέρτομος ώλετο τέχνη
εν σοι παυσάμενη πάσα και αρξαμένη. (366)

5: for the motif see pp. 87–90.
6: cf. 371. 4.

367 and 368 both underline the admiration felt, not just by his own faction, but by the people as a whole for Constantine's achievements:

Εισέτι μεν ζώοντι πόλις ποτέ Κωνσταντίνω
εικόνα χαλκείην βαιόν έκρινε γέρας·
ήδεε γάρ πας δήμος, όσους επί κύδεϊ νίκης
αιέν αεθλεύων αμφέθετο στεφάνους.
ώς δέ θάνεν, ποθέουσα φίλον τύπον άνθετο τούτον,
όφρα και εσσομένοις μνήστιν έχοι καμάτων. (367)

2: for βαιόν γέρας see p. 92.
4: cf. the epigram from the base of a statue to the Theban poet Creon, ὃς πλείστους θνητών αμφέθετο στεφάνους (Preger, Inscr. Graec. Metr. 140. 2). αιέν αεθλεύων means 'while still competing'; cf. pp. 206, 212.
5: for the text see p. 273.

Οι Βένετοι Πρασίνοισιν εναντίοι αιέν εόντες
εις έν ομοφροσύνης εξεβόησαν όρον,
ώστε σε, Κωνσταντίνε, λαβείν επιτύμβιον εύχος
πάσιν αειδόμενον, πάσιν αρεσκόμενον. (368)

Number 369 has no special link with the following or preceding poems, except for its emphasis on the extent of Constantine's fame (quoted above, pp. 61–2, with full discussion). But 370 and 371 share a very obvious link: both mention that Constantine's statue stood next to the statues of 'kinsmen', two according to 370. 2 ('it was fitting for three to stand in one place'; on the text see below, p. 274):

Εγγύθι της σφετέρης γενεής λάχεν εικόνα τήνδε·
έπρεπε γάρ τρισσοίς ειν ενί χώρον έχειν,
οί και ενί σταδίοις αρετής κλέος είκελον εύρον,
νηρίθμων στεφάνων εσμόν ελόντες ίσον. (370)

OTHER CHARIOTEERS

Τὸν Φαυστινιάδην πόλις ἄνθετο Κωνσταντῖνον,
γείτονα μὲν γενεῆς, κρέσσονα δ' ἡνιόχων.
δὴν γὰρ ἀεθλεύσας οὐκ ἤμβροτεν, ἀλλ' ἐπὶ νίκῃ
παύσατο, σὺν νίκῃ καὶ πάρος ἀρξάμενος,
ὃν καὶ κοῦρον ἐόντα παλαίτεροι ἡνιοχῆες
στεψάμενοι σταδίοις εἶσαν ἀγωνοθέτην.[1]   (371)

2: cf. 338. 4.
4: cf. 366. 6.

That Constantine's statue did indeed stand next to one other member of his family, his father, is confirmed by an epigram on Uranius (48. 1–2) describing how his statue stood next to Faustinus and 'Faustiniades' (obviously deriving the quaint patronymic from 371. 1). Perhaps 370 and 371 stood on the side of Constantine's base that faced the statues of his father and the other kinsman.

Number 371 is linked to 372 by a theme only otherwise found (in the Constantine epigrams)[2] at 43. 3–4: as a youth Constantine was a match for the veterans; now a veteran himself, he is a match for the youths:

Σοὶ τόδε, Κωνσταντῖνε, τεὴ τρόφος ὤπασε Νίκη
παιδόθεν ἑσπομένη πᾶσαν ἐφ' ἡλικίην.
πέντε γὰρ ἐν σταδίοις δεκάδας τελέσας ἐνιαυτῶν
οὐδ' ἴσον οὐδ' ὀλίγον εὗρεο λειπόμενον·
ἀλλ' ἔτι κουρίζων τε καὶ ἄχνοος ἄνδρας ἐνίκας,
ἥλικας ἡβήσας, γηραλέος δὲ νέους.   (372)

1: cf. 363. 4.

[1] Properly speaking, the agonothete was the man who provided (i.e. paid for) the games and in return enjoyed the honour of presiding at them. By the sixth century (in the capital at least) this expensive distinction was reserved for the emperors and consuls alone. However successful Constantine was, it is incredible that he should have financed circus games, and in any case it is out of the question that the 'senior charioteers' could have been empowered to 'elect' their financial sponsor. I suggest that, once the private agonothete in the old sense had disappeared, the financial implications of the word also disappeared, and it came to be applied just to the man who presided at the games. Normally at important meetings this will have been the Emperor, consul, or city prefect, but it is easy to believe that on occasions a charioteer might be accorded the honour. The unusual feature in Constantine's case, according to 371. 5, is that he was chosen while still a youth. The implication is that this honour was normally reserved for a veteran driver.

[2] It is found earlier, in 364, from the base of Faustinus, and (probably later, see p. 205) in 358. 1–2 and 359. 3–4 from the last base of Porphyrius.

140 THE LOST MONUMENTS

Number 374 simply describes Constantine's greatest feat (twenty-one victories by *diversium* in one day—quoted with discussion below, pp. 209). But3 73 and 375 alike describe the πόθος of the people of Constantinople for him, and, looking forward to future generations, lament that there will never be another like him:

Ἤθελε Κωνσταντῖνον ἀεὶ πτόλις ἡνιοχεύειν,
ἤθελεν, ἀλλὰ πόθῳ οὐκ ἐπένευσε Φύσις.
ἔνθεν ἑῶν τόδ' ἄγαλμα παραίφασιν εὗρεν ἐρώτων,
ὄφρα ἑ μὴ λήθη καὶ χρόνος ἀμφιβάλῃ.
ἀλλὰ μένοι ποθέουσιν ἔρως, ζῆλος δ' ἐλατῆρσι,
κόσμος δὲ σταδίοις, ἐσσομένοις δὲ φάτις.
καί τις ἰδὼν μετόπισθε χερείονας ἡνιοχῆας
ὀλβίσσει προτέρην, ἥ μιν ἴδεν, γενεήν. (373)

Ἔγρεο, Κωνσταντῖνε, τί χάλκεον ὕπνον ἰαύεις;
σεῖο δίφρους ποθέει δῆμος ἐνὶ σταδίοις,
σῆς τε διδασκαλίης ἐπιδευέες ἡνιοχῆες
εἴαται ὀρφανικοῖς παισὶν ὁμοιότατοι. (375)

1 : cf. Τίς πόθεν ἠὲ τίνων τὸν χάλκεον ὕπνον ἰαύεις, an epigram of Janus Lascaris quoted from Chardon de la Rochette, *Mélanges de critique et de philologie* i (1812), 243–4, by L. Robert, *Hellenica* iv (1948), 47, n. 8. χάλκεος ὕπνος is of course Homeric (for late examples see Viansino's commentary on Paul Sil., *AP* vii. 563. 1 (his no. 5)) but I have not been able to trace any other example of the exact formula common to 375. 1 and Lascaris. This, coupled with the fact that Lascaris published the *editio princeps* of the Anthology, makes it virtually certain that he was directly echoing 375 here. For other humanist quotations from and translations of the charioteer epigrams see J. Hutton, *The Greek Anthology in Italy to the Year 1800* (1935), 624, 648–9.

That there is some system in the arrangement of these epigrams will (I think) be granted. That the system is the work of the designer of Constantine's monument rather than the compiler of our collection will perhaps command less ready assent. Yet if our compiler had taken it into his head to arrange the charioteer epigrams artistically, why confine himself to the Constantine epigrams? The bulk of his material, the Porphyrius epigrams, were left undisturbed just as they came from their respective monuments. There are many circumstantial details in the Constantine epigrams, and there seems no reason to doubt that all, like the Porphyrius epigrams, are authentic inscriptional

OTHER CHARIOTEERS 141

poetry. If so, then there is no alternative to the hypothesis advanced above: all come from one and the same monument.

(K)

As for the Uranius epigrams (49, 376, 377, 48, 378), there can be no doubt that the first three at least come from the same monument, for all allude to the same unique occasion in Uranius' career. He had apparently been awarded a statue from the Greens when young, and then driven twenty years for the Blues, receiving two statues from them, one while he was still competing and the second on his retirement. Then he had come out of retirement to drive again for the Greens, who gave him another statue when he finally retired again. It is only by studying all three epigrams together that the whole story can be made out and all three properly understood. The fullest of the three is (significantly) the first of the whole group:

Σοὶ καὶ ἀεθλεύοντι μόνῳ λήξαντί τ' ἀέθλων
τοῦτο γέρας Νίκη δὶς πόρεν, Οὐράνιε,
δήμου ἀπ' ἀμφοτέροιο· σὺ γὰρ πάρος ἐν Βενέτοις μὲν·
εἴκοσι κυδίστων στέμμα φέρεις ἐτέων.
παύσαο δ' ἱπποσύνης· Πρασίνων δέ σε δίζετο δῆμος·
τοῖσδε σὺ μὲν νίκην, οἱ δ' ἄρα σοὶ τὸ γέρας. (49)

5: for δίζεσθαι of the factions seeking the services of charioteers cf. too 341. 4.

Taken by itself this poem might seem to imply (as it did to Jacobs and Beckby) no more than that Uranius had won just one statue from each faction: from the Blues while competing, and from the Greens on his retirement. It is true that παύσαο δ' ἱπποσύνης in l. 5 precedes the request of the Greens (Πρασίνων δέ σε δίζετο δῆμος), but this might have been put down to looseness of expression. Number 376, however, makes it quite clear that he had won a statue from each while still competing: and that he had now won a second from the Greens. There is no hint of the second statue from the Blues, which has to be inferred from the first couplet of 49, reconsidered in the light of 376:

Ἀμφοτέροις εἷς μοῦνος ἀριστεύσας παρὰ δήμοις
κῦδος ἀπ' ἀμφοτέρων ἔλλαχεν Οὐράνιος
εἰσέτι διφρεύων· τὸ δέ οἱ γέρας ἤλυθε πρῶτον
ἐκ Πρασίνων, οἷς δὴ γείτονα χῶρον ἔχει.

αὐτοὶ καὶ σταδίοιο πεπαυμένον ἤγαγον αὖθις
ἐς δίφρους νίκης μνωόμενοι προτέρης.

Number 377 merely refers to Uranius' emergence from retirement:

Παυσάμενον σταδίων βασιλεὺς ἐπ' ἀγακλέι νίκῃ
αὖθις ὑπὲρ δίφρων βῆσεν ἀεθλοφόρων
Οὐράνιον δήμοισι φέρων χάριν· οὐ ποθέει γὰρ
ἡ πόλις Οὐρανίου νόσφιν ἀεθλοσύνας.
τοὔνεκα διφρεύοντα τὸ δεύτερον ὑστατίης τε
νίκης καὶ προτέρης στῆσεν ἀγασσαμένη.

But the other epigrams can assist us to understand the last couplet aright. Beckby takes τὸ δεύτερον with στῆσεν, 'erected a second statue of', objecting that it is far-fetched to construe it with διφρεύοντα. Far-fetched or not, it is clearly the meaning required by the context. Uranius had officially retired once (49. 1, 5; 376. 5; 377. 1); so this was now the second stage of his competitive career (the technical meaning of διφρεύειν, below, p. 206).

Number 48 provides no further details about his various statues, but does, like the others, come from one put up by the Greens:

Ἶσον κυδαλίμοις Φαυστινιάδῃ τε καὶ αὐτῷ
Φαυστίνῳ βασιλεὺς στῆσε παρ' ἀμφοτέροις
Οὐράνιον, τῷ δῆμος ἀμετρήτους διὰ νίκας
ἠγαθέου Πέλοπος θῆκεν ἐπωνυμίην.
"ὡς αἰεὶ τὸν ὁμοῖον ἄγει θεὸς ὡς τὸν ὁμοῖον·"
τούσδε τις εἰσορόων φθέγξεται ἀτρεκέως.

5: *Od.* xvii. 218.

The first couplet states that Uranius' statue stands beside those of Faustinus and 'Faustiniades' (i.e. Faustinus' son, Constantine). Now we know that Faustinus drove for the Greens (382. 4, 383. 2, and p. 203 below), and from various passages we know also that statues of charioteers stood in the ground of the awarding faction. For Uranius compare especially 376. 4:

ἐκ Πρασίνων, οἷς δὴ γείτονα χῶρον ἔχει.

370. 1–2 is further confirmation that the statues of Faustinus and Constantine stood together; so there is no cause to doubt

that 48 commemorates one or other of his Green statues. Theoretically, it might be the first one they had awarded him in his youth, but there is nothing in favour of such an alternative, and in view of the numerous blocks of four, five, and more epigrams from Porphyrius' monuments (not to mention the fourteen from Constantine's), it seems most natural to assume that it does come from the same block as 49, 376, and 377.

By the same token, there is no adequate reason to refer the last Uranius epigram, 378, to any of his other, lost, monuments, despite the fact that it deals mainly with just his driving prowess:

Οὐράνιος Νίκαιαν ἔχει πέλας ὁπλοτέρην τε
'Ρώμην, τῆς μὲν ἐών, τῇ δ' ἔνι κῦδος ἑλών.
νικᾷ δ' ἀμφοτέρωθεν, ἐπεὶ περιδέξιος ἦεν
τῇ καὶ τῇ προθέειν ἠὲ παρεξελάαν.
τοὔνεκα καὶ χρυσῷ μιν ἀνεγράψαντο μετάλλῳ,
κυδίστῳ κτεάνων κύδιμον ἡνίοχον.

Actually there is a strong reason for referring it to his last monument. If the metals used for the other charioteer statues are anything to go by, gold would be astonishing for an early reward of a young man. Five out of Porphyrius' seven were bronze, Constantine's too was bronze, and there is nothing to suggest that either Julian or Faustinus was honoured in any more precious metal. It was not till his fourth statue that even the incomparable Porphyrius was raised up χρύσεος ἀντ' ἀρετῆς, χάλκεος ἀντὶ πόνων (46. 6). So the gold statue of Uranius mentioned in 378. 5 would be more understandable as the final compliment to a grand old man of the hippodrome.

(L)

There is little to be said here about the one epigram on Julian (45, quoted below, p. 207), except to emphasize that it does not occur among the runs of epigrams on Porphyrius, Constantine, and Uranius, as it does in the selection in *AP* xv (Σπ), but all on its own at the end of the Uranius block. And it can be added that even in the more confused sequence in L it stands on its own; not, however, at the end, but between the groups on Constantine and Uranius.

The result of our analysis (achieved, I hope, without undue

special pleading) is that the Planudean series breaks up (not counting Leontius) into eleven blocks. These eleven blocks once adorned eleven monuments in the hippodrome: one each of Constantine, Faustinus, Julian, and Uranius, and no fewer than seven of Porphyrius.

No direct confirmation is to be sought in the order of the epigrams in L and Σ^π. But no refutation either, and some indirect support. First, however, a more general point.

While L omits slightly more than half the epigrams in Pl., it contains no epigrams not in Pl. Coupled with the fact that Σ^π too has nothing not in Pl., this suggests that the tally in Pl. is complete, or virtually so. For if L and Σ^π had been drawing on a fuller collection than that in Pl., then it is unlikely that both would have chanced to single out only epigrams later to be selected by Pl.—especially since L took as many as twenty-six.[1]

Now for the order of the epigrams in the two MSS. The selection in Σ^π is of course too brief to permit any firm conclusions, but the order is not quite so random as it might seem at first sight.

41, 42, 43:	on Constantine, from block J
44:	on Porphyrius, from block D
45:	on Julian, from block L
46, 47:	on Porphyrius, from block C
48, 49:	on Uranius, from block K
50:	on Porphyrius, from block E

The three instalments of Porphyrius come from three different blocks: the only two Porphyrius epigrams to stand together come from the same block, just as do the three Constantine epigrams that stand together. The three on Constantine are the first, second, and fourth in the Planudean block on Constantine, and it is very easy to see why the fourth was picked rather than the third (xvi. 365). The first line of 365 is identical with the first line of the preceding poem 42. Someone who wanted only a sample three of the fourteen Constantine epigrams did not want two of them to be virtually the same. So he took the first three that suited his purpose.

These facts, while not proving, are certainly consistent with

[1] On the possibility that some epigrams did get lost at some stage in the tradition see below, p. 225.

OTHER CHARIOTEERS

the view that the compiler of Σ^π drew on a collection arranged in blocks like that in Pl.

Now for L. Here too, while the order of individual epigrams is slightly different, there are clear traces of the Planudean blocks, though the blocks themselves (as in Σ^π) are in a different order.

The following table divides the Laurentian material between the Planudean blocks. As a further aid to the reader I have added in brackets after the poems numbered xv. 41–50 a second number to indicate their place in the full Planudean series: i.e. xv. 44 is 346a, because it recurs after 346 in Pl.

335, 338, 337, 336, 339:	Porphyrius, block A
353, 355:	Porphyrius, block F
44 (= 346a):	Porphyrius, block D
348:	Porphyrius, block E
361, 358, 359, 360, 362:	Porphyrius, block H
347:	Porphyrius, block E
363:	Faustinus, block I
43 (= 365a), 366, 41 (= 364a), 371, 374, 373:	Constantine, block J
45 (= 378a):	Julian, block L
49 (= 375a), 48 (= 377a), 377, 376:	Uranius, block K

A comes first, complete if differently arranged inside itself. Then, oddly enough, F. Of the earlier Planudean blocks, B and C are omitted, but D and E are both represented, though later in the series. It is no doubt a coincidence, but it is interesting to recall that F *is* second in the chronological order of the blocks (p. 163). The one epigram from I (Faustinus) is carefully placed between long runs on Porphyrius and Constantine, and the one on Julian (L) between runs on Constantine and Uranius, instead of after Uranius as in Pl.

The only exception to this observance of the Planudean blocks is the breaking up of 348 and 347 from E. And even here it is illuminating that they are divided by a block, this time the whole of H, for once in virtually perfect Planudean order.

The arrangement of 361 perhaps gives us the key to Planudes' *modus operandi* (or that of his source) when compiling the series in L. Confronted with a sequence of fifty-four epigrams on charioteers, he decided to take about half, which he picked out as he went. When he glanced down the column containing F, the first to catch his eye was 361, which he copied at once. Then on closer inspection he decided that he liked the rest too, and copied them all, for once in the order of his exemplar.

I would suggest, then, that the order of L's exemplar was in fact the same as that in Pl. (and its source), and that the divergences of L itself are due to the method Planudes employed at that time. The alternative, that L's order for (say) block A of 335, 338, 337, 336, and 339 is the true one and the 335, 336, 337, 338, 339 of the Marcianus the result of some such procedure, seems unlikely in itself in view of the evident signs of a general carelessness in L. Then there is the evidence of the extant monuments: the two epigrams preserved on the old monument are on opposite faces—and so appropriately numbered 340 and 342. Had they been directly consecutive in Pl. this might have licensed the suspicion that Pl. occasionally made small alterations in the order of his exemplar. Then there is the new monument: on the left face stands 351 alone, then on the back 352–3, and on the now scorched front face must have stood the two missing epigrams 354–5. The only divergence from perfect Planudean order clockwise round the monument is that 356 (alone on the right-hand face) comes between 352–3 and [354–5]. This is more likely to be due to the original collector than to Planudes, for Planudes could have had no idea which epigrams came together on which face, and had he been rearranging, might as easily have intercalated 356 between 352–3 or 354–5 as replaced it at the end.

The division of 348 and 347 in L must then be regarded as a result of the process of hopping about we have on other grounds unmasked in its compiler, the only case where he hopped over the division between blocks.

In conclusion. It seems that certainly L and probably Σ^π drew on a collection arranged in the same order as the one in Pl. And since we have already seen reason to suppose that all three were copied from different exemplars (that is to say, they descend by different routes from the original collection), the evidence of L and Σ^π lends strong support to the presumption that the collection in Pl. is fully and accurately copied from the exemplar of Cephalas (or 'Cephalas auctus') where Planudes found it.

That Cephalas himself tampered with the order of the original collection seems unlikely. His anthology embodies substantial portions of its three most notable predecessors: the *Garlands* of Meleager and Philip of Thessalonica, and the *Cycle* of Agathias. Evidently he transferred large blocks from these collections direct into his own anthology, whence they were taken over in turn by later anthologists and are still clearly traceable in *AP*.[1] For example, analysis of the longer Meleagrian sequences in *AP* (especially v, vii, and xii) has alone sufficed to disprove the Palatine lemmatist's assertion that Meleager's *Garland* was arranged on an alphabetical principle. His system was partly one of thematic links between poems, partly alternation between the more famous poets.[2] Precisely the same double system is traceable in the Agathian sequences; Agathias' method can be seen particularly well from *AP* v. 216–302.[3] The arrangement of Meleagrian heterosexual and homosexual erotica in *AP* v and xii respectively is so similar that Wifstrand has persuasively argued that the two sequences were originally united in Meleager's *Garland* itself.[4] It was presumably Cephalas who divided them up according to sex—but without otherwise materially disturbing their original arrangement. That the longer extracts from Philip's *Garland* have not been rearranged admits of an even clearer proof. For Philip did use an alphabetical classification: that is to say by the initial letter of the first word of each poem. With such a method the slightest editorial rearrangement would stand out at once. Yet even in the longest Philippan sequences (e.g. *AP* ix. 215–312) there is not one example of a letter out of place (a beta among the alphas, or a nu among the mus). The only exception really does prove the rule: *AP* xi. 24–46 are in *reverse* alphabetical order, from omega to alpha.[5]

[1] There is a handy recent analysis of the sources of *AP* and the character and extent of Cephalas' collection in F. Lenzinger, *Zur griech. Anthologie* (Diss. Bern 1965), part 1.
[2] C. Radinger, *Meleagros von Gadara* (1895), 88 f., R. Weisshäupl, *Serta Harteliana* (1896), 184 f.; for further discussion see *GRBS* ix (1968), 324 f. (and note especially Basson's neglected argument—decisive in my judgement—quoted at p. 324 n. 6). It is inexcusable that Beckby (i², p. 70) should reject this abundantly proven point in favour of 'der wohl auf guter Überlieferung beruhenden Notiz des Palatinus'. The Palatine lemma obviously arose from a confusion with Philip's *Garland*, which *was* arranged alphabetically: see my article, pp. 330–1.
[3] A. Mattsson, *Untersuchungen zur Epigrammsammlung des Agathias* (Diss. Lund 1942), 1 f., and cf. too Lenzinger, op. cit. 22.
[4] *Studien zur griech. Anthologie* (Lund 1926), 5 f.
[5] On the arrangement of Philip's *Garland* see now E. Hirsch, *Wiss. Zeitschr. Halle* xv (1966), 401 f., and my own reconstruction in *GRBS* ix (1968), 331–49.

But perhaps the best illustration of Cephalas' method is the series of epigrams on philosophers *AP* vii. 83–133, all but four anonymous in *AP*. The whole series is in fact lifted, with two exceptions, from Diogenes Laertius' *Lives of the Philosophers*, where we discover that thirty-four of them are by Diogenes himself, others by Callimachus, Antagoras, Zenodotus, and Xenophanes.[1] No fewer than forty-eight out of the fifty-one stand in *AP* in exactly the order in which they are scattered evenly throughout nine books in Diogenes. The three exceptions are 106 on Epicurus and 108–9 on Plato; why they should have got out of place is anybody's guess (perhaps omitted in error and then replaced at the wrong point). The two poems not from Diogenes, 131–2, were probably added from some other source because, being about Protagoras, they followed naturally after 130, also about Protagoras. More striking than these minor irregularities is the fact that the rest of the series, a nondescript collection of poems in a variety of metres by a variety of authors (mostly unknown to the Palatine scribes), passed intact through however many stages it was that resulted in the text of *AP*. The Palatine scribes themselves certainly had no idea that they were dealing with a regular collection by Diogenes, for they do not ascribe a single one to him. The lemmatist added to just one (vii. 89)[2] the remark: 'Diogenes quotes this in his *Lives of the Philosophers* as his own', against which the so-called 'Corrector' patronizingly noted: 'except that they are all by Diogenes'. Evidently the Corrector recognized the series, but even he does not seem to have checked with a text of Diogenes, for curiously enough, in our MSS. at least, the poem in question is there ascribed to Callimachus.[3]

There are, it is true, long sections of *AP* where it is clear that Cephalas thoroughly mixed up his material into a thematic arrangement of his own.[4] But no less often he simply incorporated whole blocks from his major sources intact, letting their original arrangement stand unaltered as his own. Why should he have

---

[1] The only discussion is by R. Weisshäupl, *Grabgedichte d. griech. Anthologie* (1889), 34 f. (for our present purpose it does not much matter whether Cephalas himself did or (as Weisshäupl believed) did not use Diogenes direct).

[2] See Stadtmueller's apparatus ad loc., with Weisshäupl, op. cit. 34.

[3] Probably correctly, though Gow and Page, *Hellenistic Epigrams* ii (1965), 205, record the doubts of F. Jacobs. Its authenticity is warmly upheld by G. Luck in *GGA* 219 (1967), 30–1.

[4] See Lenzinger's helpful Tafel 1 (after p. 63).

treated the block of charioteer epigrams differently? Either he would have split them up and rearranged them completely along with other material, which he clearly did not do. Or he would have left them undisturbed. One or two poems *may* have been omitted, whether deliberately or by accident, whether by Cephalas or by one of his successors. One or two *may* have got displaced. But Cephalas' treatment of long sequences from the *Garlands*, Diogenes, and elsewhere suggests that such omissions and dislocations would be minimal. And the order of the epigrams on the extant monuments suggests that in this case they may well be non-existent.

V

THE CHRONOLOGY OF PORPHYRIUS

Only one attempt has been made to assign Porphyrius a date more precise than 'late fifth or early sixth century': that of Vasiliev. I hope to show that it is about twenty years out.

There are just two firm dates in Porphyrius' career: Malalas describes him in 507 (9 July, to be precise) as 'a certain Calliopas, a charioteer ἀπὸ φακτιοναρίων from Constantinople', who took over the stable of the Greens, which happened to be vacant at the time. Malalas then describes how Porphyrius led his fellow Greens in an attack on a synagogue in the suburb of Daphne, killing many worshippers.[1]

φακτιονάριος (*factionarius*) was the title given the most senior of all the charioteers, those who drove for the Blues and Greens. Those who drove for the Reds and Whites enjoyed only the inferior rank of μικροπανίτης. An ἀπὸ φακτιοναρίων was someone who had once been a φακτιονάριος, just as an ἀπὸ ὑπάτων or ἀπὸ ἐπάρχων is an ex-consul or ex-prefect.[2] So by 507 Porphyrius had already won the highest honours in Constantinople.

In 515 Porphyrius was back in Constantinople fighting for Anastasius against the usurper Vitalian, as we learn from the epigrams of monument E.[3]

Vasiliev's chronology[4] is based partly on his (as we shall see, mistaken) combination of xv. 44 with Malalas frag. 43, partly on his (equally mistaken) view that Porphyrius drove for Blues or Greens according to which colour the reigning Emperor happened to support. After beginning with the Blues, he argues, Porphyrius soon changed to the Greens, whom Anastasius supported (or so Vasiliev thought), and then back again to the Blues after the accession of Justin I (518–27) who (like Justinian after him) supported the Blues. In fact Porphyrius changed colours more frequently than this theory would be able to allow.[5]

[1] pp. 395–8 Bonn; see *Circus Factions*, Ch. VII, for a full discussion of the affair.
[2] See *Circus Factions*, Ch. II.   [3] Above, p. 126.
[4] *DOP* iv (1948), 41 f.   [5] See below, p. 243.

THE CHRONOLOGY OF PORPHYRIUS 151

Then, taking rather too literally Woodward and Wace's dating of the old monument on artistic grounds to 'about 500', he inferred from the representations of Porphyrius thereon that he was at the time 'a man of mature age' (p. 49). Thus he found him to be 'about 40' at the time of the Antioch riots of 507 (p. 48), 'over 40' during Vitalian's rebellion of 513/15 (p. 44), and 'over 60' by Justin's reign in the 520s. This last is presumably an inference from the fact that monument F (xvi. 358–62) was put up by the Blues when Porphyrius was sixty, and the assumption that the Blues were favoured by Justin I.

Fortunately, there is another chronological indication, so far unexploited. There are clear echoes of Christodorus' ecphrasis of the statues in the bath of Zeuxippos in *A. Pl.* 344. Here are the relevant lines of the poem:

Τίς τελέθεις, φίλε κοῦρε, γενειάδος ἄκρα χαράσσων;
"ὦ ξένε, Πορφύριος..."
ἔπρεπέ σοι Λύσιππον ἔχειν ἐπιμάρτυρα νίκης
τοσσατίης πλάστην ἴδμονα, Πορφύριε.

First, with γενειάδος ἄκρα χαράσσων compare Christodorus (= *AP* ii. 212), ἄνθει λαχνήεντι γενειάδος ἄκρα χαράσσων, and 278–9, ἁπαλοῖς δὲ νεοτρεφέεσσιν ἰούλοις | οἶνοπος ἄκρα χάρασσε γενειάδος.

It should be obvious that the author of our epigram has borrowed this extravagant phrase directly from Christodorus—and clumsily too. For in Christodorus the meaning is made quite clear by the datival phrases ἄνθει λαχνήεντι and ἁπαλοῖς ... ἰούλοις respectively. Our poet has only borrowed half the original, a phrase which, taken by itself, is barely intelligible.

Christodorus, as F. Baumgarten correctly noted,[1] was borrowing in turn from Nonnus (*Dion.* xxv. 403). But Baumgarten did not observe that it is not a case of straightforward borrowing, but of 'creative imitation', if one may use such a phrase of such a poetaster. Nonnus wrote here:

ἁλλόμενος περὶ κύκλα νεότριχος ἀνθερεῶνος
ὄγμῳ πουλυόδοντι παρηίδος ἄκρα χαράξας,

which means (I gratefully make use of Rouse's Loeb translation):

[1] *De Christodoro poeta Thebano* (Diss. Bonn 1881), 57.

'darting at his face tore the cheeks and downy chin with sharp rows of teeth'. χαράξας is being used in a quite different sense here, and the downy chin is in a different clause. What Christodorus has done is to combine (probably unconsciously) this passage with another, *Dion.* x. 179–80 (missed by Baumgarten),

οὐδὲ οἱ ἁβρὸς ἴουλος ἐρευθομένοιο γενείου
ἄχνοα χιονέης ἐχαράσσατο κύκλα παρειῆς,

where ἐχαράσσατο (middle here) is used in the sense 'mark', as down marks the cheek, exactly as in Christodorus (the second imitation is confirmed by Christodorus' use of the clausula of *Dion.* x. 180 in line 14 of *AP* ii: λασίης δὲ συνείρυε κύκλα παρειῆς).

It is plain from the rhythm of his own lines, his use of ἄκρα, and the active of χαράσσω, that the first of the Nonnus passages was uppermost in Christodorus' mind. Yet it is from the second passage that he takes the meaning and voice of the verb appropriate to down. The likelihood of anyone else chancing to make precisely this bizarre and linguistically dubious conflation of the two passages of Nonnus is obviously very remote. It must, then, be Christodorus whom the author of our epigram is directly echoing. But what in Christodorus was at least comprehensible because of the allusions to down is now not even that, except for readers who remembered their Christodorus.

Secondly, with line 5 of the poem,

ἔπρεπέ σοι Λύσιππον ἔχειν ἐπιμάρτυρα νίκης,

compare Christodorus, 195:

δεξιτέρην δ' ἀνέτεινεν ἐὴν ἐπιμάρτυρα νίκης.[1]

And for ἐπιμάρτυρα in this sedes compare too Christodorus 387:

κηρὸν ἀνεπλάσσαντο, σοφῆς ἐπιμάρτυρα μολπῆς.

Lastly, the word ἴδμων in the last line of the poem. LSJ quote only one example, *AP* vii. 515. 5, by Leontius Scholasticus (who has been shown already to have been familiar with these very

[1] Or, as I would suggest in the light of l. 387 (quoted in the text above), δεξιτέρην δ' ἀνέτεινεν, ἐῆς ἐπιμάρτυρα νίκης. Compare too (in each case in the same sedes) ἐῶν ... μελάθρων (l. 4), ἑὰς ... χεῖρας (l. 141), and ἐὴν ... πάτρην (l. 417). The heavy pause after the third element given by the Palatinus would be rare (see P. Maas, *Greek Metre*, § 98); there are only five examples in the rest of the poem (193, 221, 272, 276, 323).

THE CHRONOLOGY OF PORPHYRIUS 153

charioteer epigrams). In fact it occurs too a number of times in Nonnus' Paraphrase of St. John (though not more than once or twice in the *Dion.*). Our poet will no doubt have read a good deal of Nonnus, but he may have been more immediately reminded of this rare and desirable word by Christodorus again, line 411:

ἔτρεφον εὐεπίης ἡρωΐδος ἴδμονα Μοῦσαι.

Furthermore, another epigram dating from the earliest period of Porphyrius' successes, 336, contains yet another likely Christodoran echo. Compare 336. 6

χάλκεος ἱδρύνθη πρῶτον ἴουλον ἔχων,

with Christodorus, 272:

μήπω πρῶτον ἴουλον ἔχων . . .

Poets normally employ ἴουλος in the plural, and where they do not, its epithets are usually λεπτός or ἁβρός (see the passages collected by Pfeiffer in his note on Callimachus, frag. 274). The commonest stock phrase in sepulchral epigrams on people who died at this stage of their development seems to be ἄρτι γενειάσκων or some variant (*AP* vii. 122. 3, Kaibel 345. 1, 100. 1, and Add. 552a. 3; cf. Theocr. xi. 10). At Kaibel 478 (= Peek 1555). 3, τοῦθτον δὲ ἀνθήσαντος ὑπὸ κροτάφοισιν ἴουλον, Kaibel correctly interpreted the first word, taken by earlier editors as πρῶτον, as τυτθόν. No other extant poet seems to use the phrase πρῶτος ἴουλος, and *a fortiori* not the formula πρῶτον ἴουλον ἔχων. So in view of the parallels in 344, it looks as if this epigram too (together with the rest of its block) may belong after Christodorus' ecphrasis.

Epigram 344, in any case, must certainly be dated after Christodorus. The first of the three borrowings is proof enough, but the cumulative effect of the second and finally the hint of the third clinch the matter. The author of the poem had read Christodorus.

It is of course very likely that a poet writing under Anastasius *should* have been familiar with Christodorus, by far the most prolific and famous poet of the reign. And it is especially likely that, as author of a work on the origins of Constantinople in no fewer than twelve books, Christodorus should have been read in Constantinople itself, where our poet obviously lived and worked.

What more probable than that one whose business was to write epigrams on statues should have been influenced by Christodorus' ecphrasis of the most extensive and famous single collection of statues in Constantinople? The exact date of the ecphrasis is unfortunately unknown, but it must have been written after Anastasius' final reduction of the Isaurians in 497: compare the allusion at line 406 to Anastasius having δηώσας σακέεσσιν Ἰσαυρίδος ἔθνεα γαίης. We know from the *Suda* that Christodorus wrote a six-book epic on Anastasius' victory. Claudian's contemporary epics never extend beyond one book, and his longest panegyric (that on Stilico) comprises just three books. The longest such work by George of Pisidia had only four books. Christodorus' poem was probably then a substantial work, the product, probably, of more than just a few weeks' work. Furthermore, it seems natural to assume that he would have completed this epic before getting down to a mere ecphrasis of some statues in which he just happens to mention Anastasius' victory in passing, a work much less likely than a full-scale epic to secure its author imperial favour.

If so, then the ecphrasis is not likely to have been written before 498. And of course there is no *need* to assume that it was written so soon after the defeat of the Isaurians as even this. There were few enough military successes in the reign of Anastasius, and a tactful poet would have continued to evoke the victory for many years after the event.

Procopius of Gaza, for example, makes much of it in his panegyric on Anastasius, recited not before 501:[1] probably not long after 501, though a date as late as 512 has been canvassed. Priscian too sings loudly of it in his panegyric on Anastasius, placed by Bury in 503,[2] but by Schanz–Hosius–Krüger in 512.[3]

Thus we certainly cannot rule out a date as late as 500 or even a year or two later still for Christodorus' ecphrasis. Still less do we have to place the epigram which echoes the ecphrasis immediately after the appearance of the ecphrasis—though it does seem natural to place it not too long after, while the charm of Christodorus' diction was still fresh in his mind.

[1] § 9; cf. C. Kempen, *Procopii Gaz. in Imperatorem Anastasium panegyricus* (Diss. Bonn 1918), xxii–xxvi; Christ–Schmid–Stählin, *Gesch. d. griech. Literatur* ii. 2⁶ (1922), 1029.
[2] *Later Roman Empire* ii² (1922), 12 n. 1.
[3] *Gesch. d. röm. Literatur* iv² (1920), 237.

Our epigram is not likely, then, to have been written much before 500—nor in all probability very much after 500. Since we can only deal in approximations at best, and round numbers are convenient, let us say 500.

In 500, then, Porphyrius could be described as a youth with the first down on his cheeks. One might be tempted not to press this, to conclude no more than that Porphyrius was a youngish man. It would be easy to quote examples where the formula is used loosely, as when Ammianus styles the future Emperor Theodosius I 'prima etiam tum lanugine iuvenis' when he was 27.[1] But the case is not quite parallel. Ammianus means to suggest, not so much that Theodosius was very young absolutely, as that he was very young to hold so important a command. But charioteers might expect to make their mark very young indeed, sometimes well *before* the appearance of their first down. The African Crescens was only 13 when he won his first victory with the quadriga (*ILS* 5285). Tatianus had won 125 victories by the time he was 20 (*ILS* 5286). The great Diocles began his career when 18 (*ILS* 5287). It was said of Constantine that ἔτι κουρίζων τε καὶ ἄχνοος ἄνδρας ἐνίκας (372. 5). Naturally one cannot extract too precise a figure from so vague a term, but it is perfectly possible that Constantine really did begin to make his mark before the appearance of his first down; that is to say when he was 15–17. Lester Piggott rode his first winner when only twelve.

In athletics, indeed, 'beardless' is a technical term. The three classes in which competitions were held bore the names παῖδες, ἀγένειοι, and ἄνδρες, the ἀγένειοι being defined as youths between 17 and 20. The limits were not absolute: indeed, it was the height of every young athlete's ambition to win in all three classes successively in the course of one and the same festival.[2]

The detailed *curricula vitae* in the inscriptions of Diocles, Teres, and other early imperial drivers do not mention any such formal classification by age, nor is it very likely that there was one. For (as with horse racing today) it was skill rather than physical strength and stamina that counted:

[1] xxix. 6. 15.
[2] See, for example, L. Moretti, *Iscriz. agon. greche* (1953), 57, 104, 227, referring for the (approximate) age-limits to Th. Klee, *Zur Gesch. d. gymnisch. Agone an griech. Festen* (1918), 44 f.

οὐ σθένος, οὐ δρόμος ἵππων
νικῆσαι δεδάασιν, ὅσον φρένες ἡνιοχῆος.

'Tis not strength nor swift horses that know how to win, but the brains of the charioteer.

So Aktaion's father to his son before the exciting chariot race in Bk. xxxvii of Nonnus' *Dionysiaca*, not unmindful of Nestor's advice to Antilochus before the chariot race of *Iliad* xxiii:

μήτι δ' ἡνίοχος περιγίγνεται ἡνιόχοιο—

a line directly echoed in one of the epigrams from the old Porphyrius base (341. 5):

μήτι δ' ἡνιόχων περιγίγνομαι.

Porphyrius is praised more than once for his σοφία, his skill (339. 1, 343. 3, 359. 4, 360. 4), Faustinus for his νόος (363. 3). 342. 3 praises Porphyrius' ἔνθεα δήνεα τέχνης, while τέχνη alone is evoked in 43. 2, 352. 4, and (linked with σθένος) at 359. 6 and 360. 4. The most explicit statement in the charioteer epigrams is 363. 1–2 from the base of Faustinus:

μητέρες εὐάθλων γεράων φρένες, οὐ κράτος ἥβης,
οὐ τάχος ἱπποσύνης, οὐ χρόνος εὐτυχίης.

So a charioteer, like the modern jockey, might well (if he was good enough) enter first-class competition in his mid 'teens. Crescens, at 13, may have been exceptional, but 16 was probably common enough. What was felt to be so unusual about Porphyrius was not that he won *races* so young, but *statues*, normally the privilege of much older men.

There is some evidence that chariot racing, like many another profession at this period, was largely hereditary. From the earlier period there is Tatianus and his father Polyneices (*ILS* 5286). From Porphyrius' day we have Constantine, son of Faustinus, and a third, unnamed, member of the family,[1] whose statue stood next to those of both Faustinus and Constantine (370. 2).

[1] Beckby in his note ad loc. (iv², p. 574) mistakenly infers that this kinsman is Uranius. But the Uranius epigrams say nothing of any relationship with Faustinus or Constantine, and Uranius' base must in any case be later than those of both Faustinus and Constantine (see p. 213).

THE CHRONOLOGY OF PORPHYRIUS

And it is suggestive that two epigrams from what I believe to be Porphyrius' first monument name his father, one Calchas:

Πορφύριον Κάλχαντος ἄναξ καὶ δῆμος ἐγείρει. (355. 1)

ἴαχε δῆμος,
τὸν Καλχαντιάδην Πορφύριον ποθέων. (336. 1–2)

At 371. 1 Constantine is called by a similar patronymic:

τὸν Φαυστινιάδην πόλις ἄνθετο Κωνσταντῖνον,

and at 48. 1–2, an epigram on Uranius, he is styled simply Φαυστινιάδης. The explanation of this interest in his father's name is, of course, that Faustinus had been no less famous a charioteer himself. Surely the same is true of Calchas. He too had been an idol of the hippodrome in his day, and so his name is tactfully evoked in the epigrams on the first monument won by his son.

According to Procopius, both the father and grandfather of Belisarius' wife Antonina had been charioteers,[1] and her mother a dancing-girl (though of a particularly low sort, Procopius gloats).[2] Nothing is said of Antonina's own profession before her marriage, but it may well be that (as Robert Graves supposed) she also was a dancing-girl. *Ben trovato* too is the remark of the narrator of *Count Belisarius* (where the gaps in Procopius are agreeably filled in): 'most of the Hippodrome people were related by marriage'.[3] There must have been many such families.

We may perhaps explain by analogy a puzzling feature of a series of curse tablets directed at charioteers from Rome in the late fourth or early fifth century. Each charioteer is identified, not merely by a sobriquet (p. 171), but by the addition of his mother's name.[4] Why mother's rather than father's? Wuensch sees a trace here of the Egyptian origin of the rite.[5] More relevant, probably (since it was the correct identification of the charioteer that mattered) was the principle *mater certa, pater incertus*.

My friend Peter Brown has referred me to an example from a source other than a curse tablet, thus raising the possibility

[1] *Anecd.* i. 11.
[2] μητρὸς δὲ τῶν τινος ἐν θυμέλῃ πεπορνευμένων, *Anecd.* i. 12.
[3] Penguin edition (1954, 1968), 50 and 54.
[4] See the index of 'Männer- und Frauennamen' to R. Wuensch's *Sethianische Verfluchungstafeln* (1891), 119. [5] Op. cit. 64.

that this style of identification by mother's name may have no connection with the procedure of cursing at all. Among the *Apophthegmata Patrum* (*PG* lxv. 164 AB) is a story about τις ἡνίοχος κατὰ τὴν Ἀλεξανδρέων, ὃς ἦν μητρὸς Μαρίας υἱός. But the mother's name is essential for the story: her son wins despite an accident, and the crowd exclaims, ὁ υἱὸς Μαρίας πέπτωκε καὶ ἐγήγερται καὶ ἐνίκησε! So this may not be a typical case, though it is certainly suggestive none the less that the crowd did know the name of the man's mother.

However this may be, do not the names of these mothers (Dionysia, Fortuna, Paschasia, Veneria...) suggest the 'stage names' of the pantomime? Could it be that in their day they had been, not charioteers of course, but dancers? It is suggestive that on one tablet we find Artemius/Hospes son of *Sapeda* driving for the Greens and Asterius/*Sapidosus* son of Irene for the Reds.[1] Sapeda and Sapidosus look like masculine and feminine forms of the same name. We shall see below (pp. 171 f.) that charioteers and dancers of both sexes often used the same stock names. Alternatively, Artemius and Asterius might actually have been related.

Actors, dancers, and charioteers were all members of the entertainment profession, and (in the eyes of the Church, if not the public at large) all equally undesirable, refused baptism, and in peril of their immortal souls. The more successful, the Porphyrii and Caramalli, will have become as rich and famous as many a bishop and prefect, and may occasionally have married 'above their station'. Theodora, it will be remembered, hooked a future Emperor;[2] Antonina the greatest soldier of the age. But for most it is not merely likely but under the circumstances almost inevitable that marriage inside the profession was the rule. The profession must have become to all intents and purposes hereditary, like the circus and theatrical families of more modern times.

Sons of charioteers will naturally have had every opportunity to learn their skills at the earliest age and under the best trainers.

---

[1] Wuensch, p. 118; at p. 65 Wuensch mistakenly gives Sapidosus as the son of Sapeda.
[2] There is much of interest on the legal position of actresses in David Daube's paper, 'The Marriage of Justinian and Theodora: Legal and Theological Reflections', *Catholic University of America Law Review* xvi (1967), 380 f.

THE CHRONOLOGY OF PORPHYRIUS 159

No doubt an important factor in the phenomenal early successes of Porphyrius and Constantine.

Now Porphyrius is described as πρῶτον ἴουλον ἔχων in an epigram from his first monument: 336. 6. Not downless, like Constantine in 372. 5, but with the first down. Then as now there must always have been both late and early developers, but the period of first down was generally agreed in antiquity to fall between the ages of 18 and 21.[1] At the time of his fourth block (C) Porphyrius is still γενειάδος ἄκρα χαράσσων (344. 1)—hardly less by now (one would have thought) than 21.

We do not know what sort of achievements were deemed to merit a statue for charioteers—and Porphyrius' honours were in any case exceptional, as the epigrams proclaim time and again. A guess may be permissible. In most modern sports much importance is attached to what a man achieves—the number of goals scored by a footballer, or races won by a jockey—in one year or season. A racing driver's ambition is to be champion driver of the year, a bullfighter's to be a 'gran triunfador de la temporada'. There is some evidence that this concept of a season played a role in chariot racing too. Several times in the inscription of Diocles reference is made to various feats performed 'uno anno' (*ILS* 5287. 13–16). The deeper causes behind Porphyrius' exceptional rewards will be analysed in a later chapter (pp.   ), but the more immediate reason may perhaps have been the uniquely decisive manner in which he established himself as champion driver of the year at Constantinople. At all events, it is hardly credible that he won sixteen-foot extravaganzas of stone and metal at more frequent intervals than once a year. It looks as if Porphyrius' poetic admirers somewhat extended the period of his first down—notoriously a peculiarly attractive time of life to ancient eyes[2]—but even so the first four monuments must surely have been erected within about half-a-dozen years. The first, that is, when Porphyrius was about 17, the fourth when he was, at the latest, about 22.

If the Christodoran echo in 336 (from block A) be reckoned as

---

[1] T. Hopfner, *Das Sexualleben der Griechen und Römer* I. i (1938), 244. Add, e.g., Peek 1970, a first- or second-century example of a 20-year-old 'first down' from Rome, and Stein, *Bas-Empire* ii (1949), 744 n. 2, for some sixth-century examples of 21-year-olds from Procopius.
[2] Elagabalus once fell in love with a charioteer at the 'beardless' stage (λειογένειος, Dio lxxx. 15. 2).

firm as those in 344 (from C), then it would follow that Porphyrius' first monument was erected after the appearance of Christodorus' ecphrasis: i.e. that he was at least 17 in 500. If we play safe and accept only the second batch of Christodoran echoes, then it is only the fourth monuments that need be dated after 500: Porphyrius would then have been 21 or 22 in 500. Since again we can only deal in approximations, let us place his date of birth in about 480. If born in 480 he would have been 27 at the time of the Antioch pogrom in 507—a display of youthful exuberance. And he would have been 35 when Vitalian was defeated in 515, surely a far more likely age than Vasiliev's 'over fifty'. Not that fifty plus would be an impossibly advanced age for a man to be fighting in battle at: but if Porphyrius *did* fight in battle at fifty plus, we may be tolerably certain that one or more of the epigrams from the monument would have said so. It was felt worthy of comment that Constantine was still driving when he was fifty (372. 3)—a fact which made him γηράλεος (ibid. 6). Epigrams from two Porphyrius monuments erected (presumably) in the period of his fifties and sixties allude to his advancing years (44. 3–6, 358. 3, 359. 3–4, 360. 1). All the epigrams on Faustinus and Julian allude to their old age (363, 364, 45). There is no hint in any one of the five epigrams from the Vitalian monument that Porphyrius was anything but in his prime. Yet what an enhancement of the 'double victory' of 515 (p. 128) if in *both* spheres Porphyrius had vanquished opponents half his age!

Since then the date of birth suggested above accords better with the only other chronological indications than does Vasiliev's chronology, pending fresh evidence (the unearthing of another monument is an open possibility) it should surely be accepted.

We come now to the new monument. The most important epigram for our present purpose is 356:

Ἄλλοις μὲν γεράων πρόφασις χρόνος· οἱ δ' ἐπ[ὶ νίκαις]
κρινόμενοι πολιῆς οὐ χατέουσι κόμης,
ἀλλ' ἀρετῆς, ὅθεν εὖχος ἀνάπτεται, ἧς ἄπ[ο τοίων]
Πορφύριος δώρων δὶς λάχεν ἀγλαΐην,
οὐκ ἐτέων δεκάδας, νίκης δ' ἑκατοντάδας [αὐχῶν]
πολλὰς καὶ πάσας συγγενέας Χαρίτων.

THE CHRONOLOGY OF PORPHYRIUS 161

I have printed the poem exactly as it stands on the stone (save for punctuation, justified below). Planudes, however, presents εἶς for ἧς in line 3 and editors have always punctuated with a full stop after ἀνάπτεται:

ἀλλ' ἀρετῆς, ὅθεν εὖχος ἀνάπτεται. εἶς ἀπὸ τοίων
Πορφύριος δώρων δὶς λάχεν ἀγλαΐην.

They have to translate somewhat as follows: 'Some owe their honours to Time; others when judged the victor require, not grey hair, but just their skill, whence glory springs. Alone of such men (τοίων) Porphyrius twice won the splendour of gifts.' So at least Beckby: Paton and Dübner failed to see the antithesis between ἄλλοις μέν and οἱ δέ, translating respectively 'Time is the cause of the honours of others, and those who are judged worthy of them . . .', 'Aliis quidem praemiorum causa est tempus; qui vero ex victoriis indicati . . .'. Paton further mistranslated χατέουσι 'lack' instead of 'need, require': his 'do not lack grey hairs, but lack that virtue on which glory depends' is *unfavourable* to the class οἱ δέ, to which Porphyrius evidently belongs. What the poet means is that Porphyrius does not need grey hairs (i.e. years of experience) like his rivals, but just his innate skill (ἀρετή).

But these errors are the more pardonable in that, with the old text and punctuation, the class of τοίων to whom Porphyrius apparently belonged was left vague, as were the unqualified 'gifts' that he alone won twice. Paton indeed, evidently sensing the awkwardness of this unqualified δώρων, did take τοίων with it ('such gifts')—but was then obliged to omit the thereby entirely isolated ἀπό from his translation.

Yet even so it is unlikely that anyone would have been bold enough to absolve the poet by conjecturing ἧς for εἶς. The antithesis between εἶς and δίς, so neat at a first glance, might have seemed to guarantee the Planudean text despite the difficulties just raised. Indeed, it is to prevent some future critic dismissing ἧς as just a stonecutter's etacism (in itself a by no means improbable error),[1] very properly corrected back to εἶς by Planudes (or his source), that I have underlined these difficulties.

A moment's thought, and ἧς will be seen to answer all our problems. All that we need to do is replace the heavy stop after

[1] Cf. ἐπιδίξαι and λάβι in prose inscriptions from the two bases (pp. 66 and 67).

ἀνάπτεται with a comma, take ἄπο (so accented), not with τοίων, but with ἧς, and τοίων as a badly needed qualification for δώρων. ἧς ἄπο is parallel to ὅθεν (for the parallelism and anaphora cf. 340. 5, ἔνθεν ἔην Πρασίνοις ἔρις ἄσπετος, ἔνθεν ἀϋτή). The charioteers who do not need grey hair (that is to say, the young ones like Porphyrius) need instead 'skill, whence springs glory, whence Porphyrius has twice won the honour of such gifts'.

But what is the 'honour of such gifts'? What can it be but statues? It is statues that are the 'honours', γεράων, mentioned in line 1. γέρας is indeed a technical (and all but invariable) term in this genre for statue—to be distinguished from στέφανος or στέφος, which is merely the (returnable) silver crown awarded to each charioteer who wins an individual race (Porphyrius is holding one in his right hand on the reliefs from both the extant monuments).

The point is important, and may as well be established properly. At 336. 7–8, from Porphyrius' first monument, we are told that ἐτέων γέρας ἦλθε θοώτερον, ἀλλ' ἐπὶ νίκαις | ὄψιμον, ἀλλὰ μόλις πολλὰ μετὰ στέφεα. There is a clear and sharp distinction between the γέρας he has only just won and the many στέφεα which are his qualification for it. Compare too 338, where the γέρας in line 1 is distinguished from the πολυστεφέας μόχθους on the basis of which Νίκη awarded the γέρας. Compare again 367. 1–4, where the failure of the people to award Constantine a γέρας in his lifetime is explained (or excused) by the claim that while he was alive nobody needed any reminding how many στέφανοι he had won. Julian only received one statue, at his retirement, but it was a reward for his πολλοὺς ... στεφάνους (45. 2).

For γέρας = statue, note in addition: 338. 1, 340. 2, 341. 3, 349. 1, 350. 7, 353. 4, 363. 1, 367. 2, 376. 3, 43. 1, 49. 2. For the verb γεραίρειν of honouring with a statue: 41. 3, 348. 3, 354. 1, 362. 1, 364. 3. For στέφανοι of individual victories: 335. 2, 361. 2, 370. 4, 379. 3. And for στέφειν of awarding them: 371. 6, A. Pl. 56. 3.

So 356. 1–2 is saying more or less exactly what the epigrams from Porphyrius' other early monuments say. Porphyrius is getting young what the others all wait till they are old for. Particularly close to the formulation of 356. 1–2 is 338. 1–2:

τοῦτό σοι ἠϊθέῳ Νίκη γέρας, ὃ χρόνος ἄλλοις
ὀψὲ μόλις πολιοῖς ὦπασε, Πορφύριε.

It is clear then that 356. 3–4,

τοίων
Πορφύριος δώρων δὶς λάχεν ἀγλαΐην,

must mean that the statue in question was Porphyrius' *second*. This is confirmed by a couplet from the epigram on the top left-hand face of the monument:

τοὔνεκα καὶ ξεῖνον πρεσβήϊον εὗρεο μοῦνος,
εἰκόνα χαλκείην δήμῳ ἐν ἀμφοτέρῳ (351. 5–6).

Porphyrius alone has a statue in 'each of the two demes'—that is to say from both Blues and Greens. Now we have seen that the monument which must be his first (A) was erected by the Blues (336. 3, 339. 2). The new monument came from the Greens: this we know not merely from 354. 4, but from all three of the prose acclamations. So Porphyrius *did* now have a statue from each deme.

As might have been expected, there are other hints in the epigrams from the new monument that Porphyrius had just changed colours. First, 351. 1–2:

ὑμετέρων κήρυκες ἀμεμφέες εἰσὶν ἀγώνων
οἱ καὶ ἀπ' ἀντιβίων, Πορφύριε, στέφανοι.

'Crowns from the enemy are unimpeachable heralds of your triumphs': confirmation that he had previously been driving for the Blues. A much more acrimonious, gloating note is sounded by 355. 3–6:

ἀλλὰ μέρει πρώτῳ σταθερῷ καὶ ἀρείονι μίμνοις,
τὴν φθονερὴν τήκων δυσμενέων κραδίην,
οἱ σέθεν εἰσορόωντες ἀεὶ νικῶσαν ἱμάσθλην
μέμφονται σφετέρην αἰὲν ἀτασθαλίην.

Stay now in the first of factions, the steady, the better faction, and consume the jealous hearts of our foes, who, seeing your whip ever victorious, ever curse their own folly.

Here we learn that it was some act of 'folly' on the part of the Blues that led to Porphyrius joining the Greens. Paton (followed by Beckby) suggests that the Blues had expelled him. This could be so: but if so, it is not surprising that they soon repented of losing the best charioteer of the day. Maybe they refused to grant him privileges or money he felt consonant with his fame, and the Greens made a higher offer. Or perhaps there was a purely personal quarrel. The only detail we know of Porphyrius' life outside the hippodrome—the slaughtering of Jews and burning of a synagogue at Antioch in 507—does not suggest a mild and submissive disposition. Stars are notoriously temperamental, especially when fame comes early.

At 355. 3 the Greens beg Porphyrius to stay with them. And on the prose acclamation on the lower left-hand face it is alleged that the Blues admitted defeat, and had been trying to woo him back (οἱ πολλάκις, Πορφύρι, ζητήσαντές σε).

To recapitulate, block A (335–9) was Porphyrius' first monument (p. 135), block F (351–6, the new monument) his second. The first from the Blues, the second from the Greens.

B (340–3, the old monument) and C (46, 344, 47), both from the Blues and both plainly from the period of Porphyrius' early youth, must come next. But in which order? I hope to be able to show that B came before C.

For B the most important lines are 341. 2–4:

δῆμος μὲν γὰρ ἐμὸς γέρας ᾔτεεν, οἱ δ' ἕτεροί με
δίζοντ' αὖθις ἔχειν, νεῖκος ἀπειπάμενοι.

οἱ ἕτεροι, the Greens, had been trying to get him back. Note αὖθις, showing that the Greens had 'had' Porphyrius in some sense already, surely an allusion to his statue from the Greens. νεῖκος is Musurus' acute and certain correction of Planudes' νῖκος. How could it help the Greens' attempt to get Porphyrius back if they renounced (ἀπειπάμενοι) their *victory* (νῖκος)? What they renounce is their *quarrel* (νεῖκος). The temperamental Porphyrius has evidently had a difference of opinion with the Greens now and gone back to the Blues as a result. Whereupon the Greens, νεῖκος ἀπειπάμενοι, attempt to entice him back again —without success, it seems, since his next monument came from the Blues again. The Blues, amusingly enough, took a leaf out of the Greens' book and in the prose acclamation on the left-hand face represent the Greens now begging Porphyrius to come back (δὸς ἡμῖν Πορφύριν...). Similarly at 340. 6. (discussed on p. 267) the Greens are represented jealously entreating the Emperor:

ὡς Βενέτους, τέρψῃ, κοίρανε, καὶ Πρασίνους.

THE CHRONOLOGY OF PORPHYRIUS 165

The atmosphere of the epigrams from C is very different. There is no hint of the impression given by both epigrams and acclamations from B that Porphyrius' return to the Blues was recent and controversial. On the contrary, both 45 and 46 emphasize the frequency with which he changed his colours:

Πορφύριος Λίβυς οὗτος· ἀεθλοφόρων δ' ἐπὶ δίφρων
μοῦνος παντοδαποὺς ἀμφέθετο στεφάνους.
Νίκη γὰρ βασίλεια μεριζομένη κατὰ δῆμον
χρώμασι καὶ πέπλοις συμμετέβαλλε τύχας. (46. 1-4)

The implication of the second couplet is that Victory is 'divided up' (μεριζομένη) between the factions according to which one Porphyrius happens to be driving for. Number 47 is more explicit:

Τοῦτον Πορφύριον Λιβύη τέκε, θρέψε δὲ 'Ρώμη,
Νίκη δ' ἐστεφάνωσεν ἀμοιβαδόν, ἄλλοτ' ἀπ' ἄλλου
χρώματος ἄκρα φέροντα καρήατι σύμβολα νίκης.
πολλάκι γὰρ δήμους ἠλλάξατο, πολλάκι πώλους. (47. 1-4)

Clearly Porphyrius has now become notorious for his frequent changes of colour. Would not such an attitude arise naturally in the period after the erection of the third statue, when Porphyrius' record stood at one from the Blues, a second from the Greens, and the third from the Blues again? At this point it might have seemed an open question which colour he would favour next time, but as it happened (so 46 continues):

ἥρμοσε δ' αὐτὸν ἔχειν Βενέτοις πλέον . . .

It is merely 'more appropriate' that the Blues should have him again. Compare too the other epigram from the monument, 344:

Τίς τελέθεις, φίλε κοῦρε, γενειάδος ἄκρα χαράσσων;
"ὦ ξένε, Πορφύριος." —Τίς πατρίς; — "Ἡ Λιβύη."
Τίς δέ σε νῦν τίμησεν; — "Ἄναξ χάριν ἱπποσυνάων."
Τίς μάρτυς τελέθει; — "Δῆμος ὁ τῶν Βενέτων."

The tone is very matter of fact. 'Which colour?' is merely the last of a series of questions posed by the ξένος. And again, the implication is that the answer might as easily have been "Δῆμος ὁ τῶν Πρασίνων". It looks as if the factions had by now become resigned to Porphyrius' vacillating loyalties.

Furthermore, in at least one of the epigrams from each of the monuments A, F, and B there is (as we have seen) clear and emphatic allusion to the uniqueness of Porphyrius' achievement: whether (as in A and B) because he had won a statue at all while still competing (it had formerly been customary to receive one only on retirement, see p. 207), or because (as in F) he was the first and only charioteer to have won a statue from both factions. This note is absent from C, as it is from all the epigrams on Porphyrius' other, later, monuments, from whichever colour. And for a simple and obvious reason. By the time Porphyrius had won his third statue from the Blues, the uniqueness of his achievements could be taken for granted. A contemporary such as Constantine might have to wait till his death at the age of fifty to win even one statue, but with two from the Blues and one from the Greens before he had grown a beard, the usual records and yardsticks had become simply irrelevant for Porphyrius. And although two epigrams from the old monument, the third (as I believe), lay special emphasis on the uniqueness of the three statues he has won so far (340. 1, 341. 1), one of the others from the same monument looks forward to a future when it *will* become the normal thing:

ἀλλ' ἐπὶ νίκαις
Πορφυρίου πολλὰς εἰκόνας ὀψόμεθα. (343. 3-4)

C, the fourth, *was* one of the 'many', an attitude reflected in the epigrams which adorned it.

To recapitulate again: Porphyrius' first four monuments (in that order) were A, F, B, and C. Thus the two extant monuments, F and B, were Porphyrius' second and third respectively. No very long interval (though apparently at least two bitter quarrels) can have separated any of them, since on the last of them Porphyrius could still be described with some emphasis as γενειάδος ἄκρα χαράσσων (344. 1). Probably then not much more than a year or two separated F from B, both put up somewhere in the close neighbourhood of 500.

No other monument of Porphyrius can be dated before E, the Vitalian monument, in 515. Nor would it be possible for either of the other two monuments we know of from Planudes' series to be dated before then. We have seen already that Porphyrius can have been only 35 in 515, whereas he was clearly an old man when D and H were put up. H, indeed, cannot be much earlier than 540, since Porphyrius was sixty at the time (358. 3).

E, then, was Porphyrius' second statue from the Greens, put up some fifteen years after the first. Now we might have expected some hint in the epigrams that the Greens had already so honoured Porphyrius, if not in the very recent past. And if we read them attentively enough we do find it—yet further proof (if more were needed) that none of these epigrams is epideictic. All were composed for a particular monument at a particular stage in Porphyrius' career, and naturally enough look back on the earlier stages of his career.

Epigram 350. 7 tells us that τοὔνεκα τοῖς μὲν [i.e. the Greens] ἔδωκεν ἄναξ γέρας, ὡς πάρος εἶχον. Paton (followed by Vasiliev) translates: 'the privileges they formerly had', and Beckby: 'die einstigen Rechte'. In itself the notion that the Emperor was restoring to the Greens some privileges he had earlier withdrawn is perfectly plausible: Emperors were often obliged to punish the factions (or at least their ringleaders) for the disturbances that periodically convulsed the capital. Yet we have seen that in the formulaic vocabulary of the epigrams γέρας never refers to undefined privileges in general: it means, precisely and invariably, a statue. What the line in question is saying is that the Emperor (who had to give permission for the erection of such statues) has allowed the Greens to put up another statue of Porphyrius like the one they had put up *formerly* (πάρος).

This brings us to the loosely defined group D (p. 130): 345, 346, 44. 345–6 offer no handle for dating, but 44 tells us that Porphyrius is an old man, coming out of retirement at popular request:

Πορφύριον λήξαντα πόνων λύσαντά τε μίτρην
καὶ πάρος ἀντ' ἀρετῆς χάλκεον ἑσταότα,
τῇδε πάλιν χαλκοῦ τε καὶ ἀργύρου ἱδρύσαντο.
πρέσβυ, σὺ δὲ ξείνων ἀντιάσας γεράων
δήμου μὲν βοόωντος ἔλες παλίνορσον[1] ἱμάσθλην,
ὡς δὲ δὶς ἡβήσας μαίνεαι ἐν σταδίοις.   (44)

---

[1] παλίνορσος in the sense 'continuing' (as distinct from 'retrograde') is poorly treated in LSJ; it is in fact common in late epic and epigrams, especially adverbially (= 'again'): Nonnus, *Dion.* 48. 857; *Par. Ioh.* 18. 128, 21. 121; Triphiodorus

Vasiliev explains δήμου βοόωντος by comparing Malalas fragment 43.[1] We learn there that in 520 there were riots in the hippodrome: after much bloodshed the Blues and Greens came to some sort of agreement, and, assembling in the hippodrome, the Greens clamoured for the dancer Caramallus, the Blues for 'a certain Porphyrius from Alexandria'. Both got what they wanted. Could it be, then, that by 520 Porphyrius had already retired, to be recalled to the arena in Constantinople by popular request?

Attractive though this reconstruction might seem, it must, alas, be abandoned, on two different but equally decisive counts.

(i) For it to be true, the monument in question would have to have been erected by the Blues, the faction who had requested his recall. Since none of the three epigrams happens to mention a colour, it might seem unreasonable to deny the possibility that the faction in question might have been the Blues. Yet I believe that a careful examination of 44 will show that it can only have been put up by the Greens.

The statue commemorated by 44 was itself made of silver and bronze (l. 3), but lines 2-3 refer to an earlier statue *in the same area* made of just bronze:

καὶ πάρος ἀντ' ἀρετῆς χάλκεον ἑσταότα
τῇδε πάλιν χαλκοῦ τε καὶ ἀργύρου ἱδρύσαντο.

Now it is clear from 48. 1-2, 370. 1-2, and 371. 2 (see further p. 142) that statues were erected (as might after all have been expected) in the ground of the faction concerned. Thus a statue erected by the Greens would stand in the area in front of the benches where the Greens sat, a statue from the Blues in front of their benches (see the diagram on p. 182).

Most charioteer statues were made of bronze. Of the seven statues of Porphyrius commemorated in the Anthology, five (A, B, E, F, and H) were of bronze, as was that of Constantine. Uranius alone was honoured with gold (378. 5).[2]

It is not surprising, then, that the author of 44 should have drawn attention to the superior quality of the statue he was com-

---

145, 282; Colluthus 217, 339, 352; Paul, *AP* v. 241. 1; Eutolmius, *AP* vii. 608. 3; and add the fragment of late epic (*c.* 400) published by H. Maehler, *Zeitschr. für Pap. und Epigraphik* vi (1970), p. 154, I recto 7, followed by τὸ δεύτερον in the next line, a nice parallel to the pleonasm παλίνορσον . . . δίς in 44. 5-6.

[1] *Exc. de Insid.*, p. 170 de Boor.
[2] See below, pp. 214f.

memorating. His faction had only given Porphyrius bronze before: now it was silver and bronze.

Whatever the date of 44, it is certain that Porphyrius was advanced in years at the time (πρέσβυ, l. 4, δὶς ἡβήσας, l. 6). Now C, a monument erected to Porphyrius when he was still a very young man by the Blues (46, 344, 47), was of bronze and *gold*:

χρύσεος ἀντ' ἀρετῆς, χάλκεος ἀντὶ πόνων. (46. 6)

A bronze-and-gold statue would obviously have been considered superior to even a bronze-and-silver one. So if the statue commemorated by 44 had been erected by the Blues, who had already long since presented Porphyrius with a gold-and-bronze one, it is hardly credible that the poet should have contrasted the new silver-and-bronze statue with earlier ones of mere humble bronze. On the other hand both Porphyrius' two statues from the Greens —the new monument (F) and the Vitalian monument (E)—both of which date from the earlier part of his career, long before he could have been called πρέσβυς, were of bronze alone (347. 3, 349. 5, 351. 6, 352. 1).

It seems clear, then, that 44 must commemorate a new statue from the Greens, a more splendid successor to their earlier efforts in bronze. So it cannot have been a statue voted by the Blues in 520. Indeed we have no evidence that Porphyrius won at the games held in 520, much less won a statue. Nor have we any evidence that he had retired by 520, and in the light of the new chronology I have proposed for his career, it seems very unlikely. If born, as here suggested, *c*. 480, he would have been only about 40 in 520. Since we know from monument H that he was still driving (and winning) when 60, it seems hardly likely that he would have retired before he was 40.

So whether 44 belongs before or after Porphyrius' sixtieth year (p. 179), it can hardly be placed before his 50s, during the 530s.

(ii) The second and equally serious objection to Vasiliev's interpretation of 44 is that it is very doubtful whether the Porphyrius of the Malalas fragment is indeed the charioteer. Malalas, at any event, was plainly under the impression that the man was a dancer. Here are his words:

τὰ μέρη ἔκραζον, ζητοῦντες τοὺς ὀρχηστάς· οἱ μὲν Πράσινοι τὸν Καράμαλλον, οἱ δὲ Βένετοι Πορφύριόν τινα ἀπὸ Ἀλεξανδρείας, οἱ δὲ Ῥούσιοι καὶ Λευκοὶ τοὺς πρώτους.

Now we all know that Malalas was a remarkably ill-informed and careless writer, and it might not seem to be asking very much to postulate a simple confusion between one sort of circus performer and another. Yet if there was one thing Malalas *was* well-informed and particular about, it was the affairs of the circus and theatre. He assigns a quite disproportionate amount of space to dancers and charioteers and factional riots, and devoted one immortal page to a very full account of the introduction of chariot-racing and the circus factions into Rome—by Romulus, of course.[1] He had already recorded Porphyrius' activity at his own native Antioch in 507 in some detail, and it would be strange indeed if he had been unaware that the man he there called Calliopas, idol of hippodromes all over the East, was also known as Porphyrius. Yet under the year 520 he refers merely to 'a certain Porphyrius from Alexandria', quite as if he was being introduced for the first time. Furthermore, 46. 1, 47. 1, and 344. 2 ali state very plainly that Porphyrius was born in Libya. Now 'Libya' is a literary and somewhat elastic term, but it seems unlikely that even a poet would have stretched it to cover Alexandria. We possess countless inscriptions celebrating the victories of athletes and gladiators at the many festivals of the Greek East throughout the Hellenistic and Roman periods. The overwhelming majority name the native city of the honorand: the prose inscriptions simply enough in prose, the epigrams as precisely as the imprecise poetical vocabulary of the genre would allow. And for an obvious and abundantly attested reason.

These performers were proud of their native cities, and prouder still of the honour they had brought them. Indeed, a common and widespread tradition of the genre was to proclaim that it was not the actual victor who was crowned, but his city; 'neque ipsi coronantur, sed patrias suas coronant' in the words of the elder Pliny (*NH* vii. 26). A recent study by Louis Robert has traced this motif in epigrams on athletes from all over the Greek world through the centuries.[2] Here is just one good hellenistic example from Athens, on a victor in the horse-races at Ilion, Colophon, and Ephesus:[3]

---

[1] p. 175 (cf. *Chron. Pasch.* i. 208–9, Cedrenus i. 528). V. Cottas, *Le Théâtre à Byzance* (1931), 5, quotes the tradition as though it were authentic: for a more realistic discussion see *Circus Factions*, Ch. IV.
[2] *Rev. de Phil.* xli (1967), 21 f.   [3] *IG* ii², 3138. 3–4.

Νικήσας δὲ ἵππων τε δρόμοις ἔργων τ' ἐν ἁμίλλα[ις]
τὴν ἱερὰν στεφανοῖ πατρίδα Κεκροπίαν.

Naturally, charioteers were no less proud of their native cities: 37. 1 proclaims that Uranius was from Nicaea, 45. 1 that Julian was from Tyre. So if Porphyrius really had come from Alexandria, third city in the Empire, it would be strange indeed if all the epigrams on one monument had branded him a humble Libyan: the more so in that in 344. 2 it is Porphyrius himself who is represented as claiming Libya for his home.

There are weighty reasons, then, for distinguishing two Porphyrii: one an Alexandrian dancer, the other a Libyan charioteer. Nor should it occasion surprise, still less incredulity, that two popular performers of the day should have borne the same name. It has long been realized that such performers regularly took professional names (*Künstlernamen*).[1] For example, at least six different pantomime dancers took the name Pylades after the famous dancer of that name in the age of Augustus, credited (wrongly, as it happens) with the invention of the art. Then there were six Apolausti, one of whom, originally called Maximinus, later took another famous name, to be known as the third of the four Parises (so far) on record.

Some names had masculine and feminine forms according to the sex of the performer. For example, Rhodos, appointed dancer of the Blues at Constantinople in 490, took the name Chrysomallus (Malalas 386). Procopius mentions two dancing girls called Chrysomallo, old cronies of the Empress Theodora (*Anecd.* xvii. 34–5). The dancer of the Reds in 490 was Helladius (Malalas, loc. cit.). Early in the next century we find a Helladius dancing for the Greens in Rome (Cassiodorus, *Var.* i. 20, i. 32), possibly, but by no means necessarily, the same man.[2] A few years later again we have three interesting epigrams by Leontius Scholasticus on a dancing girl called Helladia (*A. Pl.* 284, 286, 287), colour unspecified. With these we may compare the pantomime represented on the comb from Antinoe.[3] Possibly, again, the same dancer, but the date of the comb is uncertain, the locale different (though charioteers and pantomimes travelled widely), and the name standard.

---

[1] Friedlaender, *SG* iv[10] (1921), Appendix XIV.
[2] So C. Pietri, *MEFR* lxxxvii (1966), 127.   [3] See above, p. 74.

It is an interesting commentary on Porphyrius' double name to note that the numerous curse tablets directed against charioteers, in their anxiety to provide the devil with sufficient information to identify his intended victims, reveal that most had one professional name, some more than one: for example, from probably fourth- or fifth-century Rome we have Εὐστόργιος ὁ καὶ Δειονύσιος, Ἀρτέμιος ὁ καὶ Ὄσπης (Hospes), Εὐγένιος ὁ καὶ Κήρεος, and Εὐθύμιος ὁ καὶ Μάξιμος ὁ καὶ Γίδας.[1] Eustorgius, Artemius, and Eugenius are all attested as charioteers on contorniates, again from late fourth- or early fifth-century Rome. As for Euthumius, not only are there numerous contorniates bearing legends such as 'Eutumius', 'Euthumius', 'Eutimi vinicas [sic]', 'Eutimi nica'.[2] He may also be the 'Eutymius auriga' who, according to his tombstone (CIL vi. 10066 = ILS 5303) died at Rome in October 439. His signum Γίδας is a puzzle: were it not written thus more than a dozen times without variant, I would have suggested interpreting it Gigas, an obvious enough nickname and attested for a charioteer by CIL vi. 33946 (ILS 5288), 'Gigas agit(ator) factionis prasinae'.

There were two polyonymous Domnini in Rome at this period—indeed perhaps rather three, all evidently exact contemporaries since all are named on the very same curse tablet. First Δομνῖνος ὁ καὶ Θώραξ υἱὸς Φορτούνας (Fortuna), then Δομνῖνος ὁ καὶ Στρωμῶσος (Strumosus) υἱὸς Βικεντίας, and lastly Δομνῖνος ὁ καὶ Ζύζυφος υἱὸς Βικεντίας.[3] Editors have assimilated the last two into a composite Domninus/Strumosus/Zizyphus son of Vicentia. But since the whole point of listing all a man's names, and his mother's too, was to ensure that the malignant spirits did not slip up, it would surely have confused them unnecessarily to refer to the same man once as Domninus/Strumosus and then as Domninus/Zizyphus a few lines later on the same tablet. The wisest course would surely have been to use all three names both times, as in the case of Euthumius/Maximus/Gidas son of Paschasia, who (just to make sure) is named in full three times on the other side of the tablet. Certainly it would be strange for a mother to have given two sons the same name,

---

[1] Wuensch, Seth. Verfluch. 119.
[2] A. Alföldi, Die Kontorniaten, Taf. XII. 7, 10, 11; XXXV. 11; XL. 3; XLII. 1, 2, 3; LXIII. 8; LXIV. 2, 8.
[3] Wuensch, op. cit. 64–5, 119.

though it might have been the name of a famous charioteering father and there were the other names to distinguish them. Alternatively there might have been two Vicentias—not an unreasonable supposition, especially if it too was a stock professional name.

One of these three Domnini may have been the 'Domninus in Veneto' of another contorniate of the period,[1] though probably not Domninus/Thorax, who drove for the Greens (unless, like Porphyrius, he changed his colour). The name T(h)orax is also attested as a charioteer's name by Ammianus, on contorniates, and on an interesting mosaic from Gerona, probably of the third century.[2]

Before we leave the subject of multiple names, there is a couplet in one of the Uranius epigrams which ought perhaps to be taken seriously rather than viewed simply as a literary compliment:

Οὐράνιον, τῷ δῆμος ἀμετρήτους διὰ νίκας
ἠγαθέου Πέλοπος θῆκεν ἐπωνυμίην. (48. 3–4)

It may have been the custom for charioteers to be awarded such names by their fans in this way, and thereafter, no doubt, Uranius was styled Οὐράνιος ὁ καὶ Πέλοψ on the curse tablets which we may be sure existed in their thousands even in the Christian city of Constantinople in the age of Justinian.[3]

Porphyrius would have been entered thereon as Καλλιόπας ὁ καὶ Πορφύριος. Of the two, Porphyrius is the *Künstlername*. Malalas calls him just Καλλιόπας in his entry for the year 507, and Porphyrius is attested as a charioteer's name by two contorniates of an unusual design. The first is a fine specimen found (though not necessarily made) at Trier, with the legend 'Porfyr' on the obverse and 'Purfyrius' on the reverse. The other, also

[1] Alföldi, Taf. V. 2, with p. 24.
[2] Amm. Marc. xiv. 11. 12; *CIL* ii. 6180, with P. le Gentilhomme, *Transactions of the International Numismatic Congress 1936* (1938), 190 f. On the mosaic see A. Balil, *Boletin de la Real Academia de la Historia* 151 (1962), 257 f., Pls. 24 f.
[3] See the material collected in Ph. Koukoulès, Βυζαντινῶν Βίος iii (1949), 68 f. (especially Amphilocius, *PG* xxxvii. 1587) and H. J. Magoulias, 'The Lives of Saints as sources of data for the History of Magic in the sixth and seventh centuries A.D.: Sorcery, Relics and Icons', *Byzantion* xxxvii (1967), 242 f. Cf. too Theodore Balsamon, *PG* cxxxviii. 592 f. (translated by F. Dvornik, *BM* i (1946), 131). On the reasons behind the recourse to magic see particularly Peter Brown, 'Sorcery, Demons and the Rise of Christianity from Late Antiquity into the Middle Ages', in *Witchcraft, Confessions and Accusations* (Association of Social Anthropologists Monographs 9), 1970, 25–7, and below, p. 245.

perhaps from Gaul rather than Rome, with the legend 'Porfuri' and a horse's name on the obverse.[1] Neither piece can be dated except on stylistic grounds, so it cannot be regarded as certain that both refer to the same charioteer. But they are probably of the fifth century rather than the sixth, and neither is likely to be our Porphyrius.

From Martial xiii. 78 we know of a first-century charioteer of the Greens called Porphyrio. And interestingly enough the inscription in honour of Avillius Teres reveals to us a famous race-horse of late first-century Rome called 'Purpurio'.[2] Four centuries later we find a horse Φορφόρεος on a curse tablet from Rome.[3] Plainly both are by-forms, with respectively too little and too much aspiration, of the same name Porphyrius (-o). Thus the association of the name with the hippodrome was long established by the day of Calliopas Porphyrius.

Calliopas too recurs, though not till a century after Porphyrius, with Calliopas Trimolaimes, driver of the Greens in 610.[4] Putting aside mere coincidence, there are three possible explanations: (a) the man took Porphyrius' now famous given name as a *Künstlername*, (b) Calliopas was already a *Künstlername*, or (perhaps more likely, since Trimolaimes is obviously a nickname already) (c) he was a genuine descendant of Porphyrius.

To return to Porphyrius the dancer. Is it likely that a dancer would have taken a name generally associated with charioteers? In fact we do often find names common to more than one branch of the entertainment profession. In the early Empire there were three charioteers and one dancer called Eutychus, several charioteers and one gladiator called Felix.[5] In the early Byzantine period we have a pantomime called Margarites (Pearl) mentioned by Malalas in 490, another on some contorniates from rather earlier in the century, then there was a female pantomime Pelagia known professionally as Margarito (V. S. Pelagiae, *PG* cxvi. 916); it is also a name borne by gladiators.[6] The pantomime's name Chrysomallus (above) is borne by gladiators at an

---

[1] Alföldi, Taf. LIX. 11; LXI. 9, with pp. 23-4; see Pl. 31. 4-5.
[2] Cf. *Bull. com.* xxix (1901), 178.
[3] Wuensch, op. cit. 21. 12.
[4] John of Antioch, frag. 110, *Exc. de Insid.*, p. 150. 13 f. de Boor.
[5] Friedlaender, *SG* iv[10], p. 200.
[6] Malalas, 386; Alföldi, *Kont.*, Taf. LXIX. 2, 3, 7: Robert, *Les Gladiateurs*, 171. 296, 301.

earlier period.¹ Uranius is the stock name for the charioteer of the Blues in the Book of Ceremonies,² and of course there is also the Uranius of five epigrams in the Planudean series. Fifth-century contorniates show a dancer called Uranius.³ Roscius, a name associated with the stage in Cicero's day, turns up as a charioteer on contorniates.⁴ From Procopius we learn of a pantomime called Macedonia, very powerful with the Blues in sixth-century Antioch (*Anecd.* xii. 28 f.), from Luxorius of another in sixth-century Carthage.⁵ Again, a charioteer Macedonius turns up on a contorniate.⁶ Finally, to the tally of the Porphyrii listed above we may add a gladiator called Purpureus from Rome.⁷

To the best of my knowledge no other dancer called Porphyrius happens to stand on record, but our records of pantomimes in the late Empire are thin.⁸ And we do have an interesting slogan chalked up on a tavern wall in Pompeii, signed 'Purpurio cum Paridianis'.⁹ The Paridiani are a local fan club for the dancer Paris, and though Purpurio (a form of the name we have met already) may not actually have been a performer himself, obviously he was a man of the dancing world.

Before taking our leave of Porphyrius the dancer, we might spare a few lines for his colleague and rival, the Caramallus demanded by the Greens. Vasiliev devoted a lengthy but unsatisfactory discussion to Caramallus, overlooking two important texts¹⁰ and inclining to the conclusion that there was only one dancer of the name. In fact there were almost certainly three, if

¹ Robert, *Gladiateurs*, nos. 81 (p. 132), 263 (p. 218); cf. too A. Wilhelm, *Sitzb. d. Akad. d. Wiss. in Wien* 224. 1 (1946), 41.
² G. Millet, 'Les noms des auriges dans les acclamations de l'hippodrome', *Recueil d'Études . . . N. P. Kondakov* (1926), 279 f.
³ Alföldi, Taf. LXII. 9.   ⁴ Ibid. LIV. 3, 5.
⁵ *Anth. Lat.*² 310. 1 Riese, with Weinreich's commentary, *Epigramm und Pantomimus* (Sitzb. Heidelberg 1944–8), 112 f.   ⁶ Alföldi, Taf. LXI. 4.
⁷ See the mosaic from Torra Nuova illustrated in R. Auguet, *Les Jeux romains* (1970), 240–1.
⁸ Though not quite so thin as the 'fasti mimici ac pantomimici' in M. Bonaria's *Mimorum Romanorum Fragmenta* ii (1956) and (still sketchier) *Romani Mimi* (1965) would suggest. Bonaria's work was well received by reviewers (e.g. Garton, *Gnomon* 1967, 362–5), but his entries on individual pantomimes in *PW Suppl.* X did not come up to the standards of Louis Robert (*Bull. Épigr.* 1969, p. 442, no. 142).
⁹ *CIL* iv. 7919, with R. MacMullen, *Enemies of the Roman Order* (1967), 168, 338, n. 7.
¹⁰ *DOP* iv (1948), 47–8. Bonaria, *Mim. Rom. Frag.* ii (1956), 143–4, lists all sources but one, though without comment.

not four or five. The Caramallus of Aristaenetus (*Ep.* i. 26), teacher of the dancer Panarete, cannot unfortunately be dated precisely because Aristaenetus himself cannot be dated precisely. On the other hand the poem of Sidonius (*carm.* xxiii. 261 f.) which alludes to a famous Caramallus can be dated more closely—and twenty years earlier—than Vasiliev supposed, to *c.* 463.[1] Obviously not even the most sentimental crowd would have recalled to the arena in 520 a dancer famous by 463! An even earlier Caramallus is attested by another contorniate issue from Rome some time in the reign of Valentinian III (425–55).[2] He could be Sidonius' Caramallus, but does not have to be. Then there is the Caramallus presented to the Greens in 490 by Longinus the brother of Zeno, τὸν Αὐτοκύονα τὸν λεγόμενον Καράμαλλον ἀπὸ Ἀλεξανδρείας τῆς μεγάλης:[3] that is to say, he took the professional name Caramallus in addition to his given name Autokyon. The young dancer presented to the Greens in 490 could just be the favourite dancer of the Greens in 520, but it hardly seems likely. Lastly, there is another epigram by that devotee of the hippodrome, Leontius Scholasticus:

Μουσάων δεκάτη, Χαρίτων Ῥοδόκλεια τετάρτη,
τερπωλὴ μερόπων, ἄστεος ἀγλαΐη.
ὄμμα δέ οἱ καὶ ταρσὰ πεδήνεμα καὶ σοφὰ χειρῶν
δάκτυλα καὶ Μουσῶν κρέσσονα καὶ Χαρίτων. (*A. Pl.* 283)

This is the text of the same anthology Σπ that we have met already. Planudes' text has Καράμαλλε for Ῥοδόκλεια, a problematic reading. For 283 is one of a series of six parallel poems by Leontius, all on dancing-girls: and a female subject seems confirmed, not merely by the feminine τετάρτη, which could be emended easily enough to τέταρτος (though despite his masculine Καράμαλλε Planudes himself has τετάρτη), but by the phrase 'tenth of the Graces'. All modern editors have preferred Rhodocleia, no doubt rightly, but they have failed to provide an even half-way plausible explanation for Καράμαλλε supplanting Ῥοδόκλεια in even a wild text. I would suggest, merely

---

[1] W. B. Anderson's edition, i (1936), lvii.
[2] Alföldi, Taf. LXXII. 7, and cf. A. Maricq, *Byzantion* xxii (1952), 366 f. (with the remarks of J. and L. Robert, *Bull. Épigr.* 1954, 99–100). To Maricq's examples of the name add the inscription from Pisidian Antioch published by Barbara Levick, *Anatolian Studies* xvii (1967), no. 51, p. 119.
[3] Malalas, 386.

THE CHRONOLOGY OF PORPHYRIUS

as an improvement on Weinreich's unlikely suggestion that Rhodocleia was a pupil of Caramallus (or one of the Caramalli),[1] that Planudes copied the epigram from a source which also contained an epigram on Caramallus, where the name will naturally have stood in the first line, and probably in the same position in the line. Under such circumstances he might easily have substituted the wrong name in error.

On the other hand there is the curious parallel of a poem by Palladas on a dancer, which appears as *AP* xi. 255 (and in five other Byzantine collections) with the name Memphi(u)s, a stock dancer's name:

Δάφνην καὶ Νιόβην ὠρχήσατο Μέμφις ὁ Σῖμος,
ὡς ξύλινος Δάφνην, ὡς λίθινος Νιόβην.

And then again 200 poems later in the same book after xi. 441 with the name Πέτρος substituted for Μέμφις. In this case it could be that the poem was reused for a dancer with a different name, and despite the awkwardness of the female context in *A. Pl.* 283, it is just possible that here too an original epigram on Rhodocleia was clumsily adapted for a Caramallus by the simple expedient of changing the name. At all events, the Planudean text of the epigram is perhaps some slight evidence for the existence of yet another Caramallus, in the period of or after Leontius.

Porphyrius may not have been so common a name for a dancer as Caramallus, but we need not hesitate, I think, to accept that there were two of them. If there were three Domnini, all charioteers, performing simultaneously in the circus of fifth-century Rome, why should not two Porphyrii have exercised their different arts in the hippodrome of Constantinople a century later? In any event, even if Malalas *has* confused his source and *does* mean to refer to the charioteer in his account of the year 520, we cannot refer xv. 44 or monument D to this occasion.

One last point. The first three lines of 44 describe how Porphyrius has been awarded this new silver-and-bronze statue after earlier bronze ones. It continues:

πρέσβυ, σὺ δὲ ξείνων ἀντιάσας γεράων,
δήμου μὲν βοόωντος ἕλες παλίνορσον ἱμάσθλην,
ὡς δὲ δὶς ἡβήσας μαίνεαι ἐν σταδίοις.

[1] *Epigramm und Pantomimus*, 103–4.

'Old man, after receiving honours from abroad...', translates Paton, followed by Vasiliev. A perfectly acceptable translation of the line taken by itself, but when considered in its context, it is a little difficult to perceive the relevance of these 'foreign honours' to Porphyrius' emergence from retirement. In any event, it has been established already that γέρας in such epigrams must refer to a statue. But if Porphyrius has been winning statues, foreign or otherwise, then in what sense has he been living in retirement?

The answer is that ξείνων here means 'unprecedented', just as at 351–5, where Porphyrius' second statue is described as a ξεῖνον πρεσβήϊον. The participle ἀντιάσας refers, not to the brief period of Porphyrius' temporary retirement, but back over the whole course of his career. We should translate: 'Old man, having *already* won unprecedented honours [alluding to the two or three statues he had already won from each of the factions], at the clamour of the people you have taken up your whip once more and rage over the stadium in a second youth.' The relevance of line 4 to the sequence of thought in the poem as a whole is now clear.

We come now to the last monument, H. Its date, as we have seen, must be *c*. 545. δῆμος ἐλεύθερος αὖθις ἐγείρει at 360. 3 alludes to the three statues Porphyrius had won from the Blues some forty years before.

It may perhaps be felt that, since D describes a return from retirement while H does not even mention retirement, D should be placed after H. Nevertheless, I have preferred to place H last because of Porphyrius' age at the time, sixty.

Charioteers were evidently a tough breed, and did not give up early. The great Diocles had been forty-two when he retired, after twenty-four years of racing. Teres, still winning in 110 and probably even later, once raced a man already famous under Nero (54–68).[1] At least one and probably both must have had a very long career. Faustinus was an old man when he retired, as was his son Constantine when death cut short his career. In Constantine's case we happen to know that 'old age' meant, precisely, fifty (372. 3). Sixty was no doubt a quite exceptional age for any man still to be braving the hazards and exertion of

[1] L. Borsari, *Bull. com.* xxix (1901), 180.

the hippodrome. But it is by no means incredible. The race track has always been unique in this respect. 'Unlike boxers, baseball players, and football pros who are called old men at 35 and are retired by 40, jockeys have been active and in fact won some of the richest handicap races while in their late fifties.'[1] Constantine's career can be exactly paralleled by those of Gordon Richards, sixteenth to fiftieth (1920–54), or Doug Smith, fourteenth to fiftieth year (1931–67). The phenomenal American Johnny Longden retired in 1966 in his sixty-first year.

That Porphyrius retired not long after his sixtieth birthday is likely enough. That he came out of this retirement to race again and win monument D in his *seventh* decade is not easy to believe. We may suspect that by the time he was sixty Porphyrius had (in the manner of sportsmen) already retired once and staged a comeback. Uranius was to do the same a few years later (p. 142). The emphasis on Porphyrius' age seems stronger in the epigrams of H than in D (assuming that 345–6 belong with D), and on balance I would assign D to some such comeback in (perhaps) his fifties.

According to Malalas there was no more racing 'for a long time' after the suppression of the Nika riot in January 532.[2] In fact this is less help than one might have hoped in dating Porphyrius' monuments, since games seem to have been restored as early as 537, if not earlier still[3] (long enough, no doubt, for poor Malalas). If Porphyrius was about 20 in 500, then he would have been 35 in 515 and 52 in 532. So a five-year gap between 532 and 537 does not help to explain the twenty-year gap between

[1] There are other parallels between the careers of ancient charioteers and modern jockeys. For example, the total number of victories won in a successful career are of the same order of magnitude. Scorpus and Pompeius Musclosus won 2,048 and 3,559 respectively (*ILS* 5287. 19 f.). By the time of his early death in 1886 the great Fred Archer chalked up 2,749, a record not broken till Gordon Richards in 1943; Richards's 4,870 was surpassed in 1956 by Longden, whose own 6,032 was overtaken in 1970 by Willie Shoemaker, still only forty. Then as now a man would aim at 100 victories in a year (see p. 66) and 2/3,000 in a career. The information about Scorpus and Musclosus is provided by the inscription of Diocles, who had himself won only 1,462. But the inscription goes on to explain that Diocles' victories, though fewer, were for much higher purses. It would appear that there existed already in ancient times the distinction which Marvin Scott draws between the jockey who 'accepts all mounts offered him' and the 'money jock' who 'is not concerned with the number of mounts he receives but with getting the best mounts in the best races' (*The Racing Game* (1968), 54, 36, whence too the quotation in the text above). Unlike his two rivals, Diocles was a 'money jock'.
[2] Frag. 46, *Exc. de Insid.*, p. 172. 30.
[3] Stein, *Bas-Empire* ii (1949), 455 n. 1.

Porphyrius' Vitalian monument of 515 and his next. Both his last two monuments could fall after the restoration of games c. 537—or one might have been before, the other after. The monument which describes him as 60 (H) must in any case belong in c. 540. Perhaps he was in retirement for some at least of the long gap after 515, before being called out of retirement by popular demand.

THE LOCATION OF THE MONUMENTS ON THE SPINA

I had already established this order for the monuments on the grounds set out above before noticing an interesting consequence which, if the argument is accepted, would lend strong independent support to these results.

If B does belong before C, then the chronological order of Porphyrius' first three monuments from the Blues would be the same as their order in Planudes' series: A, B, C. And the next three monuments in Planudes' series (accepting my assignment of D to the Greens) are Porphyrius' three from the Greens in *reverse* chronological order: D, E (the Vitalian monument), and F (the new monument). This would surely be a very odd coincidence. Is it not rather a direct consequence of the location of the monuments on the spina?

The spina of the hippodrome of Constantinople has caused scholars a certain amount of trouble. The Byzantines called it εὔριπος,[1] κρηπίς, or τοῖχος,[2] the latter two terms clearly implying that it was a wall of some sort. But the excavations of 1927 revealed no trace of a wall, and the excavators went so far as to conclude that the spina was separated from the surrounding

---

[1] On the identification of the spina with the euripus see R. Guilland, *Jahrb. d. Öst. Byz. Gesell.* vi (1957), 29–32 (= *Études topogr.* i (1969), 445–7), or (better) C. Mango, 'L'euripe de l'hippodrome de Constantinople: essai d'identification', *RÉB* vii (1949), 180–93 (unknown to Guilland: P. Lemerle's summary rejection of Mango's thesis, ibid. viii (1950), 233, seems to me unjustified). The identification has now received strong confirmation in the new inscription from Thessalonica published by C. H. V. Sutherland, *Roman Imperial Coinage* vi (1967) 89 n. 1, attesting the decoration of a 'euripus' with statues by a mint official. Not of course a 'canal' (Sutherland), but the spina of the hippodrome of Galerius, useful support for the tetrarchic date Sutherland suggests for the inscription.

[2] Guilland, op. cit. 26 (443).

THE LOCATION OF THE MONUMENTS 181

arena by nothing more than a wooden fence.[1] This is implausible in itself (the chariots would have been constantly crashing into the statues and columns, damaging priceless works of art as well as themselves) and contradicted by a text to which attention was first drawn by R. Byron.[2]

Robert of Clari, who visited Constantinople in 1204, describes the spina as 'a wall which was a good fifteen feet high and ten feet wide' ('une masiere qui bien avoit quinze piés de haut et dis de lé').[3] Buondelmonti in 1422 saw only a 'non altus murus',[4] but if Panvinio's view of a deserted and silted-up hippodrome is correctly dated to not long after the Turkish sack, then the apparent contradiction is easily explained. The level of the ground has continued to rise, and is now some 4 to 5 metres higher than when the arena was in regular use. On the analogy of the hippodromes of Toledo, Mérida, and Thessalonica, which have the same over-all proportions as the Constantinopolitan hippodrome, one would expect the length of the spina to have been approximately 230 metres.[5]

On this high wall Robert saw (without unfortunately giving any details) 'statues of men and women and horses and oxen and camels . . . all made of copper'. This is paralleled by Clavijo's description quoted above (p. 7)—and the animal sculptures are borne out by Nicetas' list of hippodrome sculptures destroyed by the Crusaders,[6] including a death struggle between a hippopotamus and a crocodile. Only three of these monuments still survive *in situ*: the obelisk of Theodosius, the so-called obelisk

---

[1] S. Casson, 'Les fouilles à l'hippodrome de Constantinople', *Gazette des Beaux-Arts* 1930, 213 f.
[2] *The Byzantine Achievement* (1929), 72 n. 1.
[3] *La Conquête de Constantinople* (Les classiques français du Moyen Âge, ed. P. Lauer 1924), 88; cf. E. H. McNeal's English translation *The Conquest of Constantinople* (1936), 109.
[4] C. Mango, *REB* vii (1949), 181 n. 7.
[5] See the calculations in Michael Vickers's forthcoming study of the hippodrome at Thessalonica (*JRS* 1972), which will contain much of value on the layout of the hippodrome of Constantinople. On other spinae in Roman circuses see H. A. Harris, 'The starting gate for chariots at Olympia', *Greece and Rome* N.S. xv (1968), 114 f. There is apparently a well-preserved spina in the newly excavated hippodrome of Tyre, complete with obelisk and even some statues (see the preliminary publication by Emir Maurice Chébab in the *Illustrated Lonaon News* for 27 June 1970, p. 24 with figs. 17 and 18).
[6] See A. Cutler, 'The *de Signis* of Nicetas Choniates: a Reappraisal', *AJA* 1968, 113 f.

of Constantine Porphyrogenitus, and the Serpent column dedicated from the spoils of Plataea.

Charioteer statues were erected in the 'ground' (χῶρος) of their respective colours. Now the turning-posts (metae, καμπτῆρες, νύσσαι) at each end of the spina were called after the two major colours: the North end after the Blues, the South after the Greens.[1] So the extremities at any rate of the spina might well have been called Blue or Green 'ground'.

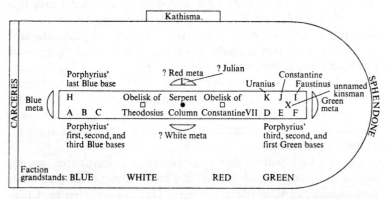

FIG. 2. Distribution of Charioteer Monuments on the Spina (purely schematic: properly the spina should be oblique to the main axis of the hippodrome)

It is not unlikely that the successive statues voted to Porphyrius by each faction were put up in a row in the order in which they were awarded. Purely *exempli gratia*, I have suggested one possible distribution in Fig. 2. We have seen that the collector copied down the epigrams from each face of each monument methodically one after another. If the monuments had been arranged in some such manner as I suggest, then it is natural that a man walking from one end of the spina to the other, collecting epigrams from monuments as he went, should have got the three early Blue monuments in chronological order and the three Green ones in reverse order. The spina was high, narrow, and evidently packed with statues, so some such methodical system would obviously have been desirable in the interests of both comprehensiveness and safety. H, put up by the Blues some forty years after their first three, may well have stood on the other side

[1] Guilland, op. cit. 28–9 (444–5).

THE LOCATION OF THE MONUMENTS 183

of the spina,[1] or at any rate somehow separated from the others, so that it was entered in the collection after the two blocks of three.

Constantine's statue, as we learn from 370. 1–2 (cf. 371. 1–2), stood next to those of both his father Faustinus and another unnamed relative. Uranius' statue stood close to those of both Faustinus and Constantine (48. 1–2). All four stood in the ground of the Greens (p. 142). Now we know that three statues of Porphyrius also stood in Green territory, and it will be argued in the next chapter that some (if not all) of these statues had already been erected by Uranius' heyday. Yet 48 says nothing of the proximity of Uranius to Porphyrius: only to Faustinus and Constantine. Presumably the Uranius–Faustinus–Constantine group stood a little apart from the Porphyrius group.

There are only two references in Byzantine texts other than the charioteer epigrams themselves to the charioteer stelae of the hippodrome: Pseudo-Codinus (see p. 111), who says nothing about their exact whereabouts inside the hippodrome, and Nicetas Choniates, who gives some very precise information.[2] Next to an unnamed martial female (? an Athene)[3] and close to the turning-post of the Reds, that is (he adds) the Eastern turning-post, stood some statues of charioteers (ἁρματηλάται ἄνδρες ἀνεστηλῶντο). If there was a Red turning-post, presumably there was a White one too, but where were they and what was their purpose? No other text referring to this or any other hippodrome ever suggests that there were more than the two normal turning-posts at each end of the spina. Nor can we assume that either Nicetas or some copyist simply confused the colours, since the additional detail that this was an 'Eastern' turning-post is clearly designed to distinguish it from the two main ones, to the North and South respectively.

Moreover, Nicetas appears to treat this Red one as a genuine turning-post, for he describes how the charioteer statues there by the gestures of their hands warned those approaching the

---

[1] According to Guilland, *BS* xxx (1969), 213, the monuments on the spina were arranged in two rows, 'disposées en file'. This may well have been so, but Clavijo, to whom he refers for support, says nothing of the sort.
[2] *de Signis* § 11, p. 865. 19 f. Bonn.
[3] The author of the *Parastaseis* (Preger, p. 60. 13 f. = p. 190. 18 f.) mentions a statue in the hippodrome which some held to be Verina, the wife of Leo I, but in his judgement was 'an Athena from Greece'.

post (προσπελῶντας τῇ νύσσῃ) that they must not relax the bit but rather apply the whip and edge their rival into the outside position.

There would seem to be two possible explanations. Either the statues are envisaged as giving advance warning about the main turning-posts coming up, or the spina was not in fact the straightforward rectangle (at least at Constantinople) that it is always shown as on gems and mosaics. The *metae* are usually represented as semi-circles, sometimes slightly detached from the main body of the spina. Perhaps at Constantinople there were two extra such semi-circles projecting from the spina at its centre, so that the ensemble was cruciform in shape (see Fig. 2).

Nicetas refers to statues in the plural standing very close (ἄγχιστα) to this Red *meta*. Hardly Porphyrius, Uranius, or the family of Faustinus, since a Red *meta* could not very well be counted either Green or Blue territory. But among them we may perhaps reckon Julian, who according to 386–7 was driver of the Reds—probably *c.* 500 (see p. 205).

The narrow spina was packed with the statuary of 1000 years by the sixth century. When a new statue was fitted into one of the few remaining places it might find itself cheek by jowl with some very choice or striking item, and it is only natural that the epigrams on the bases of such latecomers should from time to time allude to their neighbours. Hence the allusions in the Constantine and Uranius epigrams. Another good illustration is provided by a pair of epigrams written for a statue of Anastasius, curiously enough made of iron. John the Lydian[1] says it was in the hippodrome and the lemmata in the Anthology fix it precisely on the spina.[2] The epigrams are not the true inscription from the base of the statue, but a pair of very clever satirical substitutes. The first will be discussed in the following chapter (p. 219); here is the second:[3]

[1] *De magg.* iii. 46.
[2] ἐν τῷ Εὐρίπῳ, both the Palatine and Planudean lemmata.
[3] There are two versions, *AP*/*A. Pl.* and John. John, a contemporary perhaps already present in Constantinople when the poems were written, might seem prima facie a better witness, though editors of the Anthology have always followed *AP* throughout. In fact the variants may be very early, since the original is not likely to have been on public show for verification very long, and I have pursued an eclectic policy. Beckby's app. crit. gives little assistance; see rather Preger, *Inscr. Metr. Graec.* nos. 224–5, or Wuensch's app. to John ad loc. The main difference is John's alternative line for 271. 1 (γείτονα δὲ Σκύλλης ὀλοὴν ἀνέθεντο Χάρυβδιν),

ἐγγύθι τῆς Σκύλλης χαλεπὴν στήσαντο Χάρυβδιν,
ἄγριον ὠμηστὴν τοῦτον Ἀναστάσιον.
δείδιθι καὶ σύ, Σκύλλα, τεαῖς φρεσί, μὴ σὲ καὶ αὐτὴν
βρώξῃ, χαλκείην δαίμονα κερματίσας. (AP xi. 271)

Because of the parsimony for which he was commonly (but unfairly) reproached, Anastasius is said to be an all-devouring Charybdis, a fit partner for the Scylla he stands next to. But Scylla is told to watch out lest Anastasius swallow even her up, turning her bronze into coin.[1] Obviously the whole point of the epigram turns on the proximity of a bronze statue of Scylla. There was just such a bronze Scylla. Nicetas describes how it suffered at the hands of the Crusaders precisely the fate our epigram had foretold.[2] And one of the recently discovered *Epigrammata Bobiensia*, bearing the lemma *in Scyllam Constantinopolitanam in circo*,[3] provides irrefutable evidence that it was already there by c. 400 (the date of the collection) at latest, and probably earlier, since the poem has every sign of being a translation from a Greek original.[4] Whether or not this lampoon was ever actually attached to the statue,[5] if only for a matter of hours, it was clearly written with the exact location of the statue in mind—and for an audience who knew its exact location.

There are some details in the Porphyrius epigrams which can only be properly appreciated if the monuments are similarly visualized *in situ*.

providing textual support with the δέ for his treating the eight lines together as one epigram. Since the two parts deal with quite separate topics I have preferred to regard them as two separate epigrams, and accordingly follow *AP* here, as too in 270. 2. At 270. 4, however, John's text (as emended by Fuss, John's first editor in 1812) seems to me markedly superior to *AP/A. Pl.* (see p. 220).

[1] So LSJ, rightly, for κερματίσας.   [2] *de Signis* 7.
[3] Ed. F. Munari (1955), no. 51 (*aeni* in l. 3 proves the statue described to have been of bronze). There is a good chance that it is this Scylla which Themistius, long resident in Constantinople, describes in his *Or.* xxii, 279b (ii, p. 70 Downey–Norman); and a possibility that it is the subject of the anonymous epigram *AP* ix. 755, though there is no pointer to Constantinople here and obviously there may have been other bronze Scyllas. There is a rather uncertain reference to a Scylla at *Patria Cpoleos* ii. 190. 14.
[4] Like so many in the collection: see (apart from the editions of Munari and Speyer) Munari in *Philologus* cii (1958), 127 f., and (on this poem) Speyer, *Naucellius und seine Kreis* (1959), 83–4.
[5] For the hanging of satirical inscriptions on statues cf. (e.g.) Suetonius, *Caes.* 80; *Aug.* 70; *Tib.* 52; *Nero* 45. And in general on Greek epigrams which parody the traditional motifs of the genre, L. Robert, *Hellenica* iv (1948), 98 (Palladas), and *L'Épigramme grecque* (Fondation Hardt 1969), 181 f. (Lucillius).

Epigram 344. 5 assures Porphyrius that only Lysippus could have done justice to the greatness of his victory:

ἔπρεπέ σοι Λύσιππον ἔχειν ἐπιμάρτυρα νίκης.

Why Lysippus? Not, I would suggest, simply because Lysippus was a great sculptor. It is true that his name occurs often in the epigrams of the Anthology—but without exception in a description of an actual statue by Lysippus.[1] Now Constantinople had a fine collection of original Lysippan bronzes. His Kairos, described in an epigram of Poseidippus,[2] and his Samian Hera were in the Lauseion, and so presumably destroyed in the fire of 475.[3] And on the spina itself stood one of his most famous works, the colossal sitting Heracles Trihesperus,[4] brought from Tarentum to Rome and thence to Constantinople, where it was thrown down but not apparently destroyed by the Crusaders, since Gilles saw it in the 1540s.[5] There was in addition an unbridled rearing bronze horse, which might well be the similar Lysippan horse described by Philip of Thessalonica (see p. 201). All these works were in bronze, like the Porphyrius monument in question. It is easy to see how naturally it occurred to the Porphyrian poet to wish that a Lysippus had been able to cast Porphyrius' statue.

It appears from 345. 1, ἐγγύθι τῆς Νίκης καὶ Ἀλεξάνδρου βασιλῆος, that Green monument D was close to statues of Nike and Alexander. And from 341. 2, ἔστησαν Νίκης ἐγγύθι Πορφύριον, that Blue monument B was also close to a statue of Nike. Perhaps the same Nike, midway between the areas of the two factions. There is no other reference to this Alexander, but let us hazard a guess. Far and away the most famous bronze Alexanders (Robert of Clari remarked that all the statues on the spina were bronze) were those of Lysippus, according to the well-known story the

[1] This can easily be verified through Beckby's Index nominum s.v. Lysippos.
[2] *A. Pl.* 275, with Gow and Page, *Hellenistic Epigrams* ii (1965), 499–500.
[3] Cedrenus, i. 564.
[4] For sources see J. Overbeck, *Die antiken Schriftquellen zur Gesch. d. Bildenden Künste bei d. Griechen* (1868), 278–9, and L. Sternbach, *Jahres. Öst. Arch. Inst.* 1902, Beibl. 82; Λυσιμάχου in Nicetas, p. 687 Bonn, must be a slip (perhaps Nicetas' own) for Λυσίππου. The epigrams on the statue by Geminus and Philip of Thessalonica (*A. Pl.* 103–4) appear to misunderstand Lysippus' purpose (Lippold, *PW* xiv. 51 f. Gow and Page, *Garland of Philip* ii (1968), 298). Agathias' epigram (*A. Pl.* 332) on Lysippus' tableau of Aesop and the seven wise men may indicate that this too was in Constantinople, though Agathias might only have been copying an earlier epigram on the work.
[5] *De Topographia Cpoleos* (1561 edn.), 89–91: cf. Cutler, *AJA* 1968, 117 n. 51.

THE LOCATION OF THE MONUMENTS

only man Alexander himself had allowed to cast him in bronze.[1] Nothing but the best was good enough for Constantine when he robbed the museums of the world to beautify his new capital,[2] and he would obviously want an Alexander. It is quite on the cards that the Alexander which stood next to Porphyrius was a Lysippus.[3]

[1] Pliny, *NH* vii. 152: Lysippus made several, Pliny, xxxiv. 63. *A. Pl.* 119–20, dubiously ascribed to Posidippus and Asclepiades or Archelaus, are on Lysippan Alexanders: see Gow and Page, *Hellenistic Epigrams* ii (1965), 146–7, 498–9.

[2] Cf. Jerome, *Chron.*, s.a. 330, 'dedicatur Constantinopolis omnium paene urbium nuditate', and p. 201 below. We can now add to the tally of statues transported to the hippodrome one of Pompey's friend Theophanes of Mytilene, no doubt moved from Mytilene to Constantinople on the foundation of the city; the base has been published by L. Robert in *CRAI* 1969, 52 f.

[3] Not necessarily genuine: it is unlikely that many Byzantines would have been able to tell the difference. On the curious attitude of the Byzantines to their incomparable store of antique statuary see Mango's paper in *DOP* xvii (1963), 55 f.

VI

THE LESSER LIGHTS

ONCE dated (as they can be) relative to the monuments of Porphyrius, the epigrams on Julian, Faustinus, Constantine, and Uranius will cast further light on the career of Porphyrius and its significance in the development of chariot-racing at Constantinople. We may begin, not this time with the epigrams from the monuments, but with a series of iambic poems (two on each charioteer) which describe paintings of Porphyrius, Faustinus, Julian, and Constantine on the ceiling of a gallery in the Kathisma. These poems, not being contemporary, are important only for what they tell us about the paintings. But before we can properly assess the date and significance of the paintings, it will be appropriate to establish the date and character of the poems.

THE IAMBIC POEMS

Early editors (followed, e.g., by Vasiliev) ascribe the poems to Thomas the Patrician, author of the elegiac quatrain which immediately precedes them (*A. Pl.* 379). This is simply an error. In both Planudes' autograph and the BM apograph all eight are left anonymous. Nevertheless it will not be irrelevant to begin by discussing Thomas' poem, partly because it provides an appropriate introduction to the iambic poems, partly to justify my exclusion of Anastasius, the charioteer commemorated therein, from the list of lesser lights given above. Here is the poem:

> Τὸν θρασὺν ἡνιοχῆα λελασμένον ἅρματος ἄθλων
> ἐνθάδ' Ἀναστάσιον κείμενον οὖδας ἔχει,
> ὃς τόσσους ἀνεδήσατο πρὶν στεφάνους, ὅσα ἄλλοι
> ἔδρακον ἡνιόχων ἤματα ἱππασίης.

According to Beckby, Thomas flourished 'um 550'. He does not offer any justification for this apparent precision: the casual reader might assume that there were solid grounds for selecting this century rather than (say) the fifth or seventh. There are none. If I had to make a guess, I should propose the ninth or tenth.

In the first place, the title which Planudes carefully records for Thomas, λογοθέτης τοῦ δρόμου, is not attested before the eighth century, and for various reasons it is unlikely that it existed before then. Of the fourteen holders of the office between the eighth and tenth centuries whose rank is attested, eight were (like Thomas) patricians. A list of the logothetes for this period recently published by D. A. Miller shows only one Thomas, holding office in about 907 and then again in 913.[1] At the time Miller was unaware of the evidence of Planudes' lemma, but he now tells me that he would refer it to this Thomas. Naturally we must leave open the possibility of more than one Thomas holding the post (the name is hardly rare), though it is suggestive that the father of Thomas the logothete of 907 and 913, Constantine the Armenian, was a (naturally amateur) charioteer (he used to race against the Emperor Michael III in the hippodrome of St. Mamas).[2] It would be understandable for his son to have followed the sport more keenly than most. If the identification holds, then our poem would be firmly anchored in the first quarter of the tenth century. Even without it we are surely in the right period.

Certainly the metrical technique of the poem points to the ninth or tenth century rather than the sixth. In line 3 Beckby writes ὃς τόσσους ἀνέδησε τὸ πρὶν in order to restore a tolerable caesura. An earlier suggestion (probably Musurus') is recorded as a 'scholion' in the Wechel edition:[3] ὃς τόσσους στεφάνους ἀνεδήσατο πρίν, ὅσα ἄλλοι. Neither is necessary, or even plausible, and Beckby's is positively damaging (in so far as it is possible for such a line to sustain further damage). In this sense and context the middle of ἀναδέω is required: see the passages quoted by LSJ s.v. I. 1, to which many additions could be made. R. C.

---

[1] 'The Logothete of the Drome in the Middle Byzantine Period', *Byzantion* xxxvi (1966), 438–70. To Miller's documentation on this Thomas add Bury, *Eastern Roman Empire* (1912), 460, who shows that he was the father of the historian Genesius as well as son of the Constantine quoted in the text above.
[2] Symeon, the continuator of George the Monk (= Theophanes continuatus, ed. Bonn), p. 835. 6 f. (making Constantine a White), and Theophanes continuatus (a later work), p. 198. 16 (making him a Green).
[3] See p. 194 n. 3 below.

McCail argued in *Byzantion* xxxviii (1968), 563 that νίκας...
ἀναδησάμενον in Agathias *Hist.* i. 15. 10 was an echo of ἀνεδήσατο νίκας in Simonides 10 Bergk. This is a possibility in view of their common use of the plural νίκας, but there are many other examples in late writers, from ἀνεδήσατο νίκην in Nonnus, *Dion.* xix. 295 and Paul Sil., *Ecphr.* 977 down to νίκην ἀνεδήσατο in the humble Marcus Diaconus, *V. Porphyrii* 2. 18. With Thomas' phrase compare Himerius, *Or.* xxxi. 3, τοῖς ... ἀναδησαμένοις τὸν στέφανον. It is obviously most unlikely that Thomas would have varied this standard formula.

Caesura-less hexameters are not uncommon in tenth-century poetry (cf. Arethas' λαμπάδ᾽ ἐλαίῳ φαιδρύνουσα φιλοπτωχείης at *AP* xv. 34. 9), and we must certainly accept 379. 3 as Planudes gives it.

Other pointers to a late date are the ugly hiatus ὅσα ἄλλοι and ἤματα ἱππασίης, without parallel in the careful and correct epigrams from the monuments, but common by the tenth century: compare (from Cometas) σεῖο ἀθρήσας (xv. 36. 1) and τεύξατο ἀμφοτέρους (37. 2).

It should in any case be emphasized that Planudes did not get either 379 or the eight iambic poems from the same source as the series of charioteer epigrams proper, 335–78. In modern editions of the Planudea, 379 (as its number suggests) follows directly after 378, but in the Marcianus they are separated by two sections of poems on other subjects, εἰς εἰκόνας βακχῶν and εἰς εἰκόνας βασιλέων. Then comes the section containing these nine poems, headed ἔτι εἰς τὰς στήλας τῶν ἐν τῷ ἱπποδρόμῳ ἡνιόχων, ὀφείλοντα τοῖς προλαβοῦσι συνάπτεσθαι. In fact εἰς στήλας is hardly an appropriate heading. Number 379 is plainly a sepulchral epigram for the tomb of a charioteer (ἐνθάδε... κείμενον, line 2), not a commemorative monument. And the iambic poems are ecphrastic: they describe paintings or mosaics.

Different as they are from the series 335–78, for the purposes of his anthology (and reasonably enough) Planudes intended that they should be assimilated to the epigrams genuinely written εἰς στήλας ἡνιόχων (as they are in all apographs, including BM 16409, and in the printed editions). But they are clearly an addendum, taken from elsewhere in Planudes' exemplar (or quite possibly even from a different source altogether, especially in view of their date).

THE IAMBIC POEMS 191

The iambic poems are not by Thomas the logothete.[1] Yet I suspect they belong much closer to his day than to that of the charioteers they describe. Vasiliev, indeed, remarks as though it were a self-evident and incontestable fact that the two on Porphyrius 'were composed soon after Porphyrius' death' (p. 41). I should place them some 300–400 years later, give or take a century.

In the first place, it is clear that all four charioteers had long been dead when the epigrams were written. This is shown not merely by the tone of the poems as a whole, but by a number of specific references. Faustinus is τὸ κλέος πρὶν Πρασίνων (382. 4), and ὁ πρὶν ἁρματηλάτης (383. 1). Constantine drove τοῖς πάλαι χρόνοις, and all is gloom since τοῦτον ἥρπασεν Χάρων (385. 1, 3). At 386. 1 all four are τοὺς πάλαι τεθνηκότας. Now there is no reason to suppose that all four died at even approximately the same time. Constantine, who lived to be fifty, was the son of Faustinus, and so some twenty-five or thirty years his junior. And it is likely, as we shall see, that Porphyrius too outlived Faustinus (and Julian) by some thirty years at least. In 381 he is a beardless youth, though we know that he lived to be at least sixty. In these epigrams all four are lumped together as τοὺς πάλαι τεθνηκότας, as though the author lived in an altogether different and distant age.

Next, metrical and stylistic features again. The convenient term 'iambic' has been used so far to describe the metre of the epigrams. In fact all eight are written in what Paul Maas more accurately christened the 'Byzantine twelve-syllable', a refinement of the old iambic trimeter to suit the Byzantine ear.[2] The classical principle of resolution depended on a distinction between vowels in point of quantity: a long vowel was felt to be equivalent to two shorts. But when this distinction began to disappear in the course of the early Byzantine period, resolution became steadily less common, till it finally disappeared altogether. An intermediate stage is represented by the epics of George of Pisidia

---

[1] That is to say, *pace* editors before Beckby, they were not ascribed to him by Planudes. It might be rash to exclude the possibility altogether, though there is nothing but their probable date in its favour.

[2] 'Der byzantinische Zwölfsilber', *BZ* xii (1903), 278–323 (brief summary in F. Dölger, *Die byzantinische Dichtung in der Reinsprache* (1948), 39 f.). Cf. too the preface to N. Panayotakis's edition of Theodosius the Deacon's poem (written in 963), Ἅλωσις τῆς Κρήτης (Heracleion 1960), 25 f.

early in the seventh century, which admit all the classical resolutions—but infrequently. Half a century before then we have *AP* i. 11 from the reign of Justin II, with as many as seven resolutions in four lines. All 32 lines of our eight epigrams have exactly twelve syllables.

As for prosody, vowels are treated freely in proper names, and though the poet is obviously trying to observe classical quantities, his divergences are not limited to the so-called δίχρονα (α, ι, υ). That is to say we find Βενέτων(ου) (380. 3, 381. 2) alongside Πρασίνων (382. 4, 383. 2), Πορφύριος (380. 3, 381. 2), and Κωνσταντῖνος (384. 1, 385. 1). Nor is this feature limited to proper names. At 386. 1 editors have always printed Lascaris' correction χεὶρ οἶδε γεννᾶν τοὺς πάλαι τεθνηκότας for Planudes' χείρ, ἴδε, γεννᾷ τοὺς πάλαι τεθνηκότας. Certainly it is a skilful and attractive emendation. But is it necessary? Its only *raison d'être* is to remove a 'false' quantity that would have seemed perfectly acceptable to a Byzantine ear. Compare Manuel Philes, ed. E. Miller, i, Cod. Esc. clxxii. 22, πλὴν ἴδε καὶ τὸ χρῶμα... (same sedes). If the poems are indeed as late as I believe, then we should probably keep ἴδε, γέννᾳ.

Modern editors have followed Brunck in 'mending' the metre of 385. 1,

Κωνσταντῖνος ἦν, ἀλλὰ τοῖς πάλαι χρόνοις,

by inserting a γ' before ἦν. It is probably not necessary.

More problematic is the question of the accentuation of the proper name. Planudes wrote Κωνσταντῖνος, both here and at the end of 384. 1. All editors since Boissonade have removed the 'false quantity' that the perispomenon might seem to underline by writing Κωνσταντίνος. This is not a question that can be answered in isolation. Planudes was not alone in writing a perispomenon in such cases, though it is not always easy to discover the facts from printed editions.

For example, Κωνσταντίνος (or -ίνου) appears regularly in E. Miller's edition of Manuel Philes (e.g. Cod. Esc. lxv. 4, lxxxiii. 9). It is only from the preface to his second volume[1] that we learn that Miller took it on himself silently to correct the accentuation of his MS.: for (e.g.) ψῦχος, where the metre required it, he always printed ψύχος, for Κωνσταντῖνος, -ίνος, etc.

[1] ii (Paris 1857), xvi–xvii.

('absurdum erat accentu circumflexo... vocales illas tunc notare...').

I do not wish to suggest that there is a clear-cut decision for editors of such texts. A case in point is the twelfth-century poet Eugenius of Palermo, whose works survive in one fourteenth-century MS. (Laur. V. 10). They were first published by L. Sternbach,[1] who followed the apparently quite haphazard accentuation of the MS.: e.g. (all at the line-end) δῦθι (i. 132), ἀμῦναι (ix. 25), ἀκτῖσι (x. 51, xxiv. 8), but also κηλῖδα (iv. 6), μῦθον (ix. 11), φῦλα (xxi. 22). At i. 68 we have διαδράναι, at vi. 78 διαδρᾶναι. The MS. has been collated afresh by M. Gigante for his edition of 1964 (published, appropriately enough, at Palermo), and (e.g.) what Sternbach read as ὠδῖνας at i. 46 and τύφος at iv. 43 Gigante saw as ὠδίνας and τῦφος. But whichever pair of eyes we trust, the general picture of chaos is not affected, and there is an obvious case for bringing some order into it. K. Horna was for writing the acute accent everywhere,[2] while Gigante decided for the circumflex (even where the MS. gave an acute). P. Speck has now renewed Horna's plea for the acute, both in Eugenius[3] and in Theodore Studites.[4]

But to the best of my knowledge there is no manuscript support for Κωνσταντίνος metri gratia in Byzantine twelve-syllable verse. There are two examples of Κωνσταντῖνος at the end of a line in the early tenth-century poet Constantine of Rhodes: AP xv. 16. 4 (predictably 'corrected' by editors) and line 55 of his ecphrasis on the Seven Wonders of Constantinople.[5] The manuscript that carries the latter work is of the fifteenth century, but the Palatinus is perhaps no more than half a century younger than Constantine himself. Then in the early eleventh century we have John Mauropous (no. 31. 38 de Lagarde) and Christopher of Mitylene (nos. 18. 3 and 55. 10). Sternbach claimed that the only manuscript which preserves this part of Christopher 18 gave -ίνος, but Horna confirmed -ῖνος, which Kurtz printed,[6] remarking in the preface to his edition that ordinary words do

---

[1] BZ xi (1902), 406–51.   [2] BZ xiv (1905), 474.
[3] BZ lviii (1965), 82.
[4] Theodoros Studites: Jamben (Supplem. Byz. i, Berlin 1969), 83–4.
[5] Published by E. Legrand (with commentary by T. Reinach) in RÉG ix (1896), 40 f.—also published separately under the title Description des œuvres d'art et de l'église des Saint-Apôtres de Constantinople par Constantin le Rhodien (Paris 1896).
[6] See E. Kurtz's edition (Leipzig 1903), xxii, n. 1.

sometimes bear an acute on the penultimate in such cases (e.g. πράσιν for πρᾶσιν), but proper names never.[1] For example, even Νῶε (Noah) is found at the end of a line. It would be interesting if this could be established as a general rule, but it would involve a good deal of laborious study of MS. accentuation, and the result would probably be inconclusive.

Planudes' own practice elsewhere in the Marcianus is not altogether consistent—nor does it agree with that of the Palatinus. Compare the first line of the anonymous iambic poem (of c. A.D. 566) ix. 804. 1,

$$\text{'}Ἰουστῖνὸν κατὰ χρέος τὸν δεσπότην$$

The Palatinus has 'Ιουστίνον, Planudes the regular 'Ιουστῖνον.

Latin names ending -atus generally make -ᾶτος in Greek.[2] At A. Pl. 35. 2,

$$Παλμᾶτον^3 ἰθυδίκην τόσσον ἀγασσάμενοι,$$

we have only Planudes, who accented the name *both* paroxytone and properispomenon! Which were his final thoughts? As it happens it is possible to decide. As D. C. C. Young realized, BM Add. 16409 was copied from the Marcianus before Planudes made his own final revisions.[4] At A. Pl. 35. 2 it gives just Παλμᾶτον. It would seem that when revising, Planudes felt unhappy about the 'false' quantity the circumflex involved, and so changed it to an acute.

However, it is significant that he did not change the circumflex on 'Ιουστῖνος at ix. 804. 5—or the Κωνσταντῖνος of 384. 1 and 385. 1. Is this perhaps because he viewed them all alike as Byzantine twelve-syllables, which he knew to be governed by somewhat different rules from an elegiac distich composed (however badly) on the classical model?

No firm conclusions can be drawn. The Byzantines do not seem to have quite made up their minds. But some at least seem to have felt able to pronounce a syllable with a circumflex accent

[1] Kurtz, pp. viii–ix.
[2] W. S. Allen, 'Tone and Stress in Ancient Greek', *To honor R. Jakobson* (1967), 55.
[3] Editors quite unnecessarily save the metre by printing Παλμᾶν, first attested in a scholion in the Wechel edition of 1600 and so probably a conjecture of Musurus (see J. Hutton, *The Greek Anthology in Italy to the year 1800* (1935), 155 f.).
[4] *Parola del passato* x (1955), 197 f., and above, p. 107.

'short' and who are we to tell them they could not? Planudes was not a mechanical copyist, but a scholar who was apparently aware of this problem. Till more evidence is available we should probably do best to follow his example and retain Κωνσταντῖνος in these two pieces of developed Byzantine work.

Perhaps the most obvious feature of the 'Byzantine twelve-syllable' is the regulation of the accent at various positions in the line. In its developed form every line ends with a paroxytone. George of Pisidia is well on the way here, but does admit a number of exceptions.[1] There are no exceptions in the 32 lines under consideration.

A proparoxytone word was sought before the hephthemimeral caesura, oxytone avoided, paroxytone tolerated. In our poems we find five proparoxytones, two paroxytones, and one oxytone.

At the penthemimeral caesura an oxytone was sought, proparoxytone avoided, paroxytone tolerated. Our poet has only two proparoxytones, but prefers paroxytone to oxytone in the ratio 19:11. This is understandable in work of the ninth to tenth century, for regulation of the penthemimeral caesura did not become strict till later. We may compare the corpus of ninth- to tenth-century poems recently published by Robert Browning, where 'the accentuation of the hephthemimeral caesurae shows a marked approximation to later Byzantine practice, while that of the penthemimeral caesurae is still relatively labile'.[2] Much the same could be said of our poems.

No less clear a pointer are the numerous and striking stylistic parallels with ecphrastic epigrams of the ninth century and later. The most obvious general feature is the insistence on how life-like the paintings are—a motif common enough, of course, in earlier ecphrastic poetry,[3] but developed to a monotonously stylized emphasis in Byzantine work. This is the more remarkable in that, much as we moderns have come in recent years to admire

---

[1] See Maas's study (op. cit.) *passim*, and (for George, briefly) A. Pertusi, *Giorgio di Pisidia: poemi* i (Stud. patr. et byz. 7), 1960, 43 f.
[2] *Byzantion* xxxiii (1963), 295.
[3] e.g. *AP* ix. 713 f. A striking anticipation of the developed Byzantine style is Philip's iambic poem on a bronze horse, *AP* ix. 777 (on which see again below, p. 202 n. 1). I suspect that Philip's iambic epigrams were not without influence (via Cephalas) on Byzantine epigrammatists. Another 'Byzantine' tendency in Philip (long noted) is towards a paroxytone line ending (Maas, *Greek Metre*, § 21). One that has not been emphasized is his avoidance of resolution: several of his poems are twelve-syllabic throughout. The whole question deserves further study.

Byzantine art, the last thing we should say in its defence is that it was lifelike. Yet it is plain from what they say that the Byzantines themselves *did* see, or affected to see, their art as naturalistic.[1] The commonest motif of ecphrastic poetry is that the saint/ virgin/prophet or whoever is so lifelike that he is on the point of speaking (or else astonishment is expressed that he does not speak, or some such variation on the theme). Most of the usual clichés duly turn up in our eight epigrams. A selective commentary on some characteristic features in them will make the point more clearly than a general exposition.

ἐν γῇ κρατήσας παντὸς ἁρματηλάτου
καλῶς ἐπήρθη καὶ πρὸς αἰθέρα τρέχειν
Πορφύριος, τὸ θαῦμα δήμου Βενέτων·
νικῶν γὰρ οὗτος πάντα γῆς διφρηλάτην
ἄνεισιν, ὡς ἂν καὶ σὺν ἡλίῳ δράμοι.[2]   (380)

For ἄνεισιν,[3] usually of Christ/prophets/beggars, etc. rising to heaven, almost always first word in the line, compare Manuel Philes, i, Cod. Esc. xxi. 3 (of Christ), ἄνεισιν εἰς φῶς εἰς παλίνζωον βίον: xxvi. 86, ἄνεισι τοίνυν εὐκλεῶς ἐριτίμως | εἰς οὐρανίους καὶ φεραυγεῖς παστάδας: cxxxix. 3, of the κλῖμαξ of John Climacus, δι' ἧς τρέχων ἄνεισιν: cxlvii. 6, ἄνεισι . . . And with the πρὸς αἰθέρα of line 2 (repeated at 382. 5) compare *Anecd. Paris.* iv. 311. 19–20, ἐκ γῆς ὁ δοῦλος σήμερον πρὸς αἰθέρα | ἄνεισι φαιδρός: Constantine of Rhodes, *Ecphrasis*, 360: ἐκ γῆς ἀναθρώσκοντα πρὸς τὸν αἰθέρα.

Ἴουλον ἀνθῶν πρῶτον οὗτος ἡνίας
Πορφύριος Κάλχαντος εἷλκε Βενέτου.
ἐκπλήττομαι δέ, πῶς γράφει χεὶρ ἐμπνόους
τούτου τις ἵππους. καὶ γὰρ ἂν πλήξῃ πάλιν,
οἶμαι, δραμεῖται νῖκος εὑρεῖν καὶ πάλιν.   (381)

3: ἐκπλήττομαι. Compare Christopher, 122. 1, ἐκπλήττομαί σου τὴν σοφὴν τεχνουργίαν.

[1] See especially Cyril Mango, 'Antique Statuary and the Byzantine Beholder', *DOP* xvii (1963), 55 ff., at pp. 65 f.
[2] Brunck, followed by all subsequent editors, 'corrected' to δράμῃ. But ὡς ἂν plus optative is acceptable even by classical standards (e.g. Goodwin, *Moods and Tenses*, § 329 f.) and it would be a rash man who tried to bring order into Byzantine moods and tenses.
[3] According to Beckby, Planudes wrote ἀνεῖσιν, ἄνεισιν being a correction of the BM apograph and (? independently) Lascaris. In fact Planudes also clearly wrote ἄνεισιν.

χείρ: χείρ, ἴδε, γεννᾷ at 386. 1. Reference to the skill of the painter's hand is especially common: *Anecd. Paris.* iv. 319. 17, τίνος σε χεὶρ ἤγειρε; Christopher, 143, χεὶρ ... ἔμψυχον ... ζέσαι. *Anecd. Paris.* iv. 319. 19, οὐ χεὶρ λιθουργὸς οὐδὲ χεῖρες ζωγράφου; ibid. 328. 10, πῶς ὑλικὴ χεὶρ τὴν ἀϋλίαν γράφει; and *passim*. Naturally enough the motif is not absent from earlier writers (see the examples collected in W. Headlam's note on Herodas, iv. 72), but hardly in quite so stereotyped a manner.

ἐμπνόους, see below on 384. 5.

σκόπει τὸ δρᾶμα μηχανουργοῦ τοῦ δόμου·
εἰ μὴ γὰρ ἐστέγαστο καρτερᾷ σκέπῃ,
πρὸς οὐράνους ἂν ὦρτο Φαυστῖνος τρέχων
ὡς ζῶν σὺν ἵπποις, τὸ κλέος πρὶν Πρασίνων.
ἆρον στέγος γάρ, καὶ φθάνει πρὸς αἰθέρα. (382)

4: ζῶν. For the motif of the εἰκών so lifelike that it seems to live compare John Mauropous, ed. Bollig and de Lagarde (*Abh. Göttingen* 1882), no. 16. 3, ζῆν δοκεῖ γὰρ καὶ τύπος; Manuel Philes, i, Cod. Esc. iii. 2, τάχα γὰρ ζῶν ἐγράφης; xxxvii. 2–3, οὐ γὰρ ὡς ἄπνους τύπος, | ἀλλ' ὡς ἔτι ζῶν; Christopher, 101, ὡς 'Ηλίας ζῇ ...

5: for φθάνω of the trip to heaven compare Manuel, cv. 3, on Elias' ascent, σὺ ψυχὴ τάλαινα, πῶς ἄνω φθάσεις, and at 384. 3 again.

Φαυστῖνος οὗτος ὁ πρὶν ἁρματηλάτης,
ὃν δῆμος εὑρὼν τοῦ μέρους τῶν Πρασίνων
τὴν ἧτταν ἠγνόησε παντελῶς δρόμῳ.
γέρων μὲν ἦν γάρ, ὡς βλέπεις—τὸ δὲ σθένος
ἦν τις νεάζων οὐδ' ὅλως ἡττημένος. (383)

4: for ὡς βλέπεις, a rather clumsy device to draw the reader's attention to the painting, compare Christopher, 102. 2, ἰδοὺ γὰρ αὐτὸς ἐνθάδε ζῶν, ὡς βλέπεις: and compare especially 50. 1 (quoted below, p. 199).

Λευκοῦ μεθέλκων ἡνίας Κωνσταντῖνος
ἂν μὴ καθείρκτο στερρότητι τοῦ δόμου,
τοὺς τρεῖς ἐνίκα πρῶτος αἰθέρα φθάνων,
πνοῆς ἄνευθεν εἶδες αἰθεροδρόμον·
τέχνη με πείθει τοῦτον ἔμπνοον βλέπειν. (384)

4: αἰθεροδρόμος is used by John Mauropous, 13. 5: cf. οὐρανοδρόμος in Constantine of Rhodes, 359.

5: τέχνη. Commonly mentioned, often together with χείρ: compare *Anecd. Paris.* iv. 319. 20, σή, δημιουργέ, χεὶρ καὶ σὴ τέχνη; ibid. 26, ἡ τῶν τύπων τέχνη δὲ νικᾷ.

ἔμπνοον. The subject regularly appears to be breathing: compare Manuel, Cod. Esc. lxxvi.1, ἔμπνους ὁ μάρτυς καὶ δοκῶν ζῆν ἐκ λίθου; Cod. Flor. xlviii.1, ἔμπνους ὁ τύπος οὗτος; Christopher, 112.1, ἔμπνουν ἀναστήλωσον αὐτὸν, εἰ δύνῃ.

6: βλέπειν. Scores of lines in such poems end βλέπων, -ειν, -εις: Manuel, Cod. Esc. ccxliv. 1, Cod. Flor. xix. 1, lxix. 1, cviii. 2, *AP* ix. 400. 2,[1] John Mauropous 2. 17, 4. 2, 5. 1 and 11, 7. 6, 8. 29 etc.

    Κωνσταντῖνος ἦν, ἀλλὰ τοῖς πάλαι χρόνοις
    λευκῆς χρόας τέθριππον ἕλκων εὐστρόφως.
    ἀφ' οὗ δὲ τοῦτον ἥρπασεν Χάρων, ἔδυ
    τὸ φῶς ἁμίλλης ἱππικῶν δρομημάτων
    καὶ πᾶσα τέρψις τοῦ θεάτρου καὶ τέχνη. (385)

    Χείρ, ἴδε, γεννᾷ τοὺς πάλαι τεθνηκότας.
    Ἰουλιανὸς καὶ γὰρ ὡς πάλαι σθένει
    ἕλκων μεθέλκων 'Ρουσίου τὰς ἡνίας·
    καὶ νῦν γραφεὶς ἔστηκεν ὑψοῦ σὺν δίφρῳ·
    τὸ νεῦμα χεὶρ μένει δέ.[2] τὴν νύσσαν δότε. (386)

4: γραφείς. This use of the aorist passive participle is common in such contexts: Manuel, Cod. Esc. lxix. 1, γραφεὶς πάλιν ζῇς· τοῦτο τῆς εὐτεχνίας: John Mauropous, no. 17, γραφέντες ζῆν δοκοῦσι καὶ λέγειν.

    Ἰουλιανὸς οὗτος ἅρμα 'Ρουσίου
    ἔχων ἐνίκα τοὺς ἐναντίους δρόμῳ.
    ἀλλ' εἰ γραφεὺς παρεῖχε καὶ πνοῆς χάριν,
    ἑτοιμός ἐστι καὶ πάλιν διφρηλάτης
    καὶ πρόσθεν ἐλθεῖν καὶ λαβεῖν καὶ τὸ στέφος. (387)

The tendency of the author to use emphatic καί (very common in

---

[1] Which is certainly not by Palladas, and far later. Some of the Byzantine parallels were collected by G. Luck, *Harv. Studies* lxiii (1958), 465–6. With line 1, ὅταν βλέπω σε προσκυνῶ, cf. John Mauropous 18. 1 (on St. Nicolaos), αὐτόν, πάτερ, σε προσκυνῶ τε καὶ βλέπω.

[2] Planudes gives τὸ νεῦμα χεὶρ μὲν εἶδε which was corrected to μένει δέ at least as early as the editio princeps. Probably rightly, but a difficulty remains. χείρ in l. 1 refers (as normally in the genre) to the hand of the painter, while in l. 5 it is apparently Julian's hand, waiting for the Emperor's signal to start. This is an awkwardness we must probably blame on the author.

such work) to pad out his metre is more than usually apparent in the last three lines of this poem. It is yet another variation on the alleged ability of the painter all but to endue his work with life, breath, voice, etc. For a similar piece compare Manuel, Cod. Esc. xii:

ἅπαντα συνθεὶς εὐφυῶς ὁ ζωγράφος
μόνην παρῆκε τὴν βοὴν τοῦ δεσπότου.
τάχα γὰρ ἂν Λάζαρος ἐντεῦθεν πνέων
ἀφῆκε φωνὴν εὐδρομῶν [? εὔδρομον] κἂν τοῖς τύποις.

But perhaps the best single parallel and commentary for all our poems is a piece by Christopher of Mitylene,[1] on a bronze statue in the hippodrome of a horse with one front leg raised high (εἰς τὸν χαλκοῦν ἵππον, τὸν ἐν τῷ Ἱπποδρόμῳ τὸ ὑπρόσθιον πόδα ἠρμένον ἔχοντα):

ἔμπνους ὁ χαλκοῦς ἵππος οὗτος, ὃν βλέπεις,
ἔμπνους ἀληθῶς, καὶ φριμάξεται τάχα·
τὸν πρόσθιον δὲ τοῦτον ἐξαίρων πόδα,
βαλεῖ σε καὶ λάξ, εἰ παρέλθῃς πλησίον.
δραμεῖν καθορμᾷ· στῆθι, μὴ προσεγγίσῃς·
μᾶλλον δὲ φεῦγε, μὴ λάβῃς τὸ τοῦ λόγου.

For the warning not to go too close, lest the horse kicks, and the graphic claim δραμεῖν καθορμᾷ, compare 381 (one more flick of the whip and they'll be off), 382 and 384 (lift off the roof and he'll be straight up to heaven), 385 (all he needs is breath), and 386–7 (ready for the signal). The same naïve stereotypes in the same stale style.

It is hardly possible to date such 'epigrams' precisely ('occasional poetry', it has rightly been said,[2] would be a more appropriate description of these prolix and predictable antitheses of everything we normally associate with the word epigram). But since such work is conspicuous by its absence through most of the seventh and eighth centuries, and largely confined to religious subjects in the ninth, it would seem both obvious and attractive to associate them with the fresh flowering of secular occasional poetry that marks the late tenth and eleventh centuries. Since

[1] No. 50 Kurtz: Paris. gr. 1182 (f. 151ᵛ) ascribes it to Psellus, whence Cougny, *Anth. Gr.* iii. 267 (p. 334). I agree with Kurtz (p. xvi) that we must accept the authority of the *Cryptensis* in favour of Christopher.
[2] e.g. by C. A. Trypanis, *Medieval and Modern Greek Poetry* (1951), xx n. 1.

they cannot be proved to come from the Anthology of Cephalas, an even later date is possible, but in view of the looseness of the accent regulation at the penthemimeral caesura, it would be safest to settle for late tenth to eleventh. Of course, if they were included by Cephalas, then they could not be later than early tenth.

Before we pass on, it should be noted that the author of these poems (they are so similar in phraseology and style that it seems inevitable to assume one author for all eight) was familiar with the original monument epigrams. For example, 385. 3–5:

ἀφ' οὗ δὲ τοῦτον ἥρπασεν Χάρων, ἔδυ
τὸ φῶς ἁμίλλης ἱππικῶν δρομημάτων
καὶ πᾶσα τέρψις τοῦ θεάτρου καὶ τέχνη

is surely inspired directly by 365. 1–3 (on the same Constantine):

ἐξότε Κωνσταντῖνος ἔδυ δόμον Ἄιδος εἴσω,
πλῆτο κατηφείης ἱπποσύνης στάδιον.
τερπωλὴ δ' ἀπέλειπε θεήμονας.

And 381. 1, ἴουλον ἀνθῶν πρῶτον, is certainly drawn from the rare phrase πρῶτον ἴουλον ἔχων at 336. 6 (p. 153). It may be that the author read the epigrams where they stood on the monuments. But it is more probable that he knew them from a written collection. Even so, in view of the late date of the 'iambic' poems, this would be no help in determining the date of the first collection of charioteer epigrams.

THE PAINTINGS

According to Planudes' lemma the paintings were on the ceiling (στέγη) of the βασιλικὸν προκυπτικόν. Earlier editors give the last word as προκύπτιον, and Boissonade,[1] followed by later editors and commentators, identified it with the πρόκυψις, a raised and curtained dais on which members of the imperial family made a dramatic ceremonial appearance. Yet this ceremony seems not to be earlier than the eleventh century,[2] and (as we shall see) our paintings are not so late as this.

[1] In the Didot edition ad loc. (ii, 1872, 640).
[2] See E. H. Kantorowicz, 'Oriens Augusti—lever du roi', *DOP* xvii (1963), 159 f., with discussion and bibliography of the ceremony.

THE PAINTINGS

In any event, it is quite clear from the Marcianus and the BM apograph that Planudes wrote, not προκυπτίου, but προκυπτικοῦ. The προκυπτικόν, I would suggest, is the same as the παρακυπτικόν or παρακυπτικά, the gallery in the Kathisma above the level of the Emperor's box whence members of the imperial family (especially the ladies) could watch the races without being seen themselves.[1] Hence the name, from παρακύπτειν, 'to peep out of' a door or window. But as Reiske showed in a learned note to his edition of the Book of Ceremonies, both προκύπτειν and παρακύπτειν are used in this meaning, in Byzantine as in earlier writers.[2] So the gallery in question was in all probability known indifferently as the προκυπτικόν or the παρακυπτικόν. Our paintings, then, would have been painted on the ceiling of this gallery, not on that of the imperial box itself, as assumed (for example) by Paton and Beckby.[3] Hence the reference to it as a δόμος at 382. 1 and 384. 2.

Now the iambic poems are probably not earlier than the tenth century. But the paintings they describe need not be so late. More probably, like countless other such epigrams, they were purely ecphrastic, written to circulate round the drawing-rooms of Constantinople, not to be inscribed on the ceiling of the Parakyptikon.

Let us take a parallel example, Christopher's poem on the bronze horse. It is certainly not inscriptional, still less the inscription to a contemporary statue. It is most improbable that a bronze statue of this nature would have been cast in eleventh-century Constantinople. It may well have been a piece of genuinely ancient workmanship, such as Constantine brought to his new Rome from all corners of the Empire.[4] Indeed, it may actually have been the bronze horse of Lysippus described in a very similar iambic epigram 1000 years earlier by Philip of Thessalonica.[5] Nicetas records how it was pulled down in 1204, to

---

[1] See above, p. 53.

[2] ii, p. 274–6 Bonn; cf. too J. Ebersolt, *Le Grand Palais de Constantinople et le 'Livre de Cérémonies'* (1910), 101 n. 1.

[3] Beckby (iv², p. 575) writes of the 'Kaiserloge (πρόκυψις) des Amphitheaters', thus perpetrating three errors in four words.

[4] On the considerable amount of antique statuary at Constantinople, much of it bronzes collected by Constantine, see Mango, *DOP* 1963, 56–7. There was at least one other Lysippan bronze only yards away on the spina itself: see p. 187 above.

[5] As suggested by J. Overbeck, *Die antiken Schriftquellen zur Gesch. der bildenden*

join Porphyrius and his colleagues in a Crusader melting-pot.[1] Christopher's poem, like Philip's, is simply an ecphrasis. So were the epigrams on the charioteer paintings.

Four considerations, I would suggest, point to the conclusion that the paintings themselves date from *c*. 500 and represent the four leading charioteers of that time.

(i) Why these four, if the paintings are substantially later than 500? Every age had its own great charioteers, and while Porphyrius might well be deemed exceptional, none of the others had rated more than one statue apiece at the hands of even their contemporaries. A tenth-century painter reduced to estimating the fame of celebrities of a bygone age from their monuments in the hippodrome would inevitably have reckoned Uranius, with four (including at least one of gold) above all the others but Porphyrius. Uranius is absent from the paintings, I suggest, quite simply because he was not a celebrity when they were painted.

Uranius' fourth statue was placed, we learn from 48. 1–2, next to those of Faustinus and Constantine. Evidently then it is later than Constantine's one and only statue erected after his death at the age of 50 (372. 3, cf. 367. 1–2) and presumably some 20 years after his father Faustinus had retired. This fourth statue of Uranius was erected when he had retired once already himself after 20 years with the Blues, so he must have been at least 40 at the time. Depending on how soon after Constantine's statue Uranius' fourth went up, he *need* not have been very much Constantine's junior (though he probably was). But it does seem reasonable to infer that he was at any rate considerably Faustinus' junior. We shall see below that there are grounds for supposing him Porphyrius' junior too. Thus the chances are high that he was not yet a top charioteer by 500.

(ii) What made the painter assign Julian to the Reds, Faustinus to the Greens, and Constantine to the Whites? The epigrams from their monuments do not say which colours they raced for. It is indeed possible to infer from a combination of two allu-

Künste bei den Griechen (1868), p. 286, no. 1505, and again by Gow and Page, *Garland of Philip* ii (1968), 364. Nicetas' account (next note), like Philip's, stresses that the horse was represented unbridled. Christopher does not mention this detail.

[1] *De signis Cpolitanis*, p. 861 Bonn. Robert of Clari, *Conquest of Constantinople*, tr. E. H. McNeal (1936), 109, confirms the presence of a bronze horse on the spina.

sions in Uranius' epigrams that Faustinus was a Green: 48. 1–3 tells us that Uranius' statue stood next to Faustinus and Constantine, and 376. 4 that it stood in Green territory. It follows that Faustinus and Constantine also stood in Green territory.

But if it was from these hints that our hypothetical tenth-century painter made Faustinus a Green, then he should have made Constantine a Green too. Yet he made him a White. Now Red and White were the two minor colours, by the sixth century simply subdivisions of Green and Blue respectively.[1] If the painter had been guessing from the Uranius epigrams, he might have made Constantine a Red if he wanted Faustinus for his Green, but hardly a White.

There are three possibilities. (*a*) A tenth-century painter assigned drivers to colours quite arbitrarily, getting Faustinus right by a lucky chance. (*b*) A tenth-century painter was conscientious enough to look up and use sixth-century hippodrome records. (*c*) The painter was a *contemporary* of the charioteers he painted, and knew their colours at first hand. (*a*) and (*b*) being improbable, we are left with (*c*).

It would appear from the location of his statue that by the time of his death Constantine was a Green. Perhaps he succeeded his father as *factionarius* of the Greens. He may have spent most of his long career as a Green, but for a spell, perhaps only a short spell but captured for us by the painter, he was a White.

(iii) Why did the painter show Porphyrius with the 'first down' on his cheeks? Much more remarkable than this, surely, was the fact that he continued to race till he was sixty. There must always have been plenty of teenage charioteers—but rather fewer sexagenarians.

And why does Porphyrius represent the Blues? He won three statues from the Greens. Is he painted a Blue just because he won one more from them? Surely because it was the Blues he was driving for when the painting was done. Since three out of the four monuments he won in his early years were from the Blues, it is more likely than not that anyone painting Porphyrius during the period of his first down would have painted him a Blue.

It is no less significant that the painter made Faustinus look

---

[1] See *Circus Factions*, Ch. IV. J. Jarry's view (following Friedlaender) that Red was linked with Blue and White with Green (*Syria* xxxvii (1960), 352) is there shown to be erroneous.

old (γέρων μὲν ἦν γάρ, ὡς βλέπεις, 383. 4). Had he just been painting 'all time greats' centuries later, why paint them at such different stages of their lives? Surely he did so for the simple reason that this is how old they happened to be at the time he painted them.

(iv) There are in existence probably hundreds of representations of charioteers—on contorniates, engraved glasses, gems, mosaics, sarcophagi, reliefs, etc. Very many of them are inscribed with the names of the charioteers (and often of their horses too).[1] It would be surprising if any of these dated from more than a year or two after the deaths of the men (or animals) represented.

Particularly relevant are the monuments on which more than one charioteer is named. For example, the Liber and Aerius mosaics discussed in Chapter I (p. 45). These mosaics probably represent actual races. Liber is also known from an inscription at Rome which commemorates him as manager (*dominus*) of his faction.[2] This is an innovation, since in the early Empire the *dominus* had been a private businessman, not a competing charioteer.[3] There is a closely parallel inscription (again from Rome) commemorating another charioteer–manager, Cl. Polyphemus.[4] So when we find a sarcophagus relief at Rome on which two of four named drivers are Liber again and Polyphemus,[5] we may make with confidence what is in any case the natural inference: that whether or not Liber and Polyphemus were exact contemporaries, their careers overlapped at a moment captured for us on the sarcophagus.

In the nature of things extant charioteer mosaics are set into floors and pavements, all that survives of the villas of circus *aficionados*. But there is one striking Byzantine parallel for a circus scene on a ceiling, not extant of course, but known to us from the *Life of the St. Stephen the Younger*. In 764 the iconoclast Emperor Constantine V (Copronymus, as later generations affectionately remembered him) destroyed the images of the six ecumenical councils painted on the ceiling of the Milion (a central cupola supported by four arches at right angles to each other), and sub-

---

[1] See Ch. I above, pp. 21, 48. The Parakyptikon paintings were no doubt inscribed in the same way, with the bare name of each charioteer.
[2] *ILS* 5296 (= *CIL* vi. 10058).   [3] See *Circus Factions*, Ch. II.
[4] *ILS* 5297 (= *CIL* vi. 10060).
[5] *ILS* 5291 (= *CIL* vi. 10080).

stituted a painting of the hippodrome and his own favourite charioteer Uranicus.[1] The Porphyrius reliefs, with Porphyrius in the centre surrounded by circus scenes and the attributes of victory, perhaps give some idea what this painting looked like.[2] Nevertheless, it was a contemporary charioteer (of course) that Constantine chose for his central figure, not Porphyrius or any of his long-dead colleagues.

To judge from the epigrams, the Parakyptikon paintings were not four separate pieces of work, each (it might have been argued) painted at a different time. Each was one element in a unified tableau. 380. 2 says that Porphyrius mounts towards heaven, 382. 2–3 and 5 that Faustinus would rise to heaven but for the roof, and 384. 2–3 that but for the roof Constantine would beat the other three to heaven. The implication is clearly that all four were so painted that they appeared to be racing *upwards*. Either then they were painted on a flat ceiling facing towards the centre; or (more probably) in one quarter each of the inside of a dome. The references to heaven in the epigrams would then illustrate yet another standard feature of Byzantine ecphrastic poetry: the comparison of a dome to the vault of heaven.[3]

If the paintings were indeed contemporary, then we have the key to the relative chronology of at any rate Porphyrius, Faustinus, and Constantine. And since we can date Porphyrius' first down, the style in which he is painted, to *c*. 500, then we can even approximate some absolute dates for Faustinus and Constantine. Porphyrius' first down coincided with Faustinus' 'old age'. Say his fifties. When Faustinus was in his fifties his son Constantine is likely to have been in his late twenties or early thirties. This would square with the fact that he is not singled out for his youth in the paintings. In round numbers, then, we may perhaps say that Faustinus was about 50 and Constantine about 30 in the year 500. Since Julian is not singled out for either youth or age, he too must have been older than Porphyrius yet younger than Faustinus.

[1] *Vita S. Stephani iunioris*, PG c, col. 1172: that it was on the ceiling of the Milion is shown by Mansi, *Concil*. xii. 196 (cf. A. Grabar, *L'Iconoclasme byzantin* (1957), 48–9). Both Migne and Grabar print οὐρανικόν (heavenly), but we must surely capitalize and interpret as a proper name (cf. the common charioteer's name Uranius, p. 175).   [2] Cf. Grabar, op. cit. 155–8, and above, pp. 19 f.
[3] For examples see O. Wulff, 'Das Raumerlebnis des Naos im Spiegel der Ekphrasis', *BZ* xxx (1930), 531 f.

There is in fact independent confirmation of such a relationship between the four charioteers in the epigrams from the monuments. The two lines of argument lend each other converging and mutual support.

THE RECORDS

A claim that is made with some emphasis on two out of Porphyrius' first three monuments (A and B) is that Porphyrius was the first charioteer to win a statue while still competing. The others had to wait till they had retired. Compare 340. 1-2:

ἄλλοις παυσαμένοισιν, ἀεθλεύοντι δὲ μούνῳ
Πορφυρίῳ βασιλεὺς τοῦτο δέδωκε γέρας.

And 341. 1-2:

αἱ πάντων ψῆφοί με καὶ εἰσέτι διφρεύοντα
ἔστησαν Νίκης ἐγγύθι Πορφύριον.

In view of these two passages it is clear that at 336. 5-6:

μεσσηγὺ δ' ἀέθλων
χάλκεος ἱδρύνθη πρῶτον ἴουλον ἔχων,

Paton was wrong to translate line 5 'in the middle of his racing career' (cf. Beckby too, 'mitten im Leben des Kämpfers'). It just means, 'while he was competing'. The same motif recurs, a little less explicitly, on another epigram from the same monument, 338. 1-2:

τοῦτό σοι ἠϊθέῳ Νίκη γέρας, ὃ χρόνος ἄλλοις
ὀψὲ μόλις πολιοῖς ὤπασε, Πορφύριε.

Porphyrius gets young what the others wait till they are old for.

Now sports writers have never been noted for their moderation, and it would be a rash man who believed all the superlatives heaped on Porphyrius in the epigrams. Nevertheless, it does seem difficult to imagine anyone repeatedly engraving on stone the claim that Porphyrius was the first and only charioteer to win a statue before retirement if there had been another fifteen-foot pile of stone and bronze a few yards away commemorating another young charioteer not yet retired. This, I think, is a straightforward factual claim which we must accept. We may compare the meticulously documented records chronicled on the bases of the monuments of Diocles[1] and Teres[2] in Rome, or the records claimed on numerous inscriptions honouring athletes victorious at the various Greek festivals of Hellenistic and early Imperial times. 'Tous ces records', as L. Robert has recently written of such claims, 'sont soigneusement distingués. Il n'y a aucune raison de prendre tout cela pour des mensonges ou des exagérations et de le traiter par une plaisanterie soupçonneuse, comme il arrive assez souvent.'[3] Despite the high-flown epic diction of the epigrams, in every case of a claim to a record the standard formula μόνος or μόνος καὶ πρῶτος known from scores of agonistic inscriptions is used (340. 1, 351. 5, 374. 1, 49. 1, 376. 1, 352. 6).

So Porphyrius was the first charioteer of Constantinople to be honoured with a statue while still competing. So great were his achievements, such his skill (σοφία) and style (χάρις), that his admirers felt unable to wait the probable thirty years until he retired before seeing him stand in bronze alongside his peers of the past. One might draw the parallel of the knighthoods awarded to English and Commonwealth cricketers: formerly restricted to retiring or retired performers, the honour has now been extended to those εἰσέτι διφρεύοντες.

It follows that, up till the precedent set by Porphyrius c. 500, the usual practice had been for charioteers to win statues only at or after their retirement. So at any rate is the clear implication of 340. 1 (ἄλλοις παυσαμένοισιν . . .).

From the very little material we have from outside the Planudean series there does not seem to be any parallel for official honorific statues of competing charioteers at Rome either. The great inscription of Diocles commemorated his retirement.

Let us turn now to the epigram from Julian's one and only monument:

Τοῦτον Ἰουλιανόν, Τυρίης βλάστημα τιθήνης,
ἡνίοχον πολλοὺς δεξάμενον στεφάνους
αὐτὸς ἄναξ καὶ δῆμος ἅπας καὶ πότνια βουλή
ἔστησαν κοινὴν ψῆφον ἐνεγκάμενοι.

---

[1] *ILS* 5287 (=*CIL* vi. 10048), with the full commentary in Friedlaender, *Sittengesch.* iv⁹⁻¹⁰ (1921), 185–96 (partial translation in N. Lewis and M. Reinhold, *Roman Civilization* ii (1955), 230–3).
[2] Published by L. Borsari, *Bull. com.* xxix⁶ (1901), 177 f.
[3] 'Deux inscriptions agonistiques de Rhodes', Ἀρχ. Ἐφημ. 1966, 109 n. 3.

γήραϊ γὰρ σταδίων ἀπεπαύσατο· πᾶσι δὲ φίλτρον
κάλλιπεν, οἷσιν ἔρως ἤνθεεν ἀντιπάλων. (45)

Here we have a clear example of one of the old-style retirement statues. According to the painting reflected in 386–7, Julian used to drive for the Reds. But this statue was erected, not by the Reds for a particular victory, but by the Emperor, the whole people, and the Senate on the occasion of his retirement.

The epigrams from Faustinus' statue are less explicit:

Μητέρες εὐάθλων γεράων φρένες, οὐ κράτος ἥβης,
οὐ τάχος ἱπποσύνης, οὐ χρόνος εὐτυχίης.
ἱλήκοι, Φαυστῖνε, τεὸς νόος, ᾧ τάδε πάντα
ἕσπεται, ᾧ Νίκη σύντροφος ἀθάνατος. (363)

Πρίν σε νέον, Φαυστῖνε, νόος πεφόβητο γερόντων,
νῦν δέ σε πρεσβυγενῆ κάρτος ἔφριξε νέων.
δεύτερα δ' εὕρετο πάντα τεὸς πόνος, ὅς σε γεραίρει
πρέσβυν ἐν ἠϊθέοις, ἐν δὲ γέρουσι νέον. (364)

There is no allusion to retirement here, but equally no suggestion that this is anything but Faustinus' first statue, won at the end of a long career. Nor (as with Julian's statue) is there any hint which faction put it up (though we know that it stood in Green territory). But the heavy emphasis in 363. 1–2 on the superiority of age and experience over mere youth and luck, and especially the allusion to statues 'well-earned' (εὐάθλων), are suggestive. Could it be that Faustinus' statue was erected after one of Porphyrius' early statues, whether it was then that Faustinus retired, or because the precedent of waiting till retirement had now been broken? It will be remembered that Porphyrius' youth is linked to Faustinus' old age in the paintings. Such an approximate conjunction is supported by what we can glean about the relationship of Faustinus' son Constantine to Porphyrius.

Once more we must compare records. The only surviving inscription on the front face of the old base assures us that Porphyrius διβέρσια δεύτερον μόνος ἐνίκησεν. This is a straightforward claim in simple prose (note the stock formula μόνος ἐνίκησεν) and there is no call to doubt that when this monument was put up, Porphyrius was the only charioteer (at least at Constantinople) to have won the *diversium* twice. Presumably this means twice in one day's racing, not twice in his career—

THE RECORDS

a point evidently too obvious for contemporaries to have required further precision.

Let us assume then that some time *c*. 500 Porphyrius defeated twice in one day with their own teams opponents he had already defeated once with his own. By ordinary standards a fine achievement, yet it is hard to believe that it could have been claimed as a *record* after the mighty feat of Constantine recorded in epigram 374:

> Πέντε καὶ εἴκοσι μοῦνος ἀέθλια Κωνσταντῖνος
> εἰς μίαν ἠριγένειαν ἑλὼν ἤμειψε μὲν ἵππους
> ἀντιπάλοις· κείνους δὲ λαβών, οὓς πρόσθεν ἐνίκα,
> τοῖς αὐτοῖς πάλιν εἷλε μίαν τε καὶ εἴκοσι νίκας.

Once again, these are no stock sporting superlatives, but a very precise claim—made the more plausible by the discrepancy (guaranteed by metre) between the figures. Constantine won twenty-five races in the morning, but only twenty-one by *diversium*, evidently dropping four.

The implication of εἰς μίαν ἠριγένειαν followed by πάλιν is that the twenty-one victories by *diversium* took place in the afternoon. It is true that ἠριγένεια is found in late poets meaning just 'day' rather than (as properly) 'dawn' or 'morning', so we should not perhaps altogether rule out the possibility that this second batch of victories took place the following day. But there is nothing in the poem to support such a notion, and if ἠριγένεια is given its proper meaning, then everything corresponds with the *diversium* regulations as we know them from the Book of Ceremonies. It could only be run in the afternoon; reasonably enough the horses were allowed to rest before racing again. There is no cause to doubt that this sensible practice went back to the sixth century. The division of racing into two sessions certainly did. In addition to the passage of Augustine[1] quoted by Friedlaender, we may add the clear distinction between 'ante meridiem' and 'post epulas' in *Cod. Theod.* xv. 5. 2 (392–5). And according to John of Antioch, there was trouble at the hippodrome one day in 514, τήν τε τῆς δειλῆς πανήγυριν ὁ βασιλεὺς ἠρνήσατο.[2] There is also the charming epigram which our old friend Leontius wrote on a restaurant strategically placed half-way

---
[1] *Confess.* viii. 6. 15.
[2] *Frag.* 214e (*FHG* v. 33b) = *Exc. de Ins.* 146. 2 f. de Boor.

between the hippodrome and the baths of Zeuxippus. After a morning's racing, he says, why not have a bath and a bite of lunch in comfort and still be back in time for the afternoon session ?

ἐν μὲν τῇ Ζεύξιππον ἔχω πέλας, ἡδὺ λοετρόν,
ἐκ δ' ἑτέρης ἵππων χῶρον ἀεθλοφόρων.
τούς ῥα θεησάμενος καὶ τῷδ' ἔνι χρῶτα λοέσσας
δεῦρο καὶ ἄμπνευσον δαιτὶ παρ' ἡμετέρῃ,
καί κε πάλιν σταδίοις ποτὶ δείελον ὥριος ἔλθοις,
ἐγγύθεν ἐγγὺς ἰὼν γείτονος ἐκ θαλάμου. (ix. 650)

Those familiar with this division of the day's racing would inevitably interpret πάλιν in the Constantine epigram 'after lunch' just as in line 5 of Leontius' poem.

So there is no valid reason to doubt that epigram 374 is an authentic contemporary claim to twenty-one victories in the *diversium* for Constantine. Of course, it can hardly have been an ordinary race meeting. Fifty races in one day would not be an impossible or even an unprecedented number (100 a day were run under Domitian).[1] But even on other occasions when there were fifty races in a day it can hardly have been usual for the same driver to compete in—much less win—every race. Nor could he have done so if they had been run over the normal distance. Domitian had to cut the number of laps from 7 to 5 to get in his 100 a day, and it is likely that they were cut even more for Constantine's *tour de force*. No doubt the whole day's racing was specially organized as a showcase for Constantine, to see just how often he could bring off what was evidently his speciality. It was natural (and appropriate) that stars should be given the maximum opportunity to display their talents. The monument of Diocles, for example, records how he won one race for 50,000 sesterces with seven horses not yoked together and another for 30,000 with no whip.[2] Obviously such off-beat contests—'numquam ante tituli scripti', as they are called—were specially concocted to show off Diocles' unique skills. One can only feel sorry for the other drivers who had to serve as pacemakers and foils for such virtuoso performances. Small credit would have gone to the four men who robbed Constantine of his grand slam.

[1] Suetonius, *Dom.* 4.   [2] *ILS* 5287. 21–2.

But however this astonishing total of twenty-one twin victories was arrived at, we cannot seriously doubt that they did happen. And when they did they put Porphyrius' humble pair well and truly in the shade. Accordingly they must be dated later than the old monument, later (that is) than c. 500. Since Constantine did only receive one statue—and that posthumously—it might at first sight look as though he ought to be placed in the 'pre-Porphyrian' era. However, the epigrams are careful to explain that he only failed to win a statue before because of 'envy':

χάλκεος οὐκ ἔστης βιόων ἔτι, Κωνσταντῖνε·
ἀντὶ γὰρ εὐκλεΐης ἤρκασε βασκανίη. (41. 1–2)

According to another one (366. 5), with Constantine

ἱπποσύνης φιλοκέρτομος ὤλετο τέχνη.

This aspect of hippodrome activity is of course only too well known even to the most casual student of Byzantine history. Echoing perhaps our epigram, another Byzantine poem, of uncertain date, speaks of the δῆμος ὅλος φιλοκέρτομος of the hippodrome.[1] Reading between the lines, it looks as though Constantine had been perhaps more prone than most drivers to excite the murderous rivalry of the factions. Note yet another suggestive allusion at 365. 3–4:

οὐδ' ἐν ἀγυιαῖς
κείνας τὰς φιλίας ἐστὶν ἰδεῖν ἔριδας.

What the circus partisan who wrote these lines could affectionately call the 'friendly strife' of the streets might be viewed rather differently by those who suffered from it. Procopius' scandalized account of the atrocities of the factions under Justinian is too well known to require quotation.[2]

We have already seen several hints of hostility to Porphyrius in the inscriptions and epigrams of his various monuments. And his part in the great Green uprising at Antioch in 507 is likely to have made him very much *persona non grata* with the Blues there. There were of course many more ordinary ways a charioteer might become unpopular: simply by winning (or losing) a crucial race in a questionable manner, for example. And anyone who

[1] *Anecd. Paris.* iv. 292. 2–3.
[2] *Anecd.* vii. 15 f. For factional violence see further below, pp. 232 ff.

has followed any modern sport will at once think of performers of outstanding ability who have always been unpopular, usually because of an 'unsporting' style. It would be idle to speculate about what Constantine might have done (or not done) to inspire the 'envy' that robbed him of a statue in his lifetime, but the thing is far from incredible in itself.

What matters for us is the clear implication of the epigrams that an explanation was necessary—however laboured and implausible: note particularly 367. 1–4. But for this alleged 'envy' Constantine not only might but should have won a statue while he was still alive and (since death anticipated his retirement) competing (and cf. αἰὲν ἀεθλεύων at 367–4).

So there is nothing in the epigrams inconsistent with the implication of the paintings that Constantine was a somewhat older contemporary of Porphyrius. Not so much older that he could not have a father whose career overlapped with both Porphyrius and himself. And not too old to smash one of Porphyrius' records.

Paradoxically (or so it might seem) the ἄλλοις παυσαμένοισιν motif, prominent on Porphyrius' third monument (B, 340. 1, 341. 1), is absent from, or at least only indirectly expressed in the epigrams from his second monument, F (cf. 356. 1–2). In fact there is no paradox. The dominant motif of F is that Porphyrius has become the first and only charioteer to have

$$\text{εἰκόνα χαλκείην δήμῳ ἐν ἀμφοτέρῳ.} \quad (351.\ 6)$$

This put all other records into the background. By the time of his third monument Porphyrius had returned to the Blues, who passed over in silence his defection to the Greens commemorated in monument F, and contented themselves with repeating the ἄλλοις παυσαμένοισιν motif.

This brings us to Uranius. It is regrettable that we do not have the epigrams from his first three monuments, but those from his fourth offer several useful dating handles.

Epigram 48. 1–2, as argued above (p. 202), implies that Uranius was younger than Constantine. Porphyrius was certainly younger than Constantine. It does not necessarily follow that Uranius was actually younger than Porphyrius, but the records claimed in his fourth monument imply that he was at any rate his junior.

Uranius won two statues from the Blues and two more from the Greens. A fine career—but overshadowed by Porphyrius, with three from the Greens and four from the Blues. Against the background of Porphyrius' achievements it is instructive to examine Uranius' proud boast:

σοὶ καὶ ἀεθλεύοντι μόνῳ λήξαντί τ' ἀέθλων
τοῦτο γέρας Νίκη δὶς πόρεν, Οὐράνιε,
δήμου ἀπ' ἀμφοτέροιο. (49. 1–3)

He does not claim to be the *first* or *only* charioteer with a statue from each faction. No one could take this record away from Porphyrius: his claim is explicitly stated in 351. 5–6, and whether or not modern scholars care to take it seriously, evidently Uranius did.

Nor does Uranius even claim to be the first or only driver with *two* statues from each faction. Porphyrius had been first here too, by the time of his second statue from the Greens (the Vitalian monument) in 515. The second Green statue that gave Uranius his pair from each (376. 3–4) must belong after 515.

What Uranius *does* claim—an unusual yet curiously precise claim—is that he alone won a statue from each while competing and another from each on retiring. And he makes this claim because it was all that Porphyrius had left him. For oddly enough, despite a premature retirement and 'come-back', Porphyrius was never awarded a formal retirement-statue. There is no hint of imminent retirement even in monument H, put up when he was sixty. No doubt he retired for good soon after this, but the event was not commemorated with a statue. So for all his seven statues to Uranius' four, Porphyrius could *not* in fact equal Uranius' record as formulated in 49. 1–3. And this, surely, is why Uranius chose to formulate it in this way and no other.

No dates can be suggested for Uranius. The concluding section of this chapter will corroborate the inference that he was Porphyrius' heir rather than rival, but again only in general terms. He need not have been Porphyrius' junior in years by very much.

Echoes of the Uranius epigrams in the work of two *Cycle* poets suggest a *terminus ante quem* of around the middle of the sixth century. First Leontius, who in *AP* ix. 630. 2 seems to pick up a phrase from 48. 4 (texts quoted above, p. 114). Second

Agathias, who when referring to the proximity of Thomas the Curator's statue to statues of the Emperor and Empress, uses the phrase χῶρον ἔχῃ γείτονα, which I am inclined to suspect he took from 376. 4, γείτονα χῶρον ἔχει. Neither poem can be dated at all closely, but both were presumably written some time between the late 40s and early 60s of the century.[1] If both really do derive from the Uranius epigrams, then his fourth monument could hardly be later than *c*. 550—and might actually be earlier than Porphyrius' last monument of *c*. 540. This would not of course affect the suggested relationship between their careers, since it is not easy to believe that Porphyrius competed regularly in his 60s. His serious achievements surely belong in the reign of Anastasius (who died in 518), while Uranius may probably be reckoned a celebrity of the reign of Justin I and Justinian.

GOLDEN STATUES

Uranius' statue was of gold, whereas nine out of the eleven won jointly by the other four were of bronze. Not only were five of even Porphyrius' seven of bronze (A, B, E, F, H : cf. 335. 5, 336. 6, 342. 1, 343. 1, 347. 3, 349. 5, 351. 6, 352. 1, 354. 1, 359. 1, 362. 2); 335. 4–6 makes it perfectly clear that up till then all such statues had been of bronze:

ἀλλὰ τόσον νίκης κάρτος ἐνεγκάμενον
ἔπρεπέ μιν χρυσέῳ ἐν ἀγάλματι, μὴ δ' ἐνὶ χαλκῷ
τοῦτον τοῖς ἄλλοις εἴκελον ἑστάμεναι.

ἔπρεπε means here 'should have been' (because of his merits), but in fact was not. Compare 344. 5,

ἔπρεπέ σοι Λύσιππον ἔχειν ἐπιμάρτυρα νίκης,

where clearly Lysippus did not make Porphyrius' statue. Number 336. 6 shows that the statue celebrated by 335 was indeed bronze 'like the others' (χάλκεος ἱδρύνθη). Compare too 43. 1–2 from the Constantine monument:

---

[1] That is to say along with the other datable poems of Agathias and Leontius: see *JHS* 1966, 9–10 and 14–16, with McCail, *JHS* 1969, 91–2. The Emperor and Empress mentioned by Agathias have always been assumed to be Justinian and Theodora, but now that we know that the *Cycle* was not published till after Justinian's death, Justin II and Sophia become equally possible. See also p. 274.

GOLDEN STATUES

χρύσεον ἀντ' ἀρετῆς γέρας ἔπρεπε Κωνσταντίνῳ,
οὐδένα τῆς τέχνης τοῖον ἐνεγκαμένης.

The parallelism of expression shows that here too ἔπρεπε means only 'should have been'.[1] There is no explicit statement in the other epigrams from the monument, though 41. 1, χάλκεος οὐκ ἔστης βιόων ἔτι, Κωνσταντῖνε, and 367. 1–2, εἰσέτι μὲν ζώοντι πόλις ποτε Κωνσταντίνῳ | εἰκόνα χαλκείην βαιὸν ἔκρινε γέρας, do create a presumption that it was bronze. They certainly confirm that bronze was the normal metal for such statues.

Appendix D will show (p. 272) that the couplet 43. 1–2 from Constantine's monument is an imitation of the Porphyrian epigram 335. 4–6. Theoretically the Porphyrius epigram could be the imitation, but, literary arguments aside, this would involve placing Constantine's death at the age of 50 before Porphyrius was 20 (335 is from Porphyrius' first monument), making nonsense of every other chronological pointer in the whole series. Furthermore, there is another example of a Constantine epigram echoing an early Porphyrius epigram: see p. 86 above for the probable debt of 373. 1–2 to 352. 1–4. At 361. 2 Porphyrius' last monument is said to have been won for him by ἑσμὸς ἀριζήλων στεφάνων. According to 370. 4 Constantine, Faustinus, and an unnamed kinsman all won νηρίθμων στεφάνων ἑσμόν. The lines are clearly connected, but since Constantine cannot on any hypothesis have still been alive when Porphyrius was 60, here it must be the Porphyrius epigram that is the imitator.

The literary debts of the Constantinian poet lead naturally to the one absolute *terminus post quem* for Constantine, the date of Nonnus (mid fifth century).[2] 373. 3, ἔνθεν ἐῶν τόδ' ἄγαλμα παραίφασιν εὗρεν ἐρώτων, is taken from *Dion.* xlviii. 870, παραίφασιν εὗρες ἐρώτων. Compare too *Dion.* xlii. 137, παραίφασίς ἐστιν ἐρώτων and 203, παραίφασιν εἶχεν ἐρώτων (for παραίφασις in the same sedes, vi. 352, xl. 115, xli. 408; Agathias, *AP* v. 285. 7). LSJ, not at their best on late Greek poetry, quote our epigram and Agathias, but not their common source in Nonnus.

We return now to the wishes expressed by their respective

---

[1] Misinterpreted in F. Buffière's new Budé edition (1970), 150 n. 1. At p. 222 n. 5 he also misunderstands 335. 5–6.
[2] Nothing more precise, alas; the first work to show knowledge of the *Dionysiaca* perhaps belongs in about 470: see my *Claudian* (1970), 7 and 11–12.

poets that both Porphyrius and Constantine had been given golden statues. But first it will be necessary briefly to trace the background against which they were written.

Forty years ago K. Scott devoted an interesting study to the significance of gold and silver statues in Emperor worship under the principate, concluding that 'during the early centuries... almost every Emperor felt under obligation to define a policy of accepting or refusing statues in precious metals'.[1] Significantly enough, the only Emperors who officially permitted them were Caligula, Nero, Domitian, Commodus, and Caracalla. If this was the policy of emperors, it might seem an obvious *a fortiori* inference that private citizens were never allowed to have them, and the one example generally quoted, the gold statues of the ill-fated Sejanus,[2] has seemed the exception that proved the rule. Hence the common belief that only those with ideas beyond their station aspired to gold. In fact this is not so. For obvious considerations of expense gold statues were never common for private citizens, but there is an even if thin scattering of them over the provinces and centuries of the Empire. Nor were they confined to those close to the Emperor, like Bassaeus Rufus, praetorian prefect under Antoninus Pius with a gold statue in the forum of Rome.[3] For we also find a gold (equestrian) statue of a *decurio* of Brescia.[4] Then there are examples from Cyme and Miletus under Augustus, and a number from Didyma.[5] From the mid fourth century on imperial permission had to be obtained before even bronze statues of governors were allowed,[6] and a law of 398 lays down fines for governors who accepted statues of bronze, silver, or marble without such permission[7]—suggesting by its omission, not (surely) that gold was exempt from those provisions, but that it was so infrequent as not to be worth including in the list.

In fact between the mid fourth and mid fifth centuries a series of gold statues were erected in Rome to high functionaries and (mostly) aristocrats. Julius Festus Hymettius had two, one in Rome and one at Carthage;[8] Avianius Symmachus, father of the

[1] *TAPhA* lxii (1931), 101 f.   [2] Suetonius, *Tib.* 65.
[3] *ILS* 1326 (=*CIL* vi. 1599).   [4] *ILS* 6716 (= *CIL* v. 4485).
[5] T. Pekáry, 'Goldene Statuen der Kaiserzeit', *Röm. Mitt.* lxxv (1968), 145–6.
[6] A. von Premerstein, *Jahresh. Öst. Arch. Inst.* xv (1912), 215–17.
[7] *Cod. Just.* i. 24. 1.
[8] *ILS* 1256 (= *CIL* vi. 1736).

famous orator, one in Rome and one in Constantinople.[1] Ammianus comments sharply on the aristocrats' fondness for overlaying the statues they so coveted with gold ('auro curant imbratteari'[2]—a practice he (pedantically but predictably) traces back to Acilius Glabrio in 181 B.C. But while gold statues apparently became commoner in the West (an index of the ostentation inseparable from senatorial *dignitas*), it looks as if they became less common in the East than they had been earlier. For Constantinople we must steer clear of sweeping generalizations, since we are virtually deprived of epigraphic evidence.[3] But there is plenty from other Eastern cities of the late Empire, and though many an epigram on a governor or prefect alludes to the bronze or marble statue which the Emperor has granted him, I know of only one example (apart from Symmachus just quoted) of a gold statue: the one voted by the Senate for the great Aurelian, holder of three prefectures and a consulate at the end of the fourth and beginning of the fifth century.[4] There must have been other examples, of course, but perhaps not many. The argument is not exclusively *ex silentio*. Had gold statues been at all common it would be hard to explain the growth and popularity of the widespread *topos* of late honorific epigrams which formed the starting point of this discussion: the apology for the use of baser metals.

We may suitably begin with the following execrable examples from, respectively, the Trachonitis and Batanea areas of Syria:[5]

εἴθε νῦν καὶ χρυσέοισιν ἀγάλμασιν ὧδε δυναίμην
ἀναστήσειν, Μαρκελλῖνε, πεποθημένον πατρίδι κῦδος . . .

εἴθε σε καὶ χρυσέῳ ἀγάλματι ὧδε δυναίμην
Τιβέριον στήσειν, πεποθημένον πατρίδι κῦδος.

Such unmetrical centos are often valuable precisely because they reveal so clearly the echoes of earlier poets and formulas of the genre which a more skilful craftsman would have been better able to adapt and assimilate into his own work. As Kaibel saw,

[1] *ILS* 1257 (= *CIL* vi. 1698).   [2] xiv. 6. 8.
[3] C. Mango, 'The Byzantine Inscriptions of Constantinople: a bibliographical survey', *AJA* lv (1951), 59 f., for the meagre tally.
[4] *A. Pl.* 73. The information on his prefectures in Beckby's note goes sadly astray, as does Janin, *Constantinople byzantine*[2] (1964), 156 n. 1. See S. Mazzarino, *Stilicone* (1942), 349 f., and A. H. M. Jones, *JRS* lviii (1964), 81.
[5] Kaibel, 896–7.

it is not difficult to recognize behind these two specimens a common model running something like:

εἴθε σε καὶ χρυσέοις ἐν ἀγάλμασιν ὧδε δυναίμην
ἀνστήσειν ... (... στήσειν) πεποθημένον Ἑλλάδι κῦδος.

It was something very like this Ur-epigram that the author of Porphyrius epigram 335 had in mind when he wrote ἔπρεπέ μιν χρυσέῳ ἐν ἀγάλματι, substituting for εἴθε the equally common ἔπρεπε formula.[1] Another variation on the model has recently turned up on a base of the imperial period from Rhodes:[2]

εἴθε καὶ ἐκ χρυσοῦ τειμαλφέος εἰκόνα θεῖν[αι]
σὴν ἐπὶ κρηπείδων εἴχομεν, Ἀντίπατρε.

A good example of a more literary nature is the inscription which Arabius Scholasticus, a contributor to Agathias' *Cycle*, wrote for the statue of Longinus, prefect of Constantinople in 537–9 and again in 542:

Εἰκόνα Λογγίνῳ χρυσέην πόλις εἶχεν ὀπάσσαι,
εἰ μὴ πότνα Δίκη χρυσὸν ἀπεστρέφετο. (*A. Pl.* 314)

Justice herself, the guardian spirit (as it were) of Imperial officials, would not have approved of gold. The formula was obviously becoming a bit of a joke, for Macedonius, another poet of the day, wrote a rejoinder, feeble enough in all conscience, but instructive for our purposes:

Παρθένος εὐπατέρεια Δίκη, πρέσβειρα πολήων,
οὐ τὸν ἐν εὐσεβίῃ χρυσὸν ἀποστρέφεται·
ἀλλὰ καὶ αὐτὰ τάλαντα Διὸς πάγχρυσα τελέσθη,
οἷσι ταλαντεύει πάντα νόμον βιότου·
"καὶ τότε δὴ χρύσεια πατὴρ ἐτίταινε τάλαντα",
εἰ μὴ Ὁμηρείων ἐξελάθου χαρίτων. (*AP* xi. 380)

Line 5 is from Iliad viii. 69. If Homer says that Justice had golden scales, how could she object to her protégés having golden statues—providing they were justly won (ἐν εὐσεβίῃ).

Two further examples are interesting in that they too play

[1] For examples see 344. 5, *AP* ix. 697. 1, Paul Sil., *Ecphr.* 326 f. Another variation is ὤφελε; see above, p. 85.
[2] G. Pugliese Carratelli, *Ann. Sc. It. At.* xxx–xxxii (1952–4), 277, no. 39; cf. J. and L. Robert, *Bull. Épigr.* 1956, no. 197.

with the theme, drawing a correlation between (alleged) rejection of a gold statue and an honest nature. First *A. Pl.* 45:

'Ρητῆρες Θεόδωρον ἐμέλλομεν εἰς ἓν ἰόντες
χρυσείαις γραφίδεσσιν ἀειμνήστοισι γεραίρειν,
εἰ μὴ χρυσὸν ἔφευγε καὶ ἐν γραφίδεσσιν ἐόντα.

Even in a painting (γραφίς) Theodorus shrinks from gold. The poem is anonymous and undated, but style, metre (hexameters κατὰ στίχον), and motif point to the fifth or sixth century. ἐν γραφίδεσσι is one of the stock formulae of late Greek poetry, especially ecphrastic.[1] ῥητήρ often means 'barrister' at this period, and it looks as if Theodorus was an (allegedly honest) barrister being honoured by his colleagues.

Then there is *A. Pl.* 313, a good example of the elaborate dialogue technique so beloved of more ambitious poets of the day:

Εἰκών, τίς σ' ἀνέθηκε;—"Λόγοι."—Τίνος εἶ;—"Πολεμαίου."—
Ποίου;—"Τοῦ Κρητός."—Τεῦ χάριν;—"Ἀντ' ἀρετῆς."—
Τῆς ποδαπῆς;—"Πάσης.'—Τῆς ἐς τίνας;—"Ἐς δικολέκτας."—
Καὶ ξύλον ἀρκεῖ;—"Ναί· χρυσίον οὐ δέχεται."

Will a wooden statue suffice for the virtuous barrister Ptolemaeus? Yes, because he doesn't accept gold.

Much cleverer than these is the first of the two satirical epigrams on the iron statue of Anastasius, a skilful parody of not only this but other stock formulas of the genre:[2]

εἰκόνα σοί, βασιλεῦ κοσμοφθόρε, τήνδε σιδήρου
ἄνθεσαν, ὡς χαλκοῦ πολλὸν ἀτιμοτέρην,
ἀντὶ φόνου πενίης τ' ὀλοῆς λιμοῦ τε καὶ ὀργῆς,
οἷς πάντα φθείρει σὴ φιλοχρημοσύνη. (xi. 270)

With the opening of line 1 compare the opening of a serious example of the genre, from an equestrian statue of Justinian: ταῦτά σοι, ὦ βασιλεῦ Μηδοκτόνε (*A. Pl.* 62. 1). ἀντὶ φόνου is of

---

[1] Nonnus, *Dion.* xii. 114, xxv. 433, *Metab.* E. 174; Paul Sil., *Ecphr.* 608; Leontius, *A. Pl.* 32. 1, Dioscorus, Heitsch, *Gr. Dichterfr.* xlii. 3. 34. A. Mattsson, *Untersuchungen zur Epigrammsammlung des Agathias* (1942), traces γραφίδεσσι in Agathias *AP* iv. 3. 118 directly to Nonnus, but more probably it was a formula of ecphrastic poetry before Nonnus.

[2] On the question of the double tradition (*AP/A. Pl.* and John the Lydian) see above, pp. 184–5.

course a parody of the normal ἀντ' εὐεργεσίης and φθείρει of the σώζει so commonly used of the alleged consequences of the honorand's administration.[1] The first element in φιλοχρημοσύνη (as with κοσμοφθόρε in line 1) suggests that it will be a word of commendation. Indeed, φθείρει σὴ φιλοχρημοσύνη (Fuss's correction of the etacism φθειρεσει φιλο- in John the Lydian) is surely a parody of the stock contemporary form of honorific address, ἡ σὴ φιλανθρωπία, ἡ σὴ μεγαλοπρέπεια, etc.:[2] 'Your Miserliness'— much preferable to *AP*/*A*. *Pl*.'s flat φθείρεις ἐκ φιλοχρημοσύνης or Wuensch's φθείρεις σῇ φιλοχρημοσύνῃ.

But the major motif of the poem is the choice of metal: iron, because it is *less* honourable than bronze. We have no information about the date of the statue, but since Anastasius reigned till 518 it might easily post-date the first two monuments of Porphyrius c. 500, both of which have an epigram on the bronze/gold motif. Our parodist was clearly steeped in the formulas of the genre as a whole: but the statue of Anastasius stood on the same spina as the Porphyrius bases, and it could well have been from their use of the motif that he got the neat idea of turning it upside down.

We return at last to Porphyrius and Constantine. There can, I suggest, be no more doubt that Constantine's statue was bronze, not gold. As for Porphyrius, 335. 5 f. has been discussed above (p. 214), and it only remains to consider 354:

> Αἰδομένη χαλκῷ σε πόλις, τριπόθητε, γεραίρει·
> ἤθελε γὰρ χρυσῷ· ἀλλ' ἴδεν ἐς Νέμεσιν.
> εἰ δὲ τέην μέλπων οὐ παύεται ἠθάδα νίκην
> εὐγνώμων δῆμος, Πορφύριε, Πρασίνων,
> ἔμπνοά σοι ξύμπαντες ἀγάλματα· πᾶς δὲ περισσός
> καὶ χρυσὸς τούτοις εἰς ἔριν ἐρχόμενος.   (354)

In fact there are two arguments here. They use bronze because gold might have incurred Nemesis. And if the Greens (εὐγνώμων δῆμος) go around singing Porphyrius' praises all the time, they will be living statues (ἔμπνοα...ἀγάλματα), and by comparison

---

[1] I have collected a number of examples in *CQ* 1970, 126.
[2] There is a good selection in Sister Lucilla Dinneen, *Titles of Address in Christian Greek Epistolography to 527 A.D.* (Diss. Washington, 1929)—though her tally could have been enlarged considerably from the countless rescripts in the Codes.

GOLDEN STATUES

(τούτοις εἰς ἔριν ἐρχόμενος) all gold would be superfluous. The Greens protest too much. One suspects that the real reason was that their funds would not run to a gold statue.

At all events, it is clear both from the numerous references to bronze and from the use of this formula on Porphyrius' first two monuments that up till c. 500 bronze had been the normal and probably invariable metal for charioteer statues. Porphyrius' third statue was bronze again, but his fourth part bronze, part gold,

χρύσεος ἀντ' ἀρετῆς, χάλκεος ἀντὶ πόνων. (46. 6)

This was his third from the Blues: the more precious metal may have been a special reward for his hat-trick (they returned to bronze for their fourth (H). The Greens used only bronze for their second statue of Porphyrius several years later in 515 (E), and then rose to silver and bronze for their third, years later again (D). The greater honour implied by the use of the more precious metal is unmistakably underlined by epigram 44 from the base: Porphyrius now stands in silver and bronze where formerly he had stood in just bronze.

In the fact that the Greens did not match the gold and bronze of the Blues for Porphyrius' second hat-trick, G. Manojlović would doubtless have found confirmation of his much-quoted (but seldom-examined) view that the Blues were drawn from the rich, the Greens from the poor.[1] Yet it was the Greens who honoured Uranius, not in bronze and gold, but in gold alone.

This brings us to Uranius:

τοὔνεκα καὶ χρυσέῳ μιν ἀνεγράψαντο μετάλλῳ,
κυδίστῳ κτεάνων κύδιμον ἡνίοχον. (378. 5–6)

Special emphasis is laid on the significance of the use of gold. Not solid gold, of course, but there is no good reason to doubt that the statue was gilded all over.[2] Even so this was an honour denied, not merely to previous charioteers (even Porphyrius), but to most of the highest dignitaries of state. The rarity of gold statues

---

[1] 'Le peuple de Constantinople', *Byzantion* xi (1936), 644; for my own account see *Circus Factions*, Ch. V.

[2] Inscriptions usually refer to *statua aurata, auro fulgens, auro inlustris, inaurata*, etc., not *aurea* or *ex auro* (cf. Pekáry, *Röm. Mitt.* lxxv (1968), 148). A solid gold statue, which must have been exceptionally rare, may well have been a privilege of emperors only.

in Constantinople at this very period is sufficiently illustrated by the 'apology for base metals' motif. The partial use of gold and silver for a charioteer statue came in with Porphyrius. But Uranius was the first to enjoy the supreme compliment of gold alone. The epigrams from his three missing monuments might have filled in some gaps in the process, yet even so it seems clear that his fourth statue represents the culmination of a steady upward spiral of competitive expense and ostentation set in motion by the successive honours paid to Porphyrius. We may compare the fashion for gold statues among the aristocrats of Rome from the mid fourth century on.[1] After the first couple of examples, exceptional cases, it evidently became impossible for those with similar opinions of themselves to be satisfied with less. No doubt later generations looked at the gold statue of Uranius and reckoned it more splendid than any of Porphyrius'. Yet without the precedent of Porphyrius he would never have won it.

[1] Listed by Pekáry, op. cit. 147–8.

CONCLUSION

ALL the monuments commemorated in this series of charioteer epigrams were erected within a period of perhaps only half a century: during the latter half of the reign of Anastasius and the first half of the reign of Justinian.
Now chariot-racing flourished at Constantinople for more than 1000 years. The hippodrome was built by Septimius Severus and was playing to packed houses by the fourth century, if not before. Not even the Crusaders could entirely extinguish what soon became, with the elaborate and vital ceremonial of the hippodrome, truly the sport of emperors. Why then is our evidence for these spectacular rewards paid to successful charioteers restricted to just this brief period?

THE SCALE AND STYLE OF THE MONUMENTS

It is difficult to resist the conclusion that with the advent of Porphyrius the scale and style of charioteer monuments became much more lavish rather suddenly. It is true that the only two charioteer stelae we have are both Porphyrius', but it would be difficult to imagine them anything but exceptional (p. 15). And not the least remarkable thing about them is the number and length of the epigrams that adorn them.

We have seen that Faustinus' career overlapped, if only briefly, with Porphyrius'. But whether or not his own monument was put up before or after any of Porphyrius', its inscriptions suggest that it belongs before the whole Porphyrian series. Porphyrius' very first monument had no fewer than five epigrams, including two of six and two of eight lines; his next (the new base) six of six lines each, not to mention a large number of other inscriptions. Faustinus' base had two simple quatrains, Julian's just the one epigram.

Now we have a considerable number of statue bases inscribed with honorific epigrams from the late Empire. There are a certain number (especially sepulchral) with three or four, or occasionally five,[1] but very few at any time or place to match the loquacity of the Porphyrius bases. Beyond question the norm was at all times one or two. There are almost no extant bases from Constantinople: only the obelisk base with its two quatrains and the base to Marcian's column with just one distich. Fortunately, however, many epigrams from such bases are preserved in the Anthology—enough to make it clear that in fifth- and sixth-century Constantinople too the norm was still one or (less often) two. From the following, for example, one epigram each: the column of Theodosius II (*A. Pl.* 65); statue of the prefect Aurelian (73); statue of Justin I (64); statues of Justin II (72, ix. 810, 812) and Sophia (813); statue of Zeno (*A. Pl.* 70); statue of the quaestor Proclus (ibid. 48). Two each from: an equestrian statue of Justinian erected in the hippodrome in 531 (*A. Pl.* 62–3); a statue of Heraclius' cousin Nicetas also erected in the hippodrome (46–7, cf. p. 255). Compare also the pair of spoof epigrams written to replace the original inscriptions from the iron statue of Anastasius in the hippodrome (xi. 270–1).

So when the bases of Julian and Faustinus were inscribed with their one and two epigrams respectively, this was the normal quota, all that a prefect or an Emperor might have expected. The proliferation of epigrams on the Porphyrian stelae was a theatrical innovation. It may be remarked in this context that the fourteen epigrams on the base of Constantine surely confirm the chronology for him suggested in the preceding chapter. He was an older contemporary of Porphyrius, who won his statue *c*. 520, some time after Porphyrius' early run of statues *c*. 500 and probably after his Vitalian monument in 515. The jump from the two epigrams of Faustinus to the fourteen of Constantine would be incredible if it had happened out of the blue. But it falls into place after the bridge of the Porphyrian stelae with their regular four–six epigrams: fourteen is simply the Porphyrian precedent pushed to a ludicrous extreme.

But if Porphyrius' monuments were larger and more lavish than Faustinus' and Julian's, what about their predecessors? And did Uranius have no successors?

Obviously there were both predecessors and successors to our

---

[1] See § VII of W. Peek's *Griechische Versinschriften* i (1955), especially his no. 1999 (= *AP* xv. 4–8), two six- and three eight-line epigrams from the same monument in second-century Nicaea (L. Robert, *Hellenica* viii (1950), 90).

THE SCALE AND STYLE OF THE MONUMENTS 225

group. The question is: did they have monuments on the scale of our group? If they did, then why are their epigrams absent from the Planudean series? It might be suggested that such monuments did once exist, but were destroyed complete with their epigrams before our collector set about copying them down. There was a particularly bad fire in the hippodrome in 497, and since none of our group can be firmly dated before then, it is certainly possible that some earlier monuments were destroyed then. But scarcely all. Two other monuments erected on the same spina as early as the fourth century survived both this and all the other fires and earthquakes to which Constantinople was so exposed virtually unscathed: the obelisk of Theodosius (one relief out of four slightly scorched but both inscriptions quite undamaged and still legible) and the much more vulnerable bronze serpent column, which retained even its fragile triple heads till *c.* 1700 and its 2,500-year-old inscription to the present day. The fire that left its mark on the obelisk base may be the same one that damaged two faces of the new Porphyrius base. But even if so it left the other faces of the new base undamaged and did not touch the old base. Nor were the monuments that did survive for the collector clustered together in a way that might explain their accidental survival from a conflagration. Porphyrius' bases, for example, were split up into at least two groups at opposite ends of the spina (p. 182), and one monument that did not apparently yield an epigram, that of the unnamed kinsman of Faustinus and Constantine, stood immediately next to Faustinus, Constantine, and Uranius. Nor would the hypothesis of an all-devouring fire account for the loss of monuments erected after our group—unless we postulate another, more selective, fire which only destroyed later monuments.

The other obvious possibility is that the collector simply did not include all the charioteer epigrams available to him. Or that his collection has not come down to us complete. It must be admitted that some monuments we know from hints in the surviving epigrams to have existed are not now represented by epigrams of their own: the first three of Uranius and the unnamed kinsman of Faustinus and Constantine. Uranius is the more substantial of the two absentees. His fourth monument had five six-line epigrams very much in the Porphyrian manner, and it is likely that its three predecessors were similarly equipped. There seems no good reason why the collector should have omitted the epigrams from these while including those from the fourth monument.

Yet even if a lacuna be granted, is it not a little too simple to assume that the epigrams of all charioteers both earlier and later than our group fell out in it together with the missing Uranian epigrams? All in just the one lacuna? For the perfectly preserved arrangement of the Planudean series as we have it makes the assumption of more than one lacuna very hard to credit. One would have expected a series of omissions (whether accidental or deliberate) to disturb the original arrangement, if not beyond recognition, at least more substantially than the present clear-cut distribution into blocks would suggest.

Indeed, for the same reason the assumption of even the one lacuna for just the Uranius epigrams is not altogether straightforward. All five of the extant epigrams fairly clearly belong together as the inscription to his fourth monument, which is at present followed by the epigram from the monument of Julian. We should have to accept that the three Uranius blocks fell out of the series without taking with them either the end of the preceding Constantinian block (there could hardly have been more than fourteen!) or the beginning of Uranius' fourth (its present five epigrams make a reasonable quota, and the first, xv. 49, is the most precise and detailed, perhaps copied down first in order from the front face). In addition, the lacuna would have to be placed at a very early stage of the tradition. For the fact that the selections in L and Σ^π include only epigrams included in the Planudean series suggests that the Planudean series as we have it is as full a collection as was available to later anthologists in their editions (variously edited and amplified) of Cephalas.

Whatever the truth about the missing Uranius blocks, the hypothesis of massive accidental loss is scarcely a plausible way to explain the absence of the predecessors of Faustinus and Julian. There is a much simpler explanation. There were no such earlier monuments—and so no epigrams either. Just as the monuments of Porphyrius may be presumed to have been much larger and grander than the monuments of Faustinus and Julian, perhaps theirs in turn had marked a similar advance on the rewards of their predecessors.

THE SCALE AND STYLE OF THE MONUMENTS

This is more than an argument from silence. In 394 Theodosius I forbade that even pictures of charioteers or pantomimes be displayed anywhere but at the entrances to the circus or theatre, as far as possible from the public squares and porticoes where his own sacred likeness might be on show.[1] It is hard to imagine Theodosius sanctioning bases like the two now extant being erected not only within yards of the fourfold representation of himself on the obelisk base, but in close imitation of that representation.[2] It seems a reasonable assumption that at least as late as 394 no charioteers stood rubbing shoulders with emperors and masterpieces of Lysippus along the spina.

None of these charioteer monuments could have been erected without imperial permission. Many of the epigrams actually refer to such permission. Often their phraseology implies that the statue was directly awarded by the Emperor: e.g. ἔδωκεν ἄναξ γέρας at 350. 7 (cf. 344. 3, 348. 3, 43. 6, 377. 1 and 48. 2). But when we find on the same monument the formula νεύματι κοιρανέης (358. 4) used for the purely formal grant of a statue to a provincial governor (e.g. Kaibel, 915. 8, from fourth-century Athens), we may probably conclude that the naming of the Emperor as sole or principal donor of charioteer monuments is likewise a formal gesture.

At some time during the century between Theodosius I and Anastasius imperial policy towards the character and location of charioteer monuments must have changed. I would suggest that it was nearer the end than the beginning of the period.

It is interesting that, while 370. 1–2 from the monument of Constantine refers to the proximity of *two* kinsmen, the monument of Uranius, erected in the same area a few years later mentions only Constantine and Faustinus (48. 1–2). Perhaps the absence of epigrams from the monument of this other kinsman is not after all due to a lacuna or a fire. Perhaps it was only a modest affair, inscribed in simple prose—perhaps even (like the charioteer monuments of Rome) in *Latin*. It could not compare with the great plinth of Constantine—or even the monument of Faustinus. This is why the Uranian poet mentions only Constantine and Faustinus as the neighbours of his hero.

---
[1] *Cod. Theod.* xv. 7. 12.
[2] See above, p. 16.

OTHER ENTERTAINMENTS

Speculation, of course. All the same there are two considerations which lend some support to the hypothesis of a sudden increase in the scale of charioteer monuments.

First, popular though chariot-racing had always been, up till the age of Porphyrius it had not been the only nor even probably the favourite form of public entertainment at Constantinople. I would suggest that from about 500 it became dominant.

Gladiatorial games had of course long been gone by Porphyrius' day[1]—though less perhaps because of imperial disapproval than simply as a result of changing taste and the sheer difficulty and expense of procuring gladiators (contrary to popular belief, gladiators had in their heyday been every bit as popular in the Greek East as in the supposedly depraved cities of the West).[2] No doubt Christianity had some effect, but moral considerations can hardly have been to the fore or the scarcely less brutal and bloody wild-beast hunts (*venationes*) would not have been allowed to continue for nearly two centuries more.

Venationes were long performed to imperial frowns—Leo's disapproval emerges clearly from the law he issued in 469 banning public entertainments on Sundays[3]—but the only Emperor with the courage to ban them altogether was Anastasius in 498.[4] Two contemporary panegyrists praise him warmly for his action—though what they say suggests that it was the danger to human life that had been causing concern rather than the cruelty to the animals or the brutalizing effect of the spectacle.[5]

Even this was not quite the end of the road. Wild-beast shows are unmistakably represented on the diptychs issued by the consuls of 506 and 517, Areobindus and Anastasius' homonymous great-nephew. Chastagnol argues that these scenes depict 'des jeux édulcorés, simples exhibitions de bêtes, avec simulacres de combats et exercices d'adresse ou d'acrobatie'.[6] This is probably

---

[1] G. Ville, 'Les jeux de gladiateurs dans l'empire chrétien', *MEFR* lxxii (1960), 273–335; A. Chastagnol, *Le Sénat romain sous le règne d'Odoacre* (1966), 20–2.
[2] See L. Robert, *Les Gladiateurs dans l'Orient grec* (1940), 1 f.
[3] *Cod. Just.* iii. 12. 9. 2 ('nihil eodem die sibi vindicet scaena theatralis aut circense certamen aut ferarum *lacrimosa* spectacula').
[4] *The Chronicle of Joshua the Stylite*, translated by W. Wright (1882), § xxxiv, p. 23.
[5] Priscian, *Pan. Anast.* 223–8; Procopius Gaz., *Pan. Anast.* 15.
[6] *Le Sénat romain*, 62.

OTHER ENTERTAINMENTS

right—though one may be permitted to wonder whether the ferocious-looking bears and lions on the Areobindus diptychs knew that they were only supposed to be engaged in a 'simulacre de combat', and on the Anastasius diptych a leopard appears to be aiming a very real bite at the leg of a fleeing *venator*. Justinian exhibited what the contemporary chronicler Marcellinus regarded as an unprecedented number of lions and leopards and 'other wild beasts' during his sensational consular games of 521[1] (while still an ambitious private citizen), and his Novel of 537 refers to 'cum bestiis pugnantes homines' (105. 1). But this Novel is in fact the last reference on record to wild-beast shows in the Cynegion, and it is on the whole likely that, tamed or not, they had been a rare sight for some time by then.

Even before 498 it had been the consul of the year alone who provided such *venationes* as were still held—and the examples listed above from after that date all refer to exceptionally well-connected and wealthy consuls at that. This means that a *venatio* might at best be seen on two days in the year[2]—and then only if the consul was both willing and able. Most were probably neither. Wild beasts were not merely enormously expensive. They were and became increasingly difficult to get hold of—witness Symmachus' feverish badgering of all his friends years in advance for help in getting hold of suitable animals for the praetorian games of his son.[3] Good circus-horses were expensive too, of course, but unlike the lions and leopards, they lived to race another day. Gutta's Victor helped his master to no fewer than 429 victories.[4] Indeed, as we have seen already, circus-horses could become scarcely less famous than charioteers.[5]

Despite the widening gap between East and West, the situation in Rome developed along the same lines at the same time. As Chastagnol has shown, there are frequent references to the circus and its games in the correspondence of Cassiodorus, but only

---
[1] *Chron.*, s.a.
[2] Even in fourth-century Antioch they were extremely rare, restricted to the programme of the Syriarch's games: see W. Liebeschuetz, 'The Syriarch in the Fourth Century', *Historia* viii (1959), 113–26, especially 122–3. The *venatio* of 363 was the first the city had seen for a long time (Libanius, *Ep.* 1399).
[3] J. A. McGeachy Jr., *Q. Aurelius Symmachus* (Diss. Chicago 1942), 104 f., and cf. J. F. Matthews, *JRS*, lviii (1968), 266.
[4] Friedlaender, *SG* iv[10] (1921), 185.
[5] See p. 47 above: *IG* xiv. 1603 is an elegant verse epitaph from the tomb of a race-horse buried on the Aventine.

one—and that very illuminating—to a *venatio*, the last on record. Maximus, consul designate for 523, wrote to King Theodoric asking for permission to give a *venatio*.[1] Theodoric agreed—but not before devoting two fulsome pages of Cassiodorus' best rhetoric to a very thoroughgoing condemnation of this 'actus detestabilis, certamen infelix . . .'. The mere fact that Maximus felt it necessary to ask—and that Cassiodorus published Theodoric's answer—shows that *venationes* were no longer a regular item even on the consular programme (it is clear from Cassiodorus' opening words that, as at Constantinople, only a consul could have entertained the idea in the first place). And it is significant that Maximus was a descendant of the Maximus who spent no less than 4,000 pounds of gold on the praetorian games of his son a century earlier.[2] Contorniate types provide unequivocal confirmation.[3] They show many times more charioteers and circus scenes than either *venationes* or gladiators (who lasted longer in the West).[4]

It took no royal edict to kill wild-beast shows in the West, and it is probable that Anastasius only accelerated an inevitable process in the East. Long before the end of Justinian's reign the Cynegion stood as silent and empty in the new Rome as the Colosseum in the old. The Byzantine never lost his taste for wild and exotic animals, and for centuries they were paraded up and down the hippodrome to cheering crowds.[5] But no blood, animal or human, was spilt to make a Byzantine holiday.[6] By the advent of Porphyrius the old style *venationes* had had their day.

The other great rival to the circus was the theatre. Not indeed the legitimate stage, dead and gone for centuries, but the mime and (above all) the pantomime. Pantomimes of both sexes became popular idols, and we know the names of many of the most famous.

[1] *Var.* v. 42, cf. Chastagnol, *Le Sénat romain*, 61.
[2] Olympiodorus, frag. 44 (*FHG* iv. 68), with Chastagnol, *Fastes de la préfecture urbaine* (1962), 283; Matthews, *JRS* lviii (1968), 266.
[3] A point curiously overlooked in Chastagnol's otherwise excellent discussion.
[4] Chastagnol, *Le Sénat romain*, 20–2.
[5] J. Theodorides, 'Les animaux des jeux de l'Hippodrome et les ménageries impériales à Constantinople', *BS* xix (1958), 73 f., R. Guilland, 'Les spectacles de l'Hippodrome', *BS* xxvii (1966), 289 f.
[6] Except for criminals, of course, who long continued to be thrown to the beasts: e.g. Theophylact Simocatta iii. 8. 9, John of Ephesus, *HE* iii. 33 and 35, pp. 223 and 229 Payne Smith.

OTHER ENTERTAINMENTS

The pantomime acted out in dumb show a sort of ballet, usually on a theme from Greek mythology.[1] It was normally a solo performance (to the accompaniment of music and/or singing), and each of the four factions had its own top dancer. It might not sound very exciting, yet an experienced pantomime could evidently do with his audience all that a modern pop singer does—and more. As early as the first century top pantomimes had substantial fan clubs, who often got out of hand. The dancers themselves were early and consistently identified as a cause of or at any rate focus for riots, and banned from cities where they had been responsible for trouble. They were expelled from Rome on and off throughout the first three centuries: by Tiberius, Nero, Domitian, Trajan, Commodus[2]—and no doubt on other occasions unknown to us. Church Fathers tend to wax indignant about most forms of public entertainment, but it is always for the theatre that they reserve their choicest invectives. Not surprisingly it was very popular.

Pantomime dancing was evidently a major feature in an obscure partially aquatic festival called the Brytae. In 499 and then again in 501 it was celebrated with even more than usual licence and bloodshed: in 501 no fewer than 3,000 partisans were killed—including an illegitimate son of the Emperor himself.[3] The following year Anastasius banned pantomime dancing from all the cities of the Empire,[4] much to the relief of Procopius of Gaza,[5] and too no doubt of the historian Zosimus, who had written poignantly shortly before the ban of all the ills the pantomime had brought since its introduction into Rome by Bathyllus and Pylades under Augustus.[6] John of Antioch, on the other hand, sadly records that the Emperor 'bereft the cities of beautiful dancing'.[7]

Of course, this ban was no more permanent than its predecessors. Pantomimes were certainly back in Constantinople by

---
[1] There is a good brief account in Balsdon, *Life and Leisure in Ancient Rome* (1969), 274f.
[2] R. MacMullen, *Enemies of the Roman Order* (1967), 171.
[3] John of Antioch, *frag.* 101, *Exc. de Insid.*, p. 142 f. de Boor; Malalas, *fragg.* 36 and 39, *Exc. de Insid.*, pp. 167–8; Marcellinus, *Chron.* s.a. 501; Theophanes, AM 5997.
[4] Joshua Stylite, *Chron.* § xlvi, p. 35 Wright, recording the beneficial effects of the ban (within a month the price of wheat and barley at Edessa fell dramatically).
[5] *Pan. Anast.* 16.
[6] i. 6. 1, with my remarks in *Philologus* 113 (1969), 108 f.
[7] *frag.* 101, p. 143. 4 de Boor.

520—and in 525 they were expelled again.[1] But it seems safe to assume that they did not perform in the years immediately following 502.

Wild-beast shows were forbidden in 498, the pantomime in 502. Just at the very time Porphyrius was beginning his long career in the hippodrome, the theatres and amphitheatres of Constantinople were at least temporarily deserted. For the time being the leisure and sporting enthusiasm of the people must have been channelled exclusively into the hippodrome. More important, perhaps, the hippodrome must have become the main arena for the long-standing rivalry between the Blues and Greens.

FACTIONAL VIOLENCE

This brings us to the second of the two factors mentioned above, linked to and in part cause of the first. Fragmentary though our sources are for the late fifth and early sixth centuries, there can be little doubt that the reign of Anastasius marked a turning-point in the growth of factional violence.

Urban unrest was nothing new in the Roman Empire, of course (Ramsay MacMullen has recently given us an admirable sketch),[2] and hippodromes and theatres had long been a focus for high passions. But there is nothing on record to compare with the series of bloody riots deliberately provoked by the rivalry of the Blues and Greens from the reign of Anastasius on.

Modern studies of the circus factions have always made the error of presenting a static picture of their activity. 'On peut dire', wrote L. Bréhier,[3] 'que pendant trois siècles, d'Arcadius à Héraclius, aucun règne n'a été exempt d'une ou plusieurs révoltes des dèmes.' Such an extravagant generalization[4] obscures two important points: factional violence such as we know it from the sixth century can *not* be traced back to the reign of Arcadius (395–408), and faction riots are *not* a regular event, but bunch together in series for periods of ten or fifteen years after long intervals of relative peace.

[1] Above, p. 168, and for the fresh expulsion, Malalas, p. 417. 1 f.
[2] *Enemies of the Roman Order*, Ch. V.
[3] *Les Institutions de l'Empire byzantin* (1949), 199.
[4] Which could easily be paralleled from most other modern writings on the factions.

FACTIONAL VIOLENCE 233

Theodosius II (408-50) is the first emperor whose factional sympathies are known.[1] On one occasion he rearranged the faction grandstands so that the Greens, his own colour, would be directly opposite him as he watched from his own box in the Kathisma.[2] Yet the mere fact that he was able to do such a thing without provoking a riot suggests that factional rivalry had not yet reached the proportions of Porphyrius' day. The first circus riot on record at Constantinople dates from shortly before the end of Theodosius' long reign, in 445;[3] there is no actual reference to the factions, but the words 'multi sese invicem occiderunt' obviously suggests a conflict between rival parties. Malalas records trouble from the Greens under Marcian (450-7) serious enough for them to be banned from holding public office for three years.[4] The next reference is in 473, when Marcellinus[5] records a 'seditio' in the circus in which 'many Isaurians were killed by the people'. The Isaurians were an alien, unpopular, and disruptive element in the life of Constantinople as a whole, so the chances are that this was not a regular faction riot, a matter between the Blues and Greens alone.

The picture changes completely with the accession of Anastasius (491), though the first signs of the change come a year or two before this, with Malalas' account of a series of three factional riots at Antioch towards the end of the reign of Zeno (476-91).[6] The point can be best made by an enumeration in tabular form:

491: a 'bellum plebeium' in which a large part of Constantinople, including the circus, was devastated by fire.[7]

Early in the reign: the Greens attacked the *comes Orientis* Calliopius at Antioch, and special measures were taken to contain the violence.[8]

493: Constantinople. Riots at the theatre followed by riots in the hippodrome, both mishandled. The first by the city prefect Julian, the second by Anastasius himself. Serious fires, statues of Anastasius pulled down, many killed.[9]

---

[1] J. Jarry's attempt to take 'factional politics' back to the reign of Constantine I (allegedly a Blue)—'Histoire d'une sédition à Siout à la fin du IVe siècle', *BIFAO* lxii (1964), 129-45—is too frivolous to merit (or indeed permit) refutation.
[2] Malalas, pp. 351-2.
[3] Marcellinus, *Chron.* s.a. 445.   [4] Malalas, p. 368. 14 f.
[5] *Chron.* s.a. 473.
[6] *frag.* 35, *Exc. de Insid.*, pp. 166 f., cf. p. 389 Bonn.
[7] Marcellinus, *Chron.* s.a. 491.   [8] Malalas, p. 392.
[9] Marcellinus, *Chron.* s.a. 493; John of Antioch, *frag.* 100, *Exc. de Insid.* p. 141

498: riot in the hippodrome at Constantinople leading to the arrest of some Greens. Anastasius replied to a request that they be freed by sending his excubitors, and fire and slaughter ensued, Anastasius himself only narrowly escaping injury. Peace not restored till a new city prefect, a patron of the Greens called Plato, was appointed.[1]

499/500: the Brytae festival mentioned above. Again apparently a case of 'over-reacting' from the city prefect (Helias); many killed.[2]

501: the Brytae again, the Greens ambushed the Blues and 3,000 were killed, including an illegitimate son of Anastasius. A new city prefect (Constantine) was involved, apparently no more successful than his predecessor.[2]

507: (a) A 'seditio' in the hippodrome at Constantinople, quelled by troops.[3]

(b) The phenomenal Green rebellion of Antioch in which Porphyrius played a leading role. A series of pitched battles, with the Blues, imperial troops, and three successive Counts of the East.[4]

514: hippodrome riot when Anastasius cancelled a race-meeting in punishment for earlier disturbances.[5]

520: the riot early in the reign of Justin I referred to above (p. 168), followed by a succession of riots (provoked from now on by the Blues rather than the Greens) till 525. Then nothing on record till the terrible Nika revolt of 532.

Then a further gap before another series of riots between 548 and 565, followed by a long interlude of peace broken only during the reign of Phocas (602–10). For our present purpose it will not be necessary to give details for these later riots: it will be enough to draw attention to their distribution.[6]

How do we explain this sudden increase in factional violence? Reference to the footnotes will reveal that most of the information comes from chroniclers of the sixth and seventh centuries (Mar-

(cf. J. R. Martindale, *Public Disorders in the Late Roman Empire* (Oxford B.Phil. Diss. 1960), 26–7: John's account perhaps refers to 491 rather than 493).

[1] Malalas, p. 394 Bonn, and *frag.* 38, *Exc. de Insid.*, p. 168; *Chron. Pasch.*, p. 608.
[2] Sources quoted above; see too Bury, *Later Roman Empire* i² (1922), 437–8.
[3] Marcellinus, *Chron.* s.a.   [4] Malalas, pp. 395–8.
[5] John of Antioch, *frag.* 103, *Exc. de Insid.*, p. 146.
[6] There is a list in Martindale, *Public Disorders*, 31 f.: see too *Circus Factions*, Ch. XI.

cellinus *comes*, John Malalas; John of Antioch, the Paschal Chronicle, and, deriving from a fuller version of the two Johns, the ninth-century Theophanes). Now such works naturally become more detailed the nearer they approach their own day, and it might be suggested that their failure to record factional riots in the late fourth and early fifth centuries should be put down to simple lack of information on their part. There would surely be something in this argument. Gregory Nazianzen implies that tempers ran high in the hippodrome of Constantinople in his day,[1] and no doubt factional disturbances of a sort go back even before Arcadius.

But this cannot be the whole answer. In the first place there is evidence for popular disturbances at this period. It is just that they did not involve the factions. Similarly there is evidence for popular disturbances not involving the factions after 491: for example, there were serious troubles at Constantinople in 496, 508, 510, and 512 provoked by Anastasius' religious policy.[2] There can be no question of the chroniclers suddenly deciding to record popular riots and attributing all to factional rivalry—an oversimplification of which many modern historians stand convicted.[3] In the second place it is not as if, having once begun to record factional riots regularly, our chroniclers continue to do so evenly up to their own times. On the contrary, we have seen that their distribution is quite irregular. It is particularly striking that John of Antioch, writing under Heraclius (610–64), has nothing to say about the factions between their last riot under Justinian (565) and the trouble they caused throughout the tyranny of Phocas (602–10). John Malalas has nothing for the middle of Justinian's reign, a period through which he had lived himself. Both give full coverage to the series of riots under Anastasius.

I would suggest then that there is no good reason to doubt the clear prima-facie implication of our sources to the effect: (*a*) that the distribution of faction riots was irregular, and (*b*), more relevant to this study, that they suddenly increased in both frequency and violence from the accession of Anastasius.

The latter conclusion is strongly borne out by a glance at the evidence from elsewhere in the Empire during the fourth and early fifth centuries. We are particularly well informed about

[1] *PG* xxxvii. 1587.　　[2] Cf. Martindale, *Public Disorders*, 27 f.
[3] See *Circus Factions, passim*.

popular disturbances at Rome in the second half of the fourth century. Virtually all of the twenty or so known examples were caused by shortage of bread or wine.[1] In 355 the people rioted at the arrest of the charioteer Filoromus,[2] but it is plain from Ammianus' account that this was not a riot of or between the factions (whom he never mentions).[3] The massacre of 7,000 at Thessalonica in 390 arose out of a riot in favour of an imprisoned charioteer.[4] Once more, however, there is no mention of the factions.

One might add a riot at Alexandria caused by a dispute over pantomime dancers.[5] Yet again no reference to the factions. Indeed, outside Constantinople and Alexandria there is no evidence for the very existence of the factions in any Eastern city before the late fifth century. Elsewhere I shall be arguing that they were not in fact introduced into Eastern cities before the fifth century.[6] But even at Rome and Alexandria, where they certainly did exist, the factions are never mentioned in connection with riots before the sixth century.

Our sources present a clear and uniform picture. Evidence for popular disturbances between the first and mid fifth centuries is by no means lacking, both in and out of the circuses and theatres. Yet before the mid fifth century nobody connects such disturbances with the Blues and Greens. After the mid fifth century, above all from the accession of Anastasius, the Blues and Greens are held responsible for almost all the violence that racked the cities of the Eastern provinces. Are we really entitled simply to assume that factional riots as we know them from the sixth century took place as far back as we wish? Why should Bréhier take them back to Arcadius—but not to Constantine, or for that matter to Augustus?

Once granted this change in the character and extent of factional violence, it remains to explain it. Martindale has suggested that Anastasius, to use the modern idiom, 'over-reacted':

---

[1] See H. P. Kohns, *Versorgungskrisen und Hungerrevolten im spätantiken Rom* (Antiquitas i. 6) 1961, *passim*, with a useful table at p. 219, and L. Ruggini, *Economia e società nell''Italia annonaria'* (1961), 155 f.

[2] Ammianus, xv. 7. 2.

[3] And in view of the number of public disorders he does record, this failure to mention the factions must be held significant.

[4] Sozomen, *HE* vii. 25. [5] Socrates, *HE* vii. 13.

[6] *Circus Factions*, Ch. IX.

by regularly sending troops against sports fans he unnecessarily 'escalated' the level of violence.¹ There is probably something in this. One might add a more general point: the almost complete absence of a police force. There had been relatively ample provision at Rome in the first three centuries of the Empire: the praetorian guard, the three urban cohorts, and the seven cohorts of *vigiles*. In the course of the fourth century all were either disbanded or allowed to disintegrate, and by its close it is clear that the prefects of Rome and Constantinople alike had no trained force at their disposal.² The implications are obvious. Minor disturbances of the sort an experienced and efficient corps of law-enforcement officers could have settled without difficulty might mushroom into a major riot. Then troops would be called in, mailed cavalry like the excubitors or (as in the case of the Nika revolt) hardened veterans fresh from the Persian frontier. It is not surprising that sports fans should resent such a disproportionate reaction: 30,000 dead was an appalling price to pay for the suppression of even so serious an affair as the Nika revolt of 532. When troops were used against an uncooperative crowd at Constantinople in 342 they met bitter opposition, 'as usually happens on such occasions', illuminatingly remarked the historian Socrates.³ This is a lesson that we have had to learn again the hard way in recent years.

Yet excessive reaction by the authorities cannot be the whole answer. Factional riots did not begin under Anastasius. They merely reached a new peak. Anastasius' repressive measures perhaps help to explain why they reached this peak so early in his reign—and why this peak, once reached, was never subsequently lowered. But nothing Anastasius did or failed to do can even begin to account for the genesis of factional violence in the half century before his accession.

There is probably no simple explanation. Indeed it is unlikely that even contemporaries would have been able to offer anything more constructive than homely clichés about the decline of morals and discipline. We may compare the unrest of the youth with which we have become so familiar in our own day. Many causes

---

¹ *Public Disorders*, 81 (the terminology is mine).
² The extraordinary modern notion that the factions themselves were constituted as a sort of police force is discussed in *Circus Factions*, Ch. VI.
³ *HE* ii. 13.

have been alleged: disillusionment with the 'materialist society', with politicians, with out-of-date universities, with 'racism' or the Vietnam war; or (even more simplistic) the idleness of students, the 'permissive society', etc., etc. No responsible historian would be satisfied with such a list, nor with any other simple formula or complex of formulas. None of them are necessary preconditions for such a movement, and still less can they explain why student protest broke out when it did.

This applies to all the traditional explanations of factional violence.[1] The manifold and damning inadequacies of the more influential modern accounts of what is misleadingly described as the 'rise' of the factions will be rehearsed in their wider context elsewhere. Most fail for simple lack of evidence. It has been claimed, for instance, that there were social and religious differences between the factions. The Blues were upper, the Greens lower class. The Blues orthodox, the Greens monophysite. There is not a scrap of evidence for such hypotheses—and much against.[2] The myth that the 'demes' are a survival of the 'deme-structure' of the old Greek polis was touched on briefly above (p. 71); it is based on bad Greek and worse history. Nor, if 'deme' activity represented (as has been alleged) a struggle for 'municipal independence' against the 'encroachments of imperial absolutism', is it easy to explain why the violence of the demes should have been directed at each other.

Least of all is it true that the Blues and Greens were political parties, the one point on which all but the most heretical modern writers are agreed.[3] This, it is alleged, is the main difference between the factions of the early and late Empire. The very reverse is the case. There were actually more political demonstrations in the theatres and circus of early imperial Rome than at Constantinople under Anastasius and Justinian.[4] Virtually all

---

[1] I have emphasized in *Circus Factions*, Ch. IX (and cf. S. Vryonis Jr., *BZ* lviii (1965), 52–5), that contemporary sources described circus partisans again and again as 'youths'. Whatever other causes there may have been for their violence, youthful 'exuberance' (or 'hooliganism', according to one's standpoint) is obviously an important factor. Traditional accounts of the factions have overlooked this elementary point.

[2] *Circus Factions*, Chs. V, VII, and *passim*.

[3] The only exceptions being A. H. M. Jones, in a cavalier footnote (*Later Roman Empire* iii (1964), 337 n. 71), and Martindale, *Public Disorders*, 63 f., whose work remains unpublished.

[4] *Circus Factions*, Ch. VIII.

the circus disturbances of which we have any information in the fifth and sixth centuries were simply irresponsible riots; to return to our modern analogy, more akin to the violence of the soccer hooligan than to that of the protesting student.

Above all, however, these theories do not explain why factional violence reached a peak when it did. For example, there were many religious as well as factional riots under Anastasius. Yet not only do our sources always distinguish them: on the whole the factional riots occur at the beginning of the reign, the religious riots towards the end. On this count alone the case for linking the increase in factional violence with Anastasius' religious policy falls to the ground.

Popular movements are seldom easy to explain even when they can be directly related to social, economic, or religious grievances which can be dated and analysed.[1] For the purposes of this study we need only acknowledge that this increase in factional rivalry under Anastasius is a fact. From 491 on faction riots were serious, expensive, and above all regular threats to life and property in Constantinople, Antioch, and other Eastern cities. Many thousands died, scores of buildings were burned and burned again. The prefecture of Constantinople became a 'hot seat', the prefect usually judged by the way he handled the factions.

If only in its persistence and intensity this was a new phenomenon. Indeed we have the express (but neglected) statement of a contemporary to this effect. 'In every city', wrote Procopius in his introduction to the Nika riot, 'the population has been divided for a long time past into the Blue and Green factions; but *within recent times* (οὐ πολὺς δὲ χρόνος ἐξ οὗ . . .) it has come about that for the sake of these names . . . they fight against their opponents etc.'[2] Procopius was born *c*. 500. He knew at first hand that factional violence did not go back further than his parents' generation.

---

[1] The nature of our evidence makes it impossible to do for ancient popular disturbances what G. Rudé has done for those of eighteenth- and nineteenth-century France and England in his pioneering studies, *The Crowd in the French Revolution* (1959), *Wilkes and Liberty* (1962), *The Crowd in History* (1964), and *Paris and London in the Eighteenth Century* (1970). For the late Republic there is P. A. Brunt's 'Roman Mob', *Past and Present* (1966), 3 f.; for the Julio-Claudians, Z. Yavetz's *Plebs and Princeps* (1969), and, more generally, MacMullen's *Enemies of the Roman Order* (1967), with a rich bibliography.

[2] *BP* i. 24. 2.

CONCLUSION

ANASTASIUS AND THE FACTIONS

If this sketch of the development of public entertainments and the growth of factional rivalry and violence c. 500 is in essentials correct, then we have a context against which the charioteer monuments gain a deeper significance.

Porphyrius was obviously a magnificent charioteer. His forty years and more at the top speak for themselves. Yet his monuments are perhaps more important for the light they cast on the factions than for the superlatives they heap on the charioteer. Porphyrius may have been the greatest charioteer who ever lived, but this is not why he received such unprecedented honours at just this moment in history—or at least it is not the only reason. Nor did Uranius receive an honour denied to Porphyrius (a gold statue) simply because he was better than Porphyrius (though he may have been). Uranius was the Porphyrius of his age, and as such could hardly be granted less and (in the nature of such things) was likely to be granted more. Similarly today, the constantly increasing earnings and acclaim of pop singers do not mean that their talent or performance is superior to that of their counterparts a generation ago (though in some cases this may be true). What it does illustrate, combined with the decline of the cinema, is the eclipse of the film star by the pop singer as a popular idol.

The increase in the material honours paid to successful charioteers from c. 500 probably reflects just such an increase in the popularity of chariot-racing—hardly surprising if its competitors had been suppressed. More important, the monuments are in themselves concrete evidence for the increasing rivalry of the factions.

The Blues broke precedent by awarding Porphyrius a statue while he was still competing—and placed it on a perhaps unprecedentedly high column decorated with elaborate reliefs and more than twice the usual number of epigrams. Naturally the Greens had to follow suit. Porphyrius was poached away and in no time stood on a similar plinth in front of the Green benches (the new monument). Once the Blues had got him back they could not leave it at a tie, and up went another ten foot plinth (the old monument). And so it went on. If the Blues used gold and bronze for their third statue, the Greens too improved on

ANASTASIUS AND THE FACTIONS

simple bronze for their hat-trick (p. 221). They went one better for Uranius' fourth statue, all gold.

Now Porphyrius' first monument dates from c. 500, his fifth from 515. Those of Faustinus and Julian belong not more than a few years either side of 500. Constantine's perhaps at the very end of the reign (Anastasius died in 518). We have seen already that imperial permission was necessary for the erection of such statues. We can now see that it must have been the *same* emperor—Anastasius—who gave permission for the first seven if not eight out of our collection, not least the first five of Porphyrius' seven. We may surely infer that Anastasius initiated a deliberate new policy towards charioteer statues.

This is a doubly paradoxical discovery. First, because of the persistent and serious trouble the factions gave Anastasius from the beginning of his reign on. Secondly, because he had a reputation for extreme parsimony, leaving behind him at his death the fullest treasury in the whole history of the Empire.[1] Why is it, then, that we find Anastasius of all emperors encouraging such unprecedented ostentation on the part of the factions? Encourage is not too strong a word. It was one thing to break precedent and allow the Blues to give Porphyrius a statue before his retirement. It was something altogether different to let the Greens put up another the following year—and then the Blues two more in quick succession, all before Porphyrius had grown his first beard. Merely to permit such extravagance was to encourage it.

The charioteer statues must be seen, I suggest, as part of Anastasius' wider policy towards the factions. During the first ten years of his reign he took an uncompromisingly firm line. Unlike all other emperors whose factional preferences are known he favoured neither Blues nor Greens, but one of the minor colours: the Reds. He did this, as Malalas expressly states, to allow himself a free hand with both the major colours.[2] Unlike predecessors such as Marcian and successors such as Justinian, he punished Blues and Greens indifferently. In 502 he took the further step of banning pantomime dancing; not on the general

[1] Stein, *Bas-Empire* ii (1949), 192–8.
[2] p. 393. 9–11 Bonn. Many modern theories about the factions rest on the assumption that Anastasius was a Green and that any policy he pursued could accordingly be reckoned favourable to 'Green interests'. The assumption is false, and it is in any case clear from the chroniclers that Anastasius treated Green rioters with extreme severity.

moral grounds that churchmen had been advocating for centuries but because of the violence it was generating among the factions. His reason for banning *venationes* we do not know. Contemporary panegyrists imply humanitarian motives, but in the context it is hard to resist the suspicion that here too it was the impetus such violent spectacles offered to the already violence-prone factions that moved him most.

This left the hippodrome, the least provocative of the three major public entertainments. And if our sources have provided us (as seems likely) with a full record of at least the more serious factional riots of the period, it looks as though Anastasius' tactics eventually paid off. Between 501 and 514 there is only one circus disturbance which might, but need not be, a faction riot on record, in 507.[1] With the exception of the one circus riot of 514, all other recorded disturbances from the second half of Anastasius' reign were of a religious nature.

Such a conclusion tells strongly against the popular modern notion that the games themselves were but a thin cloak for the social, political, and religious activities of the factions. On the contrary, like many emperors before and after him, Anastasius saw clearly that, whatever more material factors might from time to time agitate the factions, it was in the tense atmosphere of the theatres and hippodromes that their discontent burst into violence. Close these arenas and the immediate source of the violence would be cut off.

During the decade 491–501 Anastasius' policy towards the factions had been basically negative: to call out the excubitors at the first sign of trouble. I would suggest that, once he had confined the activity of the factions to the hippodrome, the Emperor conceived a more positive approach. Their rivalry had to be accepted as a fact of life, however regrettable. But could it not be diverted into more peaceful channels? Whether the initiative in this new policy towards charioteer statues came from the factions themselves or Anastasius, it cannot have been long before Anastasius saw the advantages of encouraging the development. By withholding or granting his own permission, he had at last a more constructive way of controlling and directing their rivalry.

[1] At Constantinople, that is. 507 is the year of the great Green uprising in Antioch, and it is quite possible that the affair in the capital was a 'sympathetic' demonstration.

Vasiliev fancied that Porphyrius' changes of colour reflected the preferences of the reigning Emperor; that is to say, Anastasius (he argued) encouraged Porphyrius to drive for the Greens while Justin I and Justinian persuaded him to change over to the Blues.[1] This is certainly wrong (we have seen that Porphyrius drove alternately for Greens and Blues under Anastasius—who was in any case himself a Red—and won a Green statue under the Blue Justinian). But there is another more serious objection as well. The essence of chariot-racing, as of any competitive sport, must surely have been competition. Fans naturally want their own side to win—but they would soon lose interest if it always won. A football match in which one side wins easily does not arouse the same excitement as a close match, and it is excitement as much as victory that the fan craves.[2] The Emperor who engineered perpetual victory for his favourite colour would soon deprive its partisans of their main reason for watching.

The very reverse of Vasiliev's view would be nearer the truth. Surely Anastasius encouraged Porphyrius to keep changing colours, precisely so that victory should be, as one of the epigrams puts it, 'divided up between the demes' ($\mu\epsilon\rho\iota\zeta o\mu\acute{\epsilon}\nu\eta$ κατὰ δῆμον).[3] We may recall the plaintive cry put into the mouths of the Greens on the old (Blue) monument: δὸς ἡμῖν Πορφύριν. When the factions had calmed down after a riot in 520, they begged the Emperor for their favourites, the Blues for Porphyrius the dancer, the Greens for Caramallus.[4] Fortunately Justin was able to produce them. After the first day of the Nika revolt Justinian tried to placate the factions by offering an extra day's racing—this time in vain.[5]

Contrary again to the popular view, it is clear that the racing (or dancing) was a major, indeed the predominant, concern of the factions. Malalas traces the Green excesses at Antioch in 507 directly to their victories in the hippodrome (won for them by their new acquisition Porphyrius) after a long run of defeats.[6]

[1] *DOP* iv (1948), 42, 44–5.
[2] Cf. Norbert Elias and Eric Dunning, 'The Quest for Excitement in Leisure', *Society and Leisure: Bulletin for Sociology of Leisure, Education and Culture* ii (1969), 78–9. And compare Marvin B. Scott's account of how jockey, track secretary, trainer, and placing judge all contribute to make 'a real horse race', defined as 'an event where the contenders are bunched close together at the finish' (*The Racing Game* (1968), vii–viii).
[3] 46. 3.   [4] Above, p. 168.   [5] Bury, *Later Roman Empire* ii², 41.
[6] p. 396. 3 Bonn. 'There is no doubt that crowd behaviour is directly influenced

So this power which the Emperor very naturally reserved to himself of assigning the stars of the day to whichever faction he chose must have been a potent, though not of course infallible, means of exercising some degree of control over them. No doubt the main reason for the relatively peaceful behaviour of the factions after 501 was the chastening effect of the terrible slaughter of that year's Brytae. But it remains a fact that the only trace their rivalry has left during the next few years is the successive monuments both factions erected to Porphyrius in the hippodrome. It was Porphyrius' unique good fortune that his remarkable talents reached their height at just this moment.

THE VICTORIOUS CHARIOTEER

The charioteer had always been a popular idol at Rome. As early as the 70s B.C. we hear of a grief-stricken fan who threw himself on the funeral pyre of his favourite driver.[1] How far beyond the sixth century A.D. chariot-racing continued at the old Rome is uncertain, but in the new at least another half millennium[2] of fame and fortune awaited the charioteer.

It was not the masses alone who venerated these heroes of the hippodrome. Senators too courted them—and even emperors. The Green driver Eutychus was too close a friend of Gaius for the liking of the praetorians (whom he forced to build stables for him).[3] The Carian Hierocles held a similar sway over Elagabalus.[4]

Naturally they made fortunes. The Red driver Lacerta could net a hundred times the fee of a lawyer, lamented Juvenal.[5] Martial alludes less bitterly to the wealth of the great Scorpus—

by what happens on the field', writes Arthur Hopcroft of soccer violence today (*The Football Man* (1968), 180).

[1] Pliny, *NH* vii. 186.
[2] I do not know enough of the period after the ninth century to know whether Runciman was justified in claiming that the professional charioteer was eclipsed by the amateur (*Byzantine Civilization* (1933), 193).
[3] Josephus, *AJ* xix. 4 (I am not sure that I can accept all that J. Gagé, 'L'étendard d'Eutychus: sur un mot de Cassius Chaerea, le meurtier de Caligula', *Hommages M. Renard* ii (1969), 275–83, extracts from this passage).
[4] Dio lxxx. 15. 1–2.
[5] vii. 114: a charioteer C. Annius Lacerta is known from a lamp found at Rome (*ILS* 5293, surely confirming the Lacerta of Juvenal's *deteriores* and Valla's Probus).

and to his gilded busts all over the city.[1] We happen to know exactly what twenty-two years of fame brought Diocles: the enormous sum of 35,863,120 sesterces in prize money alone.[2]

There was another, rather different, reason why the charioteer was held in awe. The curse tablets which so warmly and exhaustively pray the demons to trip, wind, maim, or otherwise disable charioteer X and all his horses (p. 172) present only one side of the picture. The fans who had them inscribed were not (by their lights) playing unfair. Was it not obvious that in order to keep winning as he did charioteer X must himself be using magic?[3] Thus it came to be generally believed that the charioteer not only consulted magicians but was one himself. Ammianus records no fewer than three charioteers who were prosecuted for magic practices at Rome between 364 and 372: one was beheaded,[4] one burned,[5] and the third, an associate of several senators, acquitted.[6] A senator faced with insistent creditors would apparently consult a charioteer as a matter of course for help in his troubles.[7] A law against sorcerers issued at Rome in 389[8] (reissued by Justinian in 534[9] and then again by Leo the Wise late in the ninth century)[10] makes special provision for charioteers.[11] Early in the sixth century Cassiodorus describes how one Thomas, newly arrived from the hippodromes of the East, rapidly established himself as champion of Italy—and as a sorcerer.[12] Amphilocius of Iconium writes of charioteers in late fourth-century Constantinople invoking demons to make their rivals trip.[13]

[1] x. 74. 5–6, v. 25. 10.
[2] *ILS* 5287: for further material on the earnings of charioteers see Mayor's note on Juvenal vii. 243 and Friedlaender, *SG* ii[10], 28.
[3] See the works cited at p. 173 n. 3 above, especially Peter Brown, *Witchcraft, Confessions and Accusations* (1970), 25–7.
[4] Ammianus, xxvi. 3. 3 (Hilarinus).
[5] xxix. 3. 5 (Athanasius).
[6] xxviii. 1. 27 (Auchenius).
[7] xxviii. 4. 25. The poison mentioned in these passages was intended for human victims, not (as Balsdon supposed, *Life and Leisure in Rome*, 318) for doping horses!
[8] *Cod. Theod.* ix. 16. 11.   [9] *Cod. Just.* ix. 18. 9.
[10] *Basilica* lx. 39. 35.
[11] The curiously complex nature of the law suggests that it was framed with reference to a particular case when a charioteer was accused of doing away with a magician suspected of being his accomplice.
[12] *Var.* iii. 51. 2.
[13] *PG* lix. 321. Constantine V's charioteer Uranicus was described by a hostile writer as φιλοδαίμων (*PG* c. 1172).

Modern writers on the factions assume that from at least the fourth century they were led by officials called demarchs. These demarchs, unlike the 'demes', did exist—but not before the early seventh century.[1] Before then—and sometimes after too—it is not any official or committee of officials who lead the factions into trouble. It is the charioteer. The leader of the Greens on their rampage at Antioch in 507 was none other than Porphyrius. The rebellion of the Greens against Phocas in 610 was begun by another charioteer, Calliopas Trimolaimes.[2] The Western Emperor Majorian (457–61) issued a law of which only the suggestive title survives: 'de aurigis et seditiosis'.[3]

Then as now popular idols have thrust upon them power and responsibility that they are seldom qualified to exercise. Naturally they were tempted to abuse their position. Until Nero stopped the practice charioteers were apparently able to get away with playing tricks on and even robbing passers-by on the streets of Rome at will.[4] Reference has already been made to riots in fourth-century Rome and Thessalonica caused by the arrest of a popular charioteer. In the latter case we happen to know the charge: homosexual advances to a general subsequently lynched in the riot. When a charioteer was burned for sorcery at Rome in 372 Ammianus remarks that he was not 'granted indulgence as an artist in entertainment'.[5] The implication is that such indulgence might have been expected—and was no doubt often granted. A law of 381 actually advises the prefect of Rome not to inflict any punishment on charioteers 'except the contest of the circus' (again reissued by Justinian).[6] It seems clear that nothing much can have happened to Porphyrius for his not insignificant role in the Antioch riots of 507. By 515 he was back in Constantinople winning statues again.

Now the charioteer was not the only popular idol of late Roman society. There was of course the Holy Man,[7] the ascetic saint, with whom not even a Porphyrius could compete. Yet among the ordinary range of mortals the charioteer soon came to outstrip all competitors.

There are, for example, many more representations of chari-

[1] *Circus Factions*, Ch. II.
[2] John of Antioch, *frag.* 110, p. 150. 13 f. de Boor.   [3] Majorian, *Nov.* 12.
[4] Suetonius, *Nero* 16 (presumably only on special occasions).
[5] xxix. 3. 5.   [6] *Cod. Theod.* xv. 7. 7 = *Cod. Just.* xi. 41. 3.
[7] See now P. Brown, 'The Rise and Function of the Holy Man' *JRS* lxi (1971), 80 ff.

oteers on contorniates than pantomimes, their closest popular rivals. And despite the enormous continuing popularity of the pantomime in fifth- and sixth-century Constantinople, it is hard to believe that a Caramallus could ever have enjoyed the material honours paid to Porphyrius.

In the eyes of moralists the charioteer and the pantomime were both equally damned, the hippodrome and the theatre both 'houses of Satan'. Such extremism is not merely unbalanced and unrealistic. It obscures a very real and important difference between the hippodrome and the theatre.

Even at a moral level there was an obvious sense in which chariot-racing was more dignified and respectable than the mime and pantomime. The male pantomime was always represented as an effeminate figure with long hair, and the female a woman of easier than average virtue.[1] Their art, too, owed much of its appeal to its suggestiveness, if not downright obscenity.[2]

The success of the charioteer, on the other hand, depended on a combination of honest toil and genuine skill such as any man might envy. And excitement must always have been enhanced by the knowledge that the charioteer (unlike the pantomime, for example) was exposed to real danger as he hurtled round the arena. Circus scenes on mosaics would not regularly show a 'naufragium' (one chariot upturned and smashed) if it never happened in real life. Malalas records the death of the charioteer Julianicus in the big race-meeting of January 563. The charioteer also put his reputation at stake in a more open and obvious way than his rivals.[3] If he raced at all he had to race to win; the more famous he was the greater the blow to his prestige if he lost.

These considerations perhaps go some way towards explaining the unique position of the charioteer in Byzantine society. But not all the way. The more ambiguous moral status of the pantomime[4] need not have affected his popularity with the general

---

[1] Actress is in fact virtually synonymous with prostitute, though as D. Daube has recently pointed out (*Catholic University of America Law Review* xvi (1967), 395 f.), there was an important legal difference.

[2] Cf. Balsdon, *Life and Leisure*, 275–6.

[3] Marvin Scott makes the same two points in his discussion of the appeal of the modern jockey (*The Racing Game* (1968), 25).

[4] Discussed by J. Bayet, 'Les vertus du pantomime Vincentius', *Libyca* iii (1955), 114 f.

public[1]—quite the reverse in all probability. Rome and Byzantium are not the only civilizations where the fame of a star in the entertainment profession might actually be enhanced by a dubious social and moral background. All classes alike envy him not only his skill and wealth but also his freedom from the social and moral restraints that bind the rest of society. Statues were erected even to female pantomimes in sixth-century Constantinople,[2] and of course Justinian actually married one.

It is probable that the pantomime came to lose the role of court favourite that he so frequently played in the early Empire,[3] but there is little positive evidence that even charioteers enjoyed the personal intimacy of emperors in Byzantine times.[4] The principal reason for the importance of the charioteer in Constantinople is in fact quite independent of the personal character and achievements of the individual charioteer.

Alone of the candidates for popular favour, the sole function and only goal of the charioteer was victory. Now victory happened also to be the pre-eminent attribute of the Emperor. The most essential feature in the imperial ideology of Byzantium as it had been of Rome was that the Emperor was victorious: *victor ac triumphator semper Augustus*.[5] Whether or not there was any question of any given emperor being either currently or ever engaged in actual warfare, *Auguste, tu vincas* was his standard greeting from his subjects, civilians and soldiers alike. We have seen already that the charioteer too was greeted with the cry

---

[1] On the appeal of actors and pantomimes to all classes see especially Balsdon, *Life and Leisure*, 279–86. Pantomimes alone were paid the compliment of honorary membership of the exclusive young men's associations (*iuvenes*), otherwise restricted to the freeborn: cf. J.-P. Morel, 'Pantomimus allectus inter iuvenes', *Hommages M. Renard* ii (1969), 525–35. On mimes, pantomimes, etc. in the imperial household see E. J. Jory, 'Associations of Actors in Rome', *Hermes* 98 (1970), 244 f.

[2] *A. Pl.* 283–8 (it seems clear from both the lemma and the epigram itself that 284 at least must commemorate a statue, though some of the others may refer to paintings).

[3] Balsdon, *Life and Leisure*, 284–5. The dancing-girls on the crown of Constantine Monomachus are something of a puzzle by any standards: see p. 38.

[4] Uranicus was said to be προσφιλής to Constantine V (*V. Steph. Iun., PG* c. 1172). Michael III's fellow charioteers were obviously amateurs (Theoph. Cont., p. 198 Bonn).

[5] It will be enough to refer to such standard works as A. Alföldi, *Röm. Mitt.* xxxix (1934), 96 f., J. Gagé, *Rev. d'hist. et de phil. relig.* xiii (1933), 370 f., A. Grabar, *L'Empereur dans l'art byzantin* (1936), 31 f., O. Treitinger, *Oströmische Kaiser- und Reichsidee* (1938), 168 f.

THE VICTORIOUS CHARIOTEER 249

tu vincas.[1] The parallelism was in fact quite explicitly drawn. Our fullest information comes from the Book of Ceremonies, but the practices there described obviously go back a very long way. When the prizes were being awarded to the victorious charioteers the factions would cry τὰ ἴσα αἰτούμεθα τῆς ἐκ Θεοῦ νίκης ὑμῶν, τὰ ἴσα, δεσπόται, τῆς νίκης ὑμῶν, νικᾷ ἡ πίστις τῶν βασιλέων.[2] The victory of the charioteer is seen as but a reflection of the victory of his Emperor. Even more explicit is the following: ὅτε νικᾷ ὁ δῆμος οὗτος (i.e. the Blues or Greens, whichever it happens to be), ὁ βασιλεὺς ἐν πολέμοις σὺν τῷ στρατῷ εὐτυχεῖ ταῖς νίκαις.[3] Most striking of all, when the victorious charioteer mounts his chariot to do a lap of honour, his faction addresses him with the words ἀγάλλου, Βένετε (or Πράσινε), οἱ δεσπόται ἐνίκησαν: 'Rejoice, Blue (Green), your Lords have conquered.'[4] In their present form, where the Emperor's perpetual victory has altogether edged out the actual victory of the charioteer, these acclamations must represent a late stage in a long development.

The essence of the practice goes back at least to the late fourth century. We have seen that on the sides of the new Porphyrius base Porphyrius is shown being acclaimed by partisans dancing

[1] See p. 79.   [2] *De Caer.* i. 69, pp. 320–3 R.
[3] Ibid., p. 322. 17 f.
[4] *De Caer.* i. 71, pp. 355. 15, 357. 11 and 17. Treitinger's suggestion (*Ostrom. Kaiseridee* 172 n. 37) that this practice was influenced by the fact that emperors themselves raced in the hippodrome (a point emphasized too by Grabar, *L'Empereur*, pp. 62–3) seems to me most implausible. We only know of two Byzantine Emperors who did so, and of these Michael III (842–67) performed in the *private* hippodrome of the palace of St. Mamas (Theophanes Continuatus, pp. 198 and 835 Bonn), and if his father Theophilus did take part in the first race of his own triumphal games in 837 (Geo. Mon., p. 707 Muralt = *PG* cx. 1017), this was obviously an exceptional occasion (cf. Bury, *Eastern Roman Empire* (1912), 261–2) and it might be unsafe to infer that he regularly raced himself (he did not do so, for example, at his first triumphal games in 831, of which *De Caer.* 507 preserves an elaborate official account). Dio remarks that even Commodus and Elagabalus confined their chariot-racing to private hippodromes (lxxiii. 17. 1, lxxx. 14. 2), as had Gaius and (at least to start with) the sportsman-emperor *par excellence* Nero himself (B. H. Warmington, *Nero: Reality and Legend* (1969), 114). It will be noticed that (with the partial exception of Theophilus) all these charioteer-emperors are among the worst of the traditional 'bad' emperors, whose acts, even if popular with the masses, are not likely to have influenced official ceremonial to the degree suggested by Treitinger. Grabar's conjecture (*L'Empereur*, 63) that the charioteer of the Victoria and Albert textile is Theophilus is very far-fetched: Byzantine emperors were not normally so represented (above, pp. 19 ff.), and Michael's charioteering is regarded as something particularly reprehensible by our (admittedly hostile) sources. Constantine VII's aside about Michael's charioteering at *De Caer.* 493. 14–15 surely implies that it was exceptional.

and playing the flute. On face A_1 of the base of the obelisk of Theodosius, it is the Emperor, represented crown in hand (like a charioteer) as victor, who is being acclaimed *in the same way* by partisans dancing and playing the flute.[1] Another relief on the new Porphyrius base itself shows the Emperor being acclaimed, the acclaimers evidently taking their cue from the victory of Porphyrius.

The link between imperial victory and circus games is earlier still. It was in triumphal costume that the Emperor presided at the consular games in the Roman circus.[2] A strange story in the *Life* of Severus reveals that figures of Victory, one for each reigning emperor, were carried in the *pompa circensis*.[3] This practice antedates the principate itself; a Victory of Cassius was once accidentally dropped during the *pompa*—a bad omen.[4] We learn from Ovid that it was a figure of Victory that led the *pompa*.[5] The first item on a newly-published circus programme from sixth-century Oxyrhynchus (the first to be found) is the word νῖκαι, correctly interpreted by the editor J. Rea as referring to the setting up of 'statues of Victory dedicated to the emperors'.[6] Add to this the fact that emperors often celebrated real victories by giving circus games, and it is not hard to see the germ of the Byzantine practice in an originally no doubt spontaneous and occasional linking of the names of Emperor and charioteer in a shared moment of victory. Against this background we can better appreciate Pliny's description of the expanded and beautified Circus Maximus of Trajan as 'digna populo *victore gentium* sedes' (*Pan.* 51).

The charioteer stelae on the spina of the Byzantine hippodrome were something more than personal testimonies to the achievements of individual charioteers. They represented a faction as well as a charioteer, and the victory that they symbolized could be seen as, not the charioteer's alone, but the Emperor's too. The favourite theme of circus mosaics is the race itself with all its excitement, one driver whipping on his team, another crashing, a third glancing anxiously over his shoulder. The reliefs on the Porphyrius stelae concentrate exclusively on the theme

---

[1] See p. 51; Pll 4, 5, 19. [2] Alföldi, *Röm. Mitt.* 1 (1935), 34–6.
[3] *SHA Severi* 22. 3. [4] Plutarch, *Brutus* 39.
[5] *Amores* iii. 2. 45: for further material, Weinstock, *PW* viii. A. 2. 2528–9.
[6] *Pap. Oxy.* 2707 (1968).

of victory. Porphyrius himself is never shown with his defeated rivals, but always alone in an idealized victor's pose, while the figures in the lower registers, clutching their inevitable crowns and palms, all underline one aspect or another of the victory that he shares with his Emperor. Indeed, the parallelism between victorious charioteer and victorious Emperor is further emphasized by the fact that the Porphyrius stelae are plainly modelled on the base of Theodosius' obelisk (p. 16), itself erected to commemorate a real imperial victory.[1]

Under ordinary circumstances one might have been surprised that a jealous autocrat should tolerate even one, much less seven,[2] such monuments being awarded to a popular favourite—honours far exceeding anything allowed to the highest ministers and generals of the day. The answer is that Anastasius was able to tolerate it, partly because, being a charioteer and not a minister or general, a Porphyrius could never be a serious rival to his Emperor; partly because the more and greater Porphyrius' victories in the arena, the more and greater the symbolic victories of the Emperor, the louder and longer the cries of *Auguste, tu vincas*. To a generally unpopular emperor such as Anastasius this cannot but have been welcome.

We have seen that the 'imperial liturgy' of the Byzantine hippodrome can be traced back to the circus ceremonial of early imperial if not late republican Rome. Yet it can hardly have reached the stage of development we see in tenth-century ceremonial by independent and spontaneous evolution. There must have been individual emperors who encouraged, focused, and refined the development. One such emperor, I would suggest, was Anastasius.

There are several pointers. First, the most obvious and singular feature of developed Byzantine ceremonial is the role of the factions, whose rivalry had by then been almost entirely sublimated into the glorification of the Emperor. One ceremonial

---

[1] The frontal charioteer motif also had imperial associations, of course: see above, p. 20.
[2] There are a few parallels for men winning a series of statues, but never as many as seven at the same place: cf., for example, the three won by Julius Nicanor, poet and magistrate of Athens (*IG* iii. 1. 642–4, and for other examples, Friedlaender *SG* iii[10] (1923), 72). The great pantomime Apolaustus won twenty-three (at least) in various cities all over mainland Greece and Asia Minor, but never more than three at any one place (for the details see L. Robert, *RÉG* lxxix (1966), 757–9).

in which the factions played a prominent (and widely misunderstood) part is the proclamation of a new Emperor. Now we have in some chapters of the Book of Ceremonies, derived from a sixth-century work by Peter the Patrician, unusually full accounts of the proclamations of Leo I (457), Leo II (473), Anastasius (491), and Justin I (518).[1] It is thus with some confidence that we can say that the first occasion on which the factions played this role was at the accession of Justin I, Anastasius' immediate successor. This can hardly be coincidence. How could circus fans acquire such a seemingly unlikely role either by accident or by their own initiative?[2] It is surely legitimate to wonder whether Anastasius may not have done something to bring this about.

We have seen already that it was in Anastasius' reign that factional violence emerged as something more than the occasional riot that could be simply suppressed in isolation. What more likely or appropriate moment for imperial policy towards the position of the factions as a whole to be reassessed? That the new policy towards charioteer statues was but one manifestation of such a wider policy has been suggested above. May it not be that this policy of exalting the charioteer to new heights was deliberately geared to a formalization of the ceremonial whereby the Emperor first shared and later monopolized the victory of the charioteer?

THE DECLINE OF CHARIOT-RACING

So it was for a variety of reasons that extend far beyond his own no doubt superlative skill that Porphyrius ushered in a new era for the charioteer at Constantinople. Porphyrius' own monuments were topped by the gold statue of Uranius. But after Uranius—what?

Planudes made a search for supplements to his main collection of charioteer epigrams. But all he came up with was the series of iambic poems on the Parakypticon paintings, Thomas the logothete's feeble epitaph on Anastasius—and an epigram on a certain Eusebius:

---

[1] *De Caer.* i. 84 f., cf. Bury, *EHR* xxii (1907), 212–13.

[2] The traditional explanation, of course, is that they acquired this power in virtue of their influence as political parties in their own right: see, however, *Circus Factions*, Ch. X.

Ταύτην Εὐσεβίῳ Βυζαντιὰς εἰκόνα 'Ρώμη
πρὸς δισσαῖς ἑτέραις εἵνεκεν ἱπποσύνης.
οὐ γὰρ ὅ γ' ἀμφήριστον ἑλὼν ἐστέψατο νίκην,
ἀλλὰ πολὺ κρατέων ποσσὶ καὶ ἠνορέῃ.
τοὔνεκεν ἀντιβίων ἔριν ἔσβεσεν, ἀλλὰ καὶ αὐτὴν
δήμου τὴν προτέρου παῦσε διχοστασίην. (A. Pl. 56)

Eusebius has been ignored so far because there are a number of respects in which his epigram is quite unlike the main series. It would seem to be 'post-Porphyrian' in that it celebrates Eusebius' third statue yet contains no hint of retirement. But unlike the other monuments there was evidently only the one epigram—and that one, moreover, almost entirely lacking the fire, the lavish hyperbole, even the elegance of the Porphyrius, Constantine, and Uranius epigrams. It simply states that this is the third statue Eusebius has won, for a decisive victory. Now none of the other five charioteers ever won a statue for just one victory, however decisive (356. 5 refers to the 'hundreds' that were Porphyrius' qualification for the honour). Line 4 reveals that Eusebius was a runner as well as a charioteer (ποσσί), a curious detail, for while we do hear of foot-races in the hippodrome, there is no other evidence that charioteers took part in them.[1]

Βυζαντιὰς 'Ρώμη (line 1) is a formula not found in any of the other charioteer epigrams. Indeed it is not found at all before the 560s. Compare Agathias, A. Pl. 80. 1, Βυζαντίδος ἐνδόθι 'Ρώμης and (perhaps also by Agathias), 72. 7, Βυζαντιὰς ἄτρομε 'Ρώμα. Much later there is also Βυζαντίδος . . . 'Ρώμης in Constantine of Rhodes, AP xv. 15. 6. It was surely on the analogy of this formula that Paul the Silentiary referred to the old Rome as Λατινιὰς 'Ρώμη in his ecphrasis of Hagia Sophia in 563 (i. 164).

Κωνσταντινούπολις was at once too long, too inconvenient, and too unpoetical for poets, for whom it appears regularly as νέα,

[1] For foot-racing in the hippodrome see Procopius, BP i. 24. 42, Vogt, De Caer. Comm. ii (1940), 168, Koukoulès, Βυζαντίνων Βίος iii (1949), 88 f., and R. Guilland, BS xxvii (1966), 26–8. But the runner is clearly distinguished from the charioteer. There was at Rome a race known as 'pedibus ad quadrigam' in which 'the chariot raced with two men up and, as soon as the driver crossed the finishing line, his companion had to sprint once round the course. Victory went to the chariot whose runner came in first' (Balsdon, Life and Leisure, p. 316). But even here the charioteer does not race himself, nor is there any evidence that this race survived into Byzantine times.

νεοθήλης, νεοπηγής, νεούργης, ὁπλοτέρη, etc. 'Ρώμη, if not simply 'Ρώμη tout court.[1] These formulas are standard in both the prose and verse literatures of the fourth to sixth centuries, while Βυζαντιὰς 'Ρώμη cannot be traced before Agathias. It may have been a formula which did not become fashionable in this most formulaic of genres until the second half of the sixth century. Another hint that A. Pl. 56 might come from a rather later period than the rest of the Planudean series.

It should also be observed that Planudes put it in his section iv. 2, εἰς ἀγωντιστῶν εἰκόνας, along with epigrams on statues of athletes in general, instead of in his very next section, the main charioteer series. Nor is this just a slip in classification, for the epigram was not included in the anthology proper, but added among the other addenda which Planudes excerpted ἐξ ἑτέρου βιβλίου on f. 97ʳ, with a repeat of the lemma εἰς ἀγωνιστάς all to itself. Evidently Planudes cannot have found it together with his main series, and did not consider it sufficiently like them to include in the same section. It may be significant that there is no lemma recording provenance. Planudes is usually careful to indicate where an epigram comes from a monument in the hippodrome,[2] and it may be that Eusebius' did not. The eighth-century *Parastaseis* mentions charioteer statues in the Senaton,[3] and there were presumably others elsewhere (in some of the minor hippodromes of Constantinople, for example).[4]

Uranius' last and most splendid monument dates from no later than the reign of Justinian. Eusebius' is the only charioteer statue of which we have any knowledge later than this—if indeed it is later. And it is difficult to resist the inference that it was less grand than those of Uranius and Porphyrius. Is this just an accident of the tradition, or does the lack of information mean that charioteer statues really did cease to be made by the late sixth century?

The truth is that few statues of any sort, whether in bronze or

---

[1] e.g. AP i. 5. 5; viii. 79. 9; ix. 808. 1; A. Pl. 378. 1; and AP vii. 612. 2; ix. 647. 1; 657. 5; 697. 3; 799. 3; A. Pl. 62. 2; 326. 2; etc.

[2] e.g. AP xi. 270–1 and A. Pl. 62–3 as well as the charioteer epigrams.

[3] § 8, pp. 24–5 Preger: ἡνίοχοι ἐν ζευξίπποις. What the last word signifies is uncertain: for two possibilities see Preger's note ad loc. On the Senate house (presumably the one by the Augusteum), Janin, *Constantinople byzantine*² (1964), 155–6.

[4] On which see Janin, op. cit. 194–6.

THE DECLINE OF CHARIOT-RACING

stone, were erected after Justinian. Indeed, it is a commonplace of Byzantine art history that 'sculpture in the round, after the sixth century, was used only for statues of emperors and occasionally members of the imperial family'.[1] Since the only (partial) exception to this generalization known to me concerns a statue erected by the factions (A. Pl. 46-7), it is perhaps worth quoting here:

Νικήταν δορίτολμον ἄναξ, στρατός, ἄστεα, δῆμος
στῆσαν ὑπὲρ μεγάλων Μηδοφόνων καμάτων. (46)

Τὸν μέγαν ἐν πολέμοισι, τὸν ἄτρομον ἡγεμονῆα,
Νικήταν ἀρετῶν εἵνεκεν οἱ Πράσινοι. (47)

There can be little doubt that this is Nicetas the general and cousin of the Emperor Heraclius, whom we know to have been strongly supported by the Greens in the civil war of 610.[2] As for his 'Mede-slaying labours', a pardonable diplomatic exaggeration is apparently involved. In 614, by means which are not recorded but do not seem to have included any fighting, Nicetas succeeded in recovering the Holy Sponge and the Sacred Lance after the sack of Jerusalem by the Persians.[3]

But this is the sort of exception that proves the rule. Nicetas' services to Heraclius were altogether exceptional—and he was a kinsman after all.[4] Otherwise I know of only one private citizen honoured with a statue after the death of Justinian: the great chamberlain-general Narses, under Justin II.[5] Under these circumstances it would be surprising if statues had continued to be erected to charioteers at all, let alone at the rate of Anastasius' reign.

So the absence of statues need not mean that the popularity of charioteers declined. And the chariot-races of the hippodrome certainly remained a key point in imperial ceremonial right down to the eleventh or twelfth century. But the sport itself clearly did decline. By the time we have any substantial amount

[1] Mango, DOP xvii (1963), 71 n. 96.
[2] Y. Janssens, Byzantion xi (1936), 528 f.
[3] Chron. Pasch., p. 705.
[4] A relationship soon further tightened by the marriage of his daughter to Heraclius' eldest son: Nicephorus, pp. 9. 7, 21. 22 de Boor. According to J. V. A. Fine Jr., Zbornik rad. viz. Inst. x (1967), 35, 'Nicephorus says between 614-16 a statue was erected to Nicetas in the hippodrome' (p. 9. 9). Perfect—if true. In fact the statue in question was erected by Nicetas to Heraclius in the Forum.
[5] Patria, p. 230. 22 Preger.

of information on it again, in the Book of Ceremonies, it was but a shadow of its former self. A very elaborate and meticulously regulated shadow, to be sure. Every move, every gesture was prescribed in detail. But there were only eight races a day — four in the morning and four after lunch. The rest of the day had been eaten up by the ever-growing ceremonial.

R. Guilland, whose long series of studies on the hippodrome are written almost entirely from tenth-century evidence, was obviously sceptical of a remark in Rambaud's dissertation of 1871 that there were twenty-five races a day under Justinian[1]—so sceptical, apparently, that he did not look up Rambaud's references or consider the evidence from the principate. As early as Caligula the number was raised from 10 or 12 to 20 or 24 a day, and from Nero down to the sixth century 24 seems to have been normal. From the fourth century on there were at Rome (and no doubt Constantinople too) two days when 48 races were run, and three more when there were 30 or 36.[2] According to Dio, Commodus had 30 races run in two hours one afternoon in 192.[3] This is first-hand information, since Dio was in Rome himself at the time and quotes it as an example of the sort of thing that was fast making Commodus bankrupt. Naturally he must have reduced the number of laps, as Domitian had in order to get the almost unbelievable number of 100 into one day.[4]

The Constantine epigram discussed above (p. 210) is firm contemporary evidence for at least 46 and probably 50 races in one day early in the sixth century. According to Malalas, on the first day of the Nika revolt (13 January 532) the factions repeated their request to Justinian up to the twenty-second race,[5] after which they changed their tactics. There is nothing in the context to suggest that 22 was the whole day's programme, and apparently the meeting of the Ides of January (the occasion in question) was only a regular annual fixture, nothing out of the ordinary.[6] So even if Constantine's 46 was exceptional (as it surely was), the 24 or 25 rejected out of hand by Guilland was probably in fact standard.[7] The decline to the eight a day of the tenth century is sharp indeed.

[1] *De byzantino hippodromo*, p. 77, cf. Guilland, *BS* xxv (1964), 235.
[2] Friedlaender, *SG* ii[10]. 46.   [3] lxxiii. 16. 1.
[4] Suetonius, *Dom.* 4.   [5] p. 474. 8 Bonn.
[6] Guilland, *BS* xxvii (1966), 28 f.
[7] The six races of the new Oxyrhynchus programme (*P. Oxy.* 2707) are obviously

The reasons for the decline are not far to seek. The cost of financing spectacles on this scale was a crippling burden. By the sixth century it had long been far beyond the means of the private agonothetes of earlier days, and even the consuls could only give their traditional week of shows with the aid of an imperial subsidy. And after 541 no more consuls were appointed—largely because no one could afford the honour any more. There was no ticket revenue, and though we do hear of gambling on races (mainly during the early principate), there was no state tote. Thus after 541 the burden came to rest with the Emperor alone—who naturally had many other calls on his purse, especially as the Empire became increasingly embroiled in expensive and inconclusive foreign wars.

It is hardly surprising that the games should have suffered. Justinian tried to keep them up to the traditional scale as long as he could, perhaps the last Emperor who was able to—though at a cost. Agathias complains bitterly that Justinian squandered on dancing girls and charioteers money he should have spent on the army.[1] But even so he must have made some economies, since it was possible for another critic to make precisely the reverse accusation: 'The theatres and hippodromes and circuses were all closed for the most part... And later he ordered these spectacles to close down altogether, even in Byzantium, so that the treasury might not have to supply the usual sums to the numerous and almost countless persons who derived their living from them' (Procopius, *Anecd.* xxvi. 8–9). This is of course an exaggeration, like so much else in the *Secret History*. Races certainly continued to be held after 550. But the cataclysm of barbarian invasions that followed Justinian's death must have made it impossible for his successors to maintain the old standards. Soon after his accession in 578 Tiberius II issued regulations curbing the extravagance of the factions.[2] Against the background

no guide to practice in the capital. But six races (separated by interludes of singing rope-dancers, mimes, athletes, dogs, and gazelles) is quite impressive for a small town like Oxyrhynchus as late as the sixth century.

[1] *Hist.* v. 14. 4.
[2] Cedrenus, i. 688. 19 f., a late source, but evidently preserving an authentic detail here, since it fits exactly into place in the development of imperial legislation about the types of purple (in this case oxyblatta) that were and were not available to private citizens: see M. Reinhold, *History of Purple as a Status Symbol in Antiquity* (*Coll. Latomus* 116, 1970), 62 f.

sketched above we can better appreciate his reasons: the behaviour of the factions (who did not have to pay for the games)[1] set a standard of extravagance that the Emperor was finding it increasingly hard to match. It is a fair guess that the reduction in the number of races was one economy that had already begun before the sixth century struggled to its gloomy close.

The monuments of Porphyrius and his colleagues and rivals give us more than a chance glimpse into the hippodrome of Constantinople. They represent a new stage in the fame of its heroes at the peak of its golden age. The monuments themselves were of a size and splendour never seen before—and never to be seen again. It is a further reflection of the unique position enjoyed by the charioteers of just this one generation that it was they whose likenesses were painted on the ceiling of a gallery in the imperial palace of the Kathisma—and left there. We hear from time to time of famous charioteers in later times: notably the Uranicus so signally honoured by Constantine V. But the Porphyrius epigrams continued to find readers down the centuries, passing from one anthology to another, and as late as the tenth century Byzantine poets might still write fresh ones. In the eyes of posterity as well as of contemporaries the age of Porphyrius was *the* age of the Byzantine charioteer.

[1] Much has been built on the erroneous assumption that the factions *did* finance the games themselves: see F. Dvornik, *Byzantina-metabyzantina* i (1946), 132, R. Guilland, *BS* xxx (1969), 1 f., and even E. Stein, *Bas-Empire* i (1959), 294. The evidence, once collected, shows beyond doubt that such matters were (as might have been expected) in the exclusive control of the Emperors: cf. *Circus Factions*, Ch. II.

APPENDIX A · Pl. AND L

The following is an illustrative list of false readings in L (omitting a few trivial slips). The readings of Pl. (here as throughout) are to the left:

43. 5: ὅν τινα καὶ μετὰ πότμον] ὃν μοῦνον μετὰ πότμον. Pl.'s text is protected, not merely by καὶ μετὰ πότμον in the very next poem (366. 4), but by the fact that καὶ μετὰ πότμον happens to be a regular formula in the sepulchral poetry of the early Byzantine period. Cf. the first line of the first of the two late fourth-century epigrams from Athens published by A. E. Raubitschek in *Hesperia* xxxiii (1964), 63 f., τοῦτον καὶ μετὰ πότμον... ; *AP* vii. 678. 5 (fifth- or sixth-century, anon.) τοὔνεκα καὶ μετὰ πότμον... In every case in the same *sedes*. For just μετὰ πότμον cf. *AP* xvi. 4. 1 (? fifth-century), Julian Aeg. ix. 447. 1, the (? fourth-century) epigram from Aphrodisias published by I. Ševčenko in *Synthronon... A. Grabar* (1968), 38 n. 56, and Nonnus, *passim* (x. 106, xi. 206, xix. 178, xlviii. 532). For more high-flown variants such as καὶ μετὰ μοῖραν (Palladas, *AP* vii. 685. 3), καὶ μετὰ τέρμα βίου (Peek, *GV* 2037a. 8, iv–v s. from Besava), see *Athenaeum* xlv (1967), 144–5.

43. 6 : ἀζόμενοι] ᾳ̣ δόμενον (ἀειδ- before erasure).

49. 1 : ἀεθλεύοντι] ἀεθλεύσαντι.

335. 2 : εὐκαμάτοις] ἐν καμάτοις.

3 : μετ᾽ ἡνιόχοισι (sic)] μετ᾽ ἠϊθέοισι.

337. 4 : αἰὲν] παῖεν.

347. 2 : διπλόον] δίπαλον.

358. 3 : ἒξ] ἐξ—unless the stroke above the *epsilon* is a rough breathing joined to a (mistaken) acute accent (").

3 : ἀνύσας] ἀνύων.

361. 2 : Καλλιόπα] Ἀντιόπα.

5 : ἄρνυσαι. ἤ] αἴνυσαι. ἤ.

363. 3 and 4 : ᾧ] ὦ.

371. 2 : γενεῆς] γενέτη.

373. 8 : ἤ] ἤν.

374. 4 : μίαν τε καὶ εἴκοσι] μίαν καὶ εἴκοσι (om. τε).

377. 2 : βῆσεν] στῆσεν (from line 6).

But the clearest illustrations of L's method are 353 and 359:

APPENDIX A

353. 1: ἠρεμέοι] ἠρεμέει.
5: κοσμεῖ] κόσμει. Accents will not of course have been present on the original, but the imperative does not make sense.
6: ἀολλίσσας] ἀολλίσας.
6: τηλίκος] ἡλίκος.

ἠρεμέοι is the correct mood and tense, but (it might have been argued) writers of the age were loose with mood and tense in their conditionals, and ἠρεμέοι could be a learned correction of an original -ει. ἀολλίσσας too is correct, but (it might have been argued) not necessarily what the poet (or stone-cutter) wrote. Similarly the confusion of τηλίκος] ἡλίκος might go back to the poet. As it happens, Pl. is confirmed in all three cases by the original inscription (see Pl. 4). Another reassuring detail is φήσαιεν in line 3. Nonnus and his successors overwhelmingly preferred the longer -ειας, -ειεν forms to -αις, -αι, etc. (cf. Keydell's edition, i, pp. 46–7*), but by any standards φήσαιεν is an anomaly, a confusion between the two unknown to Veitch or LSJ. It is surprising, perhaps, that it escaped normalization by a nineteenth-century Dutch grammarian, but the reading of Pl. (and L too, for once) is confirmed by the inscription.

Now 359:
359. 1: Νίκα] Νίκη.
3: ἀλκᾶ] ἀλκῇ.
6: τέχνας] τέχνης.

Epigrammatists loved to fly off into semi-Doric, whether on paper or stone. It seems clear that this is what our poet did in 359, only to have his dialect 'normalized' by L—or rather partly normalized, for he left μορφᾶς ... ζαθέας in line 2. Whether we should normalize the σοφίη in line 4, given by Pl. as well as L, is less certain. The question of how far to push consistency in pseudo-Doric epigrams is one of the most 'tiresome and insoluble' problems to confront an editor of the *Anthology* (Gow and Page, *Hellenistic Epigrams* i (1965), xlv). I should be prepared (with hesitation) to pass it as an inconsistency of the author (thinking, perhaps, of the σοφίης he had written in the companion epigram, 360. 4). For another eliminated Doricism see p. 268 below on 342. 2. By the same token we ought perhaps to retain the hyperionicism ἐγερσιθέητρε in both Pl. and L at 361. 1 (editors always print Ascensius' -θέατρε).

336. 3–5:
> αὐτὰρ ὁ δεξιτεροῖσιν ἀνακτορέοιο θοώκου
> ἡνία καὶ ζώνην ἱππότιν ἀνθέμενος,
> κεῖθεν ἐπισπέρχων ἐλάᾳ ...

L has ζεύγλην for ζώνην—mistakenly, I believe, but it is an interesting

APPENDIX A 261

reading. In *Mnemosyne* xiv (1886), 414, van Herwerden pointed out that ζώνη was being used here in the meaning normally borne by ζεύγλη, namely 'yoke-strap', the loop attached to the yoke through which the horses' heads were put. Van Herwerden did not propose actually emending to ζεύγλη, but had he known that there was MS. authority for it, he might well have—and others may do yet.

Paton and Beckby take ζώνη as a belt worn by Porphyrius ('driving belt', 'Rossgurt'). Now it is true that charioteers did wear a special belt (see p. 25 n. 4), part, together with the helmet and tunic, of their official outfit (see p. 43). Nor is it impossible that there should be allusions to this belt in honorific epigrams on charioteers. But why in company with the *reins* rather than the other parts of the outfit? And why call it ζώνη ἱππότις when in the context ζώνη alone should have been enough to indicate which part of the charioteer's equipment was meant (Constantine Porphyrogenitus refers to it merely as ζωστόν)? Contrast 44. 1, where the reference of μίτρην is obvious without further qualification, and λύσαντά τε μίτρην readily understandable as an allusion to retirement. Surely ἱππότις was intended to distinguish this belt from other belts. It is a belt for the horses, not their driver.

Yet if the presence of ἱππότις confirms the meaning 'yoke-strap', it also rules out the possibility that the poet actually wrote ζεύγλην. In the context who *could* the ζεύγλη be for but the horses? The only circumstance in which it would make sense for the poet to have added the qualifying ἱππότις is if he was using ζώνη in an unusual meaning, where it was necessary to show that it was not Porphyrius' belt but the horses'. ζώνη itself does not appear to occur elsewhere in this sense, but ζωστήρ does, in the preface to Agathias' *Cycle*:

μή τις ἐπαυχενίοιο λιπὼν ζωστῆρα λεπάδνου
βάρβαρος εἰς βασιλῆα βιημάχον ὄμμα τανύσσῃ. (*AP* iv. 3. 47)

Like our poet, Agathias too felt it necessary to qualify the bare noun, this time with the defining genitive λεπάδνου.

L's text here is not then just a careless error: it must be the result of deliberate emendation, by someone (not necessarily Planudes) who had realized that ζώνη was being used in a meaning normally borne by ζεύγλη.

In view of these examples of carelessness or tinkering in L, we should probably be best advised to accept the guidance of Pl. where there seems little to choose between L and Pl.

338. 1: πολυστεφέας] πολυστεφάνους.

4: εὕρετο] εὕρατο.

In itself the first aorist is well attested and unexceptionable (cf. Veitch and LSJ): in epigrams, Antiphilus, ix. 14. 1, and the second-century

APPENDIX A

A.D. inscription xv. 7. 7. On the evidence of MSS. Callimachus appears to use both forms indifferently (*AP* xii. 150. 1, *Hy*. ii. 98, iv. 323). In the present series Pl. writes εὕρετο again at 364. 3 and 372. 4, but εὕραο at 351. 5. Inconsistency on the part of the poet again? Not this time. The stone gives εὕρεο. It looks as though Pl. (or his source) preferred the first aorist, and was prone to substitute it for the second: at 338. 1 when writing L, twenty years later at 351. 5— and also (e.g.) at Anyte, *AP* vii. 492. 6 (Gow–Page 757), where P has εὑρόμεθα, Pl. εὑράμεθα; at Palladas, *AP* x. 46. 4, P has εὑρόμενος, Pl. and L both εὑράμενος.

4: κρέσσονας] κρείσσονας. Similarly at 371. 2 L gives κρείσσονα for Pl.'s κρέσσονα. On the other hand Pl. gives κρείσσονας at 341. 6, which it would perhaps be rash to alter. The epigrams extend over a period of perhaps as much as half a century and, for all their similarities of style and vocabulary, are likely to be the work of several different poets. We can hardly look for more than consistency inside individual groups (if that). At the same time it must be recognized that Pl. is especially unreliable in matters like this. For example, papyri suggest that Callimachus preferred κρέσσων (Pfeiffer's *index vocab.*, p. 176), and at *AP* v. 6. 2 both P and Pl. give κρέσσονα: yet at vii. 525. 4, while P has κρέσσονα again, Pl. has κρείσσονα. At *A. Pl.* 283. 4 (Leontius Scholasticus) Σᵖ has κρέσσονα, Pl. κρείσσονα. Cf. too Gow and Page, *HE* 1091 n.

There are, however, two passages where Beckby prefers L to Pl., and actually prints its readings in the text of his second edition. In both cases I believe that he was wrong to do so.

(i) 361. 5–6:

μοῦνος δὴ νίκης γέρας ἄρνυσαι. ἦ παρὰ πᾶσι
δόξαν ἔχεις ἀέθλων ἆθλα λιπεῖν ἑτέροις.

'You alone win the reward of victory: indeed in the judgement of all you have the glory of contests to leave prizes for others.' All does not look well, and the difficulty seems to centre on ἀέθλων.[1] Lumb emends to ἀθλέων (participle from ἀθλέω), and translates: 'we all believe that you, when you enter, leave all the *hard* work to the others', explaining, 'i.e. they work hard but never win, a splendid compliment.' I must confess it seems a rather feeble compliment to me,[2] and in any case ἆθλα must in the context mean 'prizes'—and δόξαν ἔχειν in such a con-

---

[1] Beckby's critical note ἀέθλων ex αἴθ- Pl [voluit ᾄθλων] casts unnecessary doubt on a perfectly straightforward reading. To my eye at least Planudes both wrote and intended ἀέθλων, which is certainly how the scribe of the BM apograph read it too.

[2] But even so preferable to van Herwerden's ἄσθμα, the justification of which I quote without comment: 'i.e. anhelitum, quod quam sit aptum de aurigis velocissimo cursu certantibus, fugiet neminem' (*Mnemosyne* 1874, 546).

APPENDIX A 263

text 'to have the honour, glory, of' (cf. LSJ s.v. δόξα, III. 2). L offers ἐθέλων, which Beckby translates, 'rühmt man doch rings dich, du lässt gerne den andern den Preis'. But he does not explain *why* Porphyrius should so 'willingly' leave the prizes to others. Surely he would want them for himself? Nor is ἐθέλων even a very appropriate word for this idea (ἑκών, rather).

I have no doubt myself that the true reading and perfect sense can be restored by merely changing one accent—not even an emendation, since there were no accents on the stone: ἀεθλῶν, 'when you compete'. So Paton, and indeed Beckby in his first edition. ἀεθλεύων, 'while' or 'when competing', is a common formula of the genre: cf. 367. 4, αἰὲν ἀεθλεύων; 371. 3, δὴν γὰρ ἀεθλεύσας; 49. 1, σοὶ καὶ ἀεθλεύοντι; 340. 1, ἄλλοις παυσαμένοισιν, ἀεθλεύοντι δὲ μούνῳ. Metrical considerations dictated here the shortened form ἀεθλῶν. The meaning (as Paton saw) is that when Porphyrius enters, the only competition is between the others—i.e. for second place. This *is* a splendid compliment.

(ii) 373. 4 f.: The monument of Constantine was erected, we read:

ὄφρα ἑ μὴ λήθη καὶ χρόνος ἀμφιβάλῃ,
ἀλλὰ μένοι ποθέουσιν ἔρως, ζῆλος δ' ἐλατῆρσι,   5
κόσμος δὲ σταδίοις, ἑσσομένοις δὲ φάτις.
καί τις ἰδὼν μετόπισθε χερείονας ἡνιοχῆας
ὀλβίσσῃ προτέρην, ἥ μιν ἴδεν, γενεήν.

ἀμφιβάλῃ Pl. (-ῃ *vulgo*), ἀμφιλάβη L, which Beckby 'corrects' to -λάβοι, just as earlier editors had 'corrected' Pl. to -βάλοι.

First the minor question of the mood. The case for an optative is based, presumably, not so much on the irregularity of a subjunctive after the past tense εὗρε in line 3 (common even in classical writers: Goodwin, *Moods and Tenses*, §§ 318–21) as on the awkward switch to the optative μένοι in line 5. But μένοι, it could be argued, does not have to be taken as a parallel clause governed by ὄφρα; it could be an independent wish, 'But may he abide . . .'. Or, if this be rejected, it should be acknowledged that ὀλβίσσῃ in line 8 ought no less to be governed by ὄφρα parallel to μένοι—with a switch back to the subjunctive again.

It need hardly be said that ὀλβίσσῃ too (Pl. again, like L, writes merely ὀλβίσσῃ)[1] has troubled editors. Only this time the accepted 'correction' (already in Lascaris' *editio princeps* and still in Beckby) is ὀλβίσσει, changing the clause into an independent statement: 'and in the future people will bless . . .' This is surely strained, and it is significant that Paton, who printed ὀλβίσσει, nevertheless translated

[1] Perhaps (but not necessarily) the orthography of the monument: cf. τέρψη at 340. 6, but Πορφυρίωι at 352. 5 and -ωι . . . -ωι at 351. 6.

ὀλβίσσῃ ('and that . . . should bless'). It might be remarked in passing that ὀλβίσσει would be a very rare future form for an -ίζω verb, whereas double σ is a normal 'epicism' for the aorist. But, more important, we should beware of imposing a false consistency in an age when use of moods was very fluid—often, no doubt, the result of deliberate stylistic variation. Cf. (e.g.) Agathias, *Hist.* v. 4. 6 (p. 169. 15 Keydell), εὔδηλον δέ, ὡς οὔτε εἰ περιῇ τις ἐπὶ πολὺ καὶ ἀδεῶς ἐνευημεροίη.

Finally, it might be added that if it be felt that a future *is* required here, then even so there is still no cause for emending ὀλβίσσῃ. For by the sixth century the aorist subjunctive was frequently, indeed almost normally, confused with the virtually extinct future indicative, especially in the third person singular (λύσει and λύσῃ being indistinguishable to the Byzantine ear): cf. most recently K. Mitsakis, *The Language of Romanos*, §§ 92 f. We shall meet this confusion again at 340. 6 and in the corresponding prose acclamation (see p. 68 nn. 1–2). On balance, it would seem wiser to leave the subjunctive in both 4 and 8.

Discounting, then, Beckby's refinement ἀμφιλάβοι, is there a case for L's ἀμφιλάβῃ? Or rather, is there a case against ἀμφιβάλῃ? The middle would perhaps have been more normal, but for the active governing a direct accusative cf. *Il.* xxiii. 97–8, ἀμφιβαλόντε | ἀλλήλους ('embracing each other')—whence Agathias, *AP* v. 237. 12—and for a metaphorical use, *Il.* x. 535, ἀμφὶ κτύπος οὔατα βάλλει ('envelop, beset'). And in the context of death, cf. the famous line ascribed to Simonides (*AP* vii. 251. 4), κυάνεον θανάτου ἀμφεβάλοντο νέφος, imitated in the sixth century by Agathias (vii. 551. 4), Jul. Aeg. (vii. 32. 2), and cf. too Greg. Naz. viii. 118. 3. ἀμφιλαμβάνω, on the other hand, is exceptionally rare and never found in poetry: LSJ, indeed, quote only two examples altogether, both from medical writers. A hack poet composing largely in formulas is surely more likely to use a common poetical word loosely than an uncommon unpoetical word loosely.

So L does not come off very well from the comparison. Not that the MS. need (or should) be disregarded entirely. As an autograph of Planudes twenty years earlier than the *Marcianus* closely affiliated to *AP* and containing material not in the *Marcianus*, it certainly deserves further detailed study.[1] Elsewhere it does offer one or two new and possibly true readings. But for the construction of the text of the charioteer epigrams it is of no value.

---

[1] See pp. 100 f. above, and *GRBS* 1970, 344 f.

APPENDIX B · Σ^π AND PL.

There are places where Σ^π is inferior. For example (Pl. again on left):

44. 3: ἱδρύσαντο] ἱδρύσιτο, a *vox nihili*.

44. 4: πρέσβυ] πρέσβυν, unmetrical and ungrammatical.

And in 43 Σ^π omits a whole couplet preserved in Pl. But these are just careless slips. There are three more serious passages.

46. 1: ἀεθλοφόροις δ' ἐπὶ νίκαις] ἀεθλοφόρων δ' ἐπὶ δίφρων. Here Σ^π is certainly superior and almost certainly correct. ἐπὶ νίκαις is a common clausula in these epigrams (336. 7, 356. 1, 358. 3; cf. 371. 3, ἐπὶ νίκῃ, and 367. 1, 377. 1), most relevantly in the immediately preceding epigram in Planudes' series. It is easy to see how any copyist, having got as far as ἐπί in the same position in the line, might have carelessly substituted the commoner νίκαις, especially if he had only just written it two lines before.

J. Basson (*De Cephala et Planude syllogisque minoribus* (Diss. Berlin 1917), 61) dismissed the whole reading as a characteristic Planudean 'interpolation'. Yet surely Pl.'s text is the result of a two-stage alteration. First νίκαις substituted in error for δίφρων: *then* the deliberate 'correction' of -φόρων to -φόροις to agree with νίκαις. I think it unlikely that both changes are due to Planudes. For we know that he checked and corrected his MS.; indeed the BM apograph was evidently taken before these final corrections had been made (p. 107). So if Planudes had merely made the slip νίκαις for δίφρων from an exemplar which gave -φόρων . . . δίφρων, he would surely have spotted his slip while checking, and been able to make the true correction. I would suggest that one stage at least of the corruption was already present in Pl.'s exemplar. He may have altered -φόρων to -φόροις, but surely not the other as well. If so, then with Pl. we are at least three removes from the original inscriptions.

47. 5: καὶ νῦν μὲν πρῶτος, τότε δ' ὕστατος] νῦν μὲν ἐὼν πρῶτος, τότε δ' ἔσχατος. The superiority of Σ^π here leaps to the eye. The two heavy initial spondees would be unwelcome in such a smooth piece of post-Nonnian verse, and the ἐών is an obvious gain. Cf. too 358. 1, πρεσβυτέρους κοῦρος μὲν ἐών. Pl.'s clumsy καί has all the appearance of a stop-gap for an ἐών omitted in the exemplar (Planudes was perfectly capable of repairing metrical gaps, and indeed not infrequently does

APPENDIX B

so: cf. P. Waltz, *Anth. grecque* i (1928), 1, and see too *BICS* xiv (1967), 59). Between ἔσχατος and ὕστατος it is hardly possible to decide (both are applied to the last charioteer and his team at Soph. *El.* 734), but if a decision has to be made, it would probably be better method to follow $Σ^π$ here too.

50. 5: καὶ διδύμης, πολύμητι, σοφῆς ἐδράξαο νίκης] καὶ διπλῆς, πολύμητι, σοφῶς ἐδράξαο νίκης. The adverb σοφῶς seems preferable to a second epithet with νίκης, and the fact that διπλόος occurs in two other epigrams from this block (347. 2, 349. 5) perhaps tilts the balance against διδύμης (which might be held, however, the *lectio difficilior*).

Lastly, 49. 6: τοῖς δέ] τοῖσδε, which is obviously correct, though at 48. 6, where τούσδε is no less obviously correct, $Σ^π$, together with both Pl. and L, offers τούς [*sic* all three despite Beckby] δέ [δὲ L].

In neither case, of course, will there have been any distinction between the readings on the original stone. It will have been different with 41. 3, where for δ' ἔθανες in both Pl. and L, $Σ^π$ has δὲ θάνες. Apostrophes are marked on the extant inscriptions: e.g. at 340. 4 (δ'), 356. 5 (δ'), and 353. 1, where the division κρίνειν δ' ἐθέλοιεν ἀέθλους of Pl. is confirmed by the inscription (δὲ θέλοιεν would, of course, have involved a violation of Hermann's bridge). Naturally there is little to be said between δ' ἔθανες and δὲ θάνες, but the poet may have preferred the unaugmented form to avoid the elision, as Nonnus would have (e.g. *Dion.* vii. 354 δὲ κέλευε for δ' ἐκέλευε): at 374. 6 Planudes has κείνῳ δὲ δόσαν, L δ' ἔδοσαν. Yet at 367. 5 (not in L) Pl. has ὡς δ' ἔθανεν. If we prefer δὲ θάνες at 41. 3, we should presumably write δὲ θάνεν at 367. 5, since both come from the same monument. Gregory of Nazianzus writes οὐδὲ θάνεν at *AP* viii. 41. 1. At Paul Sil. *A. Pl.* 278. 5 editors all print Pl.'s εἰ δ' ἐθέλεις: I should be inclined to prefer $Σ^π$'s εἰ δὲ θέλεις.

There are only ten epigrams for which we have $Σ^π$ as well as Pl., and in those ten epigrams there are at least two and probably three or even four errors in Pl. There are forty-four epigrams for which we do not have $Σ^π$, and we must face the probability of a similar proportion of error in these.

APPENDIX C · THE INSCRIPTIONS

At 340. 6 Pl. has:

ἔνθεν ἔην Πρασίνοις ἔρις ἄσπετος, ἔνθεν ἀϋτή·
"ὃς Βενέτους τέρψει, κοίρανε, καὶ Πρασίνους",

which Paton translates: 'Hence arose a keen rivalry on the part of the Greens, hence a shout of applause for him, O King, who will give joy both to Blues and to Greens.' It is far from clear why an epigram from a monument by the Blues should state so confidently that Porphyrius is about to please the Greens as well as the Blues, nor is the construction easy. Hence Brunck's ὡς ... τέρψαις (i.e. ὡς Βενέτους [sc. τέρπεις], τέρψαις, κοίρανε, καὶ Πρασίνους, 'As you delight the Blues, O King, so may you delight the Greens.') Boissonade preferred ὡς ... τέρψεν.

The monument reveals that what the poet actually wrote is ὡς ... τέρψῃ, i.e. ὡς Βενέτους [sc. ἔτερψεν], τέρψῃ, κοίρανε, καὶ Πρασίνους, 'Just as Porphyrius has delighted the Blues, so may he delight the Greens.' I take the subjunctive form τέρψῃ as being equivalent in meaning to the by now defunct classical optative, a common Byzantine usage. Kaibel, less plausibly, took it for a future, another Byzantine usage. Less plausibly, because while the author, obviously a partisan of the Blues, might well represent the Greens *wishing* that Porphyrius *might* win for them, he would hardly have put into their mouths a confident prediction that Porphyrius *will* win for them.

This interpretation (and punctuation) is fully borne out by the relevant portion of the prose acclamation lower down on the same face of the monument:

δὸς ἡμῖν Πορφύριν, | ἵν᾽ οὓς Πορφύριν |
ἔτερψεν εἰς Βένετον, τέρψει καὶ εἰς Πράσινον.

See the discussion above, pp. 67–8; here τέρψει does stand for the subjunctive, after ἵνα. Here too we find the wish that Porphyrius might win for them placed in the mouth of the Greens. There can be no doubt that the τέρψῃ of the monument (construed as a wish) is correct. Yet it has been a curiously long time percolating through to editions of the Anthology. It is understandable that it missed the Didot edition, the relevant volume of which appeared only one year after Kaibel had identified the epigram on the monument (1872). More surprising that it remained unknown to Paton (who certainly knew of the existence of the monument, since he includes a sketch of the front face at v. 300) and to Beckby (who has now incorporated it in his second edition). And certainly inexcusable that Vasiliev should have reproduced both text and translation from Paton when he purported to be quoting the text of the monument. Nor does the sorry tale end here. Woodward and Wace made the blunder of assuming that Brunck's ὡς ... τέρψαις was the reading of Planudes (p. 80 n. 1), and Tabachovitz[1] seems to have thought that Planudes' τέρψει was Paton's conjecture! More surprisingly R. Keydell used the τέρψει of the prose inscription to support Pl.'s τέρψει for the epigram, forgetting that we have the original inscription for the epigram as well.[2]

342 : Despite the fact that the other epigram (342) on the old monument is better preserved (p. 132), its readings remain unknown to editors of the Anthology. Admittedly Kaibel included only 342 (and its corresponding prose acclamation) in his *Epigrammata Graeca* (1878) —all that Henzen had published in 1847—but the remaining inscriptions were all published by Mordtmann in 1880, and again by Woodward and Wace in 1912. Beckby discovered the existence of the monument between his two editions, but was under the impression that 342 was 'fast völlig zerstört' on the stone. In fact only eleven letters are missing—and three divergences from Pl. gained. For lines 1–2 Pl. offers:

αὐτὸν Πορφύριον μὲν ἀπηκριβώσατο χαλκῷ
ὁ πλάστης, ἔμπνουν οἷα τυπωσάμενος.

The stone gives ἀπηκρειβώσατο in line 1 and ἔνπνουν in line 2. Of course, there is a sense in which Pl. is correct and the inscription itself incorrect, but the point is not merely a trivial matter of orthography. It means we must recognize that Pl. (or rather the man who originally collected the epigrams from the monuments) felt at liberty to correct the orthography of the inscriptions. Thus the relative consistency of orthography in the MS. tradition may be illusory, imposed by the collector.

And his 'corrections' may not always have been corrections at all. For example, at 356. 3, where Pl. has εἰς for the ἧς of the stone. The source of Pl.'s erroneous text may well be deliberate alteration of ἧς in the belief that it was an etacism for εἰς.

The third error in Pl.'s text for 342. 2 is a similar normalization. The whole line is beyond doubt a direct imitation of a line from a 'Doric' poem by Archias, *AP* xv. 51. 2, ὁ πλάστας ἔμπνουν θῆρα τυπωσάμενος. Pl. gives πλάστης: the stone has πλάστας. Since it is the only Doric form in the poem, our collector (or some intermediary between him and Planudes) had little compunction in 'correcting' it,

[1] *Eranos* 1958, 162.   [2] *BZ* 1959, 364.

APPENDIX C 269

in this case obscuring more than an orthographical point. We have seen already that L (or again, more probably its source) made a further assault on the Doricisms at a later stage.

To pass on to the readings from the new monument:

351. 5: εὗραο] εὗρεο, discussed above, p. 262.

352. 3: ὄγκον ὁμοῦ καὶ κάλλος. ὅπερ Φύσις... No editor has queried the singular relative ὅπερ after the double antecedent. The stone gives ἅπερ, which is plainly correct. On the other hand, εὐόρκοις ὑπὸ χείλεσι at 352. 5, condemned by van Herwerden ('quid hoc sit, non intellego', *Mnemos.* ii (1874), 346, writing τόδε for ὑπό), is confirmed by the stone. ὑπό+dative is not infrequent in late poets as little more than a metrically convenient expansion of the bare dative (see LSJ s.v. ὑπό, B. 4 *ad fin.*)

356. 3: εἰς] ἧς, certainly correct, but since the point is important for the dating of the monument, it has been discussed in context at pp. 160–2 above.

APPENDIX D · EMENDATIONS

In the light of the two preceding appendices we can hardly have absolute faith in the text of the epigrams for which we have only Pl. and Planudes' own earlier efforts in L. There are in fact a number of cases where corruption is sufficiently plain to require emendation, and it seemed most convenient to discuss them together:

341. 3-4: δῆμος μὲν γὰρ ἐμὸν γέρας ἤεεν· οἱ δ᾽ ἕτεροί με | δίζοντ᾽ αὖθις ἔχειν νῖκος ἀπειπάμενοι.

3: It is not just the δῆμος as a whole which has put up the statue, but Porphyrius' δῆμος, as opposed to οἱ ἕτεροι, the other δῆμος. We must therefore accept Brunck's ἐμός.

4: Our collector at his correcting again. Musurus' νεῖκος is demanded by the context (p. 164). But, dealing as he was with poems where there is such frequent mention of victories (cf. Νίκης in l. 2 and *passim* in the other epigrams), the collector took νεῖκος here to be an incorrect spelling for νῖκος, without inspecting the immediate context closely enough.

343. 2: ἄνθετο νικητὴς κοίρανος Αὐσονίων. Almost certainly we should accept the common correction νικητὴν (sc. Porphyrius) assuming that it was attracted into the nominative by κοίρανος, just as ἐμός at 341. 3 was attracted into the neuter by the γέρας following. However, I should not like to rule out altogether the possibility that the text is sound. The vocabulary of these epigrams is very formulaic, and νικητής is not elsewhere applied to a charioteer. I do not wish to suggest that the word is not common in agonistic contexts as a whole, for it is: but we should also bear in mind that it is commonest of all at this period as an element in imperial titulature, νικητὴς τροπαιοῦχος ἀεὶ Σεβαστός (*victor ac triumphator semper Augustus*). It was so stock a title that normally no specific victory was required to justify it, but in view of the allusion at 341. 2 to the statue of Nike by which Porphyrius' statue stood, it is perhaps possible that we have here two hints of a recent victory by Anastasius. On the other hand, it could be that it was precisely this use of νικητής that assisted in the corruption of an original accusative into a nominative to agree with κοίρανος. Since the part of the monument where 343 stood is broken off, we are never likely to know.

350. 3: ἂν ἄναξ] ἄρ᾽ ἄναξ Jacobs. ἂν (also the reading of L) makes no sense, and is the easiest of corruptions before ἄναξ.

APPENDIX D 271

362. 6: ἀέθλων] ἀεθλῶν. There was no accent on the stone, and the collector or some later copyist supplied the wrong one (p. 263).

378. 5: τοὔνεκα καὶ χρυσῷ μιν ἀνεγράψαντο μετάλλῳ. Brunck's χρυσέῳ is highly probable. In general, because epigrammatists of the day seem to have preferred the epic flavour of uncontracted forms, e.g. with the same synizesis and in each case of statues, χρυσέην at *A. Pl.* 71. 2 and 314. 1; χρυσέοισιν ἀγάλμασιν at Kaibel 896. 4; χρυσέῳ ἀγάλματι at Kaibel 897. 1). More particularly because of the Porphyrius epigram 355. 5 ἔπρεπέ μιν χρυσέῳ ἐν ἀγάλματι, which the author of 378 almost certainly had in mind.

Next two less certain examples:

335. 5 (though the whole poem must be quoted):

> Πορφύριον Κάλχαντος ἄναξ καὶ δῆμος ἐγείρει
> πολλοῖς εὐκαμάτοις βριθόμενον στεφάνοις,
> πᾶσι μεθ' ἡνιόχοισι νεώτατον ὅσσον ἄριστον.
> ἀλλὰ τόσον νίκης κάρτος ἐνεγκάμενον
> ἔπρεπέ μιν χρυσέῳ ἐν ἀγάλματι, μὴ δ' ἐνὶ χαλκῷ   5
> τοῦτον τοῖς ἄλλοις εἴκελον ἐστάμεναι.

First a small point: despite Beckby's note, it is obvious from his accent that Planudes intended (what editors rightly print) μὴ δ', not μηδ'.

Next, μιν in the same line. In view of the second pronoun τοῦτον in l. 6 editors have usually printed Stephanus' μήν. But in *Mnemosyne* xiv (1886), 414, van Herwerden suggested the different solution of retaining μιν and emending τοῦτον to τούτῳ (agreeing with χαλκῷ). τοῦτον I should be reluctant to lose. τούτῳ seems to me both weak in itself and uncharacteristic of the genre. The regular pattern is for οὗτος or τοῦτον (usually in the first line) to designate the honorand himself. See the indexes of first lines in *AP* (Beckby or Dübner) or in the collections of Preger and Kaibel (and Peek, *GV* i, for epitaphs); for some further illustrations, J. and L. Robert, *REG* lxxviii (1965), 105, and L. Robert, in *L'Épigramme grecque* (Entretiens sur l'antiquité classique xiv), 1969, 206–7. Note from the charioteer series alone: 45. 1, τοῦτον Ἰουλιανόν ...; 46. 1, Πορφύριος Λίβυς οὗτος ...; 47. 1, τοῦτον Πορφύριον. It is rare to find the pronoun as late as the last line, but note the last couplet of 349: τόπερ λάχε χάλκεος ἥρως | οὗτος ὁ τεθρίπποις κῦδος ἑλὼν ἀρετῆς. Our epigram begins with just Πορφύριον, and, taken by itself, a last line beginning τοῦτον would seem to be very appropriate.

On the other hand, I am hardly less reluctant to see μιν go. First there is what is surely an imitation of this line in the later epigram

from a Uranius monument (p. 143), 378. 5: τοὔνεκα καὶ χρυσέῳ μιν...
More important is the matter of punctuation. Editors have always punctuated with a comma after l. 3 and full stop at the end of l. 4. At first sight the apparent link between τόσον and ὅσσον in lines 4 and 3 might seem to support this punctuation, but the function of ὅσσον is surely limited to linking νεώτατον and ἄριστον. Compare too Paton's translation of 4: 'winner of as many victories as any'. Is this really what the Greek implies, and, if so, is it really a very appropriate compliment (one would have expected '*more* victories than the others')? Further, as van Herwerden remarked (loc. cit.), lines 2 and 4 are virtually identical in content. Line 2 explains why the Emperor and people have put up a statue to Porphyrius, and it would be very feeble to come back to a repetition of the same reason in 4 after the different point made in 3.

Much neater (as above, following van Herwerden) to punctuate with a full stop after 3 and take 4 with 5–6. This division seems to me confirmed by a parallel not noticed by van Herwerden, a direct echo from the monument of Constantine:

χρύσεον ἀντ' ἀρετῆς γέρας ἔπρεπε Κωνσταντίνῳ,
οὐδένα τῆς τέχνης τοῖον ἐνεγκαμένης. (43. 1–2)

The τοῖον ἐνεγκαμένης phrase explains ἔπρεπε here just as τόσον... ἐνεγκάμενον would explain ἔπρεπε (with the suggested punctuation) in 335. 4. For a parallel to the relatively rare full stop at the end of the second hexameter cf. 44. This punctuation would of course rule out μήν, which could not possibly come as late as seventh word in its sentence.

I would conclude, then, that despite the resulting incoherence the poet added the formulaic τοῦτον for emphasis after he had already written μιν—much as if he had written Πορφύριον in place of μιν. For a close parallel cf. *A. Plan.* 72, from the first year of Justin II:

τὸν δ' ὑπὲρ εὐνομίας ἐριθηλέος ἐνθάδε τοῦτον
ἐξ ὑπάτου μίτρης στῆσεν ἄνασσα πόλις. (5–6)

Here too editors have not been happy about the τοῦτον after τὸν δέ (or rather, surely, τόνδε), and Jacobs toyed with the idea of a τούτων governed by ἄνασσα. Once more, however, it would disturb a formula: ἄνασσα, βασιλίς, βασίλισσα, βασίλεια κτλ. πόλις are standard periphrases in the literature, both prose and verse, of the Empire for first Rome and then Constantinople. The only sort of qualification that could readily be tolerated would be a πάντων perhaps, or a phrase like Bassus' κόσμου παντὸς ἄνασσα πόλις (*AP* ix. 236. 6)—hardly an undefined τούτων in the previous line.

These two examples of a redundant τοῦτον in a similar context ('this

APPENDIX D

statue here') perhaps prop each other up. I would translate 335 as follows: 'The Emperor and people raise up Porphyrius son of Calchas, weighed down with many well-won crowns, the youngest and best of all charioteers. But it were more fitting for him (μιν), winner of so great a mass of victories, to stand here (τοῦτον), a statue of gold, not bronze like the others.' So my only correction of Pl. here would be over the question of punctuation.

367. 5: ὡς δὲ θάνεν (sc. Constantine) ποθέουσα (sc. the city) φίλον τύπον ἄνθετο τοῦδε (Constantine again). Now since Constantine begins the line as the subject of θάνεν, he makes a rather awkward and unexpected second appearance in the genitive at its end. Quite apart from this what one would expect in such a context is a reference, not so much to Constantine himself, as to the statue to which the epigram is supposed to be drawing our attention. I venture to suggest that what the poet wrote is the conventional τοῦτον (or perhaps, rather, τόνδε). Apart from the examples of οὗτος/τοῦτον just discussed, cf. 361. 1, οὗτος, ἐγερσιθέητρε, τέος τύπος.

349. 3: πολλάκι γὰρ δῆμος προφερέστερα ἔργα κομίζων | ἤνεσε... No editor has ever been troubled by this line, yet there are several problems. (1) What does it mean? Hardly 'for often the people, their attention turned to exploits more than usually brilliant' (Paton, presumably thinking of the Homeric ἔργα κομίζειν = 'attend to affairs'). (2) προφερής is normally used of people or animals. The example LSJ s.v. II quotes, 'of plants and young persons, forced, premature, precocious', is obviously metaphorical, quite different from ἔργα. (3) The hiatus, otherwise unparalleled in such technically competent post-Nonnian work (of the other examples in the series, 350. 4, 354. 2, and 373. 2 are venial by comparison, and 335. 5 would have been passed by Nonnus himself).

My first thought, comparing 348. 2 (from the same base) where the Greens are described as δῆμος ὁ πρῶτα φέρων, was to write προφερέστερος, which would dispose of (2) and (3), but does nothing for ἔργα κομίζων. But discussion with Alan Griffiths has convinced me that the text is probably sound and the elision a deliberate epicism, by analogy with the Homeric πολεμήϊα ἔργα (Od. xii. 116) et sim. Even so, it must still be interpreted in the light of 348. 2. προφερέστερα ἔργα κομίζων is an unhappy and incoherent conflation of two Homeric tags, intended as a high-flown variant on πρῶτα φέρων and meaning simply that the Greens are the better of the two factions. Compare too the comparative at 355. 3, where the Greens are called ἄρειον μέρος.

370. 2: ἔπρεπε γὰρ τρισσοῖς εἰν ἑνὶ χώρῳ ἔχειν. 'It was fitting that three should stand in one spot.' ἔχειν could just be made to yield the sense 'stand', but Brunck's χῶρον is obviously preferable, especially in the

light of 376. 3-4, τὸ δὲ οἱ γέρας ἤλυθε πρῶτον | ἐκ πρασίνων, οἷς δὴ γείτονα χῶρον ἔχει. Cf. too A. Pl. 41. 3-4 (Agathias), on a statue of an official put up close to statues of the Emperor and Empress: ὄφρα καὶ αὐτῇ | εἰκόνι χῶρον ἔχῃ γείτονα κοιρανίης. εἰν ἑνί would then be absolute, 'together', as frequently in late poets: Nonnus, xiv. 203, xxxi. 281, xxxviii. 215; Agathias, AP vii. 572. 5; Paul, AP v. 293. 12, vi. 65. 9; anon., A. Pl. 66. 1 (like so many 'Nonnisms', it does not in fact originate with Nonnus: cf. the epigram on Claudian, Kaibel 879. 1, and Leonidas Alex., AP ix. 42. 1). Under the circumstances, the corruption of χῶρον to χώρῳ was almost inevitable.

In conclusion, a case where the text has been wrongly altered: 350. 4: ἀνακτορέῳ] ἀνακτορίῳ, Keydell (BZ lii (1959), 364), followed now by Beckby (iv², p. 772 n.). But both leave ἀνακτορέοιο at 336. 3 (also the reading of L). At 358. 4 Lascaris' correction κοιρανίης for the κοιρανέης of Pl. (and L, it can now be added) has been generally accepted. Yet at (e.g.) A. Pl. 41. 4 Planudes uses the correct spelling κοιρανίης, and perhaps we ought to allow the possibility that in all three cases from the charioteer epigrams the use of the -εη form reflects the orthography of the monument. In favour of the alternative, that they are Planudean 'corrections', note the following line from a poem of Planudes' own (Maximi Planudis Epp., ed. M. Treu (1890), 204), καίπερ ἐνὶ μεγάροισιν ἀνακτορέοις προσεδρεύων.

It is perhaps also worth mentioning 367. 4, ἀμφέθετο στεφάνους, where Beckby's doubly misleading note reads: 'ἀμφέτθετο Pl. em. Lasc.' Trifling slip though it would have been, Planudes did not in fact make it: the reading of the Marcianus is unquestionably ἀμφέθετο. In any event one cannot accurately speak of Lascaris 'emending' Planudes, for he did not use the Marcianus (see above, p. 108)— though he does seem to have had some knowledge of the BM apograph (Gallavotti, 'Planudea', pp. 35-6).

ADDENDA

p. 1 : Henzen refers to the man to whom we owe our first knowledge of the old base simply as 'sig. Abeken' (*Bull. Inst.* 1847, 122). It was no doubt through familiarity rather than ignorance that Kaibel (1871) and Mordtmann (1880) likewise dispensed with his initial, but ignorance is plainly behind Vasiliev's 'a certain Mr. Abeken' (*DOP* 1948, 32).

Fortunately, his identity is not even now lost beyond recall: Heinrich Abeken, Prussian theologian and politician, best known as 'Bismarck's pen'. The letters and journals of which his widow published extracts in 1898 reveal that he spent summer 1845 exploring the Holy Land (where he must have copied the other inscription which Henzen published for him, of Zenobia and Vaballathus in Palmyra) before visiting Constantinople. Here he was 'cordially received by Sir Stratford Canning, the British Ambassador' (*Bismarck's Pen: the Life of Heinrich Abeken*, edited from his letters and journals by his wife, authorized translation by Mrs. Charles Edward Barrett-Lennard and M. W. Hoper (London 1911), 76)—a connection which no doubt helped to gain him access to the Seraglio. It was only to be expected that one who had at Berlin been a pupil of Boeckh as well as of Schleiermacher and Neander should have had both the interest and the ability to copy Greek inscriptions.

After this Abeken returned to Rome, where he had spent the years 1831-8 as chaplain to the Prussian legation—and as part-time assistant to his patron K. von Bunsen in the administration of the newly founded German Instituto di Corrispondenza Archaeologica.[1] What more natural than that he should have entrusted his inscriptions for publication in the *Bullettino* of the Institute to its promising young epigraphist W. Henzen?

According to his widow, Abeken's journals were particularly full for the period of his eastern travels. It may be that they contain valuable details about the excavations of 1845. It is to be hoped that someone who reads this note may be able to trace their present whereabouts.

p. 44: Two passages of Chrysostom are relevant to the crowning of athletes and charioteers by the Emperor in person. According to *In Ep. ad Phil. hom.* xii (probably delivered in Constantinople: cf.

[1] By an odd coincidence the second secretary and librarian of the Institute was *Wilhelm* Abeken. Demonstrably not our man, for he died in January 1843, two years before the discovery of the Porphyrius base.

ADDENDA

J. Quasten, *Patrology* iii (1960), 447-8), in the case of those who especially distinguished themselves, οὐ στεφανοῦσιν ἐν τῷ σταδίῳ κάτω, ἀλλ' ἄνω καλέσας ὁ βασιλεὺς ἐκεῖ στεφανοῖ (*PG* lxii. 272). *In Ep. ii ad Cor. hom.* iii (probably referring to Antioch: Quasten, p. 445) likewise describes how on occasions it is the Emperor ἄνωθεν rather than a κῆρυξ κάτω who crowns the victor (*PG* lxi. 413). Thus the passage of Ammianus quoted in note 3 need not imply that Gallus descended to the arena to crown Thorax.

p. 54: Malalas p. 340. 16 shows the *praepositus* standing next to the Emperor in the Kathisma under Valens.

p. 74: Possibly not Δάζις λέγω{ν}, νικᾷ ... but Δάζις λέγων· νικᾷ ... That is to say, Δάζις λέγων is perhaps a lemma referring to the partisan represented on the relief immediately below: 'This is Dazis, saying "Long live the Greens".'

pp. 74-5: Add a newly published example from Phthiotic Thebes (P. M. Lazarides, Πρακτ. Ἀρχ. Ἑταιρ. 1969 (1971), 21, with pl. 23*a*): + νηκᾷ ἡ τύχη Πρασίνων τῶν ὀρθοδόξων + (for other graffiti mentioning the 'orthodoxy' of the Greens see *Circus Factions*, Ch. VII). And three more, unpublished, from the seats of the theatre at Carian Aphrodisias (kindly supplied by Charlotte Wrinch, with the permission of Kenan Erim and Joyce Reynolds): + νικᾷ ἡ τύχη τῶν Βενέτων (seventh block, row 12); νικᾷ ἡ τύχη τῶν Βενέτ(ων) (eighth block, row 13); νικᾷ ἡ τύχη τῶν Πρασίνων κ(αὶ) τὸν μίμον τοῦ Πρασίνου (south wall of northmost door in skene).

p. 179: According to the *Guinness Book of Records* (18th ed. 1971), 273, the oldest jockey ever was Levi Barlingame, 'who rode his last race at Stafford, Kansas, U.S.A., in 1932 aged 80'. At the other end of the scale, Frank Wootton (English champion jockey 1909-12) rode his first winner in South Africa at the age of 9. To bring the modern victory totals up to date, the record per annum is now held by Herve Filion with an amazing 485 in 1970, and Willie Shoemaker rode his 6223rd winner on his fortieth birthday (19 August 1971).

p. 184: Michael Vickers points out that the absence of such central metae both in circus representations on mosaics and on extant spinae strongly tells against my suggestion. Perhaps the Red and White metae did not actually protrude from the spina.

p. 207: A Reader of the Press, with that varied learning which is their characteristic, acutely points out that Worrell was knighted at, not before his retirement (at least from Test cricket).

BIBLIOGRAPHY

This is not a full bibliography of the book, but a list of those works I have found most useful or important. Items cited once or twice in passing are omitted, as also are almost all books and articles relating to the circus factions and circus institutions, for which see the comprehensive bibliography to my forthcoming *Circus Factions*.

ALFÖLDI, Andreas. *Die Kontorniaten* (Budapest 1943). See p. 20 n. 2.

—— 'Die Ausgestaltung des monarchischen Zeremoniells am römischen Kaiserhofe' and 'Insignien und Tracht der römischen Kaiser', in *Mitteilungen des Deutschen Archäologischen Instituts, Römische Abteilung* 49 (1934), 1–118 and 50 (1935), 1–171. Now reprinted together under the title *Die monarchische Repräsentation im römischen Kaiserreiche*, with a full index by Elisabeth Alföldi-Rosenbaum, by the Wissenschaftliche Buch-Gesellschaft Darmstadt, 1970.

AUBRETON, Robert. 'La tradition manuscrite des épigrammes de l'Anthologie grecque', *RÉA* lxx (1968), 32–82.

—— 'Michel Psellos et l'Anthologie palatine', *L'Antiquité classique* xxxviii (1969), 459–62.

—— 'L'archétype de la tradition planudéenne de l'Anthologie grecque', *Scriptorium* xxiii (1969), 69–87.

BALSDON, J. P. V. D. *Life and Leisure in Ancient Rome* (London 1969).

BECKWITH, John. *The Art of Constantinople*[2], London and New York, 1968.

BELTING-IHM, Christa. 'Ein römischer Circussarcophag', *Jahrbuch des römisch-germanischen Zentralmuseums Mainz* viii (1961), 195–208.

BROWN, Peter. 'Sorcery, Demons and the rise of Christianity: from Late Antiquity into the Middle Ages', *Witchcraft Confessions and Accusations*: Association of Social Anthropologists Monographs ix (1970), 17–45 (= *Religion and Society in the Age of Saint Augustine* (1972), 119–46).

BRUNS, G. *Der Obelisk und seine Basis auf dem Hippodrom zu Konstantinopel* (*Istanbuler Forschungen* 7), Istanbul 1935.

BURY, J. B. 'The Ceremonial Book of Constantine Porphyrogennetos', *English Historical Review* xxii (1907), 209–27 and 417–39.

CAMERON, Alan. 'The *Garlands* of Meleager and Philip', *GRBS* ix (1968), 323–49.

CAMERON, Alan. 'The date of Zosimus' *New History*', *Philologus* cxiii (1969), 106–10.

—— 'Michael Psellus and the Date of the Palatine Anthology', *GRBS* xi (1970), 339–50.

CAMERON, Averil and Alan. 'The Cycle of Agathias', *JHS* lxxxvi (1966), 6–25, cf. ibid. lxxxvii (1967), 131.

CHASTAGNOL, A. *Le Sénat romain sous le règne d'Odoacre: recherches sur l'épigraphie du Colisée au Ve siècle* (Antiquitas iii. 3), Bonn 1966.

EBERSOLT, J. 'A propos du relief de Porphyrios', *Revue archéologique* 1911, ii, 76–85.

—— *Constantinople byzantine et les voyageurs du Levant* (Paris 1918).

—— *Mission archéologique de Constantinople* (Paris 1921).

FIRATLI, Nezih and ROLLAS, Andrée N. 'Les nouvelles trouvailles de Topkapi Saray', *İstanbul Arkeoloji Müzeleri Yıllığı* (*Annual of the Archaeological Museums of Istanbul*) xi–xii (1964), 199–206.

GAGÉ, J. 'ΣΤΑΥΡΟΣ ΝΙΚΟΠΟΙΟΣ: la victoire impériale dans l'empire chrétien', *Rev. d'hist. et de philos. religieuses* xiii (1933) 370–400.

GALLAVOTTI, Carlo. 'Planudea', *Bollettino del Comitato per la preparazione dell'edizione nazionale dei classici greci e latini* vii (1959), 25–50, and viii (1960), 11–23.

GOTTWALD, Joseph. 'Das byzantinische Kugelspiel im Kaiser-Friedrich-Museum zu Berlin', *Archäologischer Anzeiger* 1931, 152–72.

GRABAR, André. *L'Empereur dans l'art byzantin* (Publications de la Faculté des Lettres de l'Université de Strasbourg, 75), Paris 1936.

—— *L'Iconoclasme byzantin: dossier archéologique*, Paris 1957.

GUILLAND, R. 'Le Velon', *Speculum* xxiii (1948), 676–82 (= *Études de topographie byzantine* i (1969) 371–4).

—— 'Les portes de l'Hippodrome', *Jahrb. d. Öst. Byz. Gesellsch.* iv (1955), 55–85 (= *Études topogr.*, i. 509–41).

—— 'La disparition des Courses', *Mél. ... O. et M. Merlier* (1955), 1–17 (= *Études topogr.* i. 542–55).

—— 'L'Arène; L'Épine; Les Bornes; L'Euripe; Le Stama-Pi', *Jahrb. d. Öst. Byz. Gesellsch.* vi (1957), 25–44 (= *Études topogr.* i. 442–61).

—— 'Le Palais du Kathisma', *BS* xviii (1957), 39–76 (= *Études topogr.* i. 462–98).

GYLLIUS (GILLES), P. *De Topographia Constantinopoleos* (1561).

HAFNER, G. *Viergespanne in Vorderansicht: die repräsentative Darstellung der quadriga in der griechischen und der späteren Kunst* (Neue Deutsche Forschungen, Abt. Archäologie, 2), Berlin 1938.

JANIN, R. *Constantinople byzantine*[2] (Paris 1964).

KAIBEL, G. *De monumentorum aliquot graecorum carminibus* (Diss. Bonn 1871).

KOUKOULÈS, Ph. Βυζαντινῶν βίος καὶ πολιτισμός Γ' (*Vie et civilisation byzantines* iii), Athens 1949.

L'ORANGE, H. P. *Art Forms and Civic Life in the Late Roman Empire* (1965).

MAAS, P. 'Der byzantinische Zwölfsilber', *BZ* xii (1903), 278-323.

MANGO, Cyril. 'L'euripe de l'hippodrome de Constantinople: essai d'identification', *RÉB* vii (1949), 180-93.

—— 'Three Imperial Byzantine Sarcophagi discovered in 1750', *DOP* xvi (1962), 397 f.

—— 'Antique Statuary and the Byzantine Beholder', *DOP* xvii (1963), 55-75.

—— *Treasures of Turkey*, Skira Books 1966.

MARICQ, A. 'Factions du cirque et partis populaires', *Académie royale de Belgique, Bulletin de la classe des lettres et des sciences morales et politiques* xxxvi (1950), 396-421.

MARTINDALE, J. R. Public Disorders in the Late Roman Empire, unpublished Oxford B.Phil. Diss. 1960.

MATTSSON, A. *Untersuchungen zur Epigrammsammlung des Agathias*, Diss. Lund 1942.

MITSAKIS, K. *The Language of Romanos the Melodist* (Byz. Archiv xi), Munich 1967.

MORDTMANN, A. D. 'Das Denkmal des Porphyrios', *Mitteilungen des Deutschen Archäologischen Instituts in Athen* v (1880), 295-308.

PEKÁRY, T. 'Goldene Statuen der Kaiserzeit', *Röm. Mitt.* lxxv (1968), 143 f.

RAMBAUD, A. *De Byzantino hippodromo*, Diss. Paris 1870.

ROBERT, Louis. 'Pantomimen im griechischen Orient', *Hermes* lxv (1930), 106-22 (= *Opera Minora Selecta* i (1969), 654-70).

—— *Les Gladiateurs dans l'Orient grec* (Paris 1940).

RODENWALDT, G. 'Römische Reliefs: Vorstufen zur Spätantike', *JDAI* lv (1940), 12-43.

SCOTT, Kenneth. 'The Significance of Statues in Precious Metals in Emperor Worship', *TAPA* lxii (1931), 101-23.

SEYRIG, H. 'Sur quelques sculptures palmyréniennes: 5. L'attelage déployé', *Syria* xviii (1937), 43–51.

TABACHOVITZ, D. 'Zu den dem Wagenlenker Porphyrios gewidmeten Inschriften', *Eranos* lvi (1958), 159–72.

TOYNBEE, J. M. C. 'Beasts and their names in the Roman Empire', *Papers of the British School at Rome* xvi (1948), 24–37.

TREITINGER, Otto. *Die oströmische Kaiser- und Reichsidee nach ihrer Gestaltung im höfischen Zeremoniell*, Jena 1938.

VASILIEV, A. A. 'Imperial Porphyry Sarcophagi in Constantinople', *DOP* iv (1948), 3–20.

—— 'The Monument of Porphyrius in the Hippodrome of Constantinople', ib. 29–49.

VOGEL, Lise. 'Circus Race Scenes in the Early Roman Empire', *The Art Bulletin* li (1969), 155–60.

WEINREICH, O. *Martials Grabepigramm auf den Pantomimen Paris* (Sitzb. d. Heidelb. Akad. d. Wiss., Phil.-hist. Klasse 1940/1, no. 1).

—— *Epigramm und Pantomimus* (ib., Phil.-hist. Klasse 1944/8, no. 1).

WOODWARD, A. M. 'Some Notes on the Monument of Porphyrius at Constantinople', *Annual of the British School at Athens* xvii (1910/11), 88–92.

WOODWARD, A. M. and WACE, A. J. B. 'The Monument of Porphyrius', Appendix to W. S. George, *The Church of St. Eirene at Constantinople* (Oxford 1912), pp. 79–84.

YOUNG, D. C. C. 'On Planudes' Edition of Theognis and a Neglected Apograph of the Anthologia Planudea', *Parola del passato* x (1955), 197 ff.

INDEX OF GREEK AND LATIN WORDS

actuarius, 44
ἀγένειοι, 155
ἀγλαΐη, 65
ἀεθλεύω, 263
ἀντίς, 73
ἀολλίζω, 93
βαιός, 92
Βυζαντιὰς Ῥώμη, 253-4
γέρας, 65, 162
δεκάς (ἐτέων), 65-6
δῆμος/δῆμοι, 71
δημόσιον, 68
εἰς Πράσινον, 67 f.
ἐλέγχω = defeat, 81
ἔπρεπε, 214-15
ἔχειν (of victories), 67
εὔριπος, 180
ζώνη, 261
ἠριγένεια, 209
ἴουλος, 153

κυλίειν ὄρναν, 63
μάρτυς, 91
μετὰ πότμον, 259
μονόπορτος, 57-8
μόνος (καὶ πρῶτος), 207-8
ναὶ τάχα, 91-2
νίκα, νικᾷ, nica(s), 45, 55, 76 ff.
νικᾷ ἡ τύχη, 74 f.
μικροπανίτης, 150
παλίνορσος, 167 n. 1
pannus, 71
παράδοξος, 82
παρακυπτικά, 52-3, 200-1
populus/populi, 71
πρόκυψις, 200
στέφανος, στέφειν, 162
τέρψις, 69
τοσσάτιος, 92
tu vincas, 77-9, 248, 251
φακτιονάριος, 150

GENERAL INDEX

This index attempts to include most significant people, places, and topics, with the exception of Porphyrius himself and his two bases, for which the table of contents will furnish adequate guide.

Abeken, H., 1
accentuation and prosody, Byzantine, 192 f.
acclamations, of factions, 30–2, 42, 74 ff., 81–2, 248–51
Aerius, charioteer, 46, 79, 204
Africa, 30
Agathias, 61, 65, 83–4, 88, 90, 94, 112, 113, 115, 116 n. 1, 147, 186 n. 4, 190, 214, 215, 253–4, 257
agonothetes, 139 n. 1
Alcaeus of Messene, 89
Alexander, Lysippan statues of, 186–7
Alexandria, 29, 79, 170, 236
Alexius III, 8
Ammianus Marcellinus, 217, 236, 245
Anastasius, Emperor, 32, 54, 150, 154, 228, 231, 233–44, 251–2
    iron statue of, 184–5, 219–20, 224
animals, shown in hippodrome, 230
Anthology, Greek, 1–2, 7, 10, 31
    Palatine (*AP*), Palatinus gr. 23, 97 ff., 120, 148, 194
Anastasius (cos. 517), 228
Antioch, 160, 164, 234, 243, 246
Antonina, Belisarius' wife, 157, 158
Aphrodisias, 59
Apolaustus, pantomime's name, 171
Arabius scholasticus, 91, 218
Arcadius, Emperor, 232, 235
    column of, 17
arch of Constantine in Rome, 40
Archer, Fred, 179 n. 1
Areobindus (cos. 506), 44, 228
Aristaenetus, epistolographer, 176
Artemius, charioteer's name, 172
Aurelian (cos. 400), 217, 224
awning, in circuses etc., 35 ff.
Ayvan Saray, gate of, 17
'Azotius', 110–11

banners, waved by partisans, 32–9
'beardless', class of athletes, 155

Belisarius, 56 ff.
benches, from hippodrome, 11, 41
Berytus, 28, 82
biga, 45
Blachernae palace, 6
Blues, 30 f., 37, 42–3, 69–76, 94–5, 111, 124, 150, 163 ff., 221, 232 ff.
British Museum Add. 16409, 97, 190, 194
Book of Ceremonies, 26, 36, 54–5, 69–70, 73, 78, 249, 256
bronze statues, 133, 168, 214, 221
bronze and gold statues, 131, 133, 169, 221
bronze and silver statues, 168, 177, 221
Brytae, festival of, 231, 234, 244
Buondelmonti, 7, 181
Byzantine prosody, 192 f.
Byzantine twelve-syllable, 191 f.

Calchas, Porphyrius' father, 136, 157
Callimachus, 61, 65, 85, 148
Calliopas, Porphyrius' other name, 122–3, 129, 173–4
Calliopas Trimolaimes, 174, 246
Calliopius, *comes Orientis*, 233
Caracalla, 19
Caramallus, pantomime, 168, 175–7, 243
Carolingian Psalter illuminations, 38, 39 n. 6
Cassiodorus, 29, 36, 229–30, 245
Cassius, tyrannicide, 250
castrensis, 54
Cephalas, Constantine, 98, 102, 105, 106–8, 109, 146–9, 200, 226
ceremonial, of hippodrome, 6, 38
circus of Rome, 37, 64, 71
circus programme, from Oxyrhynchus, 250, 256 n. 7
chariot, motif of frontal, 17–28, 251 n. 1
charioteers, 156–9, 172–5, 206 ff., 244 ff.

GENERAL INDEX

chlamys, chlamydatus, 54–5
Christodorus of Coptus, 85, 94, 105, 106, 151–4, 160
Christopher of Mytilene, 193 f., 199, 201
Chrysoloras, Manuel, 7
Chrysomallo(s), dancer's name, 171, 174
Clavijo, 7
coinage, of the Latin Emperors, 5; of early Byzantine Emperors, 24
Commodus, 80
Constantine I, 109–10
Constantine V, Emperor, 204–5
Constantine IX, Monomachus, 38
Constantine, charioteer, 32, 61–2, 86, 88, 92, 110, 120, 136–41, 155–7, 178, 202 ff., 209–12, 214–16, 224, 256
Constantine the Armenian, 189
Constantine of Rhodes, 193, 253
Constantinople, 28, 30
Constantius II, 19, 22, 23, 24
contorniates, 20, 40, 49, 62–3, 72, 78, 172–4
Corippus, 42, 54, 78 n. 1
Cosmas Indicopleustes, 38
coronation of charioteers, 44, 46, 49 n. 1
Crescens, charioteer, 155
cricketers, knighthoods of, 207, 276
crown, 17, 21, 24, 28, 51, 53
Crusaders, 5, 181, 185
cupids, *see* putti
curse tablets, 157–8, 173, 245
Cynegion, 229–30
Cyzicus, 29

dancing girls, 34, 38–9
Daphne, courtyard of, 55, 58
Daphne, suburb of Antioch, 150
David, in Byzantine art, 38–9
demarchs, 246
Dazis, 74 f.
'demes', so-called, 71, 238
Diocles, charioteer, 15, 66, 155, 159, 178, 207, 210
Diocletian, 73
Diogenes Laertius, 108, 148–9
'Dionysiac cycle' of MS. illustrations, 39
Dionysius of Halicarnassus, 37
diptychs, consular, 24, 44
diversium, 31, 43, 133–4, 140, 208 f.

dominus factionis, 204
Domitian, 210, 216, 256
Domninus, charioteer's name, 172–3, 177
Doricisms, 260, 269

Easter (Paschal) Chronicle, 57
Emesa, 29
Emperor, represented on horseback, 23
in quadriga, 23, 26
Emperor worship, 216 f.
Epigrammata Bobiensia, 185
epigrams, style, formulas of, 60 ff., 83–94
Eugenius, charioteer's name, 172
Eugenius of Palermo, 193
Eusebius, charioteer, 253–4
Eustorgius, charioteer's name, 172
Eutychus, name of charioteers and dancers, 174, 244
Eutymius, charioteer, 172

Fabius Pictor, 371
factionarius, 150
factions, of circus, 3, 30 f., 41, 119, 211, 232 ff.
and see 'Blues' and 'Greens'
Faustinus, charioteer, 136, 139, 156, 160, 178, 202 ff., 223, 241
Felix, name of charioteers and gladiators, 174
festivals, sacred, 29, 170, 207
at Constantinople, 29
Julius Festus Hymettius, 216
Filoromus, charioteer, 236
fires, in Constantinople, 5, 225
'first down' on cheeks, 155, 159
Flachat, 9
flutes, played by partisans, 33 f.
flute-players, 33 f., 42
foot-races in hippodrome, 253

Gafsa, in N. Africa, 40
gates of Kathisma, 55 ff.
George of Pisidia, 154, 191, 195
Gilles, Pierre, 7, 10–12, 36
gladiator stelae, 15, 43, 53
gladiatorial games, 228
gold statues, 93, 218 ff.
Grand Palace, 6, 56 ff.
grandstands of factions (demoi), 41 f., 44
Greens, 30 f., 37, 42–3, 67–76, 94–5, 111, 150, 163 ff., 221, 232 ff.

GENERAL INDEX

Gregorius Magister, 109
Gregory Nazianzen, 62, 65, 89, 102, 106, 113, 235, 266
Gutta, charioteer, 47-8

Helias, city prefect under Anastasius, 234
Helladia (-us), pantomime's name, 74, 171
helmet, of charioteer, 43
Henzen, W., 1
Heracles Trihesperus of Lysippus, 186
Heraclius, 5, 37, 255
heralds, 81
hexameter, κατὰ στίχον, 83
Hierocles, charioteer, 244
Hilarinus, charioteer, 45-6
hippodrome of Constantinople, 3, 27, 36, 56-8, 181, 223, 233
'covered' hippodrome, 36
Holy Apostles, Church of, 8-9
Holy Man, the, 246
hortator, 46
hundreds, of victories, 66, 179
Hypatius, usurper, 56 f., 126

iambic (Byzantine twelve-syllable), 83, 191 f.
inscriptions, virtual absence of at Constantinople, 217
Isaurians, in Constantinople, 233

John of Antioch, 231, 235
John Comnenus, 56
John of Gaza, 105-6
John Mauropous, 193 f.
jousting, 6
Julian, charioteer, 120, 143-4, 160, 162, 171, 184, 202 f., 207-8, 241
Julian, city prefect under Anastasius, 233
Julian the Egyptian, 84-5, 87-8
Anicia Juliana, 113
Julianicus, charioteer, 247
Justin I, 150, 224, 252
Justin II, 22, 83, 224
Justinian, 29, 57-8, 150, 211, 224, 229, 241, 245, 246, 256-7

Karea, gate, 56
Kathisma, 33, 41, 49 ff., 188, 201, 233, 258
Koeck, Pieter, 7

'Kugelspiel', 33 f., 42, 48, 52 ff., 58-60, 62-3

Lacerta, charioteer, 244
Laurentianus XXXII. 16, 97 ff., 144-6, 226
Lascaris, Janus, 108, 274
lemmata in Byzantine anthologies, 112
Leo the Wise, Emperor, 245
Leontius Scholasticus, 84, 91, 114-16, 124-5, 152, 171, 176-7, 209-10, 213
Liber, charioteer, 45-6, 79, 204
Libya, Porphyrius' birthplace, 131, 170
Longden, Johnny, 179
Longinus, prefect of Constantinople, 91, 218
lot-casting machine, 39 n. 6, 63
Lysippus, statues by in Constantinople, 186-7, 201, 214

Macedonius (-ia), name of pantomimes and charioteers, 175
Macedonius the consul, 84, 93, 218
Maenads, 39
magic, 173 n. 3, 245
magister officiorum, 54
Malalas, John, 1, 57, 68, 71, 77, 123, 150, 168, 169-70, 233, 235, 243
Manuel I, Emperor, 9
Marcellinus *comes*, 229, 235
Marcian, Emperor, and factions, 233; column of, 17, 59, 113
Marcianus gr. 481, 96 ff., 144-6, 188, 190, 194
Margarites (-o), name of dancers and gladiators, 174
Martial, 47, 71, 86-90, 244
Maurice, Emperor, 22-4
Maximus (cos. 523), 230
medallions, imperial, 19, 22-3
Mehmet, the Conqueror, 8-12
Meleager's *Garland*, 84, 89, 108, 147
metae, 182 f.
metre of epigrams, 83-4, 106, 191 ff.
Michael III, Emperor, 189, 249 n. 4
Midrash, Byzantine, 39
Milion, the, 109, 204
monophysitism, and factions, 238
moods, confusion of, 68
mosaics, 21
Mundus, general, 57
Musclosus, Pompeius, charioteer, 179 n. 1

GENERAL INDEX

Narses, statue of, 255
native city, prominent in agonistic inscriptions, 30, 170
Nero, 36, 79, 249 n. 4
Nicaea, 29, 30, 171
Nicetas, cousin of Heraclius, 224, 255
Nicetas Choniates, 181, 183–4, 185–6, 201
Nicolaus Mesarites, 56
Nicomedia, 28, 73
Nika revolt, 56 ff., 126, 179, 234, 237, 243
Nikai, see Victories
Nonnus, 62, 84, 89 n. 1, 91–2, 93–4, 105, 113, 151–3, 156, 190, 215, 260, 266

obelisk of Constantine VII, 6
obelisk of Theodosius, 7, 12, 16, 26, 34, 39, 40, 42, 44–6, 49 ff., 59, 113, 225, 250–1
organ (of circus), 34, 64
Ovid, 6, 23

paintings, on Prokyptikon ceiling, 200 ff.
Palatinus gr. 23, 97 ff.
Palladas of Alexandria, 83, 177, 198 n. 1
palm leaf, motif of, 17, 21, 43, 45, 53
Palmyra, 18–19
panegyric, 35
Pantocrator monastery, 9
pantomime dancers, 15, 21, 24, 49, 230 f., 247 f.
pantomime dancing, 230 ff.
Panvinio, Onufrio, 6, 181
Parakyptikon, the, 52–3, 200–1, 205, 252
Parastaseis, the, 109 f., 254
Paridiani, 175
Paris, pantomime, 87 ff.
  pantomime's name, 171
Parisinus gr. 2744, 97
Parmenio, epigrammatist, 61
patrons of factions, 75
Paul the Silentiary, 61, 83–4, 88 n. 1, 105–6, 253, 266
perspective, 19, 27
Peter Barsymes, 91
Peter the Patrician, 54, 77
Philip of Thessalonica, 83, 108, 147, 186, 195 n. 3, 201
Phocas, Emperor, 22, 234–5, 246
Photius, 109

Piggott, Lester, 155
Planudean Anthology, 96 ff.
Planudes, Maximus, 7, 8, 97 ff., 120, 145–6, 190, 192, 194–5, 253–4, 274
police force, at Rome and Constantinople, 237
Polyphemus, Cl., charioteer, 204
pompa circensis, 23, 37, 250
pop singers, 240
Porphyrius, pantomime, 168 ff., 243
praepositus sacri cubiculi, 54–5
praetorian prefect, 54
prefect of city, 54–5, 239
Priscian, 154
Procopius of Caesarea, 42, 56 ff., 157, 171, 211, 239, 257
Procopius of Gaza, 154, 231
professional names of charioteers, pantomimes, etc., 171 f.
Pseudo-Codinus, 111, 183
Ptolemaeus, barrister, 219
Purfyrius, Purpureus, Purpurio, by-forms of Porphyrius, 174–5
putti, 24–5, 43, 46–7

quadriga, see chariot
quaestor, 54

Ravenna, 44
record totals of victories won in careers, 179 n. 1
records established by charioteers, 206–14
Reds, 42, 150, 183–4, 202–3
relics, Mehmet's collection of, 9–10
Richards, Gordon, 179
Robert of Clari, 181, 187
Rome, 20
  riots at, 236
Bassaeus Rufus, 216

saint, ascetic, 3
St. Eirene, 2
St. Polyeuctus, 113
St. Sabina, in Rome, 40
St. Sophia, in Kiev, 34–5, 37
sarcophagi, imperial, 4–12
  illustrated with circus scenes, 46–7
Sassanian motifs, 18–19, 24, 26
satirical inscriptions, 184–5
scale, inconsistency of in early Byzantine art, 40
Scorpus, charioteer, 47–8, 86, 244–5

GENERAL INDEX

sculpture, decline of 254-5
Scylla, bronze statue of in hippodrome, 185
season symbolism, 39
Sejanus, 216
senate (of Constantinople), 55
Seraglio, 4, 8, 9, 11
Serpent column, 6, 181, 225
Severus, Septimius, 223
Shoemaker, Willie, 179 n. 1, 276
Sidonius Apollinaris, 44, 176
Σ^π, 98 ff., 120, 144, 146, 176, 226
Smith, Doug, 179
Socrates, historian, 237
Sol, 19, 24
Solomon, in Byzantine art, 38-9
sphendone, 35
spina, 6, 7, 111, 180 ff.
Stama / Pi, 50 f.
student disorders, 238
Suleiman, the Magnificent, 7
Sylloge Euphemiana, 112
L. Aurelius Avianius Symmachus, 216-17
Q. Aurelius Symmachus, 229
symmetry, in late Roman art, 40, 46

Tatianus, charioteer, 155
Teres, charioteer, 15, 66, 155, 178, 207
Tertullian, 71, 79
textiles, 22, 24-6, 46
Theodora, Empress, sister of Zoe, 38
Theodora, Empress, wife of Justinian, 158, 171
Theodore Studites, 193
Theodoric, King, 230
Theodorus, barrister, 219
Theodosius I, Emperor, 227
Theodosius II, Emperor, and factions, 233
Theophanes, chronicler, 57
Theophanes of Mytilene, statue of, 187

Theophilus, Emperor, 55, 249 n. 4
Thessalonica, hippodrome of, 181, 236
Thomas, charioteer, 10, 245
Thomas the Curator, 214
Thomas the logothete, 188-9, 191
Thorax, charioteer's name, 173
Tiberius II, Emperor, 22-4, 257
toga, togatus, 54-5
Tribunal, of Constantinople, 37
tunic, charioteer's, 25
Tychae, 28-30
Tyre, 29, 171
hippodrome of, 181 n. 4

unaugmented form of aorist, 266
Uranicus, charioteer, 205, 245 n. 13, 258
Uranius, charioteer, 30, 115, 120, 141-4, 171, 173, 202, 212-14, 222, 240, 252
stock name of dancers and charioteers 175, 205 n. 1

velum, a flag, not awning, 35 f.
venationes, 228 ff., 242
Via Flaminia, 45
Via Imperiale, 45
Victories, 17, 28, 30, 44
victories, number won by charioteers, 66, 179
victory, theme of, 26, 53, 55, 248-52
violence, of factions, 232 ff., 252
Vitalian, rebel, 126-30, 150, 160

Whites, 42, 150, 183, 202-3
whip, 17, 21, 24, 26, 45-6, 94

Zeno, and factions, 233
Zeuxippus, baths of, 210
Zoe, Empress, 38
Zosimus, historian, 231

1. Tyche of Nicomedia above triumphant Porphyrius, with *A.Pl.* 356

2–3. Front and back faces of the new base, with *A.Pl.* 352 and 353

4-5. Right and left sides of the new base, with *A.Pl.* 351 and 356

6. Dancing partisans, with two prose acclamations (left side)

7. Emperor and party in Kathisma, with *A.Pl.* 353 (back face)

8. Porphyrius being crowned by a Victory (front)

9. Acclamation from right side

10a. *A.Pl.* 351 (right side, top)

10b. *A.Pl.* 352 (back, top)

11. *A.Pl.* 335; 338; 337; 336; 339; 353. 1–4 in *Laur.* XXXII. 16 (written by Planudes 1280/3)

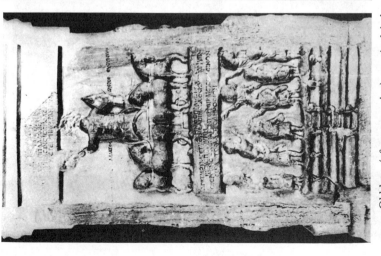

12–14. Old base (after restoration). 12. Acclaiming partisans beneath triumphant Porphyrius (left side). 13. Porphyrius and attendant putti (back). 14. The *diversium*, beneath Porphyrius and attendant Victories (front)

16. Dancing partisans, victorious charioteer (a) on horseback and (b) in quadriga (right side)

15. Dancing partisans, lot machine, racing quadriga (left side)

17. ? Kathisma, above arch (front)   18. Racing quadrigae (back)

15–18. The 'Kugelspiel', a marble object used for some sort of ball game

19. Dancers and musicians celebrate the Emperor's victory (front, A1)

20. Barbarians supplicate the Emperor with offerings (back, B1)

21. Left face, B2

22. Right face, A2

19–22. The four faces of the base to the obelisk of Theodosius

23. Relief below face A2 of the obelisk base: racing horsemen and coronation scene above racing quadrigae

25. Mosaic from Dougga, Tunisia: the charioteer Eros

24. Mosaic from the Via Flaminia: Liber wins

26. Medallion with quadriga and other circus motifs from the Aachen–Cluny textile

27. Quadriga medallion from the Münsterbilsen textile

28. Fifteenth-century view of the hippodrome of Constantinople published by Onufrio Panvinio

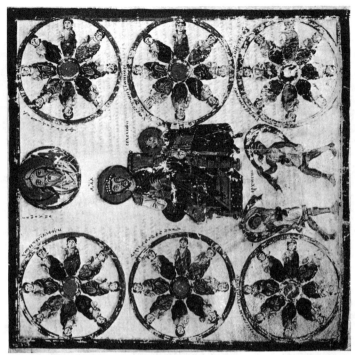

29. David, Solomon, and dancers: miniature from MS. Vatic. gr. 699

30. David and dancers: miniature from a Carolingian Psalter (Bibl. Nat. Cod. 1152)

31. 1–2. Two late Roman engraved glass bottoms (originals lost, reproduced from the engravings in Cabrol/Leclercq, *Dict. d'Arch. chrét.* vi. 2 (1925), figs. 5725–6). 3. Gold consular medallion of Constantius II (Berlin). 4–5. Medallion in niello from Trier; legend 'Porfyr' on obverse and 'Purfyrius' (with 'Fontanus', presumably the lead horse) on reverse (Alföldi, *Die Kontorniaten*, no. 575, and p. 24). 6. Charioteer on contorniate holding crown, whip, and palm, with details of tunic clearly visible and palms and crown beneath quadriga (Alföldi, no. 218); legend 'Eutymius'. 7. Pantomime accompanied by cupid waving crown; legend 'Margarita vincas' (Alföldi, no. 419). 8. Lot machine with charioteer on either side (Alföldi, no. 169). 9. Charioteer as in 6 but facing front and above horses' names in monogram; legend 'Bonifatius' (Alföldi, no. 414). 10. Movable hippodrome organ (Alföldi, no. 427). 11. Pantomime dancer with chorus (Alföldi, no. 411). 12. Bracelet medallion formed from a consular medallion of Maurice (Dumbarton Oaks).

OTHER TITLES IN THIS HARDBACK REPRINT PROGRAMME FROM SANDPIPER BOOKS LTD (LONDON) AND POWELLS BOOKS (CHICAGO)

ISBN 0-19-	Author	Title
8143567	ALFÖLDI A.	The Conversion of Constantine and Pagan Rome
6286409	ANDERSON George K.	The Literature of the Anglo-Saxons
8228813	BARTLETT & MacKAY	Medieval Frontier Societies
8111010	BETHURUM Dorothy	Homilies of Wulfstan
8142765	BOLLING G. M.	External Evidence for Interpolation in Homer
9240132	BOYLAN Patrick	Thoth, the Hermes of Egypt
8114222	BROOKS Kenneth R.	Andreas and the Fates of the Apostles
8203543	BULL Marcus	Knightly Piety & Lay Response to the First Crusade
8216785	BUTLER Alfred J.	Arab Conquest of Egypt
8148046	CAMERON Alan	Circus Factions
8148054	CAMERON Alan	Porphyrius the Charioteer
8148348	CAMPBELL J.B.	The Emperor and the Roman Army 31 BC to 235 AD
826643X	CHADWICK Henry	Priscillian of Avila
826447X	CHADWICK Henry	Boethius
8219393	COWDREY H.E.J.	The Age of Abbot Desiderius
8148992	DAVIES M.	Sophocles: Trachiniae
825301X	DOWNER L.	Leges Henrici Primi
814346X	DRONKE Peter	Medieval Latin and the Rise of European Love-Lyric
8142749	DUNBABIN T.J.	The Western Greeks
8154372	FAULKNER R.O.	The Ancient Egyptian Pyramid Texts
8221541	FLANAGAN Marie Therese	Irish Society, Anglo-Norman Settlers, Angevin Kingship
8143109	FRAENKEL Edward	Horace
8201540	GOLDBERG P.J.P.	Women, Work and Life Cycle in a Medieval Economy
8140215	GOTTSCHALK H.B.	Heraclides of Pontus
8266162	HANSON R.P.C.	Saint Patrick
8224354	HARRISS G.L.	King, Parliament and Public Finance in Medieval England to 1369
8581114	HEATH Sir Thomas	Aristarchus of Samos
8140444	HOLLIS A.S.	Callimachus: Hecale
8212968	HOLLISTER C. Warren	Anglo-Saxon Military Institutions
8223129	HURNARD Naomi	The King's Pardon for Homicide – before AD 1307
8140401	HUTCHINSON G.O.	Hellenistic Poetry
9240140	JOACHIM H.H.	Aristotle: On Coming-to-be and Passing-away
9240094	JONES A.H.M	Cities of the Eastern Roman Provinces
8142560	JONES A.H.M.	The Greek City
8218354	JONES Michael	Ducal Brittany 1364–1399
8271484	KNOX & PELCZYNSKI	Hegel's Political Writings
8225253	LE PATOUREL John	The Norman Empire
8212720	LENNARD Reginald	Rural England 1086–1135
8212321	LEVISON W.	England and the Continent in the 8th century
8148224	LIEBESCHUETZ J.H.W.G.	Continuity and Change in Roman Religion
8141378	LOBEL Edgar & PAGE Sir Denys	Poetarum Lesbiorum Fragmenta
9240159	LOEW E.A.	The Beneventan Script
8241445	LUKASIEWICZ, Jan	Aristotle's Syllogistic
8152442	MAAS P. & TRYPANIS C.A .	Sancti Romani Melodi Cantica
8142684	MARSDEN E.W.	Greek and Roman Artillery—Historical
8142692	MARSDEN E.W.	Greek and Roman Artillery—Technical
8148178	MATTHEWS John	Western Aristocracies and Imperial Court AD 364–425
8223447	McFARLANE K.B.	Lancastrian Kings and Lollard Knights
8226578	McFARLANE K.B.	The Nobility of Later Medieval England
8148100	MEIGGS Russell	Roman Ostia
8148402	MEIGGS Russell	Trees and Timber in the Ancient Mediterranean World
8142641	MILLER J. Innes	The Spice Trade of the Roman Empire
8147813	MOORHEAD John	Theoderic in Italy
8264259	MOORMAN John	A History of the Franciscan Order
8116020	OWEN A.L.	The Famous Druids
8131445	PALMER, L.R.	The Interpretation of Mycenaean Greek Texts
8143427	PFEIFFER R.	History of Classical Scholarship (vol 1)
8143648	PFEIFFER Rudolf	History of Classical Scholarship 1300–1850
8111649	PHEIFER J.D.	Old English Glosses in the Epinal-Erfurt Glossary
8142277	PICKARD–CAMBRIDGE A.W.	Dithyramb Tragedy and Comedy
8269765	PLATER & WHITE	Grammar of the Vulgate
8213891	PLUMMER Charles	Lives of Irish Saints (2 vols)
820695X	POWICKE Michael	Military Obligation in Medieval England
8269684	POWICKE Sir Maurice	Stephen Langton
821460X	POWICKE Sir Maurice	The Christian Life in the Middle Ages
8225369	PRAWER Joshua	Crusader Institutions

ID	Author	Title
8225571	PRAWER Joshua	The History of The Jews in the Latin Kingdom of Jerusalem
8143249	RABY F.J.E.	A History of Christian Latin Poetry
8143257	RABY F.J.E.	A History of Secular Latin Poetry in the Middle Ages (2 vols)
8214316	RASHDALL & POWICKE	The Universities of Europe in the Middle Ages (3 vols)
8154488	REYMOND E.A.E & BARNS J.W.B.	Four Martyrdoms from the Pierpont Morgan Coptic Codices
8148380	RICKMAN Geoffrey	The Corn Supply of Ancient Rome
8141076	ROSS Sir David	Aristotle: Metaphysics (2 vols)
8141092	ROSS Sir David	Aristotle: Physics
8142307	ROSTOVTZEFF M.	Social and Economic History of the Hellenistic World, 3 vols.
8142315	ROSTOVTZEFF M.	Social and Economic History of the Roman Empire, 2 vols.
8264178	RUNCIMAN Sir Steven	The Eastern Schism
814833X	SALMON J.B.	Wealthy Corinth
8171587	SALZMAN L.F.	Building in England Down to 1540
8218362	SAYERS Jane E.	Papal Judges Delegate in the Province of Canterbury 1198–1254
8221657	SCHEIN Sylvia	Fideles Crucis
8148135	SHERWIN WHITE A.N.	The Roman Citizenship
9240167	SINGER Charles	Galen: On Anatomical Procedures
8113927	SISAM, Kenneth	Studies in the History of Old English Literature
8642040	SOUTER Alexander	A Glossary of Later Latin to 600 AD
8222254	SOUTHERN R.W.	Eadmer: Life of St. Anselm
8251408	SQUIBB G.	The High Court of Chivalry
8212011	STEVENSON & WHITELOCK	Asser's Life of King Alfred
8212011	SWEET Henry	A Second Anglo-Saxon Reader—Archaic and Dialectical
8148259	SYME Sir Ronald	History in Ovid
8143273	SYME Sir Ronald	Tacitus (2 vols)
8200951	THOMPSON Sally	Women Religious
8201745	WALKER Simon	The Lancastrian Affinity 1361–1399
8161115	WELLESZ Egon	A History of Byzantine Music and Hymnography
8140185	WEST M.L.	Greek Metre
8141696	WEST M.L.	Hesiod: Theogony
8148542	WEST M.L.	The Orphic Poems
8140053	WEST M.L.	Hesiod: Works & Days
8152663	WEST M.L.	Iambi et Elegi Graeci
822799X	WHITBY M. & M.	The History of Theophylact Simocatta
8206186	WILLIAMSON, E.W.	Letters of Osbert of Clare
8114877	WOOLF Rosemary	The English Religious Lyric in the Middle Ages
8119224	WRIGHT Joseph	Grammar of the Gothic Language